AMERICAN ORIGINALS

PAUL K. CONKIN

AMERICAN ORIGINALS

Homemade

Varieties of

Christianity

THE UNIVERSITY OF NORTH CAROLINA PRESS / CHAPEL HILL & LONDON

The paper in this book meets the guidelines
for permanence and durability of the Committee
on Production Guidelines for Book Longevity
of the Council on Library Resources.

Library of Congress Cataloging-in-Publication Data

Conkin, Paul Keith.
American originals: homemade varieties of
Christianity / Paul K. Conkin.
p.   cm.
Includes index.
ISBN 0-8078-2342-2 (cloth: alk. paper)
ISBN 0-8078-4649-X (pbk.: alk. paper)
1. Christian sects—United States.   I. Title.
BR516.5.C65   1997
280'.0973 — dc20   96-35270
                                                    CIP

01   00   99   98   97   5   4   3   2   1

CONTENTS

94295

PREFACE

North America provided special opportunities for religious innovation. In the English colonies and then the United States, plenty of space, the desire for immigration and population growth, and the eventual absence of an established church all combined to provide opportunities for religious prophets and reformers. Some of these broke from the boundaries of Christianity, but none of the new, non-Christian religions ever gained a large following. Because of the heritage of Europeans in America, most religious innovations remained within Christianity, if broadly defined. At the very least, the most successful new prophets or reformers believed that Jesus was the promised Messiah and that in some sense he opened a new path to salvation.

To write a book on American originals is to confront all manner of definitional and boundary problems. Every new Christian sect in America had some European progenitors or anticipations, although least so for Mormons and Christian Scientists. Universalists, Unitarians, Adventists, and restorationists all had doctrinal roots in the past or cousins back in Europe. Modern Pentecostals have had counterparts in Britain and elsewhere. Thus, I do not claim that all aspects of any of the religious groups treated in this book were original or peculiarly American. I do believe that they now represent quite distinctive versions of Christianity and that they have a special home in America, however much they borrowed from abroad.

My topic is not specific denominations, but distinctive types of Christianity, whether represented in America by only one denomination or by many. Yet even this guideline faces problems, as best illustrated by the present Disciples of Christ. They derive from the broader Restoration movement, still reflect in doctrine and practice some of the distinctive features of that movement, but have become so ecumenical and have so loosened the bases of separate identity as to be virtually a part of the Christian mainstream. A majority of Unitarian-Universalists no longer claim a Christian identity and thus have moved, or are moving, outside the boundaries of Christianity. The doctrinal divisions within Pentecostalism are deep and perhaps intractable. Some doctrines of the Mormons are so original and so far from any traditional Christianity that many orthodox critics deny their Christian profession.

I have not attempted a history of all original forms of Christianity in America, just the largest and most influential. I believe that my six clusters or groupings encompass well over 90 percent of Americans who have embraced new or original forms of Christianity. But the other 10 percent includes several identifiable sects, some very small, some quite bizarre. Yet even tiny sects most often fit within one of my six categories. That is, they are most often distinguished by apocalyptic, spiritualistic, humanistic, restorationist, or ecstatic beliefs and behaviors. Some are fascinating hybrids, such as the Christadelphians, who combine restorationist, Adventist, and Anabaptist doctrines. One communal group, the Shakers, made up (a handful of survivors still make up) a quite original American religion, even though its dominant prophet, Ann Lee, immigrated from England. The doctrines about her, and the unique institutions of the Shakers, were American inventions. The Shakers were unique, not because of their communalism, but because of some doctrines closely tied to it. The Hutterites, the largest communal sect in both the United States and Canada, are, in doctrines and values, model Anabaptists. Their roots are in Europe. So were the doctrines of the Amana Society, the Harmonists, and others. Thus, unlike some other scholars, I do not find, in a community of goods, a proper grouping category for American Christian sects.

Neither do I find such in race or ethnicity. This does not mean that Christian movements are exempt from cultural influences. Even within a confessional tradition, the understanding of essential doctrines as well as the nuances of self-expression in iconography and music will vary according to culture. Thus, in ways not always easy to define, Hispanic Catholics in America differ from those of English and Irish derivation. These differences largely reflect the assimilation of aspects of earlier Indian religions. But any religious tradition will reflect cultural influences. In a sense, every expression of Christianity has an ethnic component. These cultural differences are additive to what is essential or definitive in any tradition. Hispanic Catholics, if they adhere to the normative doctrines of the church, are as much Roman Catholics as are Italians.

In the United States, race has some additional dimensions. African Americans derive from many areas of West Africa, each with a different language and religious heritage. In most areas of North America these African peoples were unable to retain their native languages or, in pure form, their traditional religions. In time, particularly in the United States, they had to learn English, but with some retained linguistic elements from the old world, and in time most would convert to various Christian confessions. At times slave owners controlled access and choice, but at times blacks were able to choose the Christian sect they preferred, although again in a context of limited options. Yet, in each case, ranging from Roman Catholicism in Louisiana to evangelical forms of Baptism and Methodism in most of the South, they retained some influences from Africa. To an extent difficult to measure, some African survivals, particularly in patterns of worship, helped shape forms of popular white Christianity. In much of the rural South a merging of religious styles soon blurred the boundaries between blacks and whites, who in most cases worshiped in the same congregations until after emancipation. Blacks eventually joined all denominations, but because of location or culturally influenced preferences, most became Baptists and Methodists in the nineteenth century, while very recently a disproportionate number have joined Pentecostal denominations. In each case, the flavor of black Christianity has been different, but no more reflective of cultural roots than white versions. Black Baptists are as authentically Baptist as whites. It makes good sense to talk about African influences on various Christian confessions in America, but no sense at all to classify black Christians, who are present in every denomination, as constituting a separate form of Christianity, at least so long as one defines a religious tradition in terms of scriptures, doctrines, polities, and moral standards.

Many of the major American originals have become world religions through effective missionary activity. The Restoration churches and Christian Science, although well represented abroad, are still primarily American movements. The Mormons, Adventists, and Jehovah's Witnesses are distinctive for having more members abroad than in the United States, and this may be true for Pentecostals. These versions of Christianity are indeed, in the fullest sense of the word, international in appeal, but they originated, and their home base is still, within the United States.

I emphasize the roots and the founding of the six largest American originals. I try to establish a distinctive identity and thus focus on the formative years. Once a movement is well established, with the essential doctrines and practices in place, I offer a much more brief and cursory history. Space allows no more than this. I have arranged the six groups chronologically, in the sense that those that developed first appear first in this book. Thus, for Pentecostals, the story of foundations is also, in effect, a story that extends to the present.

By "originals," I mean much more than simply new denominations. Hundreds of small splinter denominations have separated from the main-line churches, but with limited shifts in doctrine or worship styles. The six movements in this book reflect new departures in basic doctrines and in practices. This means that they have broken with major commonalities among the state churches of Europe and their non-established offspring in America. In this sense they have been heterodox. But to so denominate them is to appeal to some conception of orthodoxy. In early American history, when several denominations in the broad Reformed tradition (Anglican-Episcopal, Presbyterian, Congregationalist, Calvinist Baptists, Methodists, and German and Dutch Reformed) dominated church membership in America, even the mother church of Western Christianity, Roman Catholicism, and to a lesser extent even the original product of the Reformation, Lutheranism, seemed heterodox to the American mainstream. So did schismatic and unorthodox sects that began in Europe but migrated to America, such as the Quakers and the several Anabaptist sects. These European imports, whether state churches or dissenting sects, helped create the religious pluralism of America as well as the anxiety attendant on a soon wide-open form of religious competition, which both inspired and permitted my American originals.

Since I argue that, on certain key doctrines or practices, the major originals in America all challenged orthodoxy, I have the crucial and difficult task of characterizing what I mean by orthodoxy. This is not easy and will, by necessity, remain in part a matter of arbitrary definitions (in some sense, all definitions are arbitrary, a matter of stipulation).

In time, the largest stream of Christianity flowed through Europe, with an eventual break between the Western churches centered on Rome and the Eastern ones centered on Constantinople. Soon after the final split between Rome and Constantinople, the Western Church splintered after 1500 into competing Roman Catholic and Protestant state churches. Representatives of all the Western European state churches and all the major dissenting sects eventually moved to the American colonies. Often unnoted in the intramural warfare between legally established Catholic and Protestant churches was a large body of shared beliefs and worship traditions. Only the small, usually persecuted sects broke with these commonalities, which dated from the first six centuries of the Church. During these centuries, the churches of the empire developed a New Testament canon (not an easy decision) and also decided, unofficially, on a closed canon (no more sacred scriptures); used Greek philosophy to refine a Christian theology with certain minimally necessary beliefs; perfected an episcopal or hierarchical system of church government; settled very divisive doctrinal controversies about the divine–human traits of Jesus and about the relationship between Father, Son, and Spirit; and matured a very rich type of worship centered on the Eucharist or Lord's Supper.

Except for polity and worship, these decisions and settlements have remained a joint legacy of Catholicism and of Lutheran and Reformed churches. They reflect not some New Testament church but what evolved over the centuries. The commonalities are best reflected in the Apostles' Creed, a creed used by Roman Catholics, Lutherans, and Reformed denominations. In this book I refer to these common beliefs and practices as "orthodox." Advocates or founders of the new American forms of Christianity all rejected some aspects of this orthodox tradition and in this sense were rebels. For example, some added new scriptures to the received canon; most rejected some aspects of the received formulas about the Trinity; some experimented radically with traditional worship practices; some endorsed new views about the advent and about divine judgment; some denied hell or affirmed universal salvation; some changed the accepted day of worship; some revived gifts of the Spirit such as healing, prophecy, and tongues; and all developed at least slightly modified beliefs about the requirements for salvation.

Salvation doctrines are most critical for an understanding of the present varieties of Christianity in America. These are very complex. All orthodox Christians affirm the following doctrines: Humans in their natural capacity are so alienated from their personal and masculine god, so full of pride and ego, that they are incapable of giving their full consent or love to him. They are sinful. This does not mean that they are mean or immoral from the perspective of some system of moral philosophy or law, but that they cannot so act as to further the will and purpose of God. They are therefore doomed to life apart from God, to some type of hell, unless God is merciful to them. Only he can choose to save humans. His chosen means of salvation is the atoning Christ. Through the sacrifice of the Christ and through the continuing agency of the Holy Spirit, God has provided, at least for some people, a pathway back to reconciliation, even though no one deserves such salvation. Thus, salvation is an unearned gift. Yet all orthodox Christians, whether Protestant or Catholic, believe that the atonement was, in some sense, conditional, at least for adults, and that some humans, but not all, will receive salvation. Those without God's grace or mercy will suffer some form of damnation, either eternal separation from God or some form of torment. It was around these doctrines that the deepest fissures entered the story of Western Christianity.

The major Reformers—Luther, Zwengli, Bucer, Calvin, Cranmer, and Knox—all believed that the condition that rendered the Christ's atonement efficacious was faith, by which they meant belief, trust, and love. The only persons truly reconciled to God are those who perceive his beauty and power and righteousness, respond in belief and trust, and then struggle to bring their conduct in line with what faith requires. They are aided in this move toward a saintlike life by the Holy Spirit, by the scriptures, by prayer, and perhaps above all by the sacraments of the Church. They know, and remember with thanks, that God alone elects to salvation. It is his initiative, the work of his Spirit, that brings one to repentance and to a new outlook. This is a rebirth that, like an original birth, is not something one chooses, but a momentous transformation of one's affections. These control all subsequent choices. At the moment of transformation, a convert does indeed respond to God in a very active way, but such a response is a product of divine initiative.

This Protestant understanding of salvation departed from the most common view within the older and, by the sixteenth century, corrupt Church. But this Pauline or Augustinian view of salvation, a very hard or pious view, had a long history in the Church, and thus Luther and Calvin believed they were reclaiming the church of the fifth century. Roman Catholics all agreed that salvation is a gift. No one earns it. But they increasingly emphasized the sacraments, not as aids for moving toward sanctification, but as the formal means by which God brings the saving grace of the Christ to humans. This begins with a remitting baptism and continues, primarily, in the Eucharist, which is a living reenactment of the passion of the Christ. Thus, unlike Protestants, they see the elements of the communion as the actual, miraculously present blood and body of the Christ, and they view the Eucharistic meal as a sacrificial ordinance. Performed by priests, this sacrament has efficacy even for the dead. Since it draws on the sacrificial tradition of Judaism, on the role of priests at the temple, the Catholic Mass centered on an altar (images of sacrifice) and on the role of a clergy whose authority descended from Jesus and his disciples. This way of understanding how God elects and sustains his saints meant a devotional life tied to forms of obedience, and thus what Luther saw as a religion of sacramental works rather than faith.

The reformers tried to replace a priestly and sacrificial approach to salvation with what they called an evangelical emphasis—on the preached Word and on the immediate work of the Spirit. They rejected the traditional Mass, with its elements of awe and mystery, and viewed baptism as a remitting ordinance only to the extent that it was confirmed by a later confession of faith. The Eucharist is a powerful sacrament for people of faith, but without faith it is not a saving ordinance. Yet, unlike many of their successors, both Luther and Calvin believed that the Christ was present in the sacramental meal (alongside the bread and wine for Luther, spiritually present for Calvin).

Eventually such Protestants would fall into another major, even watershed, disagreement about salvation. Many Lutherans, some reforming Calvinists in Holland, and a growing faction in the English Church rejected the most rigorous or Pauline understanding of salvation. This trend, already embraced by sectaries such as the Anabaptists, climaxed in the English Church in the doctrines of John Wesley. We now refer to the polar positions as Arminianism and Calvinism. But the labels are misleading, since many disciples of Calvin moved to an Arminian position, including Arminius himself. Here the subtleties defy any easy or simple explication. As the divisions deepened, professed Calvinists at Dort, in Holland, and then at Westminster, near London, worked out fighting confessions. The label "Calvinism" soon designated the doctrines affirmed in these assemblies. Such latter-day, or scholastic, Calvinists offered an uncompromising defense of the following doctrines: God fully determines who will be the beneficiaries of his grace, and not because of any foreknowledge of any virtue in those whom he elects. This is because those ungifted with his grace have no virtues or merit. Thus, all humans in their natural capacity are sinful or depraved. Salvation is conditional on grace and the faith that results from the divine initiative. One can do nothing on one's own to merit salvation. But when God, working through the Word and the Spirit, chooses an individual, then his grace (his beauty) is simply irresistible. One is overwhelmed with a new insight, a new understanding, and new likes and dislikes. Finally, such a saving work by God is permanent. The saints, however much they may entertain doubts or fall into disobedience, will persevere—once in grace, always in grace.

Those called Arminians disagreed. To illustrate their point of view, I take the extreme position of Wesley. But note that up to the time of salvation, Arminians agreed that humans are depraved, that they cannot save themselves, and that a divine initiative is necessary for salvation. But at the point of salvation they affirmed a different conception of the atonement, and with this an array of different, avowedly anti-Calvinistic doctrines. Wesley and most who later accepted the label "Arminian" believed that the death of Christ fully atoned for the inherent sinfulness of humans. Thus, infants were in the kingdom already. A remitting baptism was unnecessary for them (Wesleyan Arminians agreed with Anabaptists on this but retained infant baptism, not as a remitting ordinance, but to attest a strong commitment by parents to rear their children within the church). Arminians believed that only when children were old enough to be responsible and to understand what God required did they become guilty, subject to divine judgment. The guilt reflected not some inherent depravity but poor character and actual disobedience. People were not inalterably bad or sinful. Because of the atonement, God had already given to all people a type of limited grace. By disobedience they lost the assurance of salvation and thus needed the rebirth experience. But note that, to them, this grace was not irresistible but something open to human choice. So, as a result, Arminians made salvation and the preservation of salvation something that involves a human input, although the divine initiative was still essential. Thus, they reversed the beliefs of scholastic Calvinists. Humans are deeply inclined to evil, but not totally depraved, at least since the atonement. God opens salvation to humans, but they are free to reject what he offers. His offer is to everyone. Salvation is dependent on one's obedience. Unforgiven sins in effect exclude a person from the church. This meant a salvation scheme more humanistic in its conception of God than the Calvinist. It meant a religion more moralistic or even legalistic than Calvinism, but one close, in many ways, to Catholicism, in the sense that one worked at one's salvation within a religious community. The consequence of these fissures in the Western churches was that newly independent Americans confronted what seemed to be three different schemes of salvation: the sacramental system of Roman Catholics, the rigorously God-centered scheme of most Lutherans and Calvinists, and the more benevolent and often sentimental path offered by latter-day Anglicans and Methodists.

These differences still existed within a larger framework of orthodoxy. The commonalities, although often overlooked in the midst of post-Reformation controversy, vastly outweighed the differences. My American originals all took additional steps to separate themselves from existing Catholic, Calvinist, and even Arminian traditions, however much they retained from each tradition. Gifted with new scriptures, led by new prophets, informed by new scholarship and new scientific knowledge, or inspired with a desire to restore an early but now corrupted New Testament church, they created authentic new versions of Christianity.

This is a work of many years. I am not a member of a church within any of the six original groups that are the subject of this book. Yet I have had more direct experience with some than with others. I attended a college sponsored by the Disciples of Christ and briefly was a member of a Christian congregation. In the past I was a member of Unitarian congregations.

Some of my kinfolk are Adventists. I have had warm personal relationships with Mormons. I have had more limited firsthand contact with Christian Scientists and Pentecostals, and this only through students. But all such direct knowledge has been helpful, and thus hundreds of people have helped me write this book, a book that will never fully please members of any one of these traditions.

I want to acknowledge special help from scholars. George R. Knight, a gifted Adventist scholar, read and offered invaluable advice on Seventh-day Adventists. Douglas Foster, Thomas H. Olbricht, and Ted McAllister offered detailed comments on my chapter on Restoration Christianity. My colleague Richard F. Haglund Jr., a scientist and very active Mormon, read and offered needed suggestions for an early version of the chapter on Mormonism. Richard Lyman Bushman, an eminent historian and also a Mormon, offered an even more rigorous and challenging critique. He helped me avoid numerous errors. None of these readers fully agreed with my interpretations. They enormously improved this book, but they are in no sense responsible for the content.

AMERICAN ORIGINALS

I

RESTORATION **CHRISTIANITY**

Christians

and

Disciples

In some sense, almost all new Christian movements have advertised their return to an early or pure New Testament Church. In America, one group of early restorationists placed crucial emphasis on such primitive purity and, unlike most other restorers, downplayed the role and status of the Old Testament. These reformers preferred names such as Christian, Churches of Christ, or Disciples of Christ for their congregations. The early history of such movements is very complex, even as the modern descendants of such reformers are deeply divided among themselves. Yet, it is possible to identify important commonalities both at the time of origin and even today.

Since several of these reformers began with an announced effort to restore the primitive New Testament Church, their work eventually gained a collective label—the Restoration movement. Today, congregations that share this heritage (to call them sects or denominations or even churches is to get entangled in the very teachings that distinguished the "movement") still represent a distinctive, albeit eclectic, tradition in American Christianity.

THE PROBLEM OF RESTORATION

The term "Restoration movement" is an inexact label for Christians and Disciples. Many in the more inclusive and ecumenical branches of the movement have never liked the designation. Yet, it reflects at least one goal of each of the founders of a tradition that soon had its own doctrines, institutions, and liturgies. The problem with the label is its generality. Almost without exception, those who have launched new sects or schismatic splinters have claimed to restore the ancient or primitive church. All the Reformation churches made this claim, and so have all successors in the Protestant tradition, broadly defined. It is possible, in a brief space, to list only the major issues involved in the restoration claim. The early reformers—Martin Luther, John Calvin, and Huldrych Zwingli—tried to restore the church of the Augustinian age, the church that followed the great councils, the doctrinal controversies these resolved, the creeds they established, and the state recognition or support that made them possible. They insisted that their reforms restored the true church, the developing and maturing church described at least in a fragmentary way in the epistles of Paul. They returned to the New Testament for instruction on issues of doctrine, polity, and worship and claimed no authority above scripture. But their reforms soon seemed incomplete for Anabaptists, Puritans, and Pietists. The first major and enduring effort to go back to primitive beginnings involved the Swiss Brethren and their Anabaptist successors (Mennonites, Amish, Hutterites, and the Church of the Brethren).

In time, the primitive or restorationist goal involved efforts to reform not just the alleged corruptions that marred the Church of Rome but corruptions that developed in the first four centuries of Christian history. These corruptions involved state churches or state-supported churches, episcopal orders, the creeds and doctrines worked out by the great councils, and a wide range of nonscriptural innovations in worship. But as events as well as careful scholarship soon attested, the New Testament did not provide an unambiguous model, and thus those reformers who placed most emphasis on a return to the ancient order were soon the ones who most sharply disagreed over doctrine, polity, and worship. In other words, restorers turned out to be the prototypal sectaries, however earnestly they hoped that a return to an early model would end sectarian strife.

Because of fragmentary or elliptical or conflicting guidelines in the New Testament, restorationists had to make critical choices about what to emphasize as essential. In time, critical scholarship would raise difficult questions about the scriptural guidelines to which they so often appealed. Since Jesus, as presented in the gospels, offered no detailed blueprint for churches, Christians had no recourse except to Paul and to the author of Luke and Acts, who seems to have been a close disciple of Paul. Thus, a rigorous restorer might challenge even the authority of Paul, or at least of some of his purported letters, or even find in him and his disciples the first corruptions of primitive Jewish Christian congregations, the Ebionites and Nazarenes.

Thus the most rigorous and radical restorationist in American religious history—Joseph Priestley—tried earnestly to go back to these first Christians and to repudiate the earliest and greatest corruptions within the church, the doctrine of a separable soul or spirit and the doctrine of the Trinity. Other Christians took very literally the church as described in Acts and thus opted for a community of goods, as did the Anabaptist Hutterites, the Shakers, and the perfectionists that John Humphrey Noyes gathered in the Oneida Colony in New York, there virtually to reverse the Shaker demand for celibacy in a bizarre experiment with a type of free love. Others embraced the charismatic gifts gained at Pentecost, followed the example of the congregation at Corinth and baptized the dead, or tried to revive such ancient ordinances as the washing of feet or the love feast. Notably, no sect ever adopted all these practices, although the Mormons came close. The point is that restorationists almost had to approach the New Testament with some selective criteria.

A few religious reformers eventually gained a monopoly on the label "restoration" in American religious history. They all shared enough common concerns to give some unity to what began as several scattered reform movements. These early efforts led by 1810 to three related, regional groupings of congregations, all of which denominated themselves simply as "Christians." This was the first American restoration stream, but one whose sluggish and often multichanneled waters still revealed the as yet incompletely mixed hues of its three founding tributaries. By 1832 some of its channels intersected and merged with another stream—the Disciples of Christ—one not nearly as long, but spring-fed, clear, and fast moving. It swept up at least half of the Christian stream. The unmerged part of this stream, the congregations soon known as the Christian Connection or as General Convention or American Convention Christians, survived until 1931, when it merged with Congregationalists to form the Congregational Christian Churches.

THE FIRST CHRISTIAN CONGREGATIONS IN AMERICA

The first self-denominated Christian congregations with American origins began in 1794. The key actor was James O'Kelly, an early Methodist lay preacher in the American colonies and a long-term antagonist of Methodist Bishop Francis Asbury. O'Kelly first challenged Asbury's authority before the formation of the Methodist Episcopal Church in 1784 and then opposed Asbury's policies when he became one of the church's first two bishops. Against the pleas of Asbury and the commands of John Wesley, O'Kelly and other southern lay preachers began administering the sacraments to their congregations just after the American Revolution. At the founding Methodist conference in Baltimore in 1784, O'Kelly opposed a tight episcopal system and in the following years fought unsuccessfully for a Methodist discipline that was republican rather than "dictatorial." These controversies led to a Methodist general conference at Baltimore in 1792 (it began the tradition of quadrennial conferences). Here O'Kelly sponsored a resolution that would have allowed Methodist ministers to appeal to the conference their appointment to unwanted circuits by their bishop. This would have limited the authority claimed by Asbury. In the political fight a wily Asbury rather easily outmaneuvered O'Kelly and persuaded a majority of Methodist ministers to defeat O'Kelly's resolution.

After this defeat, O'Kelly, joined by a minority of colleagues, withdrew from the conference and from Asbury's authority. These dropouts proudly proclaimed themselves Republican Methodists. At this point no doctrinal issues were involved, and over the next two years both Asbury and O'Kelly tried in vain to find a way of healing the breach. The new Republican movement climaxed rather quickly, with several of the deviant ministers returning to the Asbury fold. The great fears of schism, which at first demoralized many Methodists, proved largely unfounded, since by 1800 it was clear that O'Kelly posed no enduring threat to the rapid growth of Methodism in the new country and new century, a growth related, in part, to the tight episcopal order founded by Wesley and supported by Asbury.

A majority of dissenting ministers were from Virginia and North Carolina. In 1792 these Republican Methodists began meeting in conferences and reluctantly began to make plans for a separate denomination. At a conference in August 1794 a committee of ministers failed to agree on the exact plan of government for their new denomination. At this point a ministerial colleague and supporter of O'Kelly, Rice Haggard, suggested that the group follow the primitive church and call themselves simply Christians. Another minister recommended that they make the Bible their only creed and confession. Since these solutions avoided factionalism, the assembly assented, and from 1794 on all but a handful of the surviving Republican Methodist congregations took the name Christian. In this founding conference they appropriately decided to give representation to laypeople.

These Christians of the South, led by no more than thirty or so ministers, remained a small sect in the new century. In doctrine and style they remained Wesleyites. At first they continued infant baptism by sprinkling, but this soon became a divisive issue. In 1810 the congregations divided into two groups, with one Virginia conference affirming adult immersion and often using the name Independent Christian Baptists. The O'Kelly faction, dominant in parts of North Carolina, remained loyal to the older Wesleyan practices, with the continued sprinkling of infants.

Just before this splintering, these southern Christians first learned of like-minded congregations in New England and sent a letter of greeting to a new Christian newspaper published in New England by Elias Smith. From Portsmouth, New Hampshire, a New England Christian conference sent a friendly reply. In 1811 Smith traveled to a Christian conference in Virginia made up of the baptist faction and without O'Kelly. At that conference the assembled Christians agreed to some form of common fellowship or union with the New England brethren. The Virginia conference was no official body, just an assemblage of no more than fourteen ministers and a hundred or so laypeople. Smith was the lone representative of the New Englanders and could hardly speak for all the congregations back home. Thus, this "union" seemed little more than an enthusiastic recognition of commonalities and an expression of hope for future cooperation. From 1811 on itinerant ministers from both regions often extended their preaching tours to make contact, and the southerners continued to communicate with Smith's newspaper. By 1811 both groups had already made contact with Christians in Kentucky led by Barton W. Stone.

The New England Christian movement was never as loose and amorphous as the one in the South. Arguably, it began in 1801 in Lyndon, Vermont. There a thirty-year-old Baptist physician, Abner Jones, suffered through an agonizing religious renewal during the New England revivals at the turn of the century and decided to give up a successful medical practice to become a soon-impoverished lay preacher. A Baptist always (he believed in the immersion of adult converts), he like thousands of others converted in the revivals soon came to doubt major tenets of Calvinism and repudiated the creed and the name of his fellow Baptists. Thus, in 1801 he gathered a small congregation of about a dozen people in Lyndon, a group that chose to call themselves simply Christians, leaving individuals free to adopt whatever speculative theology they believed consistent with the New Testament. Jones quickly took to the roads and trails of New England, an itinerant in the cause of such primitive Christianity. Doctrinally he was a freewill Baptist and fervently evangelical in the sense that he preached the need of a spirit-induced conversion. He sought and gained ordination in 1802 in a Freewill Baptist association, but with the reservation that he would denominate himself not a Baptist but only a Christian. In the same year he organized a second Christian congregation in Hanover, New Hampshire.

In 1803, when preaching in Portsmouth, New Hampshire, Jones first met Elias Smith, who soon would displace Jones as the dominant spokesman of a new movement. Smith, who was born in Lyme, Connecticut, but grew to adulthood in Woodstock, Vermont, was also an unorthodox physician (herbalist), a Jeffersonian Republican, and a former Baptist minister who had already repudiated Calvinist doctrines. He moved to Portsmouth in 1802 after a brief flirtation with Universalism. His opposition to orthodox medicine, to the dominant Federalism of New England, and to the orthodox clergy made him an effective rebel wherever he traveled. He had already, apparently without knowledge of Jones, determined to found a fully New Testament church, and in 1802 he met in a small conference at Sanbornton, New Hampshire, to draft articles or a covenant for a new Christian movement. Here Smith affirmed the type of simple, New Testament Christianity preached by Jones and in early 1803 formed his own small Christian congregation in Portsmouth. He surely already knew about a small Sandemanian congregation founded earlier in Portsmouth by Scottish restorationist Robert Sandeman, but its rigid dogmatism, separatism, and antievangelical style would have had little appeal to Smith. Smith, more gifted but less emotionally stable than Jones, was a man of changing moods and frequent controversies (he later twice defected to the Universalists). He joined Jones in preaching tours, and the two were able in a decade to organize at least fourteen Christian congregations. In 1808 Smith began publishing the *Herald of Gospel Liberty*, often claimed by members of his movement as the first Christian newspaper in America (a challengeable claim, since at least three evangelical periodicals already existed in New England and New York).

In the New England context, these new Christian congregations seemed quite heretical, a threat to orthodox Congregationalists or Calvinist Baptists. Neither Smith nor Jones had a classical education or any sophistication in theology. They used what they believed to be common sense in interpreting the Bible. They were as evangelical and as fervent in preaching at revivals, in trying to save souls, and in affirming an affectionate or spiritual Christianity as O'Kelly's ex-Methodists. But from the beginning the New England Christians not only repudiated creeds (in some sense, so did all the restorationists) but remained much more tolerant of doctrinal diversity than Campbell's later Disciples. Both Jones and Smith rejected any substitutional view of the atonement and found the traditional Trinity formula incomprehensible. They affirmed a type of Arianism. Smith, for example, believed Jesus a mediator between God and humans, subordinate to his father, yet divine and quite distinct from humans. In the New England context, almost everyone referred to this view as unitarian, and even some of the later Boston Unitarians would refer to the Christians as evangelical Unitarians. Since these views on the Trinity were close to those of Barton W. Stone in Kentucky, the New England Christians soon acknowledged a commonality with those in the West, and soon migrating New England Christians joined Stoneite Christian congregations in Ohio.

The Christian movement would not follow Smith into Universalism, and thus he eventually left his own congregation. Yet, salvation doctrines were clearly in flux in the early movement. By 1804 both Jones and Smith had agreed on the doctrine of annihilationism, or that the wages of sin would be death, not eternal torment (the view of later Adventists). Earlier than any other American sect save the Shakers, these New England Christians accepted women as preachers and evangelists. Orthodox clergymen ridiculed Smith because he accepted the ministry of a woman, Nancy Cram, in 1811. Neither annihilationism nor the so-called unitarianism of Smith and Jones became obligatory doctrines in this creedless movement, but at least avowed unitarians remained in the church throughout the nineteenth century. These New England Christians joined with the American Unitarian Association (AUA) to establish a joint seminary at Meadville, Pennsylvania, in 1844, but offered such limited support that it eventually became a fully Unitarian institution.

Although all the restoration leaders talked of Christian unity, the New England Christians alone were willing to embrace, in fellowship, Christians with a rather wide diversity of doctrines. This made them more ecumenical, more willing to explore various merger proposals, than the later Disciples. But such openness and a lack of any centralized denominational authority also made these Christians very vulnerable to new religious fashions. Not only Smith but several other ministers moved to Universalism. Because Smith and Jones were millenarians, convinced that the advent of the Christ was near, many New England Christians accepted the predictions of William Miller and furnished over half the leadership of the early Seventh-day Adventists. Others joined the popular spiritualist movement that preceded the Civil War.

It is worth noting that the home country of both Smith and Jones (backcountry New England) was a seedbed for new American Christian religions. William Miller lived on the New York-Vermont border near Poultney. Ellen G. White, the prophetess of Seventh-day Adventism, was from Gorham, Maine. Both Joseph Smith and Brigham Young as well as dozens of other early Mormon leaders were born in Vermont. Hosea Ballou, the leading architect of nineteenth-century Universalism, was born in New Hampshire and for years served Universalist churches in central Vermont.

Mary Baker Eddy grew up in the Merrimack valley of New Hampshire. Thus Christians, Universalists, Adventists, Mormons, and Christian Scientists all had roots in rural New England.

THE STONEITE CHRISTIANS

The third wing of the emerging Christian movement began in Kentucky and southern Ohio. Its history is enormously complex, for almost none of the characteristics of the very first independent congregations survived until the gradual union of half or more of these Christians in the West with the Disciples of Christ after 1832. Barton W. Stone was a very important catalyst of revolt against Presbyterianism in central Kentucky, but until 1812 he was not clearly a more important leader than at least two other colleagues. It is impossible, in a brief sketch, to do justice to this story.

Stone was born in Maryland of Anglican parents, grew up in southern Virginia, and moved into the Presbyterian Church only when he came to study at David Caldwell's academy outside Greensboro, North Carolina. He came in the midst of a regional revival that began at Hampden-Sydney College in 1787. He soon experienced an agonizing period of religious conviction, which led finally to conversion under the guidance of James McGready and William Hodges, both later architects of the western revival. He remained an adoptive Presbyterian, a bit of an alien in the Scotch-Irish culture. Committed to the Presbyterian ministry, he at least twice succumbed to doubts and indecision. In a year of teaching in Georgia in a Methodist academy, he first encountered a minister who had earlier been a Republican Methodist or Christian. After gaining a license back in North Carolina, Stone vacillated before deciding to join his friends in the West in the summer of 1796. He went first to the Cumberland area, to renew his friendship with McGready and other former mentors. From there he moved to central Kentucky, accepting a trial assignment to the then-vacant congregations of Cane Ridge and Concord. He finally settled in Cane Ridge in 1798, with ordination in the fall. The Presbyterial records show nothing unusual about his ordination, which would seem to mean that he subscribed the Westminster Confession. Later he claimed, as against the memories of most colleagues present, that he announced publicly that he subscribed to the confession only as it agreed with the scriptures, a key point in all subsequent Christian-Disciples hagiography. He rejoined his former colleagues at a communion in Logan County in the spring of 1801 and came back to report to his two congregations, even as a series of explosive sacramental meetings in central Kentucky built toward a climax, which in a sense came at his own Cane Ridge sacrament in August 1801.

Stone's later, almost bitter anti-Calvinism may have reflected long-term doubts partially reinforced by the revival experience. Clearly, the youthful, maturing Stone was swayed by the already developed religious culture at Cane Ridge and Concord. These congregations, in part by a self-screening process, had become distinctive in Kentucky for their egalitarianism, their moral rigor, and a very affectionate or spirited form of worship. The Cane Ridge congregation took a strong and early stand for temperance and petitioned the presbytery in the strongest possible language against slavery (only after his Cane Ridge ordination did Stone emancipate his slaves and begin advocating emancipation and colonization). Yet, none of these views was inconsistent with Calvinism. Stone's dissent on key doctrines seemed to reflect his characteristic approach to the Bible—a commonsense, reasonable reading of the text that was little influenced by scholarship. He was very close to Elias Smith in his approach to the Bible. Stone, who always stressed what was logical or reasonable, could not suffer mysteries, such as those that seemed to underlie the orthodox understanding of the Trinity, and his sense of a benevolent God made it impossible for him to grasp either the logical coherence or the psychological appeal of Calvinist doctrines such as depravity and election.

Stone's demystifying bent even led him to defend a new understanding of saving faith—the one doctrinal position that moved him closest to a view earlier affirmed by Robert Sandeman and later accepted by Alexander Campbell. For Presbyterians or other evangelicals, faith entailed much more than simple belief or intellectual assent to the scriptures; it meant special religious affections and unswerving trust or love, or what was impossible for anyone to affirm without the prompting of the Holy Spirit and thus the special initiative of God. Stone increasingly conceived of faith as belief, as a willingness to accept the reliability of New Testament witnesses, who offered the evidence that Jesus was indeed the Messiah or Christ. This belief was the faith that redeemed, when humans confessed and acted consistent with such beliefs. But Stone never denied, as did Alexander Campbell, the active role of the Spirit in bringing sinners to repentance; everything he observed in the revivals attested to this.

Stone's suppressed doubts about Presbyterian doctrines surfaced in 1803. In that year five Presbyterian ministers withdrew from the jurisdiction of the Kentucky Synod rather than suffer two of their group, Richard McNemar and John Thompson, to undergo an examination because of charges that they were Arminian in doctrine. Both McNemar and Thompson were former members of Stone's congregation at Cane Ridge. They gained a classical education at an academy established by the first Cane Ridge minister, Robert Finley. McNemar had been an elder in the Cane Ridge congregation before Stone became pastor in 1798, and McNemar made his commitment to the ministry in that congregation. The doctrinal controversy originated in the Washington Presbytery, a new presbytery based largely in new settlements in Ohio and northern Kentucky. There both McNemar and Thompson, along with McNemar's brother-in-law, John Dunlevy, also from Cane Ridge, ministered to large congregations, each of which reflected the intensely revivalistic subculture that had developed at Cane Ridge. Of the five original rebels, only Robert Marshall, from a congregation south of Lexington, was not a part of this immediate Cane Ridge subculture. He was a longtime friend of McNemar and, along with five or six other Presbyterian ministers, of approximately thirty in the synod, part of a now clearly identified revivalist faction.

After the synod tried and failed to find a basis of reconciliation with the five, it suspended them from the ministry and warned their congregations against their teachings. At this point the five, who insisted that they had not withdrawn from the Presbyterian Church but only from the jurisdiction of the synod, decided to bind together as a Springfield Presbytery (a nonlegal procedure, as they well realized, and thus their presbytery was not eligible for recognition by the Presbyterian General Assembly). Since they were able to persuade most members of their congregations to support them, the new presbytery had at least fifteen congregations in Ohio and Kentucky. The name Springfield had symbolic meaning. One of the two ministers charged, John Thompson, was pastor of the Springfield congregation outside Cincinnati, and it was there, earlier in 1803, that the Washington Presbytery, with the revivalists in a majority, had refused to hear charges against McNemar and Thompson.

The Springfield Presbytery never functioned as such within the Presbyterian system. The original five ministers accepted into ministerial fellowship two young men but did not ordain them, both out of a developing conviction that such was unscriptural and because they lacked any authority. In the second conference of these ministers at the Cane Ridge church in June 1804, the group decided to dissolve their so-called presbytery. McNemar wrote the half-serious, half-whimsical "Last Will and Testament of the Springfield Presbytery," a document that later became famous in the Disciples movement (Elias Smith would print it in the first number of his *Herald of Gospel Liberty*). In it McNemar endorsed a rather well-developed restorationist or primitive platform: that all institutions of merely human origin should dissolve into the one body of Christ, that no one should claim titles such as "reverend," that only the members of a congregation could govern a church or choose ministers, that the Bible had to be the only creed, and that the sweets of gospel liberty should replace paternalism within the church. The document also reflected strong millenarian expectations. McNemar sensed a new era aborning. The congregations, once again, followed their ministers, beginning with Cane Ridge, and thus declared their independence of any denominational government.

The ministers decided to accept only the name "Christian" for their now independent congregations. This was much more significant than the problem of labels might suggest. It aligned them with the O'Kelly faction in the South and with the choice just made in New England by Jones and Smith. Rice Haggard, the former Methodist minister who first persuaded rebellious Methodists to accept this label in 1794, had traveled to Kentucky to meet with the five dissidents and to persuade them to adopt the correct name. He would return shortly to Virginia for a few years and then move permanently to Kentucky as a minister in the Christian churches. In 1804 he wrote a pamphlet defending "Christian" as the only scriptural label for those in a New Testament church (congregations often took the name Church of Christ) and denouncing the use of any human-derived labels. In this direct way the western Christians began with a significant tie to those in the East.

At first the tie was little more than one of name and polity. At the time of the break with Presbyterianism, the five ministers were part of a developing revival faction within the Kentucky Synod and were clearly soft on key Calvinist doctrines. Even in 1801 the revivals had begun to fragment the Presbyterian clergy. All wanted revival. All tried to minister to their flock as best they could, however chaotic the meetings or wild the exercises. But the ministers soon disagreed as to what role they should take, either in trying to stimulate or to smother the level of emotional intensity. A majority of Presbyterian ministers tried to maintain order, to downplay the extreme exercises, to keep the physical effects in correct perspective (incidental to the work of the Spirit), and to correlate the intense feeling with a correct understanding of Christian doctrine (that is, with the Westminster Confession). Stone reflected a middle position. He never tried to stimulate the exercises. He was a calm, reasonable preacher. But he believed the exercises were the work of the Spirit, and he did nothing to restrain his own congregations, which gained local fame for the regular occurrence of swooning and crying out, rhythmic motions, and a type of holy laughter or singing. McNemar and Thompson enthusiastically embraced all the new exercises and, borrowing techniques from Methodist ministers, used their pulpits to inspire or inflame audiences. In the next three years their services, particularly their intercongregational communions, became wilder and wilder, with not only jerking and swooning but barking like dogs and formalized dancing. This style, almost as much as freewill doctrines, alienated those ministers and congregations from the main body of Presbyterians. Issues of style lay behind the overt doctrinal charges brought against Thompson and McNemar.

It is difficult to describe the first Christian congregations in Ohio and Kentucky. The great revival was at its peak. The religious situation was extremely volatile and complex. Within a year, opponents referred to the more revivalistic ministers as New Lights, drawing on eighteenth-century precedents. And at least McNemar and Thompson soon accepted and justified the label. They claimed direct visions and inspirations from God and applauded charismatic gifts among their members, particularly prophecy and exorcism. They adopted dance as a substitute for the more extreme and degrading forms of barking and jerking. In the falling or swooning, people purportedly glimpsed a heavenly kingdom and were overwhelmed even by its fragrances. McNemar was sure this all presaged the imminent return of the Christ and fanned the millenarian expectations of his congregation to the breaking point. As of 1805 one might have predicted that these Christians in the West would become America's first Pentecostal denomination, for such seemed the trend in these first two, heady years of "Gospel liberty." But in 1805 three Shaker missionaries came from New Lebanon, New York, and very soon converted McNemar, Dunlevy, and a young protégé, Malcolm Worley, plus the most recent ministerial addition to the Christian cause, Matthew Houston. This meant the defection of all the wild ones save Thompson and Marshall, who shortly began to repent their own excesses.

Even before the Shaker defection, Stone began to enunciate a set of doctrines that seemed completely heretical to Presbyterians. In a series of essays he tried to clarify his developing antitrinitarian views and his rejection of any substitutionary version of the atonement, or doctrines affirmed across the whole Catholic-Protestant spectrum. Also, after careful Bible study, he and almost all his followers submitted to immersion. Stone never made this a condition of membership, but by 1830 only a handful of western Christians remained content with their childhood sprinkling. These doctrines and practices proved very disturbing to Marshall and Thompson, as did the lack of any formal discipline in the almost anarchic congregations (they could not even act in concert to resist the Shakers). Thus, both ministers recanted and successfully applied for readmission to the Presbyterian Church in 1811. This left only Stone of the original five rebels. From 1812 on he remained the single most influential voice for the new movement in the West. After the death of his first wife, he moved briefly to middle Tennessee and helped found there the first congregations in what would later become a center of the Restoration movement.

After assuming his leadership role, more by default than by choice, Stone was more emphatic than ever in his antitrinitarian crusade. By popular labeling, which he sometimes accepted, his Arian or subordinationist position (Jesus was not God, but the son of God, created before all worlds, and fully divine) made him a Unitarian, a position that soon gained him support and endorsement from New England Christians but that stigmatized his congregations in the West. Once again, Stone never made acceptance of his theological speculations a condition of membership. Several ministerial colleagues did not share his views, and possibly few lay Christians accepted or even understood his Arianism, a position that always seemed largely incidental to the evangelical appeal of the movement.

From 1812 to 1832 the three branches of the Christian churches grew rather slowly, with those in Kentucky and Ohio expanding most rapidly. The loose contacts and affinities among the three groups did not constitute unity or approximate the coherence that one expects in a denomination, although local congregations met in conferences. The Christians of New York and New England began meeting in the United States General Convention by 1815. It tried, with small success, to unify all the Christians, and at least some delegates from Virginia attended the convention. None came from the western Christians. Thus, an envoy from New York went west in 1825 to try to establish stronger contacts. But his effort to get a united western convention failed in 1826, apparently because the Stoneites felt that they had not had a large enough role in planning it. At the urging of eastern Christians, in 1827 Stone, who had moved several times since 1812, established a new journal, *The Christian Messenger*, at his home at Georgetown, Kentucky. It joined the New England *Herald of Gospel Liberty* as a national organ, since Christians all over America subscribed or sent communications to it. With the gradual ascendancy of the immersionists in the South, all the Christians in the three scattered movements became, in effect, a very evangelical freewill Baptist sect, distinguished from other freewill Baptist associations only by their name and their rejection of all creeds. Stone's so-called Unitarianism and the antitrinitarian views widely affirmed by New England Christians both distinguished and in the larger Christian population stigmatized these Christians.

For most historians of the Disciples of Christ, the story of these Christian sects all but ended in 1832 with the informal union of a possible majority of western and southern Christians with the Disciples. The innovations of the earlier Christians simply blended at that point into what became a highly competitive Disciples movement. But not all Christians accepted the union. Over half of Stone's Ohio and Indiana congregations remained independent and rejected Campbell's doctrines, while the union involved only a few congregations in New England and in Virginia and North Carolina.

THOMAS AND ALEXANDER CAMPBELL

Most historians of the Restoration movement focus on Alexander Campbell, with only secondary attention to O'Kelly, Jones, Smith, or Stone. In the perspective of later developments, this makes sense. Campbell, more than anyone else, shaped the Disciples movement that matured after 1832. But it is good to remember that Campbell was a latecomer. He was a child in Ulster when O'Kelly and Haggard formed the first Christian churches. The opening events in the long road to a Disciples movement came only in 1809, the year Alexander Campbell arrived in America, and only in 1830 did Campbell's Reformed Baptists dispense with their association and their Baptist name to become simply Disciples of Christ. But it was Campbell, much more than anyone else, who molded a set of distinctive doctrines and practices for the movement.

Thomas Campbell, the father, and Alexander Campbell, the son, were belated Scotch-Irish immigrants to America. Thomas, who taught in his own academy in Ulster, was also a preacher in the narrow, rigorous Anti-Burgher wing of the Scottish Seceder Presbyterians (Associate Synod). He decided to emigrate to the United States in 1807, in part for health reasons. His wife and children were to follow, but because of a shipwreck in 1808, they had to delay their trip until 1809 and spent a year in Glasgow. In the unexpected delay, young Alexander, well-tutored already in the classics by his father, was able to study for a year at the University of Glasgow. When he, with mother and siblings, arrived in New York in 1809, he was only twenty-one. Important in shaping both father and son was their excessively scholastic Presbyterian heritage. The Seceders were rigorous confessionalists, suspicious of any doctrinal innovations in the Scottish Kirk. In Scotland, Northern Ireland, and the United States they professed an evangelical faith keyed to the work of the Spirit, but they resisted hymn singing (they used only psalters) and rejected all new forms of revivalism. They particularly condemned the disorder and the acrobatic exercises that accompanied many American revivals. The scattered members of the Associate Synod in America became known as antirevivalists. By background and experience Thomas and Alexander Campbell had no taste for a highly affectionate or ecstatic form of Christianity, and in this one sense they remained faithful to their Seceder roots.

Upon arriving in America in 1807, Thomas Campbell sought a ministerial placement from the just-convening Associate Synod. His talents and college education made him a valued addition to a small sect that had never adequately staffed its few congregations in the United States. The synod assigned him to what then seemed a virtual frontier, small congregations along the western borders of Pennsylvania, near the village of Washington and a stone's throw from the narrow wedge of western Virginia (now West Virginia) and the Ohio River. This tristate area nurtured the early Disciples movement. Thomas was quickly in trouble with his presbytery. He admitted to his communion table regular Presbyterians without a minister and announced doctrines that led his colleagues to suspect his conformity to required doctrine and polity. Charged by his presbytery with errors, some of which suggested the position later taken by Disciples, he did not answer to the satisfaction of his ministerial colleagues. On appeal to the synod, he had to accept censure but was reinstated as a minister. His jealous presbytery would not assign him to a congregation.

By this time Thomas was sick of narrow party divisions and scholastic distinctions, which he had too long suffered in Ulster. In his first protest to his synod he had aired some of those concerns. Now, without a congregation, he could only preach to neighbors and did so in homes or fields. Encouraged by some of his neighbors, he joined with them to form the Christian Association, which they at first did not conceive as a church. The members, if they wished, retained their ties to their old denominations. But, clearly, this association of friends soon took on all the functions of a church. Eventually the members built a log meetinghouse on Brush Run, outside Washington, Pennsylvania. During the spring and summer of 1809 Campbell wrote and presented to his association a "Declaration and Address," a type of platform or constitution for the association and also a plan for achieving the unity of all churches. Even as he awaited copies from the printer, he greeted his long-delayed family.

Later Disciples, particularly the more liberal or inclusive ones, honored Thomas Campbell's declaration as the founding document of their movement. Above all, Thomas decried the spirit of party or faction. Divisions among Christians obstructed the mission of the church. Most divisions reflected matters of private opinion or human interpretation and thus were not essential. He hoped his association and other like-minded groups might begin a movement back to a unified church, for in the highest sense of the word there was only one church. The church was made up of all who professed their faith in the Christ and obeyed what the Christ commanded. It was the obligation of such Christians to make the church one in fact. The way to do this, he argued, was to follow the New Testament in what it prescribed and to resist any human innovations in areas where it offered no guidelines. Later, Disciples would turn this advice into a formula: "Where the Scriptures speak, we speak; where the Scriptures are silent, we are silent." By such advice Campbell introduced the restoration theme. His little association would have no terms of communion except those expressly taught by Jesus and his disciples in the New Testament, meaning no human creeds or doctrines. He seemingly granted to individuals a broad latitude for private interpretation or theological speculation, but behind his openness to private differences lay an assumption basic to all the early restoration leaders, that on all the essentials of Christian communion the New Testament was simple and unambiguous. He reflected the commonsense outlook of contemporary Scottish philosophy and at times almost paraphrased John Locke's book on toleration. As it turned out, the New Testament did not offer an unambiguous guide, and the more Christians tried to follow it the more likely they were to fall into sectarian strife. From 1809 on, Thomas Campbell generally deferred to his son Alexander. He never contributed another major document to the movement but in letters and sermons remained more irenic, more open to differences, than his often legalistic son.

While Thomas fought his battle with the Associate Synod in America, young Alexander began to rebel against Seceder orthodoxy at the University of Glasgow. In a symbolic gesture he deposited his leaden token but did not take communion at his Seceder congregation. More critical, he became an eager student of Scottish independency and of early restoration efforts within Scotland. In various ways and at various times two small sects directly influenced the work of Thomas and Alexander Campbell in the United States. In 1725 a Presbyterian minister in Scotland, John Glas, formed an independent (noncovenanting) society and in 1727 was suspended by the Church of Scotland. He thus began his own effort to restore the primitive church. He founded noncreedal congregations (a few remain in Britain) usually called Churches of Christ, instituted at first monthly and eventually weekly communion, defined faith as simply acceptance of the testimony of New Testament witnesses that Jesus was the Christ whose death atoned for human sinfulness, and, as some Anabaptist groups, revived several early ordinances of the primitive church (the love feast, the holy kiss, and foot washing). Robert Sandeman, the son-in-law of Glas and soon the major theologian of the movement, emigrated to New England and founded his first congregation at Portsmouth, New Hampshire, in 1765. A disciple had formed a similar congregation in Danbury, Connecticut, a year earlier. Eventually the Sandemanians, as they were called in America, had seven or eight very rigid and exclusive and soon schismatic congregations, all of which finally expired in the nineteenth century. These Sandemanian congregations fell into factionalism after Sandeman's death in 1771. One splinter from the Danbury congregation eventually affiliated with the Disciples.

This one institutional connection to the later Disciples was not very significant. Much more important were the contacts that both Thomas and Alexander Campbell had with such restorationists back in Ulster. Later, Walter Scott, the most effective preacher in the early Disciples movement, became a member of one of these Scottish-type Churches of Christ before he joined the Disciples. Except for their continuation of infant baptism, Glas and Sandeman anticipated almost every doctrine and practice of the later Disciples. Some of the language of both Thomas and Alexander Campbell was almost identical to that of Sandeman. In New England, Sandeman's beliefs seemed very threatening to most ministers, not the least because he so emphatically condemned all the existing denominations, or what he called popular Christianity. The one doctrinal issue that led to the most debate was his lean and simple concept of faith as mere belief, with none of the affectional elements present in evangelical churches.

The Sandemanian churches repudiated any creeds or confessions, tried to adhere to the simple and direct meaning of the New Testament, and came as close as any church to reviving every aspect of New Testament worship. They made communion the center of Sunday worship, sang only metrical psalms, ordained multiple elders or bishops (to them the titles were interchangeable), called on various elders for morning prayers or sermons, emphasized free pews and freewill offerings, closed their communion to outsiders, gathered in homes for the love feast, and exercised very strict church discipline. Sandeman seemed, to the evangelical ministers that absorbed most of his denunciations, arrogant and self-righteous, even as the Sandemanian congregations claimed to represent the only New Testament, and thus acceptable, church in all of New England. This sectarian bent and exclusivity appealed to the more conservative elements among later Disciples, with one small faction in the present Churches of Christ still insisting on a New Testament order of worship that is very close to that of the Sandemanians.

In Glasgow Alexander Campbell also attended a free congregation influenced not so much by Glas as by two related reformers, the eminent and wealthy brothers Robert and James Haldane. The Haldanes tried, much as Glas, to restore the primitive church, but they first used their wealth to seek reforms in the Scottish church. In 1799 the Haldanes established their first separate congregation in Edinburgh, where they followed the Glasites in their primitive practices but, unlike Glas, ultimately decided to shift to the baptism of adult converts by immersion. In Ulster Thomas Campbell had met one of the brothers and participated with them in a common evangelical society. In Glasgow Alexander Campbell became a friend of Greville Ewing, who served as pastor of the largest and most wealthy Haldanite church in the city. Ewing, unlike the Haldanes, still defended infant baptism, and thus at the time of his move to America Alexander Campbell had not yet repudiated his own Presbyterian baptism. After the Campbells moved to America, a reforming minister in Scotland, George Forrester, already sympathetic to the Haldanites, migrated to Pittsburgh, Pennsylvania. There he established an independent Church of Christ in which the later Disciples leader, Walter Scott, would be baptized, and which Scott briefly served as a minister.

By the time he arrived in America, young Alexander was intellectually ready to join Thomas in the Christian Association and gladly applauded the declaration. He continued his studies under his father's direction but now in further preparation for the ministry, although it is not clear what institutional affiliation he envisioned. He gave his first sermon in 1810 (at age twenty-two). From the beginning he was an effective, although not an inspiring, preacher. His bent was careful, logical analysis. He was never as penetrating in theological speculation as Barton Stone. Instead he was a born lawyer or debater, careful in research and preparation, and in this sense scholarly, although his biblical scholarship remained at mid-level (textual but not critical). Campbell's role in the ministry made up only one aspect of his career. He soon married well and exhibited keen acquisitive or entrepreneurial skills. Through various ventures, from land speculation to royalties on hymnbooks, he became one of the most wealthy men in his tristate area. Through his first wife he gained ownership of and moved to a large farm in the northern wedge of Virginia, the site of the later Bethany, a town he named. His farm was only a few miles from the Brush Run congregation in Pennsylvania.

Campbell became one of the most distinguished men of western Virginia. He became a popular lecturer on a range of topics and gained election to the 1829–30 Virginia constitutional convention, at which he failed in his efforts to gain greater representation for western Virginians and gradually to eliminate slavery. In his entrepreneurial and public role he was a broadly learned, cosmopolitan figure. But as an editor and publisher or as a religious leader he could seem more parochial or dogmatic. At times he could be contemptuous of people who disagreed with him.

When, in 1812, the Brush Run Christian Association decided to become an independent church, it elected Alexander Campbell as its first minister. The congregation was locally distinctive in celebrating weekly communion. Because of a growing conviction that it was scripturally mandated, the whole Campbell family and several members of the congregation chose to be baptized by immersion in 1812. Although at the time Campbell had not yet matured his doctrine of baptismal remission (first announced in 1823), this acceptance of baptism made the little congregation Baptist. With certain written reservations, it joined the western Pennsylvania Red Stone Baptist Association, apparently in 1815 (after the regular Presbyterians had rejected an application for ministerial fellowship from Thomas Campbell). At this time the doctrines of the Brush Run congregation were probably loosely Calvinistic. Thomas Campbell continued to refer to himself as a Calvinist, but it is not always clear exactly what he meant by the label. From 1813 to 1830 Alexander Campbell slowly matured his doctrines, most explicitly non-Calvinistic, within the unlikely context of two Baptist associations. As he did so, he developed what was to be most distinctive about the beliefs of later Disciples.

As Alexander Campbell began his ministry, he was a conspicuous ex-Seceder. By temperament and background he distrusted a religion tied to feeling or to an explosive conversion experience. Thus he was accounted a "rational" Baptist. He was also an avowed opponent of creeds and any episcopal authority but was open to a loose association with other congregations, or what he gained when he and his congregation joined the Red Stone Association. Campbell rose rapidly to preeminence among Baptist ministers, largely because of his education and debating skills. In an 1816, belatedly scheduled sermon before a joint Baptist gathering he began enunciating doctrines that gradually alienated him from traditional Calvinist Baptists. In this sermon on the Mosaic law, Campbell drew a sharp distinction between covenants or dispensations. He argued that the church rested entirely on the authority of Jesus and the New Testament. Jesus fulfilled the old law, and in none of its details, not even its moral aspects, did it have continuing authority for Christians (the broad moral principles enunciated in the ten commandments and as taught by Jesus did apply to Christians, but not on the authority of Moses and Sinai). This declaration of a fully New Testament church seemed largely innocuous, since Christians did not follow many ritualistic laws observed by Jews. But most Christians, and particularly those in the Calvinist tradition, picked and chose among Old Testament commands. For example, Presbyterians used Old Testament types to justify infant baptism (the counterpart of circumcision), while Baptists joined most Christians in using Jewish precedents to strengthen their appeals for tithing and applied certain Jewish sabbatarian laws to Sunday, or what Campbell called the Lord's Day, but which most Protestants inappropriately called the Christian Sabbath. This selective reliance on the Jewish scriptures also supported earlier attempts to merge religious and civil law, as had the Puritans in New England (echoes of this remained in blasphemy and Sunday laws). Implicit but not yet overtly stated by Campbell was leeway for Christians to work on Sunday, although Campbell would insist that Christians make the Lord's Day one of worship and devotion, certainly not one of work and recreation. Thus in his early years Campbell opposed all Sabbatarian legislation, which seemed to him a violation of the separation of church and state, a principle that he always advocated.

Campbell soon became a famous debater. He participated in five widely publicized, weeklong contests, including one with famous agnostic and reformer Robert Owen. In his first two scheduled, publicized debates in 1820 and 1823 he defended adult baptism by immersion against Presbyterian ministers. By the end of those exchanges he had moved to his most controversial doctrine—baptismal remission, a principle keyed to what became the Disciples's benchmark New Testament passage, Acts 2:38. Peter, just after the coming of the Holy Spirit, commanded the multitudes to repent and be baptized in the name of Jesus the Christ for the forgiveness of sins and in order to receive the Holy Spirit. This clearly set the purpose of baptism—the remission of sins. But it left open a dozen possible interpretations.

Campbell never quite settled on a completely unambiguous understanding of baptismal remission. By 1823 he had already repudiated the Calvinist doctrines of complete depravity and limited atonement. Thus, unlike Roman Catholics, he never interpreted remission to mean a washing away of the sin of Adam or of any inherent sinfulness. Infants suffered no such disability; neither did people who never had a chance to hear the gospel. The guilt that needed forgiveness had to be guilt incurred from willful disobedience (this is the Anabaptist view). Thus, for Campbell, baptism remitted the accumulated guilt of adult converts, those who now believed the New Testament and chose to follow it into the Church of Christ.

What was never fully clear, and what was at the heart of the most vigorous criticism of Campbell by other Protestants, was the causal status of baptism. Here Campbell showed some ambivalence, much more so than some of his more rigid disciples, including even Walter Scott. Clearly he did not attribute any efficacy to baptism alone and thus did not interpret baptism as a remitting sacrament in the Roman Catholic sense. On the other hand, he saw baptism as essential in the steps leading to salvation, thus viewing the ordinance as more critical than most Baptists, who saw it as the first act of obedience for converts, linked closely with regeneration as a symbol of the burial of an old person and the rising of the new but not in itself necessary for salvation. For Baptists, a new convert who intended to be baptized but died in the meantime had no reason to fear damnation. Campbell, in the 1823 debate, distinguished baptism not as the efficient cause for forgiveness (this is belief and true repentance) but as a formal cause, but still a literal and not just a symbolic medium for the washing away of sins. Since Campbell himself was not only a confessing Christian but had been ordained before he decided to be immersed, his doctrine of baptismal remission seemed to mean that he had earlier deceived himself, but in a famous 1837 letter he conceded that those who believed but were ignorant of the proper form of baptism were in the Church, an inclusiveness not accepted by many of his successors in the movement. Obviously, if they correctly understood that baptism was necessary, they would obey the Christ. Notably, at the time of his own immersion he had not yet developed his doctrines about baptismal remission, and by the standards of some of the more rigid exclusivists in his later movement even he lacked the proper baptism (the right method but for the wrong purpose).

It was not only the remitting role of baptism but its priority to the gift of the Holy Spirit that challenged normative evangelical beliefs. Campbell denied that the Holy Spirit was a gift to other than Christians, those already baptized and in the Church. It was a promise to Christians alone, and thus, contrary to the doctrines affirmed by all the Reformed churches, the Holy Spirit could not work directly within an individual and thus bring sinners to repentance. Only in the sense that the Spirit informed the Word did it apply to sinners, which in effect made the path to salvation one of hearing and understanding and believing the New Testament. In this claim Campbell began to undercut any spiritualistic or supernatural interpretation of conversion, with its intense, emotional, crisislike features.

Faith, to Campbell, meant belief based on the New Testament witness that Jesus was the Messiah. It resembled any type of empirical or inductive belief, any belief based on inferences from facts, but such was the nature of the object of such belief that it elicited an active and moving response from humans. In the tradition of Locke and the commonsense philosophers he knew back in Scotland, Campbell believed that humans were born with no innate ideas, that they learned entirely through experience. This led to his emphasis on the evidential strength of the accounts in the New Testament. The road to belief and repentance was quite similar to a persuasive course in history. It meant reading or hearing the New Testament to the point of conviction and then a reasonable and trusting response to the now clearly documented lordship of Jesus. Then came the repentance, baptism, and commitment to Christian obedience that made one a member of the Church. At this point one received the help of the Spirit, but a Spirit that worked not miraculously but through human faculties. Campbell knowledged the special, miracle-sustaining gifts of the Spirit enjoyed by the early apostles but believed these were present only in the Apostolic age (in this one case he used reasonable arguments to reject prevalent aspects of worship in the Pauline congregations, such as healing and speaking in tongues). Not only did Campbell reject any explosive or supernatural conversion but any charismatic or ecstatic conception of life after conversion. His was, in this sense, a cold and not a hot religion, although one should not discount the elements of love and joy that marked the process of repentance and baptism in Disciples revivals.

THE DISCIPLES MOVEMENT

The movement begun by the Campbells had a slow start. Even as late as 1823, when Campbell had matured his major doctrines and practices, it included only three closely related congregations (the original Brush Run church, a small congregation at a school taught by Thomas Campbell in Pittsburgh, and a colony congregation from Brush Run at what later became Wellsburg, Virginia, on the Ohio River). Only in 1823 did the movement make the first step toward independence and rapid growth. From 1815 on, Brush Run had been part of the Red Stone Baptist Association, but Alexander Campbell's doctrinal views and his strong statement of them increasingly alienated Calvinist Baptists. Fortunately for the Campbells, two sympathetic Baptist ministers had taken the lead in forming a small Baptist association—the Mahoning—in the Western Reserve of Ohio in 1820. Just before his likely expulsion from the Red Stone Association in 1824, Alexander Campbell and his small congregation at Wellsburg joined the Mahoning Association, and by this new ministerial fellowship he maintained his right to preach as a Baptist. For a brief time Brush Run remained in the Red Stone Association, while Thomas Campbell's small congregation had no affiliation (the Red Stone Association had rejected its application for fellowship).

Just before this shift and after the success of a published version of his first debate, Alexander Campbell established a monthly magazine, *The Christian Baptist*, at his home in Bethany. In this magazine Campbell fervently promoted his doctrines and in good debating style tried to refute, at times even ridicule, his clerical opponents. This made his journal and his baptismal doctrines increasingly controversial, often to the despair of a more benign Thomas Campbell, who still hoped for Christian unity, not a new sect to add to the competition. In these Baptist years Alexander Campbell launched vicious attacks on every form of ecclesiastical organization and every formalized clergy. He denied any special ministerial authority based on university training, on any form of ordination, and on any purported special calling from the Holy Spirit. He affirmed the complete separation of church and state and urged Christians to avoid participation in benevolent or missionary societies. He approved only the simplest form of meetinghouse, denounced instrumental music, and preached the radical equality of all Christians. He would later moderate these views, but in his periodical he provided plenty of ammunition for those Christians who, by 1900, wanted a completely purified Church and who dropped their fellowship with the Disciples to become the Churches of Christ.

The Mahoning Association, made up in 1824 of approximately sixteen churches in Ohio plus the Wellsburg congregation across the river in Virginia, was a loose association of independent congregations. Most were already quite sympathetic to the beliefs of Campbell. The association was distinctively more freewill than Calvinistic. Soon members of these churches were widely known as Reformed Baptists. In 1824, after his debate of 1823, Campbell completed a two-month preaching tour in Kentucky and won several Baptist congregations and ministers over to his reforms, including one congregation in Louisville that gave up its creed and confession and began celebrating communion each Sunday. But for a time all these reformed congregations continued to use the Baptist name, as did Campbell himself, although enemies often referred to his congregations as Campbellites. Neither Alexander nor Thomas wanted to create a new sect. But cooperation with Baptists became more difficult when the Campbell reforms seemed to alienate half the Baptist churches in Ohio and Kentucky from their traditional doctrines and practices. The competition grew hot largely because of the success of a young minister, Walter Scott, engaged as a missionary by the Mahoning Association in 1827.

Walter Scott was almost as critical to the emergence of a separate Disciples movement as Alexander Campbell. Scott, appropriately, was a Presbyterian from Scotland, an immigrant to America at age twenty in 1818. He was a graduate of the University of Edinburgh and by profession a teacher when he arrived in America. While teaching in an academy in Pittsburgh, he became an associate of George Forrester, a disciple of the Haldanes. In Pittsburgh Forrester had established a small independent Church of Christ very similar to the Sandemanian congregations in New England. In this congregation Scott began his tutelage in primitive Christianity and soon submitted to immersion. At Forrester's premature death, Scott took over both the academy and the congregation. During this ministry he visited a Scotch Baptist church in New York City that taught baptismal remission but was otherwise unwilling to adapt the primitive pattern as Scott understood it. In 1821 Scott first met Alexander Campbell in Pittsburgh and almost immediately became his disciple. A man of shifting moods and not nearly as aggressive as Campbell, he urged Campbell to publish *The Christian Baptist* and became its most faithful contributor. In his first series of articles he sketched a plan for spreading the Christian faith and in it hinted at his later schematic "plan of salvation." In 1826 Scott left his school and congregation in Pittsburgh to take over an academy in Steubenville, Ohio, just across and up the river from Wellsburg. Because of Campbell's friendship, he addressed the Mahoning Association in 1826, and in 1827 it elected him as its first paid evangelist (he was not a Baptist but a member of a small Haldanite congregation). Scott immediately closed his local academy, left his wife and children, and embarked on his "experiment" in spreading the "ancient gospel."

After some early frustrations Scott developed a simple, effective mode of preaching. He exploited the widespread popular confusion over doctrines and thus doubts about personal salvation. To confused people he presented a reasonable, itemized plan of salvation open to anyone who would comply with a series of points or steps, which Scott often grouped in five so that even schoolchildren could count them off on the fingers of one hand. The steps never amounted to a rigid formula, and Scott often changed the exact wording. Three of the steps were critical, for they responded to the query, What must one do to be saved? Scott had a formalistic answer: believe, repent, and be baptized (one of his five-step formulas was "believe, repent, be baptized, gain the remission of sins, and receive the Spirit," although eventually the most popular formula would be "hear the Word, believe, repent, confess, and be baptized"). This seemed simple, clear, and doable. In the Reformed churches the beginning requirement—faith— was not a matter of choice, since it involved trust and love. Even belief, in one sense, was not a choice, since one could not believe any and all propositions. Belief, as Scott insisted, was a matter of evidence, and evidenced belief alone constituted faith. He insisted that the only proposition that one needed to believe and confess was simple: Jesus was the Messiah. In the cultural context, most of his audience already believed this. Even if they did not, they had enough respect for the New Testament to give credence to the historical evidence Scott could cite to support the belief. Thus, by existing commitments or by response to evidenced arguments, almost anyone could fulfill the first step. Scott knew this and exploited the point, particularly among people who had waited in vain for the work of the Spirit, for that explosive moment of grace that purportedly marked conversion.

Thousands of concerned, frightened, even despairing folk found something beguiling and liberating in Scott's message. They gladly professed belief, repented their past disobedience, and came forward for baptism. It was so reasonable and promised so much. Of course, entrance into the church was only a beginning, and the rigorous, demanding discipleship preached by Scott was not easy to sustain. But the huge, intimidating first step was easy, and one could hazard the future with hope based on the promised guidance of the Spirit that followed baptism and gained meaning in the larger community of the faithful. With this message Scott won a thousand new converts the first year and often just as many in each of the next thirty years. These were largely people heretofore unbaptized, not Baptists who bought into Campbell's reforms. Other preachers, mostly Baptists won over to the movement, tried to duplicate Scott's tactics, with the result that by 1830 the movement was expanding rapidly, particularly in Ohio and Kentucky, which meant that it overlapped with and in some areas competed with Barton Stone's Christian churches (this was true in Steubenville).

In 1830 Scott and Campbell moved outside the Baptist fold. In a sense they had captured the Mahoning Association from within, but by the very success of their missionary efforts (up to 200 congregations by 1830) they created a fearful and defensive reaction among most other Baptist associations. Particularly for the dominant Calvinist Baptists, the doctrines of Campbell were anathema, as was a new, largely borrowed translation of the New Testament in 1826 by Campbell, in which he translated key words to support his own doctrines, particularly on baptism. For smaller, looser freewill Baptist associations, Campbell's closely reasoned doctrines often proved irresistible, and several freewill Baptist congregations and even a few small associations accepted the Reformed Baptist faith.

In 1825 the Red Stone Association finally forced out the Brush Run congregation and others of like mind because they would not subscribe to Calvinist confessions. Ohio Calvinist Baptists tried to lure away members from Campbell's churches by establishing a rival to the Mahoning Association. By 1830 the Campbells were widely reviled in Baptist publications. Campbell had been content to work within an association so long as he felt free to preach his own doctrines, but by 1830 he felt more beleaguered than liberated. In effect, the Mahoning Association by 1830 was only nominally Baptist, since its congregations all reflected the doctrines of Campbell and embraced the plan of salvation so effectively preached by Scott. Besides, local Reformed Baptist congregations in Kentucky had already separated, often peacefully, from their Baptist associations. The symbolic separation came in August 1830 when the Mahoning Association voted to dissolve, a move Campbell neither planned nor desired but reluctantly accepted. Soon, although at various times in different congregations and different regions, the newly separate congregations took the name "Disciples of Christ," which Campbell preferred for a variety of reasons, including the prior assumption of the name "Christian" by Stone and others, and because of the unitarian virus he associated with the New England Christians.

With the break, Campbell dropped his earliest and now misnamed journal, *The Christian Baptist*. A few months before, he and Scott had launched a less polemical, more scholarly journal, the *Millennial Harbinger*. The title reflected his growing hopes in an early millennial age. But Campbell was never consistent in his views of a coming millennium. He wrote editorials for his new journal right in the midst of the Millerite movement. He meant by "millennium" a thousand-year period of great bliss and happiness for the church. But he did not believe that a miraculous or magical return of the Christ would inaugurate this great age. By later, inadequate labels he often seemed the prototypal postmillennialist. He believed that the restoration of the New Testament church, now well begun, presaged an early age of Christian unity. At times he even talked of this reformation as the beginning of a millennium. He was a creature of the mid-nineteenth century. He rejoiced in all the examples of material progress, and despite periods of disillusionment with and disengagement from American party politics, he was usually an enthusiast for what he called American democracy. This joined with a clear racial theory: the great role of Anglo-Saxon civilization, which was to him the hope of the world. Thus he usually looked forward to religious, moral, and political reforms that would prepare the way for the direct government of the Christ. With the disillusionment that came with the conflict over slavery, he muted some of his earlier dreams of an imminent millennium and then talked about 2000 as the likely year. But it is important to note that Campbell was neither a coherent dogmatist nor a rigorous theologian. One can quote him to quite different effect according to time and place. Typically, on the great, ongoing battle between Calvinists and Arminians, he repudiated both polarities but never very clearly clarified a middle way between the two.

The *Millennial Harbinger* became his and the movement's most influential organ and, in time, the most famous product of Campbell's pen. In it Campbell played the role of a de facto bishop (some colleagues even playfully used the title), trying until the Civil War to mediate disputes and to maintain, as a test of fellowship, the central doctrines that he gave to the movement. In the loose congregational system, preacher-editors became the molders of opinion (this led to the frequent joke that the Disciples did not have bishops, only even more powerful editors) and at times also the source of divisions. Alexander Campbell, as editor-bishop, could be at times a moderating peacemaker, helping cement bonds between widely di-

verging ministers and congregations. But he could also be narrow, dogmatic, even testy when he sensed a challenge to basic doctrines or to his
status in the movement. He was quite ruthless in denouncing and helping
drive from fellowship an eloquent Nashville minister, Jesse B. Ferguson,
who argued for a mild form of universalism (a second-chance theory,
meaning that those who died before the gospel would have another opportunity to repent). Campbell's *Millennial Harbinger* became his disciplinary
tool, since it circulated most widely and had more prestige than the dozens
of other regional publications that developed within the movement.

But the publication of the new journal marked a transition in Campbell's tactics if not his doctrines. He soon saw the need for some type of cooperation or organization. He embraced higher education and founded his
own college at Bethany. Walter Scott had already presided over Bacon College in Kentucky, with its well-chosen name reflecting Scott's emphasis on
a simple form of empiricism. Campbell, after early reluctance, supported
organized missionary activity. He rejected extreme forms of separatism and
ultimately urged Disciples to vote. He was a member of the American
Bible Society. Finally, he was at times inclusive or irenic in his approach to
other Protestants, albeit increasingly rabid in his anti-Catholicism and fervent in his emphasis on an Anglo-Saxon role in Christianizing the world.

By 1831 the Stoneite Christians and Campbell's Disciples already mixed
and competed in several areas of Ohio and Kentucky. Campbell in his trip
to Kentucky in 1824 met with Stone, and the two had corresponded, with
Stone more generous toward Campbell than the reverse. In 1831 their literary exchanges were sharp, revealing some jealousy over their respective
roles in restoring the New Testament church. Stone confronted the Disciples in his own backyard. He had as a neighbor in Georgetown, Kentucky, a Disciples minister, John T. Johnson (his brother Richard served as
vice-president of the United States under Van Buren), who preached at a
church just outside town. The two congregations often shared communion. Johnson and the more elderly Stone became fast friends, with Johnson becoming a coeditor of Stone's *Christian Messenger*. The hope for some
type of union between the two movements matured in their local discussions in 1831. Soon involved in the informal dialogues was another early,
more colorful Kentucky Disciples minister, "Raccoon" John Smith, who
hailed from the mountains of east Tennessee. A close associate of Stone
from the Cane Ridge community, John Rogers, consulted in behalf of
the Christians. The preliminary talks led to more formal discussions at
Georgetown at Christmas 1831 and to a planned proclamation of union at
the Lexington Christian Church on New Year's Day 1832. Johnson and
Smith represented the Disciples. Campbell was not present and was in no

direct sense an architect of the so-called union, which he did not at first welcome with good grace. Stone, after his decades-long efforts to unify all Christians, not further divide them, was ecstatic and proved willing to make almost any needed compromise on behalf of the union effort.

The union, a small, local event with problematical significance at the time, became important only because of subsequent events and hard work by the architects of what was little more than an expression of hope. The four ministers began an immediate effort to persuade competing local congregations to merge. After two years of efforts to appease competing factions, Stone was able to complete a merger of congregations in Lexington and heralded this union in his magazine. He did everything he could to persuade Christian congregations to recognize the union and to accept a joint identity (in most areas the two did not have competing congregations). The union was not a negotiated merger with announced terms and conditions. In fact, the result was in many cases a near-capitulation of Christians on doctrinal issues. The merging Christian congregations continued to call themselves Christians, not Disciples (Stone and Campbell debated the issue), but slowly dropped or subordinated any doctrines that clashed with those of Campbell and Scott. The new denomination that coalesced in the 1830s (despite demurrals from both Christians and Disciples, it was such in function even though not in claim) long remained a largely mid-American church, with its greatest strengths in the states bordering the Ohio and Tennessee Rivers and, after subsequent migrations, in Missouri and Texas. In these areas its followers competed as equals with the Baptists and Methodists and in time outgrew the Presbyterians. By the Civil War the Disciples had approximately 200,000 members, according to their own most reliable estimates.

Since the Disciples soon dominated the united movement, the Christians had to give up a great deal. What the two movements shared was an avowed commitment to the New Testament pattern and an opposition to parties and creeds and denominational labels. They both professed a concern for church unity, although in the crunch only the Christians were willing to make concessions to achieve it. By 1832 almost all Christians accepted adult baptism, while Stone and some others accepted a mild doctrine of baptismal remission but never made this a test of fellowship. The Christians early moved to weekly communion (a few already practiced this). The major differences involved matters of style as well as doctrine. The Christians, born of the great revivals and of a very hot religion, often seemed to advocate the opposite evangelical extreme from the calm, rational scheme of salvation preached by Scott. This difference of style involved only one doctrinal issue—the role of the Holy Spirit before and after conversion. On this neither Stone nor, in all likelihood, most Christians of his generation ever accepted Campbell's belief that the Spirit was a gift only to Christians after the purifying effects of baptism. Stone, typically, did not see this as an essential doctrine that should divide the churches. Finally, many Christians had taken very seriously Stone's Arian views on the Trinity and his heterodox beliefs about the atonement. Those who would not concede on these issues, or at least be silent, could never accept the union and thus remained part of the Christian Connection. Stone simply stopped airing these doctrines, or what he generally conceded were mere speculations. This did not fully allay Campbell's fears, and in fact the Disciples, as had the Christians, would for years face charges of unitarianism. Campbell had always condemned both Arians and unitarians but did not want to become ensnared in abstract arguments concerning the Trinity (a word he avoided, since it was not in the New Testament). On difficult issues, such as the nature of the Christ or how to interpret the predestinarian passages in Romans, Campbell characteristically rejected dogmatic certainty.

The united Christians-Disciples made up an eclectic movement. Campbell, although an effective defender of Protestant Christianity in the broader sense, did not want to classify the restored church even as Protestant. It was just Christ's Church. In American Christianity the Disciples did not fit any broad, grouping categories—Catholic, Reformed, Wesleyan, Lutheran, Anabaptist, spiritualist, or Adventist. They shared some affinities with most. Although overtly opposed to his parent Presbyterians on most points of doctrine and polity, Campbell not only retained some of the dogmatic temper of Seceder Presbyterians at their best but remained at least nominally orthodox on the most basic Reformed doctrines (the Trinity, atonement, and the certainty of damnation for those unjustified by faith, which of course he defined in his own distinctive way). In overall doctrine and practice, the Disciples were closest to the Brethren or Anabaptist churches—in their rigid congregationalism, in a lay ministry, in the simplicity of worship, in adult baptism, in freewill or complete atonement doctrines, in their strong defense of the complete separation of church and state, and in a practical, moralistic, and devotional approach to religion. But save for a few sectarian congregations, most in Tennessee, the early Disciples did not accept a radical pacifism or a complete separation from the world and of course disagreed with the Brethren on the purpose of baptism and in rejecting all creeds and all names save "Christian" or "Disciples." They shared freewill doctrines with Methodists; preached an equally rigorous or ascetic morality (hostility to dancing, the theater, fine clothes, drinking, and card playing); but rejected Methodist episcopacy, creeds, and mode of baptism.

In a limited sense, the Disciples moved back toward Rome—in their insistence on one church, in their conflating of salvation and church membership, in their key doctrine of baptismal remission, and in the centrality of weekly communion in their worship. This did not mean any respect for the Roman Catholic Church, since Campbell and other Disciples leaders often took the lead in anti-Catholic organizations and in propaganda against Rome. Campbell's somewhat ambiguous doctrine of baptismal remission came closest to the position of Luther. His movement shared few affinities with the emerging Adventist movement, although a few early Disciples, including Stone and Scott, at least briefly flirted with the advent speculations of William Miller, while one early Disciples minister, John Thomas, capitulated completely to Miller's views. The Disciples were unique in their simple, historically oriented conception of faith and in the very limited role they attributed to the Holy Spirit, and alone among Protestants in their weekly communions.

The Christian congregations that rejected union have not fared very well in restoration historiography. The 1832 union, in a sense, forced the remaining Christians into closer contact. The failure of the merger effort in much of Ohio saddened Stone, particularly when former colleagues accused him of betrayal. One of his closest friends from Cane Ridge and the first young minister he converted to the early Christian movement, David Purviance, not only rejected the merger but led the remnant of Christians in Ohio. Clearly, these resisting Christians were most appalled at Campbell's baptismal doctrines but also believed that the Disciples demanded closed communion and thus posed an obstacle to further ecumenical cooperation. In the first of many ironies, their very commitment to a broader type of Christian unity prevented their union with the seemingly more exclusive Disciples.

After 1832 the scattered Christian congregations did begin to resemble a national church. At least the Ohio and northeastern congregations moved to more active cooperation. The scattered Christian congregations in the West remained small in number (only around 200 in 1832). In Virginia and Carolina the Christians had met frequently in their local conferences, which were so loose as to be closer to revival meetings than business conferences. In 1832 the northeastern congregations briefly dissolved but then shortly thereafter revived an annual general convention, with a few delegates attending from at least one conference in eastern Virginia. Gradually the center of membership shifted toward the Midwest, with the annual convention meeting increasingly in Ohio. But in no literal sense did it represent most of the southern conferences. The popular label—Christian Connection—well expressed the very loose commonalities and lack of denominational organization that characterized the continuing movement.

Organizational efforts increased after 1850, but the slavery issue precluded one national church. By 1850 the General Convention was committed to forming a college. Some of the most eminent members of northern congregations matured these plans, which led in 1852 to the chartering of Antioch College at Yellow Springs, Ohio. In a major coup, the trustees wooed the now-famous father of public education, Horace Mann, to move from Massachusetts to assume its presidency. Mann, of Unitarian background, had not joined any church, and it is clear that his beliefs were on the liberal side of even Unitarianism; but he joined the Christian Church in Antioch, in part because of its open membership and ecumenical aspirations. Unfortunately the General Convention could not provide adequate financial support for the college, leading to major Unitarian intervention and the gradual lessening of Christian ties to what soon became an independent liberal arts college. By the early 1850s the General Convention was almost as inclusive in membership and as flexible on doctrines as New England Unitarians; it espoused a liberalism not duplicated among the congregations in Virginia and North Carolina. But until 1854 these southern congregations considered themselves a part of the Christian Connection as a whole, and a few conferences continued to send delegates to the annual meeting.

In 1844 the North Carolina and Virginia conferences took the lead in organizing a Southern Christian Association. It had only three strong conferences in its home territory, but a few struggling state conferences in the Deep South. It also tried to form closer ties to the General Convention. Alas, this effort failed. In 1854 the General Convention met in Cincinnati (soon the site of its few offices), with some Virginia delegates present. The meeting sharply divided over a strong antislavery resolution (pushed by abolitionists from New England). When it passed, not only southern but some midwestern delegates walked out. Two years later the Southern Association re-formed as the Southern Christian Convention, with no formal ties to the General Convention. Such had been the looseness of ties all along that this scarcely amounted to any schism. Fraternal relationships continued between the two major conventions. But the weak Southern Convention had to go its own way, and with almost no growth over the next three decades (inexact figures suggest a church of no more than 10,000 members). It did establish some academies and in 1889, in North Carolina, established Elon College, which became the most important institution of this small southern denomination. Although many of its ministers had defended slavery, these Christian churches were distinctive in the South for their inclusiveness, ecumenism, and doctrinal liberalism. Some ministers continued to affirm the Arian views of Stone and Elias Smith.

In 1890 the northern and southern conventions agreed to reunite in what became the American Christian Convention. But once again this was more nearly a union of sentiment than of church government. The Southern Convention continued to be the primary organization for the southern congregations. Only in 1922 did these southern congregations fully merge with the American Convention, then renamed the General Convention of the Christian Church, with a membership of approximately 120,000 in 1,250 congregations. Both the northern and southern conventions had made ecumenical cooperation a primary goal. Thus both northern and southern branches held major talks with Freewill Baptists (almost identical doctrines and practices), while the General Convention worked out several types of cooperation with Unitarians (a shared polity and an antitrinitarian position) and discussed a merger with northern Presbyterians. In the twentieth century, when most of these Christian congregations had become much more liberal and less evangelical in style, their merged convention, although small, worked more assiduously for an alliance of several mainline denominations than any other American religious group, and from these efforts began the successful discussions that led to its 1931 merger with the Congregationalists. This same impetus lay behind the later merger of the resulting Congregational Christian churches with the product of two merged Germanic denominations—the Evangelical and Reformed Church—to create in 1957 the present, very ecumenically oriented United Church of Christ. So far as the early restoration congregations aspired to Christian unity and saw a restoration of the primitive church not so much as an end in itself but as the platform that offered the greatest possibilities of unity, then the present United Church of Christ is the most appropriate heir of the early American Restoration movement. But insofar as the early restoration congregations committed themselves, above all else, to the recovery of the primitive church, with unity a desired result but in itself always subordinate to a properly constituted church, then the United Church of Christ might seem, in its openness to various forms of church government, to various forms of worship, and to various doctrinal positions, a complete betrayal of that heritage. In what amounts to an ironical historical outcome, the United Church of Christ is now involved in promising merger discussions with the liberal branch of the early Disciples movement.

SEEDS OF DISUNION: THE CHURCHES OF CHRIST

Except on a few key doctrines and on a common approach to worship, the Christians-Disciples were never really united. Deep tensions always lay beneath the surface agreements, making this movement perhaps the most schismatic in American religious history. The fault lines ran in all directions. Visible long before the union of 1832 was the potential tension between two goals—unity and restoration. By placing priority on unity and accepting flexibility on doctrines, Stone made possible the union. From then on the movement revealed a spectrum of attitudes toward other confessions, ranging from the most narrow sectarianism and separatism among a minority of congregations, mostly rural and southern, to a more accommodating stance by congregations, often located in Ohio and Indiana, which, without sacrificing distinctive doctrines and practices, moved ever closer to the Protestant mainstream, accepted more of the wealth and fashions of the world, involved themselves in politics and social reforms, and often assumed leadership in ecumenical efforts. By the early twentieth century the more sectarian congregations gradually separated into a distinct fellowship, the Churches of Christ, while most of the more liberal congregations kept the label "Disciples of Christ."

Several issues invited such internal conflict and helped solidify developing factions. At the time of the union the Disciples had to confront an early schism in Ohio. One of the most beloved ministerial colleagues of Alexander Campbell, Sidney Rigdon, took the idea of restoration to an extreme that appalled Campbell. Rigdon's congregation at Kirtland, Ohio, tried to follow the early church in a literal way and adopted a community of goods. Campbell, with some caustic language, used his journal to try to prove that the New Testament really justified private property (Campbell was already acquiring his private fortune), and, possibly influenced by this rebuke, Rigdon very shortly joined the early Mormon movement and carried with him a few ministers and half of his own congregation.

A second, more rigorous restorationist preacher, John Thomas, moved far enough from Alexander Campbell's doctrines in 1837 to gain a ringing denunciation and withdrawal of fellowship from Campbell. Thomas, an immigrant from Britain to Cincinnati in 1832, was very quickly converted to the Disciples by Walter Scott and briefly met with Campbell. He moved to Richmond, Virginia, and there began denouncing Campbell and most Disciples for a lack of rigor in restoring the primitive church. At first he was excessively rigid, in Campbell's estimate, in his insistence on the rebaptism of all converts who had not been baptized by immersion for the remission of sins, in eschewing any professional ministry, and in adopting an extreme pacifism and separatism. These emphases brought him very close to the Anabaptist denominations. At the same time he became a fervent Adventist. Not only did he anticipate the early advent, but he eventually became a corporealist, rejected all Trinity formulas, looked forward to a literal resurrection only of correct believers at the time of the advent, and affirmed death and not eternal torment as the punishment for nonbelievers. In 1864 Thomas chose the name "Christadelphian" (which means brethren in Christ) for his scattered congregations (they would not use the word "church"). The movement remained very small, with most of its congregations in Virginia and along the east coast, and in Arkansas and Texas. But it was large enough to be schismatic. It remains divided into two small denominations, with the quite honest names of Amended and Unamended Christadelphians. By 1900 all the groups scarcely numbered over 2,000 (no more than 6,000 today). But it remains the only sect that blends an extreme restorationist or primitivist bent with separatism and Adventism. In its one bid for some national visibility, this small sect claimed as members the paternal grandparents and, as a youth, the father of Lyndon B. Johnson, who himself joined a Disciples congregation.

Rigdon and Thomas were the exceptions—Disciples who thirsted for too much restoration for Alexander Campbell. Subsequently the leading source of division would be those in the movement who seemed, to their brethren, too worldly, too prosperous, too accommodating, and thus too far from primitive Christianity. Ironically, in the view of some, even an aging Alexander Campbell betrayed the purity of the early movement.

The early Disciples, consistent with their radical congregationalism, denounced all forms of overarching church authority along with clerical orders. Its ministers or preaching elders were technically laypersons, and in the early years almost all preachers joined other employment with their ministerial duties. Some congregations continued the older Sandemanian pattern of having various elders conduct all aspects of the Sunday worship. Even to this day, many in the movement insist that all Christians are ministers and use euphemisms such as "full-time Christian service" to distinguish those who have professional religious training and who make church or mission work their primary vocation. Local congregations and ministers early met in conferences and conventions, but these had only an advisory role. This meant, in effect, that leadership and power devolved onto key ministers, particularly those that developed their own periodicals and influenced lay affairs through articles and editorials. In a pattern earlier established by Baptists, the Disciples, as individuals or as congregations, cooperated in supporting a number of academies and colleges, including several for women. Although not the oldest, the college with the greatest early influence among Christians was Bethany (1840), established by Campbell on his own farm and under his direct control for the rest of his life, except for extended periods when he lectured in Europe or other parts of America.

Only in 1849 did Disciples meet in a called but voluntary national convention and form the American Christian Missionary Society (Campbell headed it until his death in 1866). A few southern ministers condemned as unscriptural even such a completely voluntary organization, much as they tried to keep Disciples from joining benevolent or humanistic societies. Although committed to female education, the Disciples, with few exceptions, rejected on biblical grounds any leadership or speaking roles for women in the church, a very different position from that accepted by the Christians in New England. Until divisions provoked by the Civil War, none of these issues led to coherent factions. The only gathering place for Disciples nationally continued to be the annual convention that made policies for the often ill-supported missionary society.

The slavery issue and sectional politics came close to fracturing the Disciples and intensified divisions that later contributed to twentieth-century schisms. The Disciples, more than any other denomination except possibly the Cumberland Presbyterians, were concentrated in the border areas between North and South, but with regional concentrations in the heavily antislavery Western Reserve of Ohio and in strongly proslavery areas of middle Tennessee. Most of the leaders of both the former Christians and Disciples were strongly opposed to American slavery. Few were abolitionists. Stone, after years of efforts on behalf of both gradual emancipation and colonization, almost lapsed into a despairing silence about the issue in the decade before his death in 1844.

Alexander Campbell always opposed slavery in America on moral and political grounds but not on scriptural grounds. He tried, with some equivocation, to impose a virtual gag rule on any agitation or, eventually, almost any discussion of the issue within the fellowship. Campbell even seemed to subvert his earlier antislavery stance and angered a minority of abolitionists in the church by arguing, over and over again, that the New Testament did not forbid servitude (unlike slavery apologists, he did not use New Testament passages to defend it). This meant that slave owners could remain within the church, although their Christian faith required a high standard of paternal concern in how they dealt with slaves. This was his gesture toward a national fellowship. As the sectional controversy deepened, Campbell and a majority of ministers, again most from the border areas or the Upper South, tried to maintain a neutral position, to plea and pray for some peaceful resolution, and to insist that Christian fellowship provided a sufficient hedge against any political division. This middle position, which allowed the church to retire from the political battlefield, left agonized minorities, including a group of antislavery ministers in Ohio who formed a separate missionary society when the American Christian Missionary Society would not take an open position against slavery and for the Union. In Tennessee the leading editor (bishop), Tolbert Fanning, moved by 1860 to a very extreme pacifism and separatism, a position that isolated the church completely from both politics and war, a tactic widely accepted by Disciples in the upper, slave owning, and eventually Confederate South. To northern abolitionists this separatism, even to the point of refusing to vote or hold public office, was simply an opportunistic tactic that, in effect, strengthened the slave power. Finally, a few ministers, most in the Deep South, defended slavery and later supported the Confederacy.

Had the Disciples had a formal denominational structure, the church would almost certainly have split over slavery and secession. As it was, the moderates were able to hold together the American Christian Missionary Society during the war but failed in 1863 to prevent approval of a pro-Unionist, antisouthern resolution. By then the congregations in the Confederate states were effectively cut off from the society, with opposition to this unionist stand largely from delegates from Kentucky or other slave regions that remained within the Union. The sectional cleavages survived the war and festered for years. These correlated closely with the later, turn-of-the-century divisions between Disciples (heavily concentrated in the North or in border areas, with more urban congregations, more affluent members, a less restrictive morality, and, in time, more cooperation or communion with other denominations) and the Churches of Christ (predominantly south of the Ohio River, more rural, more impoverished, more rigidly sectarian and separatist, more resentful of wealth and privilege, and less open to ecumenical cooperation or compromise on primitive purity). Those cleavages reflected not just the divisions of the Civil War or the issues fought for in the war, but long-term doctrinal and theological differences that dated from the 1832 union and were exacerbated by the effects of the war on the southern economy, and the defensive, antiestablishment attitudes that developed in the post–Civil War South.

In the immediate postwar years three centers of conservative opposition to new innovations among largely northern Disciples presaged a later separation. In Indiana an outspoken populist and primitivist with the memorable name of Benjamin Franklin (a distant relative of his more famous namesake) used his periodical, the *North American Review*, to lambast almost every innovation made by more "fashionable" congregations. Above all, he led the battle against missionary societies (he had earlier supported them), which he believed unsupported by the New Testament.

In Nashville and middle Tennessee, one of the strongholds of the Restoration movement, Tolbert Fanning had begun, before the war, what became after 1865 the most influential periodical in the South, the *Gospel Advocate*. After the war its new editor and emerging leader of Tennessee Disciples, David Lipscomb, used his journal in a successful appeal for relief funds to help impoverished Disciples in the South and gained such influence as to become, more than anyone else, the arbiter of opinion among ex-Confederate Disciples, of which at least half were in Tennessee or among former Tennesseans who had settled in Texas. Just after the war Lipscomb was a mild opponent of joint mission efforts and slowly became, at times because of southern loyalties, an effective opponent of most of the innovations already more shrilly attacked by Franklin (joint societies, expensive sanctuaries, organ music, the easing of membership requirements, ecumenical outreach, settled and salaried ministers, and an early receptivity to biblical criticism or to Darwinism). Finally, the rapidly growing Disciples movement in Texas was deeply splintered in the postwar years. Here a few editors were even more rigid and purist than Franklin.

Although the factions battled one another in their periodicals, the Disciples seemed to thrive on controversy. In many ways the postwar years were a golden age, with more rapid growth than any other time in Restoration history. From 200,000 members in 1860 the membership doubled by 1875 and exploded to well over a million by 1900. Many northern members were affluent, and some urban churches in effect joined the evangelical mainstream, at least in the sense of social respectability. James A. Garfield, a sometime Disciples minister, gained the United States presidency in the election of 1880, and even southern editors, ideologically at an opposite pole from the progressive wing that he represented, could not hide their sense of pride. But growth and new forms of organization within the church helped reveal some of the deep ambivalence present even in Campbell and aggravated the ever-present problem of identity, which has always haunted the Restoration movement.

The two goals—New Testament purity and Christian unity—did not easily cohere. Stone had epitomized the goal of unity and had compromised almost all doctrines in behalf of this goal. Thomas Campbell leaned toward this position. Alexander Campbell, in his Reform Baptist years, had moved far toward a separatist and purist stand but after 1832 had adopted a moderate or middle position that maintained some tension between the two goals. Benjamin Franklin first and best reflected the purist bent and thus wanted to exclude from membership and communion those who did not in every respect duplicate the New Testament church. Soon baptism became the most important test of purity. Stone never wanted to make the method or purpose of baptism a test of membership. Campbell clearly insisted on immersion and hoped that converts understood the remitting role of baptism. Yet he was willing, at least in his later years, to accept as members other Baptists who had not, at the time of baptism, understood correctly its remitting role, and to grant that even those not immersed, out of ignorance of what the New Testament commanded, could be regenerate Christians. Franklin and eventually many rigid ministers in Texas were not nearly so generous. They would not open either membership or the communion table to people immersed for the wrong purpose, which meant Baptists, and would not concede that unimmersed people could be in the Church. This meant very exclusive congregations, and it was such exclusivity in behalf of purity that marked the later Churches of Christ.

In the immediate postwar years voluntary missionary societies were the focus of conflict, the most visible symbols or markers of divisions within the movement. After about 1880 instrumental music became an even more clear marker, a symbol of purity to those who would not countenance organs or pianos. The issue had not been important before the war. Other Protestant denominations had long rejected instrumental music, and only two urban Disciples congregations had organs. But the more affluent urban congregations, largely in the North but also in southern cities such as Memphis and Nashville, began to introduce music into their new meetinghouses and their worship. In almost every case the same congregations participated in the Parliament of Religions at the 1893 Columbia Exposition, joined in statewide societies or conventions, continued to support the old Christian Missionary Society and to add new female mission societies, gladly adopted Sunday schools or such interdenominational organizations as Christian Endeavor, took a lead in the movement that led eventually to the Federal Council of Churches in 1908, and, above all, moved to more and more inclusive membership standards.

It would be a mistake to view the separation of the Churches of Christ as a reaction to modernism, if modernism meant a ready acceptance of biblical criticism, compromises with Darwinism, or any rejection of the historical credentials of scripture. As late as the split, none of the major editors or leaders had moved this far. Yet the Disciples did have an early flirtation with a type of liberalism. One minister in St. Louis, R. C. Cave, rejected biblicalism and opened church membership to everyone. His congregation forced him to resign in 1889. Many younger ministers attended the major, liberal seminaries and soon created a visible but never clearly defined progressive element in the church. The editors of the more purist periodicals, such as the *Gospel Advocate* and its many imitators, aired these issues, only to condemn the liberals. They saw, correctly, that such compromises of the old restoration culture would gradually erode all that was distinctive about their movement.

The factions hardened in the 1890s, leading to an odd type of schism. The Disciples by then had an embryonic denominational organization, with a convention and missionary society at the center and voluntary social agencies, several colleges, and some type of local organization in most states. But none of these agencies had any legal authority, while the purist congregations simply did not participate in them. Thus from 1890 to the present, the key term of distinction in the movement has remained the tantalizing word "fellowship." Ministers and congregations can announce a withdrawal of fellowship from those they dislike, which means no more mutuality or sense of brotherhood. It is a type of shunning. As early as 1889 a small group of Disciples in Illinois, reflecting the purist position of a deceased Benjamin Franklin, first urged sympathetic congregations to withdraw from the main Disciples fellowship but gained few supporters. They were only a decade too early. In the 1890s a reluctant David Lipscomb in Nashville moved to this same position. He more than anyone else helped establish a distinct identity for dissenting congregations, a majority in the Upper South or in Texas.

Lipscomb reacted to an accumulation of liberal innovations and never saw music as the critical issue. Events in Tennessee affected him directly. In 1890 the more liberal Tennessee congregations established a convention and launched a new and competitive periodical. In 1895 the brother of R. C. Cave became minister of the Nashville Vine Street congregation, which two years later added an organ. Lipscomb was also pushed toward a more exclusive stance by radicals in Arkansas and Texas. By 1895 many ministers had announced that they were no longer a part of an emergent Disciples denomination, and in 1897 Lipscomb publicly announced his departure. By 1904 he had compiled a list of ministers who agreed with his separation, or what amounted to a formal recognition of a new fellowship. Those who wanted to join in this fellowship uniformly rejected intercongregational organizations and instrumental music. In 1906 the director of the United States Census Bureau wrote to the *Gospel Advocate* asking how to deal with the seemingly splintered Disciples movement. Lipscomb assured him that what had been one movement was now two, and he used his ministers list to define the boundaries of what he called the Churches of Christ. The census report did not come out until 1910. Only in 1911 did the Disciples *Yearbook* acknowledge the loss of these congregations. At the time many Disciples in the North probably little noted the separation, since only about 150,000 of a denomination of 1.1 million had departed. Many of the more progressive congregations had long wanted to be rid of the exclusivists and purists. But in the next eighty years this small splinter would become much larger than the parent Disciples.

The separation was in part a southern phenomenon, despite a scattering of Churches of Christ in such non–Confederate states as Indiana and Missouri. Old Civil War allegiances still had predictive power. In Tennessee almost none of the congregations in Unionist upper east Tennessee joined the Churches of Christ, even though on some of the doctrinal and social issues they were in agreement with Lipscomb. In middle Tennessee only three or four liberal congregations in Nashville and its environs remained with the Disciples. The rest separated, creating what remains to this day the most densely concentrated (as a percentage of total church membership) cluster of Churches of Christ.

The members of Churches of Christ have continued to reflect the most rigorous restorationist or primitive elements in the early movement. They have remained emphatically non–ecumenical, unwilling to risk any compromises of purity in behalf of a wider fellowship. This self-conscious sectarian posture meant that such conservative restorationist churches remained distinctly outside the Protestant mainstream, although not as much as the Anabaptist denominations, which they resemble in so many ways. Yet the Churches of Christ are today deeply divided, to the extent that several incipient fellowships are visible. Since all the factions are radically congregational, it is impossible to give adequate names to or draw boundaries among the various groups, which some within the movement number up to twenty or more.

The number of factions can be misleading. Notably, it is historians within the movement that are so painfully aware of factionalism. They have been participants in the intramural skirmishes. From an outside perspective, what is most apparent are the commonalities and continuities that still define the Churches of Christ. So far, such outside perspectives are few and far between. No American fellowship of such size and significance has attracted so little outside scrutiny. Textbook treatments are uniformly brief and caricatured. Thus almost all significant scholarship is by members or ex-members of these churches. It is notable that today the Churches of Christ have a growing intelligentsia and some able historians. They have carefully plotted the developing tensions but by their very closeness to events have often assumed, but not emphasized, the commonalities.

What unites Churches of Christ are the core doctrines and practices that go back to the beginnings. Walter Scott lives on. At the heart of this religion, not only in Churches of Christ but in conservative Disciples and in the Christian Churches and Churches of Christ, is a plan of salvation and a standard approach to worship. These distinguish Churches of Christ from other conservative Protestants and from most evangelical denominations. The plan often seems formulaic and can become very legalistic. In a virtual litany Churches of Christ still ask people to hear, believe, repent, confess, and accept baptism for the remission of sins. The baptism is most distinctive, but unique is the reasonable, practical, staged steps that precede it, with no role for the Holy Spirit. As in all freewill approaches to salvation, this plan focuses responsibility on the individual. Its enumerated steps and its simplicity promise a type of security. One knows what one must do. The discipleship that follows is demanding, since members of the Church of Christ affirm and try to live the same demanding and abstentious life advocated by conservative evangelicals. One can, by persistent disobedience, lose one's promise of salvation and move out of the Church. One is quite aware of when such apostasy occurs, for the rules are reasonably clear, the verbal and behavioral markers quite visible to fellow Christians.

This means that such Christians, like Roman Catholics, focus not on inner markers of conversion but on the requirements of daily discipleship, on living a rather patterned life within the church. This helps maintain a distinctive religious culture without the emotional or even ecstatic peaks and valleys of evangelical Christianity. Adherence to what members of Churches of Christ view as the one New Testament plan of salvation, and most of all to New Testament baptism, sets them apart from other Christians and gives them a special type of assurance, a feeling not necessarily of superiority but of exclusive correctness. Built on such bases of confidence and self-assurance, such Christians are often kind and compassionate, try very hard to reflect the spirit of Jesus, and maintain close families and nurture strong character.

The pattern of worship is also distinctive. Everywhere, Churches of Christ meet on Sunday morning for prayer, unaccompanied song, teaching the Word, fellowship (today the offering, but in the nineteenth century this sometimes involved the actual placing of alms on tables in the front of churches), and the communion service. The arrangement of these five elements may vary from one congregation to another, but they are always present. The weekly communion (a memorial and not a sacrament) is no longer as distinctive as in the past (some Protestant churches have moved to weekly communion), but the a cappella singing is distinctive and symbolically very significant. It, more than any other aspect of worship, testifies to how fully they honor even the "silences" of the New Testament, and by so doing distinguish themselves from all the other "lax" branches of the Restoration movement. Unlike the Anabaptists, whom they resemble in so many ways, members do not use distinctive dress or speech to set themselves apart from nonobedient Christians.

These continuities with the early Restoration movement, to an extent, transcend the issues that divide the Churches of Christ. Since some of these tensions run deep, it may well be that a somewhat precarious fellowship will soon give way to multiple and smaller fellowships. Such fragmentation seems endemic in all restorationist and congregational forms of Christianity and in some cases is a source of new vitality and growth. But the fatal or irresolvable schisms may not come as soon as predicted. Churches of Christ emphasize their congregational democracy and quarrel continuously about what types of intercongregational cooperation is consistent with such a polity. Yet, what is most apparent to an outsider is the degree of uniformity, in belief and worship, within at least the vast majority of Churches of Christ. If one wants diversity, one finds it in episcopal denominations such as the Episcopal Church or the United Methodist Church. Bishops and hierarchies seem to accompany diversity; uniformity seems to mark radically congregational churches. This is so not only for Churches of Christ but for sister Restoration fellowships and for Anabaptists. The recent turn by the Disciples to a tighter denominational organization has accompanied a greater diversity in beliefs and worship.

This may seem paradoxical. It is not. Any participatory democracy that works over time, any congregational polity that endures, will necessarily rest on widely shared beliefs and values so habitual as often to be unnoted, passed on effectively generation after generation. Another way of saying this is that such nonhierarchical types of human bonding are either explicitly or implicitly totalitarian, in the nonpejorative sense that a shared opinion has to prevail. Such communities always have informal modes of social control that lead to the ostracism or exclusion of dissenters. Such exclusion rests on broad communal support and does not depend on an elite leadership, although in most cases it needs intellectuals to articulate and focus such communal opinion. Such intellectuals influence the broader fellowship through periodicals and what, in the Churches of Christ, substitutes for conventions or conferences—well-publicized, annual lectureships at most of their colleges.

To a remarkable extent so far, the large center group of Churches of Christ has been able to maintain such internalized beliefs and values. These congregations have such informal networks of communication and such effective spokespersons and opinion makers as to maintain an unusual degree of uniformity, at least in a pluralistic American setting. They have changed through time but have so managed change as to deny fellowship to, stigmatize, or at least isolate those who have too strenuously resisted all change or those liberals or radicals who have tried to push ahead too rapidly. Over and over again the majority of congregations have been able to keep most members in line with the prevailing orthodoxy. The informal modes of applying communal authority have been most apparent to individual ministers who stepped out of line, met a fraternal rebuke from fellow ministers or in the major periodicals, and never again gained a pulpit in a mainstream congregation.

With this backdrop it is easier to evaluate the bases of factionalism. The separate Churches of Christ exploded in half a century from scarcely 150,000 members to around 2 million in the peak years of the early 1960s. This growth came during the period of deep tensions within the mainstream denominations and the growth of reactive evangelical or self-denominated fundamentalist movements. Churches of Christ had to resist, even when in many ways capitulating to, these evangelicals, creating several points of tension that came to a head in internal battles over eschatology and soteriology (in the loose language of the time, over premillennialism and the role of grace in salvation). At the same time, the small, separatist, predominately pacifist, countercultural, largely rural, often impoverished, and class-conscious congregations led by David Lipscomb at the turn of the century had matured into a prosperous, middle-class, socially and economically conservative denomination by 1950. In most respects it no longer bore prophetic witness to the evils of the surrounding culture but had bought into most of the consumptive, capitalistic, and intensely nationalistic values of conservative Protestantism. These shifts often paralleled an almost virulent anticommunism and a gradual shift of members of the Churches of Christ from the Democratic Party (tied to southern loyalties or an antiestablishment outlook) to an overwhelming support for Republicans.

Such shifts invited controversy. In the 1950s, Harding College in Arkansas became notorious when its president, George Benson, identified sinister communist influences behind almost every new innovation in American society and tried to enlist Churches of Christ in his crusade in support of a libertarian, free-market system. He was the Joseph McCarthy of the movement, while a powerful, somewhat erratic preacher, Foy E. Wallace Jr., helped drive premillennialists from the fellowship and actively opposed racial integration, inviting comparisons with George C. Wallace. But in the same years the Churches of Christ were upgrading and seeking regional accreditation for their colleges and universities (of around twenty, a few, such as Pepperdine, Abilene Christian, and David Lipscomb, are gaining at least regional distinction). Urban congregations began to attract affluent or powerful members, including corporate executives or successful politicians. Larger urban and suburban congregations built magnificent meetinghouses and supported a very able, well-educated (many with Ph.D.'s) and entrepreneurial ministry. Such trends assured the emergence of a rather clear body of "progressives," who offended the majority by suggesting radical new ideas about biblical scholarship or about economic and social policies.

Two divisive issues bared the problems of finding a New Testament model for modern congregations. In two respects the dominant majority of Churches of Christ have remained loyal to Campbell: on millennial doctrines and on the role of the Holy Spirit. The issues are too complex to develop in this limited space, but clearly the first and most divisive issue was what everyone, with some confusion, called premillennialism. Among conservative evangelicals a schematic, dispensationalist view of the advent of Jesus (a future event in some sense affirmed by all sides) gained widespread support and won many converts within the Churches of Christ by the 1920s. Here several issues merged, including even the role of the Holy Spirit. In effect, a minority of ministers and congregations came to believe that we lived in the last, awful period before Jesus returned to a doomed earth to greet a saving remnant of disciples and to inaugurate his own perfect kingdom, which would endure for a thousand years before a final resurrection and judgment. This scenario, at least in a general way, conforms to Revelation 20–22 and thus has strong New Testament endorsement. But, much as Luther and Calvin before him, Alexander Campbell had been leery of such a literal eschatology and had, at least in optimistic moments, believed that the restoration of New Testament Christianity would in some sense help usher in the kingdom. He rejected schematic Adventist doctrines, such as those of the Christadelphians. Also, his hopes for Anglo-Saxon expansion and his celebrations of American institutions belied the deeply pessimistic scenario of most Adventists. Views close to those of Campbell remained popular among most members of Churches of Christ, who needed this issue to maintain clearer lines of demarcation from evangelicals or from avowed or organized fundamentalists, even when members of the Churches of Christ supported almost all their moral and legislative goals. In time, after intense intramural debates, the majority in effect so stigmatized the premillennialists as to force them out of the movement (less than a hundred congregations survive).

More enduring factions reacted to an implicit denominationalism. One group objected to Sunday schools and particularly to female teachers in them, while a largely overlapping group condemned individual communion cups (the one-cuppers), which clearly violated the description of Jesus' Last Supper. The largest faction of this type, with over 1,200 congregations today, is the strict anti-institutionalists. All along, some Churches of Christ had been leery of fine meetinghouses, colleges, salaried and settled pastors, and radio and television ministries. In particular, they found no biblical vindication of congregational support for missions, higher education, or orphanages. They condemned a familiar pattern in the main-stream of the movement: contributions from several congregations to a large congregation that in turn used such accumulated funds to support foreign missionaries, colleges, or radio and television ministries. Today the "antis" are a recognized part of the Churches of Christ, at least from the center perspective, but in a sense they do not share fellowship with the broad majority of congregations.

The deepest but less coherent divisions today involve theological issues and problems of biblical interpretation. Churches of Christ have had dif-ficulty relating grace and God's initiative in salvation with their step-by-step, legalistic approach. Creeping evangelicalism, particularly among some soon-stigmatized college ministries, illustrated a recurring and com-plex issue. Closely tied to this was the seemingly dated nature of a rational, historical approach to New Testament witnesses and a conception of faith as simple belief. For intellectuals in the movement this was the least believ-able, at times even the most embarrassing, legacy of the founders. Suffice it to say that almost all philosophical currents of the post–World War II years have tended to undercut such a literal historical view of the Bible. In fact, no other approach to biblical understanding, no other canons of scriptural interpretation, are as much out of vogue. Even if one retains a belief in an inspired Bible, the complications introduced by even the most conserva-tive scholarship still leave enormous interpretive problems and make any claim to one New Testament pattern seem naive. This controversy has in-formed the progressive or revisionist factions in the Churches and has led to a vital and creative dialogue among intellectuals. But it has also fright-ened the older, more traditional ministers and, in so far as these issues have percolated down to the congregational level, has begun to lessen the surety and security of members.

In retrospect it is clear that Stone and Campbell were very selective in their reading of the New Testament. They did not follow the scenario that ends the Book of Revelation, as Adventists reminded them. They also ig-nored or downplayed the works of the Spirit. Uneasy with miracles, except those required to demonstrate that Jesus was the Messiah, suspicious of any form of spiritualism, and wary of the elements of emotionalism in evangel-ical revivalism, the founders seemed to have all but eliminated the third person of the Trinity. Some internal dissidents or reformers within the Churches of Christ have stressed the vitality of spiritual experience, while a tiny minority has been attracted to Wesleyan forms of holiness or to the charismatic movement in mainstream churches (the most publicized case involved singer Pat Boone). After all, the Church at Corinth, whose prac-tices are first recorded in the New Testament, not only illustrated the five components of worship emphasized by restorationists, but its members also enjoyed the gifts of the Spirit. They prophesied, healed, spoke in tongues, and interpreted tongues. Paul commended these gifts, if expressed in an orderly way. Of course, most Protestants, and with them Stone and Campbell, chose to believe that such gifts were appropriate only in the Apostolic age, before Christians had the New Testament as a guide. But such an interpretation did not itself rest on any scriptural authority. Nonetheless, with almost excessive rigor and zeal, the mainstream Churches of Christ have anathematized such spirituality, particularly glossolalia, and denied fellowship to congregations that accept it.

The battles continue. Equally stigmatized have been overly rigid dogmatists, including those in the so-called Crossroads movement (often called the Boston Church of Christ and identified today as the International Churches of Christ). These congregations emphasize rigorous discipleship through a close and even mind-controlling monitoring of converts and rely on an emergent hierarchy of authority. Youth groups have challenged the smug accommodations with modernity by the older generation (it is hard to find a pacifist in the center movement), while women have begun to push for very moderate demands in some congregations (some would like at least to become deacons, a position held by women in the early church and accepted by some nineteenth-century Disciples). Although some large congregations have supported effective missions to the poor, the movement as a whole has resisted a social gospel, and only belatedly and with some reluctance did southern churches accept racial integration, even though David Lipscomb had denied that any true Church of Christ could reject for membership anyone on racial grounds. Almost hidden—almost a separate fellowship—are the all-black Churches of Christ, who long received paternal aid from white congregations and who seem, except on economic issues, more conservative than white congregations. But who on the outside knows? One compelling topic for a historian would be a detailed study of black Churches of Christ. For example, how have blacks in over 1,200 congregations accommodated the least ecstatic and least spiritual form of Christianity? What, if any, African traditions have survived and in subtle ways created a unique version of Restoration Christianity? The same questions about ethnic survivals might be posed for a small fellowship of Spanish-speaking Churches of Christ.

THE FINAL DIVISION: CHRISTIAN CHURCHES
AND CHURCHES OF CHRIST

The separation of the Churches of Christ cleared the way for the Disciples to move ever closer to mainline northern denominations. Because of their ordered, reasonable path to salvation, the early Disciples were clearly non-evangelicals. Yet, in time, the more ecumenical Disciples, as distinguished from the more purist Churches of Christ, became less distinctive in their salvation doctrines. At least in the North, former evangelicals, such as Congregationalists, Presbyterians, and even Methodists, gradually accepted, at least in a de facto way, an orderly path to salvation that differed little from that among Disciples. In the twentieth century more and more Disciples congregations loosened membership requirements, accepted the validity of baptism in other denominations, and opened their communion services to other Christians. At the same time, mainline denominations reaffirmed the critical role of ordinances such as baptism and the Lord's Supper, as well as the centrality of the church. Many Disciples ministers were influenced by new biblical scholarship and by theological innovations, such as neo-orthodoxy. Many joined Methodists, Congregationalists, Presbyterians, Episcopalians, and northern Baptists in social action outreach, and some congregations were among the first to accept women into the ministry.

In a pattern duplicated by both southern and northern Baptists, the Disciples gradually developed a de facto presbyterian polity. Legally, congregations remained autonomous or independent, but not so in practice. The annual convention (today a biennial general assembly) long remained a mass convention. All who wanted to could participate. But to guide the convention, the Disciples in 1916 established a delegate-based committee on recommendations that soon effectively controlled the agenda of the convention, which in 1917 became the International Convention of Disciples of Christ. The board of directors of the convention and a president served as the executive wing of what was becoming a well-ordered denomination. They directed the varied boards and agencies of the church. Gradually the Disciples were able to form conventions in each state, with a state secretary and a small bureaucracy. Although technically each congregation called its own minister, in fact almost all congregations worked through state secretaries, meaning more centralized guidance in the training and screening of ministers. In many cities the Disciples developed a local organization, or the equivalent of presbyteries. Although the agencies, in theory, were supported by voluntary contributions from congregations, in fact the Disciples moved in 1935 to a unified system of giving, with the allocation of funds largely determined at the center. Whether church leaders would admit it or not, and some did, the Disciples had become all but indistinguishable from other denominations by the end of World War I.

Such organizational changes and, more particularly, the policies adopted by centralized agencies, created new forms of factionalism. This led to a long, complex internal battle that eventuated, after 1960, in another rather fuzzy division and a new fellowship that insisted, above all, that it was not a denomination. Even to name it involves controverted issues, but generally the congregations that asserted their independence from the Disciples are known by the unwieldy title (conventional but not official) of Undenominational Fellowship of Christian Churches and Churches of Christ (CCCC).

One can trace the origins of such a second division among Disciples back into the nineteenth century. Many congregations that rejected the pacifism and political separatism of Fanning and Lipscomb gradually adopted organs in worship but consistently opposed liberal doctrinal innovations. Once again periodicals and publishing companies became involved. In the post–Civil War era, a Cincinnati paper, the *Christian Standard*, had generally opposed separatists such as Lipscomb. Its influential, long-term editor, Isaac Errett, supported missionary societies and did not want instrumental music to be a test of fellowship. In 1873 Errett expanded his periodical into a religious publishing house, Standard Publishing, and began the sale of literature for congregations. He died in 1888 with his journal still identified as liberal, at least as compared with Lipscomb's *Gospel Advocate*. His son, Russell Errett, was much more conservative, particularly on doctrinal issues, and by 1900 had converted the *Standard* into a leading voice against liberalism and modernism. He was supported by John W. McGarvey, who long headed the largest training school for ministers, the College of the Bible, at what is now Transylvania University in Lexington. McGarvey for years wrote a column in the *Standard* on biblical criticism, largely to lambast all incursions of the higher criticism, or what he called infidelity or "destructive criticism."

As so often in Restoration battles, nonreligious issues often intruded. The owners of a competing journal in St. Louis, the *Christian-Evangelist*, which supported the emerging liberal or modernist wing of the movement, developed a publishing business that competed with the soon-powerful Standard Publishing Company in Cincinnati. In a sense the battle among Disciples was also an intense, competitive struggle between two publishing houses. In time Standard won and has remained a privately owned but very influential voice in the CCCC. By 1910 the publishing house in St. Louis faced intimidating debts. At that point a wealthy benefactor bought it and gave it to the Disciples, which from then on had what was, in effect, a denominational publication board. Another seemingly extraneous issue also reflected other than religious competition. When the *Standard* lambasted the acceptance of tainted gifts for missions from a monopolistic John D. Rockefeller, the main supporter of such a seemingly ethical response was a competing oil baron, Thomas W. Phillips of Pennsylvania, one of the great benefactors of the Restoration movement.

From the turn of the century until a climactic struggle in the mid-1920s, the Disciples suffered the same divisions that racked mainstream Protestantism, particularly in the North. The issues were complex in each denomination, and the labels attached to the contending sides, modernist and fundamentalist, cry out for contextual definitions. A new leadership tied to young and better-educated ministers developed among Disciples. Young men attended major universities such as Yale or the new University of Chicago. They responded to intellectual trends, identified with colleagues in other mainline denominations, and were increasingly embarrassed by the more sectarian or divisive aspects of their movement. They absorbed new, scholarly information about the Bible. Out of honesty they could not accept the commonsense biblicalism of Stone and Campbell. They wanted a more inclusive movement and wanted to fulfill the old goal of Christian unity through different forms of cooperation with other Christians. As in most denominations, the ministers moved far ahead of the majority of the laity and at times practiced a type of duplicity in camouflaging what they were about. They gathered at their new seminary, the Divinity House at the University of Chicago, and formed an elite or exclusive theological discussion group, the Campbell Society. As they gained leadership roles, a gulf developed between the leading agencies of an emerging denomination and the broader constituency the agencies were supposed to represent but which was, in fact, a constituency they tried to lead and mold in new ways.

Soon the signs were all about. Among the Disciples, the one most potent symbol of change, or what conservatives saw as betrayal, was open membership, or admitting to fellowship people who had not received proper baptism. This issue focused the problem of biblical authority, since the movement had always argued that baptism by immersion for the remission of sins was a critical aspect of the New Testament plan of salvation. If there were any essential doctrines, surely this was one. Only a few congregations practiced open membership before 1910, but others reflected an ecumenism that clearly pointed in that direction. Disciples led the successful effort to form the Federal Council of Churches and won convention support for membership in it. Disciples missionaries in China formed working alliances with other Protestants. Socially active Disciples joined in broader moral reforms, beginning with temperance. One of the most prominent of many Disciples journalists, Charles C. Morrison, took over a small periodical, renamed it the *Christian Century*, and turned it into the leading proponent of Protestant liberalism and unity. It soon became the leading antagonist of the *Standard*.

By 1919 the *Standard* had begun rallying effective opposition to what its editors saw as modernist trends in the central agencies of the Disciples. The smoking gun, from its standpoint, were policies sanctioned by a newly unified mission agency, the United Christian Missionary Society (UCMS). It seemed that in China, at least, missionaries had adopted open membership. Beginning in 1919 the conservatives, who undoubtedly reflected the majority view of laypeople, began meeting in congresses before the International Convention. A pattern soon developed. They introduced resolutions upholding the traditional membership standards, the convention as a whole voted in their favor, but then the various agencies always seemed to find ways of diluting their intent. From the standpoint of those who headed the agencies and boards, and particularly the UCMS, such resolutions came perilously close to creedal tests and violated the principle of free conscience. Thus they found ways to allow individual missionaries to evade the policies of the convention. In a pattern duplicated among northern Presbyterians and Baptists in the same years, investigations, committee reports, and divisive resolutions dominated the annual conventions, with the level of bitterness increasing almost yearly. In a sense both sides appealed to unity. The conservatives were most concerned with unity within the fellowship and begged for such a degree of respect for the traditional doctrines of the movement as to include everyone. On the other side, the so-called modernists were most concerned with the unity of the church as a whole and with such polices in the Disciples movement as to further ecumenical cooperation.

The climax came in 1925 and 1926, at the same time and with the same result as in northern Baptist and Presbyterian denominations. The liberals won. In 1925 the conservatives planned carefully, packed the convention floor, and won passage of seemingly clear resolutions requiring closed membership in the agencies of the church (they could not do anything about individual congregations). But the leadership diluted the impact of such resolutions, carefully planned the 1926 meeting at Memphis, politically outmaneuvered the conservatives, and despite some verbal compromises, clearly won the battle in behalf of membership inclusiveness. From this point on, many of the leading conservatives did not actively participate in the International Convention, although some joined in commissions that sought means of healing the informal split. After 1926 the conservatives withdrew support from most of the official agencies of the denomination and began creating their own "free" organizations, supported informally by members and congregations. By 1930 the Disciples movement effectively had a dual organizational system, with little contact between the two groups (separate colleges, mission efforts, periodicals, and publishers). In 1927 the independents, as they now began to call themselves, organized the first North American Christian Convention (NACC). It met periodically until 1950, when it became a carefully planned annual assembly, the most visible symbol of unity in what became the CCCC. Unlike the International Convention, it did not conduct business and resembled a huge fellowship meeting, with great singing and preaching.

The bitter experience with the International Convention led the independents increasingly to repudiate any central organizations (they had formerly tried to reform the existing agencies). At the core of their "free" fellowship were extensive mission efforts funded by congregations, often through informal advisory committees, and a growing number of regional Bible colleges (numbering thirty-three in 1990, after several marginal institutions had failed). Two or three of these colleges predated the independence movement but later affiliated with it. Most were new, many were underfunded, and some had low academic standards. Here most young men (no women were admitted to the ministry, but some trained for mission assignments) gained whatever training they received for the ministry (the academic achievement of CCCC ministers is still below that of both the Disciples and the Churches of Christ). Only one Disciples liberal arts college (Milligan in Tennessee) affiliated with the independents, and this occurred after World War II. Today the CCCC has three seminaries, only one with recognized quality. Most of its Bible colleges have accreditation within an association set up by the National Association of Evangelicals, and a few have gained regional accreditation.

At times the independence movement clearly overlapped the larger fundamentalist movement of the 1920s. William Jennings Bryan was invited to give an antievolution speech before one of their early, preconvention congresses. Some of the independents embraced biblical inerrancy, and a few ministers supported or held offices in the larger evangelical movement. But not all, for this was as strange an alliance, as alien to the Restoration tradition, as the ecumenical cooperation embraced by Disciples. Creeds, different conceptions of faith, the role of Holy Spirit in conversion, and different baptismal and communion traditions would have seemed to make such an alliance inconceivable. One can now detect within the CCCC some deep divisions over issues such as inerrancy, the degree of cooperation among congregations, and the role of women. Its loose organization, or lack of organization, both disguises and encourages such divisions. The final break with the Disciples came only after 1960. By then, independent ministers and leading laypeople, some from the largest and most wealthy Christian or Disciples congregations (including the largest of all, P. H. Welshimer's First Christian congregation in Canton, Ohio), had declared their complete separation from the Disciples. As early as 1955 they began compiling their own list of independent ministers, and individual congregations began requesting the Christian Churches (Disciples of Christ) to remove their names from its yearbook. By the mid-1960s over 3,000 congregations had made this request and considered themselves the continuing, faithful part of the original Stone-Campbell movement. A series of consultations on internal unity ended in 1968, when the split was clearly irreversible.

The final separation, or really the certification of what had happened years before, paralleled major structural changes under way among the Disciples. These changes simply confirmed what the independents had claimed all along: the Disciples had forsaken the nondenominational values of Stone and Campbell. Some Disciples, but far from all, agreed with this accusation (sharp divisions remain in the Disciples over the role of centralized agencies). Beginning in 1961, even as the independents began to affirm a separate fellowship, a crucial Disciples committee began an extended study of polity. It matured a plan for restructuring that, in effect, created a formal denomination. The convention accepted the report in 1967 and implemented it in 1968. The former Christian Churches (note the plural) became the Christian Church (Disciples of Christ). The International Convention, already a de facto delegate body, became a representative general assembly (with delegates from each congregation). This large and unwieldy biannual assembly yields most effective power to an annual council, and it in turn delegates authority to an executive council. The architects of the new design desired something close to the organization of the United Church of Christ or of southern Baptists. Legally, congregations remained autonomous, but for the first time they had to accept the new polity in order to gain a listing in the *Yearbook* and thus to gain representation in the general assembly. This meant a carefully screened list of affiliated congregations. Those unwilling to accept the new denominational structure had to leave the reorganized denomination. From over 8,000 congregations listed in 1967, the *Disciples Yearbook* of 1971 contained barely 4,000. A majority of the departing congregations had already identified with the CCCC. But probably over 1,000 congregations, often led by older ministers, rejected the restructuring. A few of these became part of the CCCC, some remained independent, and many later rejoined the Disciples.

The separation of the CCCC was never as clear and neat as that of the earlier Churches of Christ. Some individuals and congregations remained ambivalent. A few would relate to both. Some Disciples ministers attend the NACC and enjoy the fellowship. A rather broad minority of Disciples resented the centralized leadership at the top and formed a subfellowship called Disciples Renewal (now Disciples Heritage Fellowship), with enough strength to defeat an assembly presidential candidate who approved the ordination of homosexuals. On the other side, the CCCC includes some ministers and able intellectuals who still regret the division, want no association with fundamentalists or contemporary evangelicals, engage in midlevel biblical scholarship, and are developing new responses to the issue of women's leadership. Yet the policies adopted by the Disciples, and the likelihood of a merger with the United Church of Christ, preclude any future reconciliation. At the same time, the Churches of Christ, which seem to have much more in common with the CCCC, will not accept a common fellowship, not only because of the highly visible issue of instrumental music, but because of a very different and matured tradition of their own. Over two-thirds of the members of the Churches of Christ are still in the South. The heartland of the CCCC is the Midwest, although this division was not sectional to the same extent as the one in 1907.

The Restoration movement is now too fragmented for any accurate assessment of its present membership. It is almost impossible to isolate the former Christian Connection members in the now-declining ranks of the United Church of Christ. The Christian Church (Disciples of Christ), like so many liberal and mainline denominations, has a declining active membership, which is today probably less than 700,000, in slightly less than 4,000 congregations. The much looser CCCC has more congregations—over 5,000—and by its own 1988 count 1.07 million members. The most conservative wing, the Churches of Christ, has more listed congregations (over 13,000) than the other two fellowships combined, in part because it has generally favored small and intimate churches. It reports an inclusive membership of over 1.6 million and an active one of 1.278 million, although some within the fellowship believe these self-reported numbers are too large, while others cite even higher figures. A degree of inflation haunts almost all self-reported membership claims, particularly by rigidly congregational churches. In any case, the often cited figure of 4 million in the combined Restoration churches is too optimistic today, since the movement as a whole is not only deeply fractured but has a declining membership.

READING GUIDE

In this and the following guides I select books that are at least reasonably accessible to most readers. I do not list unpublished Ph.D. dissertations, even when they were very useful to me. I do not list the most basic primary sources, such as new scriptures. It seems obvious that one interested in Mormonism would consult *The Book of Mormon* or *Doctrine and Covenants*, or would read *Science and Health* as a background to understanding Christian Science. I include what seem to me to be the most reliable or useful books on each religious tradition. Most are secondary sources; a few include primary documents. Thus, the lists are very selective, but some of the books chosen for each religious tradition include detailed bibliographies.

No book fully encompasses the history of all the restoration churches. The three main, semiofficial histories of the Disciples either ignore or treat only cursorily the Christian Connection churches. Also, the divisions since 1906, first into two and then, after 1960, into three major branches, have left interpretive problems. All three share the same origins and nineteenth-century history, but authors from each branch have a different perspective on this history, one that in each case supports their own contemporary doctrines and practices. Unfortunately, until very recently, the most comprehensive, scholarly histories of the movement have reflected a clear bias in favor of the more liberal Disciples.

The first of these comprehensive histories had as one of its authors a major leader in the more progressive wing of the Disciples, Winfred E. Garrison. His father had edited the *Christian-Evangelist*, the most liberal early twentieth-century Disciples periodical. He, with Alfred T. DeGroot, wrote in 1948 *The Disciples of Christ, a History* (St. Louis: Bethany Press). A later, official history with the same progressive perspective encompassed the structural changes that turned the Disciples into a denomination: Lester G. McAllister and William E. Tucker, *Journey in Faith: A History of the Christian Church (Disciples of Christ)* (St. Louis: Bethany Press, 1975). In 1981 Leroy Garrett published a more informal but informed history, *The Stone-Campbell Movement: An Anecdotal History of Three Churches* (Joplin, Mo.: College Press Pub. Co.). Garrett knew well all three branches of the movement and tried to be fair to each; but his dominant motif was unity, and thus he most respected those leaders in either branch who worked for cooperation or at least dialogue across the somewhat blurred sectarian boundaries.

The first scholarly histories of the Disciples movement written from one within the Churches of Christ were by David E. Harrell Jr., *Quest for a Christian America* (Nashville: Disciples of Christ Historical Society, 1966) and *The Social Sources of Division in the Disciples of Christ, 1865–1900* (Atlanta: Author, 1973). As his titles suggest, Harrell focused not on doctrine or practice but on the economic and social context that led to the separation of the Churches of Christ. He, more than any other scholar, emphasized both economic or class differences and also the powerful influence of sectional divisions and the Civil War. The only blow-by-blow account of Disciples history, and particularly the events that led to the Churches of Christ, is in a personal, at times polemical, chronicle by Earl I. West, *The Search for the Ancient Order*, 4 vols. (Indianapolis: Religious Book Service, 1949–79). Robert E. Hooper has written the standard history of the Churches of Christ since the division at the turn of the century: *A Distinct People: A History of the Churches of Christ in the Twentieth Century* (West Monroe, La.: Howard Pub. Co., 1993). The most recent and most sophisticated interpretation of this tradition is in a book by a scholar already distinguished for his work on primitivism, Richard T. Hughes, *Reviving the Ancient Faith: The Story of the Churches of Christ in America* (Grand Rapids: Eerdmans, 1995).

The CCCC is so young as to share most of a common history with the Disciples. Yet, three excellent histories reflect its outlook. James D. Murch, an active protagonist in the independence movement and one close to evangelicals or fundamentalists, wrote his *Christians Only: A History of the Restoration Movement* (Cincinnati: Standard Pub. Co., 1962) at the point of a final break. Henry E. Webb, in a graceful and eloquent book, *In Search of Christian Unity: A History of the Restoration Movement* (Cincinnati: Standard Pub. Co., 1990), and James B. North, in a scholarly and very readable *Union in Truth: An Interpretive History of the Restoration Movement* (Cincinnati: Standard Pub. Co., 1994), provide the most detailed and revealing histories of the long road to CCCC separation. It is significant that all three of these authors still use the term "Restoration movement" and that they all published with Standard in Cincinnati.

The movement begun by Stone and Campbell has attracted a wide array of biographies (of Stone, Thomas and Alexander Campbell, and Walter Scott) and scholarly monographs, including a large number of unpublished dissertations. The writings of both Stone and Campbell are voluminous. Less accessible are historical studies of the nonmerging wings of the early Christian movement. The only history of the few Sandemanian congregations in America and their British roots is by Lynn A. McMillon, *Restoration Roots* (Dallas: Gospel Teachers Publications, 1983). Most details known about the life of James O'Kelly are in an old, nonacademic celebration by Wilbur E. MacClenny, *The Life of James O'Kelly and the Early History of the Christian Church in the South* (Raleigh: Edwards and Broughton, 1910). The only detailed history of the southern wing of the Christian Connection is by Durward T. Stokes and William T. Scott, *A History of the Christian Church in the South* (Elon, N.C.: n.p., 1973). The fullest history of the early Christian movement in New England is in Michael G. Kenny, *The Perfect*

Law of Liberty: Elias Smith and the Providential History of America (Washington, D.C.: Smithsonian Institution Press, 1994). Charles H. Lippy has written the only recent history of the tiny Christadelphian movement, *The Christadelphians in North America* (Lewiston, U.K.: Edwin Mellen Press, 1989). Unfortunately, the last detailed history of the Christian Connection dates from 1912.

2

HUMANISTIC **CHRISTIANITY**

Unitarians

and

Universalists

Among the most pervasive issues to engage religious rebels or reformers in America were the doctrines and formulas associated with the Trinity. Even more central were the unending debates over salvation doctrines. Given the traditions of the Western Church, two of the most radical doctrines had been, from New Testament times on, a rejection of the divinity of Jesus and a belief in some form of universal salvation. As the brief introductions below suggest, both of these beliefs—heresies from the perspective of the orthodox—had a long history. In no sense was doctrinal unitarianism or universalism a product of American reformers. And, to an extent rarely recognized by most Americans, neither doctrine would be distinctive to those American Christians who adopted the labels "Unitarian" or "Universalist." For example, Christian Scientists are both unitarian and universalist in belief. A major wing of Pentecostalism is unitarian. Jehovah's Witnesses are unitarian and virtually universalist. Most apocalyptic sects reject any hell or eternal torment. Most early Adventists were at least heterodox on the Trinity issue. Some leaders of the early Restoration movement were Arian and at least close to being unitarians.

Neither were the Unitarian and Universalist churches in America without European precedents. Nonetheless, the Unitarian and Universalist denominations in America were largely indigenous, rooted originally in New England puritanism and shaped doctrinally and institutionally by American religious innovators. Of all American originals, they were the most humanistic and, except for the Mormons, usually perceived as the most radical.

THE EUROPEAN ORIGINS OF UNITARIANISM

As doctrines, a unitary conception of God and a belief in the full humanity of Jesus have long histories. Much of this history had little impact on Americans. The fragmentary evidence we have of the early Jewish Christians suggests that they retained a rigorous Jewish monotheism; that they adopted only one gospel, attributed to Matthew; and that they viewed Jesus as a fully human messiah, not a god. He was the son of Joseph and Mary (no virgin birth), born in their home in Bethlehem without any miracles. This means that the first Christians were unitarian, if one defines unitarian as belief in a unitary god and in the strictly human nature of Jesus. But the evidence is thin, and the later history of the two Jewish sects—the Nazarenes and the Ebionites—is obscure. In the early church such a unitarian view did not prevail or possibly even survive. But neither did the early church profess the later trinitarian formulas as perfected in the great councils at Nicaea and Constantinople.

By the time of the great church councils, the unitarian position had no visible supporters. In the fourth century the most appealing subordinationist view of Jesus was Arianism. Arius assumed the subordinate, or begotten, status of Jesus. Otherwise, Jesus was the Christ, the divine Logos, created before time and fully divine. The Arians lost, but Arian doctrines had continuing appeal and survived surreptitiously in parts of eastern Europe, possibly all the way to the Reformation. Ironically, almost all the leading founders of the Unitarian movement in America were more nearly Arians than true unitarians (they believed in a preexistent, divine Christ, and not that Jesus was in all ways a mere human).

The Reformation was mother to almost every imaginable heresy. In the chaotic religious ferment, unitarian doctrines gained open even if much reviled and persecuted advocates. Yet it is much easier and more correct to talk about dissent from the Athanasian formula than to identify true unitarians. One of the most famous early dissenters, Michael Servetus, emphatically rejected the traditional Trinity formula but still referred to Jesus as a god. He was not quite a true unitarian, although later he was much honored as a unitarian martyr (he died at the stake in Calvinist Geneva). Among the Brethren or true Anabaptists a near-Pelagian freewill position and a simple and literal biblicalism made the Nicene creed seem incomprehensible, meaning that many Anabaptists ignored the orthodox Trinity doctrine and flirted with Arianism. The spiritualist Caspar Schwenkfeld moved close to a unitarian conception of Jesus. In Transylvania, where ancient Arian views may have lived on, a Reformed faction had moved to an overt unitarian position by 1560. Its leading theologian, Francis David, advised the only unitarian king in the history of Europe, John Sigismund. David believed that the idea of the Christ, the Logos, had been in the mind of God eternally, but that Jesus was begotten of the Virgin Mary and only at that point came into being as a true son of God, with both human and divine characteristics. This early version of unitarianism has survived in Transylvania, and in the twentieth century Transylvanian Unitarians have established many contacts with their now much more liberal American cousins.

In a limited way, unitarians in Poland provided inspiration for early English unitarians. In a pluralistic Poland, one wing of the Reformed Church split from its parent body in 1556. This sect, called the Polish Brethren or Minor Reformed Church, closely resembled the Swiss Brethren who split from the Swiss Reformed Church, or the original Anabaptists. Its members were complete separatists and pacifists but unique among the Brethren groups for their open rejection of the traditional or orthodox understanding of the Trinity. Their ablest theologian, Italian exile Faustus Socinus, soon gave a popular and much reviled label to the sect—Socinianism— a word that long stood for any unitarian doctrine. Socinus was an unambiguous unitarian; he affirmed that Jesus was a human and none other. Only a fellow human could serve as the appropriate mediator between God and humanity. Only a human could suffer, die, and rise again (gods do not die), and in this way provide a means of salvation. Socinus made use of a press at Racow in Poland to publicize his views. Surreptitiously his tracts circulated throughout Europe, arousing great apprehension and fear on the part of the orthodox. His Racovian catechism became the foundational document of Unitarian Christianity. His views became well known in seventeenth-century Holland and in England in the period of the Puritan revolution. The Socinians, hopeful of a friendly reception, dedicated a 1614 edition of their catechism to James I, who promptly ordered it burned. The first widely identified Socinian (he was not) in England, John Biddle, published an attack on the traditional Trinity in the midst of a developing civil war in 1644, but he chose to attack the divinity of the Holy Spirit. The next year Parliament enacted a death penalty for those who denied the orthodox version of the Trinity.

In the eighteenth century many "rational" Christians, whether Anglican, Presbyterian, Congregational, or English dissenters, found the orthodox Trinity formula obscure and irrational. Inspirationists such as the Quakers and Shakers effectively bypassed, when they did not repudiate, the orthodox Trinity doctrine. Such views, if not made a point of controversy, were quite acceptable in some Anglican and liberal Presbyterian congregations, particularly in Britain, where many of the surviving Presbyterian congregations eventually moved to Unitarianism. Arian views were almost conventional, since such a famous Christian as Isaac Watts, the hymn writer, endorsed a form of Arianism. The most influential Arian to emerge in the Anglican Church was Samuel Clarke, who was much read by liberal ministers in New England. He eventually left the church and so edited the *Book of Common Prayer* as to eliminate all traditional Trinity formulas.

It was within an Anglican context that Arianism and even a form of Unitarianism first found an institutional home in America. In 1782 the wardens of the oldest Anglican church in Boston (King's Chapel) elected a young Congregational minister, James Freeman, as lay reader (the revolution had left the Anglican church an orphan, without a means of procuring priests). His views were close to those of Clarke or, eventually, those of Socinus. His congregation supported him in a complete revision of the prayer book, with a wording modeled on that of Clarke's. It simply left out all references to the traditional Trinity. The congregation wanted an inclusive liturgy acceptable to trinitarians, Arians, and Unitarians. Since this congregation eventually ordained Freeman and joined the new AUA in 1825, it gained the distinction of being the oldest Unitarian congregation in America, although it did not at first so denominate itself. It kept its prayer book and its highly formal liturgy and to this day is an anomaly in American Unitarianism.

The first organized British Unitarian movement developed, appropriately, among dissenting congregations in England. These independent congregations, the descendants of earlier Puritans and Separatists, were bound by no creeds or confessions and, locally, flirted with every imaginable heresy. In 1719 a controversy among dissenters over Trinity formulas led to a schism among English congregations, with the liberal minority including many doctrinal Arians and unitarians. But they did not make these doctrines the test of fellowship or the basis of their identity. Out of these more radical dissenters would come Joseph Priestley and an overtly Unitarian version of dissent. But even before this, a mild, peaceful Anglican minister, Theophilus Lindsey, fought against doctrinal tests (subscription) in the English church without success and finally led his congregation out of the church in 1774. He, much as Freeman a decade later, adopted a liturgy modeled on that of Clarke. His congregation became a gathering place for radicals and scientists, including both Priestley and Benjamin Franklin. Lindsey became a close friend of Priestley, who because of his fame as a scientist and his polemical theological books, became the best-known English Unitarian and in a sense also the first American Unitarian.

Joseph Priestley came from a formerly Puritan family and had to complete his education at a dissenting academy. He entered the dissenting ministry, even as he became a serious student of natural philosophy. While he gained fame as a scientist (he wrote a book on electricity and discovered oxygen), he served different dissenting congregations, becoming a notorious religious radical. In 1780 he moved to Birmingham for what would become the most fruitful and controversial decade of his life. There he became minister of the New Meeting, possibly the largest dissenting congregation in Britain. In 1782 he was able to bring together much of his earlier controversial writings about Christianity, from dozens of tracts or small books, into one powerful two-volume polemic, *An History of the Corruptions of Christianity*, which converted Thomas Jefferson to Priestley's form of Unitarianism. This volume raised a storm of controversy. By 1790 the vehement condemnations of Priestley by the orthodox gained a new and sinister political content. As one would have expected, Priestley enthusiastically endorsed the early French Revolution. As a consequence, a mob burned his church and his home and laboratory. He fled to London and in 1794 emigrated to America, where he was greeted as a martyr to religious freedom and republicanism.

Priestley well summarized his mature religious views in the *Corruptions*. He wanted to restore the early, primitive church, one uncorrupted by Greek and pagan ideas. The two great subsequent corruptions of this early church involved two noxious and related doctrines: the Greek concept of a separate soul or spirit and the orthodox doctrine of the Trinity. Priestley wanted to restore the corporealism or materialism of the ancient Jews. He rejected Arian views of Jesus (divine, preexistent, and immaterial) as emphatically as trinitarian ones. To him, Jesus was simply a human with a special mission, a mission that required a human (on this he agreed with Socinus). Since Priestley rejected any spiritual substance, he had to reject any concept of incarnation. This, in turn, led him to reject all versions of a substitutional atonement. Jesus lived an exemplary life, taught us our duties, but above all rose from the dead. The resurrection was central to Priestley, for it gave promise that righteous humans, who die and decay (no immortality), can also come back to life to live in the coming kingdom. These doctrines, close to those of Thomas Hobbes, combined with a profound sense of divine providence (a type of necessitarianism), placed Priestley in the doctrinal tradition of most modern Adventists (materialism, soul sleep, a literal resurrection). But he spent most of his writing trying to demonstrate the errors in the existing orthodox churches. With some looseness and sophistry he tried to establish the unitarian origins of the Church and then lambasted the Greek mysteries, the pagan influences, that corrupted the simple beginnings. These arguments, including the materialism, proved completely persuasive to Thomas Jefferson. For the first time he realized that his religious views and his understanding of Jesus were not heterodox but consistent with those of the uncorrupted early Church. Without attending carefully to all the nuances in Priestley's works, Jefferson acclaimed himself a Unitarian Christian and dismissed the so-called orthodox as corrupted Christians.

Priestley found anything but a utopia in America. In this final decade of his life he lost to death a beloved son and then his wife, suffered tormenting illnesses, and attracted harsh political criticism. He eventually built a new home at Northumberland, Pennsylvania, but this was on a failed land venture launched by his sons. He still knew a type of peace in his last four years, rejoiced in the election of his friend Jefferson to the presidency, and at his death in 1804 had unbounded hopes for the new American republic. Other dreams remained unfulfilled. Plans to build a great academy at Northumberland collapsed. His reformed or Unitarian Christianity was not as appealing in republican America as he had anticipated. He held services in his home at Northumberland, celebrated the Lord's Supper, but only a handful of people ever attended, although enough to establish this short-lived society as the first self-denominated Unitarian congregation in America. His first lecture series in Philadelphia in the spring of 1796 seemed very promising. Vice-President John Adams attended every lecture, as did many members of Congress, and President George Washington had Priestley to tea and at least expressed an interest in his doctrines. Before the lectures ended, Priestley helped establish an enduring, English-type Unitarian congregation in Philadelphia. But he could not serve as its pastor (lay readers had to suffice). A second series of lectures in 1797 was less well attended. Yet he died confident that God's providence would prevail and that a true, simple, reformed Christianity would eventually reign in America. Jefferson was even more optimistic. As he learned of the expansion of Unitarianism in New England, he became confident, before his death in 1826, that in only another generation Unitarianism would become the religion of America, a free and uncorrupted Christianity that best fit a free republic.

In most respects Priestley's version of Unitarianism deserves only a footnote in American religious history. It had limited appeal. Although New England liberals admired Priestley and a few read his books, none bought into his unique theological system. The founders of New England Unitarianism, so called, were more often Arians than unitarians. They were as offended by Priestley's materialism as were orthodox Calvinists and as resistant to his necessitarianism as to Calvinist predestination. Politically they were almost all Federalists, bitter enemies of Jeffersonians and of all deists and political radicals. Finally, although many of the New England liberals reflected a form of rationalism, they also revealed a soft, sentimental aspect. Lurking in the wings were the Transcendentalists, or those modern-day Platonists who were at the opposite extreme from a materialistic Priestley, and for this reason all the more radical in their religious views.

THE FOUNDING OF AMERICAN UNITARIANISM

In 1800 Unitarianism was scarcely visible in America. Only two congregations, Priestley's small Philadelphia society and King's Chapel in Boston, openly affirmed a unitarian position. Meanwhile, liberal Congregationalists, who would later and for complicated reasons accept the Unitarian label, were increasingly gaining almost complete dominance over the churches in the Boston area. None of the liberals foresaw or wanted a schism in the established churches, which stretched back to the earliest Puritan settlements.

These ministers chose the label "liberal," which invites confusion today. They meant it to convey their openness, catholicity, or generosity to diverse doctrinal positions. In a sense they represented the New England version of latitudinarianism. To some extent they had all repudiated orthodoxy, which in New England meant the Calvinism of their progenitors. All were loosely Arminian in doctrines, and after 1740 many had been willing to admit this. Some flirted with both universalist and Arian doctrines, but few either publicized such views or wanted to make such doctrines the basis of sectarian controversy. More than any other group of ministers, they wanted to preserve the existing order and in political and social outlook were on the side of order and deference. It was their enemies, orthodox in doctrine but often more republican and egalitarian in politics, who forced a confrontation and in 1825 a type of separation. This story has gained as much historical attention as any other in American religious history.

The early Puritan congregations in America rejected any confessions and creeds. They were free churches, formed around congregational covenants written and subscribed to by local members. Yet the early congregations reflected a remarkably homogeneous population and thus a working consensus on most doctrinal issues. The towns and congregations were very democratic in the sense of political participation but were quite exclusive and, for the deviant, repressive to the point of village totalitarianism. The free church tradition, in New England as in England, almost ensured diversity through time. But the fragmentation came more slowly in New England, in part because of selective emigration. Early conflict gave way to a rough uniformity of faith and practice that prevailed for a century. The first open break came with the revivals of 1734–42, or what some call the Great Awakening. The revivals created so many fissures in New England religious life that no easy classifications fit. The most evangelical or revivalistic factions often separated, with overtly New Light congregations forming the backbone of subsequent Baptism in New England. The less separatist evangelicals formed a faction led by Jonathan Edwards within Congregationalism. Opponents of revival excesses included both traditional Calvinists and an emergent and self-identified liberal faction, led at least in publications by Charles Chauncy, longtime minister of the famous First Church in Boston, and Jonathan Mayhew, two ministers that one might list as the grandparents of both American Unitarianism and Universalism.

This liberal faction eventually became the New England Unitarians. The first stage of a developing controversy involved battles over revivalism and key Calvinist doctrines. The liberals openly repudiated such resented and generally misunderstood doctrines as complete depravity and double predestination. They found such doctrines an insult to the loving and benevolent god they affirmed and a horrible indictment of human nature. But such doctrinal revision was no more important than subtle issues of class and cultural values. The liberals, by and large, represented the more affluent and socially prominent citizens of New England. They clustered in Boston and in the smaller towns of eastern Massachusetts and were scarce in most of western Massachusetts and Connecticut. The ministers, almost without exception, were Harvard (not Yale) trained, although many orthodox ministers also had degrees from Harvard. Culturally they were closer to the intellectual fashions of the day, more cosmopolitan in outlook, more secure in wealth and social standing, and more accepting of the world. They were often quite moralistic, even inclined to transform the Pauline scheme of salvation into a moralistic substitute, but they did not value holiness and spirituality as much as did the evangelicals. In other words, they accommodated the world, whether in their justification of wealth and enterprise, their infatuation with modern science and literature, their celebration of reason and good order, or their acceptance of worldly amusements and symbols of class standing, such as fashionable dress. In all these ways they were the very opposite of the followers of John Wesley, even though their campaign against Calvinism often involved similar doctrines. They represented a humanistic and not a pietistic or evangelical form of Arminianism. They were not sectaries at heart, but just the opposite. Only with great reluctance, and perhaps with a sense of compromised dignity, did the liberal ministers engage in vulgar doctrinal controversies. They did so only when their honor was at stake.

An open break came only in the new century. Much in post–Revolutionary America worked against any schism among Congregationalists. The liberals were as concerned as the orthodox about Deism and infidelity and were as faithful in support of the Federalists against the dangerous Jeffersonians. The postwar years marked a dull period even for the orthodox, with few revivals in any Congregationalist churches. Defending religion itself, not one doctrinal position, was the order of the day, particularly in the "dead" 1890s. Thus even the orthodox did not have the zeal needed for a frontal attack on quite visible signs of major heresies among the twenty to thirty identified liberal ministers and congregations. In 1784 Charles Chauncy published a defense of universalism that included a type of purgatory as a mode of punishment after death. God was not bent on vengeance but reformation. Even earlier Jonathan Mayhew had criticized the Athanasian Trinity formula and opted for a form of Arianism, a view widespread among the liberals by 1800. Both men rejected a substitutional atonement. But none of the liberals were, technically, unitarians, and none defended Joseph Priestley. They did not want controversy or to be identified with such a radical. In 1784–85 the liberals as much as the orthodox denied their pulpits to a visiting Unitarian of the Priestley persuasion. In Boston only James Freeman of King's Chapel had direct contact with English Unitarians, and it was he who helped publish an American edition of Priestley's *Corruptions*.

The religious situation changed rapidly after 1800. Widespread revivals erupted in Congregational churches throughout New England, although most were quite decorous in comparison with those of 1740 or with contemporary Baptist and Methodist revivals. These revivals reinvigorated the orthodox, who soon had such able and eloquent leaders as Lyman Beecher and Jedidiah Morse. They welcomed a fight with the liberals. The first occasion for open conflict came in 1805, with the election of the Hollis professor at Harvard (the oldest and most distinguished theological chair in America). The controversy brewed for two years before the fellows of the Harvard Corporation, divided four to two on the side of the liberals, elected a liberal, Henry Ware of Hingham, to the professorship and, subsequent to this and against the vehement protest of Jedidiah Morse, also appointed a liberal as president. The orthodox had lost Harvard. It is significant that, at this point, the doctrinal label thrown at the liberals by the orthodox was Arminian, not unitarian, although Morse "exposed" Ware's heterodoxy on the divinity of the Christ. The loss of Harvard was only symbolic of a very hard truth the orthodox had to face. They now clearly controlled only one of nine congregations in Boston. The oldest Puritan churches were in the liberal camp; the most prestigious Congregational parishes in America had deserted Calvinism.

After 1805 the factions hardened, largely because of the action of Morse. The liberals remained catholic and wanted to maintain harmony and institutional cooperation. In a powerful protest against liberal trends, the orthodox violated an old New England tradition by refusing to exchange pulpits with the liberals. Divided congregations had to choose between the two developing factions. No middle way remained viable. A few congregations split into liberal and orthodox factions, with the majority retaining control of the parish church. In a crucial decision in 1820, the Massachusetts Supreme Court ruled, in the Dedham case, that the members of the total parish, not the communicants or members of the congregation, controlled the property of the still-established church. This meant, in many towns, that nonmembers and liberals kept control of the local church and forced the orthodox to separate. Such fractures divided, for the first time, the established ministers of New England, those who still received state support or those generally still referred to as the ministers of the Standing Order. Such divisions, among other reasons, helped smooth the way for the disestablishment of the church in Massachusetts in 1833. But except for their efforts to hold on to parish property, the liberals still refused to fight, even at times to defend their own cause. It took another event to bring them into the open.

Morse continued his attack on the liberals. In 1808 he helped found Andover Seminary as a safe option for young men corrupted at a heretical Harvard. Then, in 1815, he thought he found a smoking gun. He read an English biography of Theophilus Lindsey, written by the leading successor of Priestley in English Unitarianism, Thomas Belsham. Belsham included a chapter on the progress of American Unitarianism. Morse published this chapter plus some letters from James Freeman at King's Chapel. Freeman shared with his English correspondents a perhaps overly optimistic evaluation of the progress of Unitarian opinion at Harvard and among the liberal ministers, where it was making a "silent but rapid and irresistible progress," and where most public worship was "carried on upon principles strictly, if not avowedly Unitarian." Morse tried to turn these revelations into a scandal. To him these publications proved that, as he had long argued, the liberals were worse heretics than anyone realized, that they were unannounced Unitarians who had secretly conspired to overthrow the true Church, and that it was his duty to expose them and their hypocrisy as a first step for expelling them from the church. He now had the proof that the defection had run to the "lowest degrees of Socinianism, to the very

borders of open infidelity." The liberals, he argued, were also part of a secret and sinister international conspiracy to overthrow true religion in New
England.

Morse made unitarian doctrine the crux of his assault on the liberals.
They were ill equipped to respond to the charge. Few, if any, were Socinians or Priestleyites, if this was what Unitarianism required. On the other
hand, few were Athanasians. Few had made this issue central to their ministry and for several reasons did not want to identify themselves with English Unitarianism. But Morse laid down a gauntlet they could not ignore.
He, in effect, accused them of hypocrisy and deceit. Their personal honor
was at stake. By the time of Morse's review the Boston liberals looked
to William Ellery Channing, a still-youthful pastor of the Federal Street
Church and already a very effective preacher, as their spokesman. Channing lacked a commanding intellect. He was not a serious biblical scholar
and was not nearly as able as the recently deceased Joseph Buckminister, a
more philosophical liberal minister and an early and informed biblical
critic. But the emerging movement had no abler spokesman, and at least
Channing could meet Morse on his intellectual level. In a private letter intended for publication, Channing offered a blistering reply to Morse. He
denied that any of the liberals were unitarians in the sense of Priestley but
were indeed such in a more general sense (he intimated a form of Arianism). On internal grounds he destroyed Morse's charge of secrecy and
hypocrisy and proved that the liberals rarely considered the Trinity issue in
their pulpits and never attacked trinitarians. They had been restrained,
worked in behalf of a broader fellowship. Finally he painted Morse as the
dogmatist, ready to split the fellowship on the basis of false fears and false
charges. Clearly, any odium for any split of the churches would rest with
the orthodox, not the liberals, who would do almost anything short of
moral compromises or dishonor to maintain the unity of the church.

The label would not go away. The former Arminians, the declared liberals, were now Unitarians (no one seemed concerned with precise definitions). After 1815 these liberals constituted, in sentiment, a separate fellowship, although one still within the loose Congregational system. In 1819
Channing decided to make a virtue of the stigmatizing label. In an ordination sermon in Baltimore at the installation of Jared Sparks, not only a liberal minister but one of the first able American historians, he read what
amounted to a declaration of independence, or what became the most
important founding document of American Unitarians. He titled his sermon "Unitarian Christianity." In fact, he defined a brand new version
of Unitarianism, one that had distinctive New England origins. The label
remained awkward. It did not fit well. No matter. Channing and his fellow

ministers would change the meaning of the word, make it fit their realities. Ironically, in two generations the movement so shifted that the label in its purest meaning (Jesus was only a man) fit very well.

Institutionally the new movement had no clear form. Nothing changed in individual congregations. They retained their old covenants. If the liberals retained control of the parish, their congregations continued to receive state support until disestablishment in Massachusetts in 1833. Nothing officially identified a Unitarian congregation, at first not even a name. Yet, in New England everyone knew which congregations were in the Unitarian camp. Of over 100 such congregations, a large share were the oldest and most prestigious in New England. In 1825 a group of ministers representing less than half the liberal congregations formed the AUA. It was not a new denomination but just a ministerial association, which at least helped identify a new fellowship. Such a loose association was about all that was possible within the traditional congregational system. The "loss" of the Unitarians was a terrible blow to Congregationalists. They lost their most prestigious congregations, at least a large portion of their ablest ministers, and more than their share of eminent members.

What were the doctrines of the new movement? Officially it had none. The Unitarians loved to chide the Congregationalists about their departure from early Puritan ideals, for Congregationalists had introduced creeds or confessions. The Unitarians thus claimed the free church tradition. If one wanted to characterize the Unitarians doctrinally in 1825, one could refer to them as rationalistic and humanistic Arminian Christians who were soft on the Trinity issue. Most were already Arians of some type, and increasing numbers of young ministers affirmed a fully human Jesus. Within this broad framework, opinions varied on almost every doctrine, although all concurred on their rejection of the five points of Calvin. What these labels too easily conceal and what critics liked to downplay is that all the early Unitarian ministers were avowed, serious, conscientious Christians who simply wanted to reform and purify the church. They still believed the Bible, when interpreted with reason and common sense, to be the Word of God. They rejected a triune God but continued to baptize in the name of the Father, Son, and Holy Spirit.

The only way to flesh out Unitarian beliefs is by reference to individuals. In New England the ministers served as spokesmen for their congregations. This does not mean that all laypeople agreed with their minister, but in time persevering ministers and congregations tended to reflect a near-consensus. Ministers attracted like-minded parishioners. Thus, about the only way to penetrate the ambiguities of an avowedly free church is through the ministerial leaders. One must start with Channing, and that is not an easy task. Channing may have been the most representative Unitarian minister. His position on doctrinal issues was mediatory and close to the center. More important, on several occasions, such as the 1819 Baltimore sermon, he tried to be a spokesman for his colleagues, to note areas of near-consensus, and to identify doctrines on which Unitarians remained in disagreement.

Channing was the son of a prominent and affluent Newport, Rhode Island, lawyer. He, of course, attended Harvard as preparation for the ministry. Notably, he at times attended the congregation of Samuel Hopkins, the disciple of Jonathan Edwards and the leader of the New Divinity movement. In one sense Hopkins's strong Calvinism alienated the young Channing, but Hopkins stressed, as no one else, the Edwardian concept of complete benevolence to God as the only acceptable form of virtue and, before almost any other minister, righteously condemned slavery. Channing later acknowledged the enduring influence of Hopkins's moral theory and his moral courage. At Harvard he almost automatically began to identify with the dominant liberals, and thus as a young minister allied himself with the liberal cause. It is difficult to explain his influence. He excelled as a preacher and essayist, not as a theologian. He had a gift for a clear, direct, eloquent style informed by great sincerity. His personality, his character, and his goodwill attracted the young men of New England, including Ralph Waldo Emerson and Theodore Parker.

In his key sermon, in which he tried to characterize the beliefs of the liberals, Channing began with the issue of authority. This would soon divide the young movement. Channing professed a scriptural form of Christianity. The authority for the liberal platform was the Bible. The Bible was a vast body of literature written over a long period of time and in human languages. It required interpretation, judgments about what each part meant. Channing stressed that the orthodox as well as the liberals had no alternative but to interpret the Bible. They had to use what he called "reason" in their interpretations. The liberals likewise used reason, but they were honest enough to acknowledge that necessity. They did not find all parts of the Bible equally authoritative. In fact, they found all manner of inconsistencies from one part to another, and, more critical, in sections of the Old Testament they found a crude understanding of God and examples of great cruelty. Thus liberals had to pick and choose among, or rank, biblical passages. Without admission, the orthodox did the same. To them, as to the liberals, all parts of the Bible were not equal, could not be equal. Some were irrelevant to modern Christians. After all, the Bible was a record of a progressive understanding of divine truths, a record of God's continuing revelation over time. Such revelation did not end with the canonical scriptures. But Channing had no doubt that the climax of such revelation was in the recorded teaching of Jesus. Thus the gospels clearly ranked highest in his estimate. He, like so many Christian rationalists, shifted the focus from the Christ of Paul back to Jesus of Nazareth and to his ministry. In this sense the emerging Unitarians were more Jesus oriented, less Christ centered. But at the time Channing and most of his colleagues still accepted, without doubt, the gospel stories, including the miracles attributed to Jesus.

It was on scriptural grounds that Channing rejected the traditional conception of a Trinity. Of course the doctrine was also, in his estimate, completely illogical, even absurd. But what doomed it, in his eyes, was the absence of any justification for such a doctrine in the record of Jesus' ministry. Jesus always conceived of himself as the dutiful son of God, not a god. Proudly, Channing claimed his movement as unitarian, in the sense that it accepted—celebrated, in fact—the perfect unity of God and the perfect sonship of Jesus. Channing also stressed the unity of Jesus; he was not two persons but one. Channing deliberately left open the issues that separated Arians (a preexistent, divine Christ or Logos) and Unitarians (Jesus was only a man, whatever the sublime nature of his teachings or his mission). He had sided with the Arians earlier, in his response to Morse, but when speaking for the movement, he wanted to leave room for people like Freeman, who was close to Priestley in his unitarianism. By this time, in the New England context, the word "Unitarian" increasingly meant any position that denied the equal divinity of the Father and the Son. Arians and true Unitarians thus united, and for most of the nineteenth century American Unitarians claimed Arius as one of their heroes. Some confusingly referred to Arianism as one type of Unitarianism.

To Channing, as for most of his liberal predecessors, the Trinity issue had not been central. It was not the unity of God but his moral perfection that Channing wanted to preach. This was his key emphasis, which he used as a weapon against Calvinists. He was most in his element when he lambasted various Calvinist doctrines. To a great extent New England Unitarian Christianity gained its identity by contrast. It was the opposite of Calvinism. Channing was not very perceptive in setting up the enemy. He usually caricatured the doctrines of Calvin (or of Augustine). The problem was that through time and among accomplished and cosmopolitan New Englanders the old language made no sense. The terms were alien and, when taken in a literal sense, repugnant. The conceptions of God and of humanity had so shifted as to make the older doctrines irrelevant. Channing, with some degree of astonishment, noted over and over again that he found sterling character, moral courage, and exemplary conduct among the orthodox. He had found such in Hopkins. He condemned not the orthodox but some of their professed doctrines—professed, not really believed—for he could not accept the fact that good people understood or accepted such cruel doctrines. They were good Christians in spite of, not because of, such doctrines as depravity and election. In ways Channing never noted—in their moral seriousness, in their attempt to combine piety and moral activism, and even in their intellectuality—the Unitarians remained good Calvinists.

Behind his critique of Calvinism was the humanism of Channing, or his reevaluation of humanity. In all areas, humans have to interpret, judge, and decide. They do this when they interpret the scriptures. They do it when they render moral judgments. They do it when they try, however inadequately, to understand divine subjects, such as the nature of God. Channing never doubted that a God existed. The problem was how humans could understand such a God. Their only alternative, one again followed without acknowledgment by even the most orthodox, was to use self-understanding to move toward an understanding of God. Of course, such understanding would always be limited and incomplete, for God in his nature was far beyond human comprehension. This did not mean, to Channing, some retreat into mysticism. It meant that humans, using what insights they had, could only apply to God the traits—of mind and will—they knew in themselves. God, as a divine person, must necessarily be understood in anthropomorphic terms, else he (even the "he" implicates human traits) becomes a complete mystery or has to be conceived as material and nonspiritual. When humans speak of the goodness of God, they must attribute to him human conceptions of justice and mercy; the only alternative is silence. They must, indeed, attribute such human virtues in their infinite perfection, but they are not different kinds of virtue.

This humanism had its own vicious circularity, which Channing could not recognize. Why not conclude that all the various gods are simply human inventions, projections of historically shifting conceptions of what is good? Channing never conceded this, for behind his humanism lay his assurance that God was the source of all things. He created humans. He gave them a moral faculty. They could therefore rely on it. Thus, when humans exercised moral judgments or attributed moral virtues to a god, they were exercising divine traits given them by God, and thus God himself anchored and secured human judgment, at least at its best. This solved all the problems. What God had implanted in human nature allowed humans to understand goodness and justice and to understand them correctly although not fully, and their understanding of such virtues gave them the concepts needed to characterize God, insofar as humans can characterize divinity.

This circular argument subtly shifted the locus of authority toward the god within, toward a form of Transcendentalism, and away from historical records and biblical miracles, although Channing never rejected external proofs. Thus he navigated easily between emerging rationalist and romantic factions in the new movement.

Channing's main quarrel with Calvinists was that they professed to worship an arbitrary and cruel deity who did not measure up to the god-given moral standards present in the conscience of all humans. Calvinists, as persons, usually followed these god-given standards and were in fact just and kind, but their theology pointed in a different direction. If Calvinists were consistent and imitated their god, they would contrive to have flawed or depraved children and then punish or even damn such children for acting consistent with their depraved nature. Or they might select a favored child, one obedient in all ways, and have him killed as a sacrifice in order to buy forgiveness and mercy for some but not all of the other undeserving siblings. To Channing, it was impossible to believe in such a god, ignoble to worship him.

Of all Calvinist doctrines that Channing despised, human depravity led the list. He confessed human ignorance and weakness and cowardice. These were ever present. But he rejected some innate or essential corruption. Typically he saw all such doctrines in moral terms. People, he affirmed, are not depraved or corrupt. They are in the image of God, spiritual creatures, only a little lower than the angels. Channing thus preached endlessly on the goodness of humankind and on its potential for growth and redemption. His focus was on the elements of divinity in humans, a divinity most clearly and perfectly embodied in Jesus. The success of his ministry probably rested on this message of hope and encouragement. He stressed what people could be, at their best, and believed a message of love more congenial to the flowering of virtue than one of fear. The message appealed to his audience, an audience capable of guilt but not able to comprehend the older doctrines of alienation and depravity. Perhaps they did not look as closely at themselves, at their innermost motives, as did earlier Puritans. The other side of such a message was a religion of duty and moral obligation, or essentially a religion of devotion and good works, not one of undeserved grace. Channing acknowledged that the liberals had varying interpretations of the exact role of Jesus' death in leading to salvation, or really different interpretations of the atonement. He would not encourage any consensus here. But he argued, quite consistently with his conception of God and humanity, that no liberal accepted a strong version of a substitutionary atonement, any penal version in which Jesus had to die to appease God, to pay back some debt, or to allow him to relent on the punishment all humans deserved.

Channing's Unitarianism and that of most of his liberal colleagues represented a somewhat vulnerable compromise. By retaining a scriptural grounding, it reflected only a small move beyond the type of rational Arminianism present in some Episcopal and Presbyterian as well as Congregational churches. The somewhat ambiguous Unitarian doctrine and rather broad support for the doctrine of universal salvation after future punishment placed these Unitarians on the leading edge of Christian revisionism. But even Channing revealed a tension between biblical authority on one hand and that of conscience on the other. So far, he used internal revelation only as a check on scriptural interpretation. He was not willing to cut loose from a historic and written authority, but he was already somewhat equivocal in his use of it. Other colleagues, including Andrews Norton, a divinity professor at Harvard and, in traditional terms, an able Bible scholar, noted such hints of subjectivism with dismay. Other young Unitarians found in this soft or Quaker side of Channing a glorious opening to a religion tied completely to the authority of the god in each person. These young people included both Emerson and Parker.

THE GOLDEN AGE OF UNITARIANISM

Until after the Civil War, Unitarians did not have anything close to a centralized polity. After the period of separating congregations, the movement grew slowly, if at all. Within a decade of the formation of the association, the ministers were increasingly divided into factions. Many had dreams of expansion, but pitifully small funds to support missionary efforts led to only a few new congregations outside New England, and these were almost always made up of migrating Yankees. Most Unitarians remained in Boston and eastern Massachusetts. Yet, the formal weakness of the new denomination should not conceal the social, economic, and political preeminence of its members. In no other period of American history and in no other Christian denomination did church members have so much cultural impact.

Because of subsequent shifts in the denomination, the youthful rebels, the innovative Transcendentalists, have gained the greatest amount of historical attention. In a sense they did represent the future of the denomination. But their attempted reforms can camouflage the period from 1825 to 1865, when almost all Unitarians remained devout Christians, still involved in a type of church life and worship that was in the older Puritan tradition. They were no longer evangelicals, in the sense that they did not emphasize a transforming rebirth experience, did not support most forms of revivalism, were somewhat diffident in proselytizing, and did not aspire to the types of purity and holiness preached by Methodists. They were very much in the world, but did all they could to shape it to fit their own moral vision. Yet, in their political activism, in their sense of stewardship and their philanthropy, in their advocacy of educational reform and at least moderate antislavery protest, and even in their openness to new scholarship and science, they reflected many more continuities with Cotton Mather or Jonathan Edwards than they often realized. Although Unitarian ministers from Channing on emphasized a humane or benevolent god and embraced a thoughtful or reasonable approach to biblical interpretations, the later Transcendental image of a cold and stale Unitarianism was unfair because it was untrue. The insights we have into Unitarian congregations reveal as much warm, personal piety as rational argument. Just as the Puritans of old, a warm and spiritual form of religion still mixed, in combinations that varied from person to person, with the intellectual components. Belief and sentiment were both present. Channing, because of his blending of piety and intellect, remained the model Unitarian.

The Unitarians were never a majority of Christians even in Boston. There they outnumbered Congregationalists, but not in New England as a whole. Rapidly growing Baptist and Methodist congregations, and soon immigrant-based Roman Catholic parishes, easily surpassed the Unitarians. The contacts with these groups were minimal but were closer and often more tense with the growing Universalist movement in New England. The largest Unitarian congregations dated from the earliest Puritan migration. Only a smaller number of Episcopal churches competed for the membership of the most affluent and eminent Bostonians. Most Unitarians were members of older New England families of English origin. They were not all wealthy or even affluent, but most had some degree of social status.

Detailed studies reveal that in the greater Boston area, Unitarians had an unprecedented and never again duplicated monopoly of cultural and economic resources. Well over half the major figures in a New England literary renaissance came from Unitarian congregations. Many remained in the church. Poets, essayists, novelists, critics, journalists, and historians were disproportionately a part of what might be called a Unitarian culture. So were early feminists, including Margaret Fuller, who remained at the fringe of the church, and Lydia Maria Child, who suffered ostracism by Unitarians because of her early and extreme abolitionism. Unitarians formed the first American literary society, the church itself sponsored the first major literary review, and Unitarians (Horace Mann in particular) led in public educational reform. In politics a disproportionate share of both elected and appointed officials in Massachusetts were Unitarian. Wealth was equally concentrated in Unitarian hands. Over one-half of the wealthiest Bostonians were members of Unitarian congregations. In almost every area of enterprise, including railroads, insurance companies, banks, and textile mills, as well as traditional shipping and merchandising, Unitarians took the lead.

One continuity with the Puritan past was the role of ministers in Unitarian congregations. They had the best education (almost always Harvard), high social status, and a crucial leadership role. They served at the will of their congregations, but many spent their whole career in one pulpit. They continued the free worship tradition of Puritanism (hymns, prayers, scripture, and sermons), with a continuation of the ordinances of baptism and communion. The ministers, through a frequent exchange of pulpits (demanded by their members), had every motive to prepare learned and increasingly eloquent sermons. In a sense the Puritan sermonic tradition reached a climax in these liberal pulpits, before demanding, very literate, and socially elite audiences. With the break from an older orthodoxy and from stereotypical sermon styles, ministers tried to cultivate literary grace and moral conviction. In a sense this sermonic tradition climaxed in the essays of Ralph Waldo Emerson.

For a few rebellious young ministers, as for Emerson, the Unitarian congregations seemed smug and self-righteous. For a few radical reformers, such as Theodore Parker, they were insensitive to most forms of injustice, despite their paternalistic and philanthropic endeavors. The elites in Unitarian pews prided themselves on refinement. They supported the arts, particularly literature, and dabbled in most forms of civic improvement and reform. Politically they had all been Federalists, and with a few exceptions all became Whigs. At times, no doubt, their charity took on the cast of paternalism, and on the most controversial issues, such as slavery, they exhibited as much caution as radicalism (most ministers and laypeople backed colonization, wanted gradual emancipation, and only belatedly moved toward an abolitionist platform). Unitarians as a whole did not join in the crusade for temperance, and the ministers in Boston, to the despair of Parker, expelled one minister who crusaded against the evils of alcohol. In retrospect their openness to the new science or to biblical criticism might seem contradictory to their generally conventional and conservative social and economic outlook. Not so, for the Unitarians considered themselves an enlightened minority who wanted to uplift the common people but who never identified with them.

Unitarians were not well equipped to expand their movement. Its elite profile did not help. Its humanistic and antirevivalist style discouraged more effective forms of proselytizing. Of particular concern to Unitarian leaders was the provincial image—the fact that Unitarianism seemed largely a parochial product of Boston and its environs. Actually, Unitarian congregations were at least thinly scattered over all of New England and into New York. But at first there were none west of the Appalachians. As Yankees moved west, they began forming at least small Unitarian congregations, usually in the developing cities of the West and even in a few cases in the South, although except for Louisville and Baltimore such congregations did not survive the Civil War. In time these western congregations would create a very different, less clearly Christian form of Unitarianism.

From the perspective of Boston, even western Pennsylvania was in the wilderness of the West. In Meadville, just south of Erie, a former Dutch Reformed minister, Harm Jan Huidekoper, converted to Unitarianism and established a local congregation. In 1844 he used some of his own funds to help establish a small, struggling seminary jointly sponsored by Unitarians and the Christian Connection, a small, New England-centered, and Arian-oriented wing of the Restoration movement. Young men who could not afford Harvard could come here for ministerial training. Eventually the Unitarians moved this seminary to Chicago and united it with a failing Universalist seminary (Ryder) connected to what soon became a failed liberal arts college (Lombard).

In three cases, young and able New England ministers moved west and helped build a Unitarian presence. In 1833 James Freeman Clarke, a Harvard graduate and an intuitionist or Transcendentalist in theology, helped form a congregation in Cincinnati. It endured but did not always thrive. After seven years Clarke returned to Boston, formed a new and very liberal congregation, and became one of the leading intellectuals in mid-nineteenth-century Unitarianism. In 1844 William Greenleaf Eliot moved to St. Louis, remaining there for the rest of his career. Typical of almost all the early Unitarian pioneers in the West, he entered actively into the civic life of St. Louis and was one of the founders of what became Washington University. His son, Thomas Lamb Eliot, helped found a Unitarian church in Portland, Oregon, just after the Civil War.

With the gold rush, Yankees flocked to California, and in San Francisco a few quickly founded a Unitarian congregation, which struggled for survival during the 1850s. In 1860 the AUA persuaded a sickly, former Universalist minister, Thomas Starr King, to move to San Francisco to rebuild this church. They hoped the climate would aid his health (it did not). He had already demonstrated his oratorical and leadership abilities in Unitarian pulpits in Massachusetts. King not only rebuilt the church, soon making it the largest Protestant congregation in California, but became the best-known preacher in the West, played a major role in keeping California in the Union, helped spread the Unitarian message into Oregon and Washington, and was so politically involved as to be invited to run for the

United States Senate. His death in 1864 was a disaster for California. Such were the memories, even the legends, about King that in the twentieth century the church eventually gave his name to their seminary at Berkeley. King, typical of the western pioneers, tried to build more inclusive congregations and cooperated more easily with Universalists (King never repudiated his original loyalties). These westerners were also less involved in the factionalism that soon divided the movement in New England.

Unitarians were never of one mind. Factional divisions were inevitable, although none of these led to any schism (the loose congregational system made it difficult to exclude anyone). The most important source of controversy was incipient at its founding. This was the basis of authority for religious belief and commitment. As it played itself out before the Civil War, this controversy took on major national significance, for one group of contenders, usually labeled Transcendentalists, would have an enormous impact on American culture.

Much less emphatically than Universalists, but almost to a person, the founding ministers had joined Channing in his appeal to the scripture and to supernatural revelation and miracles. The Unitarians wanted to restore a purified Christianity—the one issue that connected them to Priestley. They never joined overt deists, who found in nature and reason the only revelation of God. But by the time of the organization of the American Unitarian Association in 1825, several intellectual developments began to place the issue of authority in a completely new light. These developments included the increasing philosophical ascendancy of types of absolute or dynamic idealism, most rooted in Germany; the impressive development of biblical scholarship, again largely in German universities; and the first intensive interest in and scholarship on eastern religions, particularly the progenitors of Hinduism and Buddhism. As young Unitarian intellectuals tried to absorb and cope with such new knowledge, they almost had to take a more critical stance toward biblical authority or, much more subversive, even challenge the authority of Jesus.

In time, Unitarians identified the often youthful rebels as Transcendentalists. The label was at best unclear; at worst, completely misleading. German idealistic philosophy and German biblical studies had an early impact on Unitarians. But idealism, as a philosophical position, had roots all the way back to Jonathan Edwards and did not, of necessity, lead even to a break from orthodoxy. Beginning with George Bancroft and Edward Everett, both before 1820, some of the brighter Harvard students and emergent liberals went to Germany for graduate work. By 1830 the trickle of such students became a stream. Some were Congregationalists, and not all the Unitarians became radicals back home. Frederick Henry Hedge went to Germany with Bancroft in 1818, studied there for four years, perfected his German, and became a student of the Lutheran reformation. Back in New England, he graduated from Harvard Divinity and became a Unitarian minister and a college professor. Hedge helped form the discussion group in Cambridge that Emerson referred to as the Transcendentalist Club (the only organization that ever gave content to the label). Yet, his intuitionist view of the foundations of faith did not lead him to reject a secondary role for scripture or to challenge the importance of the institutional church.

Few Unitarian ministers were committed to serious theology. Few had the time for serious scholarship. But as the factions formed, it was clear that the more radical young men, particularly those most willing to challenge the authority of either nature or the Bible in grounding religious faith, were in the Germanic or, as their enemies identified them, pantheistic tradition. The vast majority of ministers were less likely to be versed in German idealism and more often found their philosophical inspiration in Scottish common sense. The idealists never captured the struggling divinity school at Harvard. There the most dominant early professor was Andrews Norton, but he resigned in 1830 to devote full time to biblical studies. He was an able scholar and had been one of the earlier polemicists in behalf of a separate Unitarian fellowship. More carefully than any of his peers he had developed arguments in behalf of a unitary God, but he remained confident that Unitarianism, as a restored and purer form of Christianity, had to find its authority in the New Testament, particularly in the miracles and the teachings of Jesus. As the new, higher criticism came to America, he was horrified, soon almost obsessed, with its speculative excesses and spent years completing what he hoped would be a scholarly refutation, his *Evidences of the Genuineness of the Gospels*, a three-volume masterpiece completed from 1837 to 1844. He was horrified at the "infidelity" of Emerson or the "pantheism" of Parker. But in so far as evidence is available, his thoroughly Christian Unitarianism remained that of a vast majority of both laypeople and ministers until after 1850, when slowly the more "advanced" ideas of the radical young ministers began to spread outward and downward from a few of the early leaders, such as Parker.

At least in retrospect, one cannot ignore Emerson. In one sense he had only a minor role in Unitarianism. He moved so far from any version of Christianity as to be all alone in the denomination. Yet he had enormous influence on a few young ministers, such as Parker. Emerson attended the new Harvard Divinity School and in a desultory way was preparing himself for the Unitarian ministry just as the new association formed in 1825. In 1828, with his Harvard M.A., he secured his first permanent pulpit at the large Second Church in Boston, the successor of the famous Henry Ware. The tragic death of his first wife, personal doubts and confusions, and a desire for greater intellectual freedom led him to contrive a minor dispute over the administration of the Lord's Supper (he refused to preside at such services) and to his resignation from this pulpit in 1831. He did not thereby leave either the church or the ministry. He remained a nominal but often inactive Unitarian for the rest of his life. For many years he accepted temporary pulpit invitations until eventually only a few were open to him because of his perceived radicalism. He always acknowledged the powerful and positive influence of Channing and credited Unitarianism with removing the bonds of Calvinism. Otherwise he was a sharp and penetrating critic of Unitarianism (and of all conventional churches) throughout his long and very unique ministry. His lectures and essays, even his poems, became his sermons; the nation as a whole, his congregation. He aspired to be the inspired poet-priest of America, not a disciple of anyone, not even Jesus.

As late as 1838 Unitarians still considered Emerson one of their ministers, although he had no permanent pulpit. By then he had settled in Concord, gathered a group of disciples, published his first book (*Nature*), and gained a measure of fame in both America and Europe. He was by then the most eminent Unitarian (both John Adams and Thomas Jefferson had died in 1826), and the Church gladly if anxiously claimed him. Thus, in 1838 the divinity school students at Harvard invited him to deliver the annual address to the senior class, although not without some apprehension and debate. Many feared what he might say. What he said became the second most important document in Unitarian history, next to Channing's 1819 Baltimore sermon. Among the students in the audience was Theodore Parker, who was lifted almost into transports by the content of the address. He alone may have completely grasped the full import of what Emerson said.

No brief summary can do justice to Emerson's "Divinity School Address." Beautiful, dense, and packed with implications, it was a condensation of his developing personal philosophy, a philosophy more directly characterized by his doctrine of self-reliance. He knew the context. He still referred to God. But his text made clear that this was not the Jehovah of scriptures, not a creator god. As throughout his career, Emerson refused to pin down his concept of ultimate reality, to give it one name. He could, in various contexts, call it Nature, or Spirit, or Oversoul, or, as in this sermon, simply a form of energy or a type of immanent virtue or moral law. It is not clear that such a reality has any existence, in the sense of things, which are only the dead surfaces of divine ideas. Ultimately, the only approach to such divinity is internal; the only true god is within. Divinity lies within each human soul, normally suppressed and unrecognized. Religion, properly conceived, involves glimmers of recognition and celebration of this immanent deity and the beatitude possible when one merges with it, consents to it, affirms it, and loves it. Emerson called this acknowledgment the religious sentiment and linked it, as always, to the moral law and to virtue. Recognition of one's true self and a grasp of the demands of moral law are synonymous.

These soaring Platonic affirmations provided the grounds for Emerson's devastating attack on conventional religions of all kinds, including Unitarianism. Religious insight involves intuition, grace, a response to the light. It has nothing to do with authority. One may honor prophets and seers, but one honors them because they turned to the light, gained inspiration, and reflected this in their lives. The light within them is not accessible to anyone else. Above all, these great prophets are not proper subjects of worship. Instead we should turn, as they, toward the light, the divine spirit, and worship what they worshiped. But the whole history of religion revealed the opposite. The prophets and seers, such as Jesus, became false objects of worship. Their flickering descriptions of the divine, translated into mundane scriptures, became authoritative creeds and confessions, cold, second-hand, unmoving, and unauthentic. Emerson honored Jesus above all seers. Jesus understood better than anyone else the mystery of the soul, saw that God was incarnate in humans, and in moments of transport referred to himself as divine, even as all persons are divine in such moments of transcending spiritual insight, when reason overtakes and subordinates mere understanding. But the church—Emerson almost said it with a sneer—was built on the authority of a god-man and on the literal idioms and tropes of his celebrations.

Implicit in Emerson's sermon was his rejection, on principle, of any external authority whatsoever in religion. It is all bogus, diverting, a source of idolatry. The chief idols of Christianity, even of liberal Unitarianism, were the Bible and Jesus. Emerson rejected all idols as well as all formalism, all liturgies, and all sacraments. He tried to inspire the young ministers. He venerated their ministerial role. He wanted them to preach the faith of the Christ, not faith in a Christ. Above all, they had to preach their faith, their self-understanding, and their intimations of redemption. None of this had anything to do with traditional Christianity, with any received doctrines, or with any traditions of worship. Their message had to come directly from their own experience, their own insights, and their own souls. No new cult, no new liturgies, and no new and pale Unitarian innovations had any value. What was left was the day of worship and an honorable tradition of preaching. This was all the young ministers needed. "The Hebrew and Greek Scriptures contain immortal sentences, that have been bread and life to millions. But they have no epical integrity; are fragmentary; are not shown in their order to the intellect. I look for the new Teacher, that shall follow so far those shining laws, that he shall see them come full circle; shall see their rounding complete grace; shall see the world to be the mirror of the soul; shall see the identity of the law of gravitation with purity of heart; and shall show that the Ought, that Duty, is one thing with Science, with Beauty, and with Joy."

This address became an instant scandal. Emerson was no longer welcome at Harvard. One can sympathize with his critics. Here was the complete antinomian, with no external foundations for his beliefs or his moral values. He claimed no such. This was enthusiasm with a vengeance, for Emerson, instead of submitting humbly to God, played god. How could a church, a religion, survive without any basic doctrines, any source of authority, any firm grasp of the truth, any gods, or any savior? Emerson broached complete religious anarchy. Andrews Norton, who in the fullness of time would seem to Unitarians both petty and dogmatic, saw quite clearly the issues that Emerson raised. Without a scriptural base Unitarianism could not remain a Christian religion. And the foundations of Christianity lurked in the gospel accounts of Jesus' ministry. His messiahship was vindicated by his teachings and his miracles. Norton was a biblical scholar. He was not about to demean the Bible by interpreting it literally. But he saw that Christians had to concur on certain historical facts and affirm certain teachings. The new Transcendentalists and German pantheists removed all solid moorings. By turning inward, by seeking their foundations in human consciousness, and by identifying religion with sentiment, they based religion on mere subjective opinion and destroyed any meaning of "religious truth."

THEODORE PARKER

Emerson led no faction. He soared beyond any of the vital issues within the Unitarian movement. Not so Theodore Parker, who remained in the church until his early death on the eve of the Civil War. Unlike Emerson, he used idealistic philosophy and theology to salvage what he believed to be an authentic version of Christianity. He was a committed churchman. Also unlike Emerson, he was a serious student of the Bible, for a time possibly the best-informed biblical scholar in America. And, as time permitted, he came close to being a systematic theologian. One can determine rather precisely what Parker believed on almost any religious issue. Finally, Parker not only joined Emerson in celebrating the moral law but spent much of his career in active, courageous crusades for justice. All in all, he was the greatest single leader of American Unitarianism. Ironically, the majority in his church, until after his death, rejected him and at times cruelly ostracized him.

Parker never quite fit within the Brahmin circles of Unitarian Boston. He was an outsider. Born on a farm near Lexington, he had none of the advantages of the young men of Boston. He did not attend Harvard as an undergraduate but entered the divinity school on the basis of home tutoring and self-education. He was a loyal son of New England, with ancestors stretching back five generations. His father fought in the battle of Lexington. Theodore was a lifelong patriot, inordinately proud of the American republic and of the freedom enjoyed by Americans. Although metaphysical fashions changed, and he reflected the changes, he admired the founding fathers and wrote essays on Jefferson, Adams, and, above all, Benjamin Franklin, who remained one of his great heroes. Although his family was not poor, it still lived on the land and knew the value of hard work. In his political outlook Parker was always more egalitarian, more aware of the life of the common people, and more sensitive to issues of class and gender exploitation than most of his Unitarian colleagues. He also made a deep commitment to the Christian ministry. No one more esteemed the calling or pursued it so conscientiously.

In 1831 young Theodore, then twenty-one, moved to Boston to earn his living by teaching in a private school, soon to begin his studies at the divinity school. As he later remembered, he was a raw boy, with handmade clothes, coarse shoes, and red lips. But such rustic externals concealed a precocious, adventuresome, and brilliant mind. Parker had already, on his own, learned at least four foreign languages and would subsequently master several more. He was already fascinated with philosophy and literature and with history and the sciences. He was a true Renaissance man, and unlike Emerson he did not dabble in various disciplines but mastered them. Although a bit rough around the edges, he easily outshone his fellow students in the divinity school and was the most inspired by Emerson's famous address. In his work on biblical subjects he began reading the serious and, to some, almost revolutionary work coming out of Germany. Within a few years he began translating the best of this scholarship into English. He not only translated the work of the pioneer scholar on the Old Testament, Wilhelm M. de Wette, but added extensive reflections of his own. From

Wette he gained an enduring insight: that the literature of the Old Testament reflected the naive and fumbling efforts of ancient writers to glimpse eternal values, values that they described in esthetic but not literal terms. Even as Parker ventured into serious scholarship, he typically taught Sunday school in the local prison every week. He was always as much an activist as a scholar and saw the two as complementary.

As a young minister Parker accepted the pulpit at West Roxbury, soon famous as the site of Brook Farm. Even as he began his ministry, it was clear that he was on the radical edge of Unitarianism, a youthful fan of Emerson. He soon entered the polemical battles that followed Emerson's 1838 address and as an antagonist of Andrews Norton. He gained notoriety only in 1842, when he was invited to give his first ordination sermon. His text, "The Transient and Permanent in Christianity," added a third enduring document to the American Unitarian tradition. He took the title from the first scandalous product of German higher criticism, a life of Jesus by David Strauss in which Strauss first charted the possible ways in which the gospel writers and Jesus' disciples created a mythological Jesus to suit the developing doctrines of the church, and thus forever concealed the real historical person. The book horrified most Germans and quickly became infamous in America. Parker's sermon was not as soaring or as abstract as Emerson's. It was not as radical. But it was clear, blunt, and unambiguous.

The sermon evoked almost universal condemnation, from Unitarians as much as the orthodox. Poor Parker. It was the first essay he published under his own name. He was proud of it, for it reflected a level of scholarly understanding and philosophical sophistication rare for one so young. He perhaps exaggerated a bit, but in his later memory it led to an almost complete ostracism. His colleagues tried to ruin him, to drive him from the church. Harvard removed him from all committees and in a sense disowned him. With the exception of only five or six ministers, no one in all New England would exchange pulpits with him. Ministers lined up to denounce or refute his heresies. The Unitarian ministers removed his name from their directory or in effect denied him fellowship. As he ruefully lamented later, he suffered Unitarian excommunication. Everyone denounced a young man "who thought the God who creates earth and heaven had never spoken miraculously in Hebrew words bidding Abraham kill his only son and burn him for a sacrifice, and that Jesus of Nazareth was not a finality in the historical development of mankind." The rejection hurt. His bitterness was still evident years later. But Parker, unlike Emerson, was not about to withdraw to his own study. He committed his life to the Christian ministry and with complete honesty determined to continue his calling and to tell the truth as he saw it. His congregation, won over completely by his fervor and eloquence and benevolence, fully supported him, and the Unitarian Association had no means to shut him up.

In his "Transient and Permanent" sermon Parker found only one permanent element in Christianity: the pure Word of God, which was alone eternal truth. In his sermons Jesus spoke this Word as no one since had spoken it (Parker never foreclosed the possibility of an equal or greater prophet in the future). The Word is eternal, but not human understandings of that Word. The actual history of Christianity is the history of such human understandings, ever variable, ever changing through time. This is the transient element. It includes all creeds and confessions, all institutions, and even all theologies. People, in their confusion, think the transient is the real content of religion, and they persecute all those who cannot accept one or another historical version of these transient interpretations. Parker loved to point out how repulsive much of medieval Christianity was to moderns, and how likely it was that the creeds and forms of his day would appear equally repulsive to his distant descendants. Theological truths change as surely through time as do scientific ones. The heresy of one age is the orthodoxy of the next (ironically, his very words eventually became orthodox for Unitarians).

Had Parker stopped with such generalities, he might not have roused such a fuss in Boston. But he felt burdened to illustrate some of the transitory doctrines. Perhaps without anticipating the effect, he fell back on contemporary scholarship, much that he alone in America had read in the original German. He raised the issue of the canon. Many doctrines accepted by honest men rested on a belief in the literal inspiration of the whole Jewish Bible. Parker rather delighted in mocking such naivete in those who took fiction for fact, believed impossible legends, relied on dreams, or even took amatory poems (such as the Song of Solomon) as symbols of the love of God for his Church. It seemed almost unbelievable to Parker, given the newly won knowledge about the origins of both the Hebrew scriptures and the process that led to their canonization, that anyone could take seriously all these oriental fables. But some people did, and they felt that their salvation depended on it. Poor Parker was often impatient with such people, particularly those who prayed for him or tried to convert him to "Christianity." In response to a woman who took a keen interest in his spiritual welfare two years before his death in 1860, Parker expressed some of the arrogance of a serious biblical scholar. The persons who labored with him and who wanted to argue with him were uniformly completely ignorant of what they talked about, namely the Bible. For whatever reason, they had not bothered to read the plentiful and revealing scholarship on the subject and for some reason did not really take the Bible seriously enough to investigate it, to devote loving scholarship to it. In the American context, he sometimes felt this way about almost all his colleagues, for even at Harvard the level of biblical scholarship was not nearly up to the German model.

Had he limited his scholarly cavils to the Old Testament, Parker might still have retained some sympathy from fellow Unitarians. Few of them staked any major doctrines on these Jewish writings. But he encompassed in his critique even the New Testament and the reliability of accounts about Jesus. He ridiculed the idea that all the writers of the New Testament books were infallibly and miraculously inspired and that they were responsible for no errors of doctrine or fact. He noted the hundreds of discrepancies, some as critical as the very different Jesus presented in Luke and John. To rub salt into the wounds of Andrews Norton, he compared all the accounts of miracles attributed to Jesus, including the Lukean account of his birth, to the myths of Hercules and Apollonius. Even Unitarians preached that believers had to believe these myths literally. And they declared these twenty-seven books, bound together by accident and caprice, as the infallible Word of God, the only certain rule of faith and practice. Openly to profess disbelief in any of its absurdities made one an infidel. Parker therefore concluded that "an idolatrous regard for the imperfect scripture of God's Word is the apple of Atalanta, which defeats theologians running for the hand of divine truth." Notably, none of the authors of the biblical books claimed such infallibility for themselves. The more modest writers would have been astounded at the idolatry involved in modern Christian reverence for them.

As a final blow Parker considered transitory the doctrines that related to the nature and authority of the Christ. He noted how denominations rose and fell on subtle interpretations of the exact relationship between Jesus and his father. Parker had no real respect for any position, including the Unitarian one. All sides rested authority on Jesus, not on the Word that he spoke (echoes of Emerson). It was as if the truths of science rested on the personal authority of Newton. The authority should, of course, rest on the words spoken, the truth revealed, and not on the one who revealed it. This was an accident of history, a function of the genius of a person. The axioms of geometry are true in themselves, not because of any special authority in Euclid. Parker also delighted to note how opinions about Jesus changed constantly. Now, with Strauss and other penetrating scholars, the whole received view of the New Testament and of the life of Jesus seemed to be unraveling in all directions. More was sure to come, and woe be to those Christians who were blind to this scholarship, whose faith rose and fell with the actions of a few councils or depended on the infallible inspiration of a few Jewish fishermen. Reared on such fragile grounds of authority, Christianity was doomed in the modern world.

In the context, these straightforward arguments seemed terribly dangerous. They clearly hit the mark, even among Unitarians. Parker was astounded and dismayed at the response. His purpose had been constructive. He wanted to shift the grounds of faith to what could endure, away from all empirically vulnerable historical or theological claims. He saw the depth and magnitude of coming challenges. He easily historicized all the traditions. But in his own way he did not want to disown this history. Far from it. This is what decisively separated him from Emerson. Much influenced by Friedrich Schleiermacher, he wanted to shift the problem of authority to experience or to the exploration of the human mind. As Parker put it, he wanted a proper metaphysical grounding, meaning a type of absolute idealism. To explore this was the proper role of theology. For Christians this theology was not necessary, for in their own vital experience they responded to the Word, ultimately in deed. This was all that was important. But they were often, quite correctly, inspired by those who came before. They honored those progenitors and found apt expression of their own deepest truths in some of the biblical texts. Above all, they joined Parker in finding the most sublime expression of those truths in the teachings of Jesus. In this sense Christianity was a historic faith, but it was a faith ever grounded in immediate human experience, not in the empirical truths of history.

Parker used this analysis to debunk all the traditional sects and all doctrinal formulations. In his way, much as Jefferson and Priestley, he wanted to return to a simple religion, to the message of the sermon on the mount. The central insights were all simple. The moral demands were not. Parker wanted to shift the basis of authority in Christianity largely to get rid of an enormous burden, all the excess baggage. His purpose was not philosophical but moral, to get people to focus on what the Word required of them. Parker was first and last an angry prophet.

Parker's reform efforts culminated in his courageous, at times intemperate, and even angry attack on American slavery. From Italy, where he was losing his battle with tuberculosis, Parker praised John Brown and the slave insurrection at Harpers Ferry; a person had a natural right to kill in behalf of God-given rights. Almost alone among the proper Unitarians, who could easily learn to detest southern slavery so long as such did not threaten profits (it often did and thus wealthy Unitarians often condemned abolitionists), Parker cited the class divisions developing in New England, the plight of recent immigrants such as the Irish, the developing city slums and attendant evils, and the elements of exploitation in the emerging factories. He early embraced the cause of women's rights (he believed in sexual differences and different likely roles but wanted complete political and legal equality). In his final, long, reflective letter to his home congregation (he had moved from West Roxbury to minister to a new Twenty-Eight Congregational Society in Boston, a congregation formed to accommodate his radical views, and where Parker became one of the most popular preachers in America), he asked God, the "Infinite Perfection," even "our FATHER and our MOTHER," to bless them forever and forever. Save among the Shakers, this was a rare, if not the only, nineteenth-century recognition of an androgynous god.

Parker's scholarship, his theological explorations, his long and arduous speaking tours on the lyceum circuit in order to enlighten people all over America, and his activities as a national reformer cannot be recounted in this brief context. But he did reflect almost perfectly a Transcendental version of Christianity. Emerson soared so far from the historical faith as to lose contact. Parker felt that his repairs, particularly the shift of authority away from any of the empirical or textual foundations of Christianity, were of the type that could save the Church of Christ from intellectual embarrassment and social irrelevance. This subordination of historical revelation to inward enlightenment was not new. George Fox preached such a message long before Parker. But it was newly sophisticated, fortified by the best of contemporary scholarship and philosophy. It had broad appeal. By the time of his death in 1860, it was becoming commonplace among young Unitarian ministers. The era of Andrews Norton was over. Even in Congregationalism, it found an echo in the theology of Horace Bushnell.

The critics were correct in one respect. This shift of authority had dangers. It made the foundations of Christianity private and subjective. Parker would have noted that it had always been so—that all authentic faith has ultimately rested on individual experience and insight, whatever doctrinal straitjackets ministers, often deceitful ministers, had tried to place on it. But the orthodox knew that it was not so simple. They had fought George Fox and other enthusiasts because they knew that a religion only of the heart would fragment in a thousand directions, and it always did. Parker did not believe he was cutting loose from a common mooring. As most idealists, he believed that a divine mind lay behind all the intimations of truth that humans are able to grasp, and that the result of a religion of authentic inspiration would be, in the long haul, more convergent than divergent, yet one that could keep open the possibilities of growth. The permanent would win out; the various transient elements would drop away. The Word would prevail in the end.

The critics said such an unanchored faith would not stop with Parker. It would eventually move all the way to humanism and atheism. It did. In the process, Unitarianism became a gathering place for people of quite varied religious commitments and in no sense, other than its remembered heritage, a Christian movement.

BEYOND CHRISTIANITY

By the end of the Civil War the AUA seemed to be an ineffective voice for a stagnant church. Unitarians then numbered at least 50,000 but enjoyed almost no growth except in a few western outposts. As a percentage of the total population, the movement declined with each passing decade (a trend that has continued to the present). For some ministers it seemed time to create a real Unitarian denomination, national in scope and with some centralized authority. Notably, the single greatest architect of a new organization was not a Bostonian but Henry Whitney Bellows, minister of the Church of All Souls in New York City. During the Civil War he had headed the United States Sanitary Commission. He repudiated the anarchic individualism of some of the Transcendentalists and wanted to emphasize the role of the institutional church. Thus, just after the war ended, delegates from congregations, lay and ministerial, met to approve a constitution for a national conference. It would meet annually, as a type of legislative body, but did not replace the AUA, which became the executive organ of the denomination.

The constitution of the National Conference helped trigger a new controversy that did lead to a small schism. A few ministers, all along, had resented what they saw as the high church outlook of Bellows. An even smaller number, possibly fewer than ten, already looked forward to a Unitarianism that was, at least, broader than Christianity. They wanted no creedal tests or even any restrictive language in any bond of union, and they also wanted the new denomination to welcome independent congregations, those neither avowedly Christian nor out of the Unitarian tradition. In 1865 they centered their protest on the reference, in the preamble to the constitution, to "disciples of the Lord Jesus Christ." The two ablest protesters were Octavius B. Frothingham, a latter-day Transcendentalist and historian of that movement, and Francis Ellsworth Abbot, a Meadville graduate, impoverished, rigorously honest and dogmatic, and already developing a new form of theism tied to evolutionary theory and the methods of the new science. The next year, after losing their battle to change the wording of the preamble, they separated and helped form the Free Religious Association (FRA). It was not really a new sect, although a few independent congregations affiliated, but a band of religious radicals able to edit a worthy journal and, for a few years, keep up a semblance of unity. Notably, one of the founders of the FRA was Felix Adler, an ex-rabbi in New York City who founded the Ethical Culture Movement (a humanistic religion with great appeal among Jews who could no longer affirm any form of traditional Judaism).

The FRA was not a serious challenge to the Unitarian movement, at least not at the time. Only three or four congregations disaffiliated. But it was, nonetheless, a prophetic little schism. The founders wanted a truly free religion, or in fact argued that no authentic religion could be bound by any creeds or dogmas. An aging, mentally declining Ralph Waldo Emerson gladly joined the FRA, as did the vaguely orientalist Bronson Alcott. Tensions soon divided the small association. It attracted some members who wanted to break the barriers of conventional morality, particularly regarding sex and marriage, which offended a puritanical Abbot. Frothingham and other intuitionists seemed philosophically antiquated to Abbot, who tried, on the basis of the implications of the scientific method, to formulate a new realism opposed to nominalism or materialism, on one side, or to a very subjective form of idealism or pantheism, on the other. Abbot's *Scientific Theism* of 1885, or what some mistakenly saw as the most radical theology ever published in America, was in reality a careful new philosophical defense of theism and a refutation of all forms of atheism and agnosticism. It had much of the flavor of an older moderate realism worked out by Thomas Aquinas and was related closely to the theistic metaphysics developed by Abbot's close friend Charles Saunders Peirce. On the intuitionist side, both Frothingham and Adler also affirmed a belief in a type of divinity, although in each case a god with little ties to the biblical tradition.

Although still theistic, the leaders of the FRA wanted to break completely from the authoritarian religions of the past, whether Judaism or Christianity. They wanted a free fellowship, indeed open to Jews or Christians if they wanted to join, but Abbot was quite clear that one could not adhere to such religious traditions, in good faith, without affirming some type of authority over individual conscience. He recognized the bland and loose nature of Unitarian Christian affirmations and in a sense condemned them for being so flaccid. He believed one should dutifully be subservient to Jesus and his church, as were consistent Roman Catholics, or else move on to full liberation, to a free religion. He, in effect, challenged the Unitarians to take this last step. Few in the church were willing to do so, but Abbot at least forced them to reconsider first principles. They had believed themselves to have a church without creeds that offered all the freedom anyone could want. Abbot demonstrated that this was not true. The issue would not go away. The major catalyst for a free, or at least more free, association came not from the dogmatists in the FRA but from more free-wheeling western Unitarians.

Before the Civil War, William Eliot at St. Louis and other western ministers had formed the Western Unitarian Conference. This at first represented only their response to the distance from New England and a concern for effective mission activities in the West. Because of new leadership after the war, the conference became not so clearly an ally of the AUA as a rebellious and at times independent competitor. It also, in its own way, replicated many of the concerns of the FRA. The dominant figure in the West was Jenkin Lloyd Jones, a son of Welsh immigrants to southern Wisconsin. A poor farm boy, he, like Abbot, had struggled to pay his way through Meadville, had joined the FRA, and had served two small congregations in Illinois and Wisconsin before moving to a church in Chicago (he renamed it All Souls), where he also became in 1875 the general secretary of the Western Conference with responsibility for building new Unitarian churches in the West, including even the distant West Coast. A vital supporter of Jones was a poetic, latter-day Transcendentalist, William Channing Gannett, from the heart of Unitarianism but a radical who dissented almost as much from the National Conference as did Abbot. In 1877 he moved to St. Paul as minister and soon helped Jones edit the journal of the Western Conference, *Unity*, a name with its own intended message. In the far West the most effective ally of Jones was a former classmate at Meadville, Charles W. Wendte, who began the long process that led in 1904 to an avowedly new type of Unitarian seminary attached to the University of California at Berkeley.

Gannett and Jones at first reflected minority views even among western ministers. But such was the effectiveness of Jones in forming new congregations that the radicals soon had a majority. In fact, in the post–Civil War years the only area of rapid expansion in the denomination was in the Midwest and West. Much as Abbot earlier, Jones and Gannett wanted a church without creeds and without any exclusive Christian identity. In 1886 in a developing civil war between those sympathetic to Jones and those with a clear commitment to a continued Christian affirmation, the Western Conference repudiated any dogmatic tests and welcomed into fellowship anyone who wanted to advance the kingdom of God. This theistic reference invited any number of definitions or conceptions of a god. Dissenting Christian Unitarian ministers in the West disavowed the policies of the conference, appealed frequently to Boston, and formed a separate Western Unitarian Association. In 1887 the AUA ceased all ties to the Western Conference, meaning at least an informal schism. The battle was now national. Reconciliation between the two contending associations in the West in 1892 helped spur a near-capitulation by the denomination as a whole. In 1894 the National Conference revised it preamble, emphasizing that nothing in its constitution was to be construed as a test of membership and specifically inviting those of different beliefs to join. Even before this, Gannett had tried to devise a formula that would please both sides. His poetic but ambiguous and hopelessly irenic summary—"The Things Most Commonly Believed Today among Us"—long found a sympathetic ear among sentimental Unitarians. In it he concluded with a reference to God, but one clearly identified as Life or Love or even something close to an Emersonian Oversoul.

As the Unitarians entered the new century, they had much cause for alarm. Active membership remained below 100,000. Because of population shifts, even in New England Unitarians, although still affluent, had lost some of their earlier social and literary prominence and most of their political clout. They had able ministers and some effective administrators but no intellectuals of the caliber of Theodore Parker. In the larger religious context they counted less and less, and they were aware of this. Despite strenuous efforts at the center to reverse this pattern of stagnation, the fortunes of the denomination did not improve until the late 1930s. The one acknowledged leader of the church in the new century was Samuel A. Eliot (son of long-term Harvard president Charles W. Eliot), who became secretary of the AUA in 1898, its first president in 1900 (and for the next twenty-seven years), and the architect of a more centralized denominational structure. After 1884 the AUA accepted congregations as members, making it more an executive organization for the churches than a ministerial fellowship (the fellowshipping of ministers remained one of its functions). The National Conference continued to be the delegate body, but finally in 1925 the two organizations merged, with the annual meeting henceforth being that of the AUA.

Slowly, often too gradually to be recognized by the leadership, the denomination shifted toward a different clientele and role. In the nineteenth century, despite growth in the West, the denomination had reflected a continuity from the past, in the stable and eminent Yankee families who continued as members generation after generation, in the New England flavor of its polity, and in the continued Whig-Republican, free-market-oriented outlook of its typical members. After 1920 the proportion of membership in New England declined, some of the most vital congregations were in cities all across the country, and the percentage of members who grew up in the church declined, slowly at first but at a dramatic pace after 1945. By the merger with Universalists in 1961, over 80 percent of Unitarians had grown up in some other denomination. The often remarked and at times ridiculed "come-outers" were completely dominant. To a somewhat lesser extent this was true of ministers, with an increasing percentage shifting from more conservative denominations to gain the intellectual freedom offered by Unitarianism. Even more than in the past, Unitarianism became an urban or suburban religion. Outside scattered, often declining village churches in New England, almost all the congregations were in larger metropolitan clusters or in smaller cities with certain identifying characteristics (sites of major colleges and universities or centers of scientific research). At the same time the membership was less and less representative of corporate executives or of people with great wealth and much more attractive to affluent, professional people. These changes in membership dramatically shifted the political profile of Unitarians toward the Democratic Party and liberal or ultraliberal social action movements. In certain respects—such as acceptance of or leadership in organizations devoted to civil rights for all minorities, to the environment, to feminism or homosexual equality, to avant garde or radical forms of artistic expression, and to internationalism—Unitarians became one of the most homogeneous and predictable denominations in America. In ways its members did not recognize, it also was among the most exclusive (its culture was such as to repel or make very uncomfortable most Americans, including those with a firm Christian commitment). Yet a type of ultimate inclusiveness, in polity and belief, is what helped attract such an almost stereotypical "liberal" membership.

The move to such an inclusive membership paralleled a gradual, now almost completed movement away from Christianity. Except for a sometimes honored heritage, the presently merged denomination is not Christian, although most (not all) members would insist that it is religious. As of 1993 the National Council of Churches of Christ in the United States stopped listing the Unitarian Universalist Association (UUA) as Christian. This rather momentous shift away from Christianity obviously had roots in the FRA and the Western Conference, but the fact that it became definitional for the denomination as a whole reflected both changes in the beliefs and values of Americans in the modern world and the shifting background of members. The move beyond Christianity was not unopposed, and a minority of Unitarian-Universalist Christians still try to maintain a countercultural voice in the denomination. The confusing context of these shifts involved what many called the humanistic controversy. It is impossible, in a brief context, to flesh out the complex issues involved, simply because so many definitions are needed.

After 1894 the National Conference offered fellowship to those who were not Christian but retained a commitment at least to some form of theism. In the first decades of the twentieth century, even theism had declining appeal, although the word "god" simply begs so many definitional problems as to make even survey data meaningless. Clearly, few Unitarians retained a belief in a personal, supernatural deity. This was an important shift. Until the 1920s the god talk among Unitarian leaders had retained much of its Christian content, even as Jesus remained a heroic if not a divine figure. Today it is impossible to characterize beliefs about ultimate reality among Unitarians. The variety is too great. The fact that some find a continued use for the label "god" may not be very important. What is important is that now the debates about a god or gods rarely implicate the Jehovah of old. But the label "humanist," gladly accepted by some of the radicals early in the century, was equally ambiguous and confusing.

The most effective advocates of religious humanism were, at first, all Unitarian ministers. Two come-out ministers from Calvinist orthodoxy, Curtis W. Reese and John H. Dietrich, both appropriately members of the Western Conference, helped define a new movement and advocated it from Unitarian pulpits. The label "humanism" may have been unfortunate, since it seemed to reflect (rightly so in many early pronouncements) an overly irenic view of humankind. The real philosopher behind the movement, the person who best expressed its foundational beliefs and even at times provided its shibboleths, was John Dewey, who later endorsed the first Humanist Manifesto of 1933. Reese and Dietrich were philosophical naturalists who rejected as unbelievable or irrelevant older forms of supernaturalism. Yet, guided by Dewey, they emphasized not a mechanistic view of nature but a nature that had matured, in humans, both mind and purpose. They repudiated any creeds or tests and wanted a broad, even universal church of humanity. They stressed that they did not exclude theists, but in fact they found most concepts of god irrelevant to the concerns of religion in a modern age. They stressed the development of character in people, ethical commitment, a political process they called democracy, and even a type of piety toward the ultimate sources of life. Beyond such general emphases, they did not seek any agreement. They wanted the Unitarian movement to be free, in the sense of Abbot in 1865, but unlike Abbot they did not see the problem of god as the central problem of religion.

As so many other radical challenges in the history of Unitarianism, the humanist platform at first triggered an avalanche of condemnation. But in time the debates dwindled, as if everyone tired of them. As so often before, the denominations moved in the direction of the humanists, and it did become a completely open fellowship. But in time even Unitarians were so influenced by the horrible atrocities of this century, or by the direct or indirect influence of neo-orthodox or existential theologians, as to move well beyond the easy optimism of the earliest humanists. The end result of this long debate was the near impossibility of Unitarians agreeing on any unifying statement of principles. Since World War II they have had to make do with various, usually vaporous, generalities. The most vacuous was a statement affirmed by the AUA in 1947. It committed Unitarians to individual freedom of belief, discipleship to advancing truth, the democratic process, universal brotherhood (later deemed politically incorrect), and allegiance to a world community.

In spite of, or possibly because of, this completely free fellowship, the Unitarians did experience a period of growth during and after World War II. In this they moved in the opposite direction from the beleaguered Universalists and thus set the stage for a merger largely on their terms. Out of the doldrums and pessimistic evaluations of the depression 1930s, the AUA appointed the Commission of Appraisal, whose 1936 report was titled *Unitarians Face a New Age*. Many would subsequently see this as a turning point in Unitarian fortunes. The head of the commission, another Eliot (Frederick May), reluctantly accepted the presidency of the association and thus the duty of implementing the reforms demanded by his commission. In a sense these paralleled the final shift to a creedless church, one no longer tied necessarily to Christianity or any form of theism. The report helped lead the denomination into more ecumenical talks, particularly with Universalists, and to efforts to found an international organization of liberal religions (at present, this is the International Association for Religious Freedom, a grouping that contains European, Australian, and Indian Unitarians, plus a few small groups that derive from other world religions). Eliot also helped centralize denominational functions. This soon led to an enlarged bureaucracy, stimulated a revival in Sunday school work (a new Department of Education), encouraged the formation of the Unitarian Service Committee and the chartering of Beacon Press, and improved standards in seminary education. Unitarians benefited from the baby boom that followed the war, from the new surge in church membership in both liberal and conservative denominations, and from the development of smaller Unitarian fellowships, some on the way to full-fledged churches, some to remain as small congregations, most without ministers. Membership did not soar but by the mid-1950s exceeded 100,000. In 1961, at the time of the merger, the membership was 104,821 in 651 congregations, and the joint membership soared to its historically highest level in the mid-1960s (an estimated 250,000) before falling sharply back in the 1970s (in 1993 the combined Unitarians and Universalists numbered around 150,000). Well before this date, the history of Unitarians was institutionally intertwined with that of Universalists.

UNIVERSALIST ORIGINS

Doctrinally, universalism has a heritage almost as ancient as that of unitarianism. Origen, the first great Christian theologian and biblical critic, affirmed the ultimate absorption of all humans back into the Logos, or one of several reasons why the Western Church later deemed his teachings heretical. By the fifth century, several churchmen interpreted the reference in the Apostles' Creed to Jesus' descent into hell as his means of bringing salvation, not only to the heroes of Israel, but to all who had lived before his crucifixion. The biblical issues are complex, but at various points the New Testament suggests that Jesus' death eliminated the penalty of sinfulness for all humans. At least enough New Testament passages support this view as to make the doctrine of eternal torment problematic.

Until the nineteenth century the doctrine of universalism usually entailed not exemption from punishment but a second chance. After death each person would have additional opportunities to repent and receive forgiveness, but not until they suffered the deserved punishment for their earthly sins. In the Calvinist tradition, universalism usually meant some form of antinomianism—one gains salvation despite what one does. Grace is all sufficient. In a freewill tradition, it entailed a proportionate repayment of debts incurred by disobedience. Thus, one charge of Luther and Calvin against the Church of Rome was that it supported a de facto form of universalism, since it routinely baptized all infants (thus remitting any penalty for Adam's sin) and provided purgatory as a second-chance opportunity for those nominally in the church but who died with unforgiven sins. But until the Reformation it is difficult to find anyone who openly defended universal salvation. Belief in some type of hell, in some form of endless torment, became very deeply embedded in Christianity and seemed to most Christians not only a biblical doctrine but a socially necessary one. The prospect of future punishment was necessary to sustain morality. Without the fear of damnation people would degenerate into barbarism and anarchy. Even in America, early nineteenth-century Universalists often faced a ban on testimony in courts, on the grounds that their lack of belief in a future punishment destroyed any assurance of truth telling.

In the post-Reformation religious confusion, no Universalist sect comparable to the Socinians emerged in Europe. Some German pietists flirted with some form of eventual salvation for all but rarely publicized such views. By the eighteenth century a covert form of universalism was widely held among latitudinarian Anglicans. Formally the Thirty-Nine Articles of the English Church did not condemn universalism, meaning that rationalists could hold such a doctrine and remain in the church. In the eighteenth century orthodox clergymen frequently condemned what they saw as widespread universalism, not only in England but in Presbyterian Scotland and in Northern Ireland. Eventually, a majority of the liberal faction in Ulster (the Non-Subscribing Presbyterians) would accept both unitarianism and universalism. But the first overt, declared English Universalists were disciples of James Relly, a dissenting minister in London. In 1759 Relly published a book defending the restoration of all to salvation. One of his disciples, John Murray, founded some of the first Universalist congregations in America. By the time of Murray's immigration (1770) several liberal ministers in New England had already seriously considered or accepted his central philosophy, and one, Charles Chauncy, had broached the doctrine to friends and had already written a manuscript in defense of it (published only in 1784).

English Universalism, when transplanted to America, was more appealing than Priestley's version of Unitarianism, but just as Priestley failed to win many converts to his version of Unitarianism, so Murray won almost no Americans to his form of Universalism. Yet, unlike Priestley among American Unitarians, Murray is still honored as the father of American Universalism, correctly or not.

Born in England in 1741 and reared in Ireland, Murray was the son of a rigid moralist, an Anglican who joined a Methodist society in Ireland. Young Murray received no college training and had to take up various forms of business, such as the rental of houses, to earn a living. His temperamental universalism reflected his personal reaction to the gloomy and harsh doctrines taught in his family and parish. His religious bent first found outlet in Methodism. He became a lay preacher. When he moved to England, he yielded to the powerful influence of George Whitefield and became a Calvinist rather than a Wesleyan Methodist. In London, in order to help rescue a young Methodist from the lures of Universalism, Murray first heard and soon capitulated to the doctrines of James Relly. He read all of Relly's books, pored over the scriptures, and soon became a devout convert, ready to preach the gospel of deliverance. He eventually had to break from his friend Whitefield, who could not tolerate Universalism. His Methodist society denied him continued fellowship. Meanwhile, his family fortunes deteriorated, a wife and child died, and for one period, as he later remembered these years, he came close to debtors' prison. Out of these woes he decided eventually to move to America, apparently for personal and economic reasons, not as a missionary for Universalism.

Murray only temporarily debarked in Philadelphia. Responsible for the cargo of a merchant ship, he then sailed for New York. Because of the accidental grounding of this ship on the south Jersey shore, Murray had to debark at a place called Goodluck Point. Here, almost miraculously it later seemed to him, he met a local lay minister of Quaker and Baptist leanings who had built a small meetinghouse. The small congregation was part of a very small Quaker–Baptist sect, followers of John Rogers of Rhode Island. It also held fellowship with the communal German Baptists at the Cloisters in Ephrata, Pennsylvania. Apparently the members already believed in some form of universal salvation, a "heresy" rather widespread among the closely related Dunkards (Church of the Brethren). Murray preached his first American sermon in this small church and then continued to New York City on his liberated ship. Word of his preaching preceded him, and he accepted several invitations to deliver sermons. He returned to New Jersey but was unable to settle peacefully in the small congregation because of numerous invitations to deliver his message. Later Universalists would elevate this New Jersey episode and the Goodluck congregation to epic status, which it scarcely deserved.

For the next decade an unordained Murray became an itinerant in behalf of Universalist Christianity. This does not mean that he proclaimed a startling new gospel. His sermons, almost always well attended but not always well received, largely involved strings of scriptural quotations with little commentary. He approached his audiences with some deference to their existing beliefs and tried to move them by indirection to the idea of a final restoration, which he often did not announce in his sermons. In city after city it was the ministers, not laypeople, who grasped the full import of his message and who tried to organize resistance against him. At first he did not try to found a new sect or church.

It is not easy to characterize Murray's doctrines. In most respects he remained a Calvinist on the order of Whitefield. He repudiated Priestley and never found many commonalities with emerging New England Unitarians. He simply believed that the atonement of the Christ encompassed all of Adam's seed, even as Adam's fall was universal. Because of the atonement and the vicarious satisfaction of God's wrath, no one faced eternal torment because of their disobedience (they did suffer the logical and often awful consequences here on earth). This view led critics to label him an antinomian. But he believed salvation was conditional on faith or belief. Those who died without faith did not immediately inherit the kingdom but would do so eventually, at the time of or after the final judgment, when after long suffering they would finally repent and believe. Even at the time of judgment, God would judge them for their unbelief, or lack of faith, not for their past sins. This "Calvinist" form of Universalism gained few adherents in America. Even before Murray died, only a few of his disciples still affirmed it. He was increasingly alienated by the doctrines of the second generation of Universalist ministers. But his growing alienation should not conceal his achievements over a long lifetime.

During his itinerant decade (the 1770s), Murray had his greatest preaching successes in New England. It is impossible to gauge the impact of his specific doctrines. He found many people sympathetic to universal salvation, but they often understood the doctrine differently or arrived at their conviction for different reasons. On their own, other Christians adopted other versions of Universalism, and Caleb Rich, who did not even know about Murray, founded a Universalist congregation in 1775 in western Massachusetts. Many, in more liberal Anglican and Congregational churches, saw no reason to make this doctrine a point of conflict or a basis of schism. Of the three most prominent early Americans to embrace Universalism—the liberal Congregational ministers and embryonic Unitarians Charles Chauncy and Jonathan Mayhew and the former Presbyterian Philadelphia physician Benjamin Rush—only Rush made the doctrine a central aspect of his religious identity. In the small towns of New England professed Universalists faced excommunication and even overt persecution.

This happened in Gloucester, Massachusetts, where Murray frequently preached and where he gained the loyalty of several devoted disciples. In 1777 his friends had to give reasons why they had absented themselves from services in the First Church (they had been listening to Murray). The church suspended them in the next year. These and other families (thirty-one men and thirty women) then decided in 1779 to write their own covenant, form a new Independent Church of Christ, and build their own meetinghouse, which they dedicated in 1780. In this process they simply followed the traditional New England pattern. Murray was their unordained minister. Because they did not incorporate the society and because Murray was not ordained, the town at first refused to release its members from parish taxes, but the Universalists eventually won exemption through legal action. Universalists would later identify this Gloucester congregation as the founding congregation of an organized Universalist movement.

In the next decade dozens of Universalist societies formed in New England and as far south as Pennsylvania. Few knew about or accepted all of Murray's doctrines, but all conceded his priority in the rapidly growing movement. His later years were a sharp contrast to his early obscurity. His work at Gloucester prospered. He was one of the most popular lecturers in America. He returned for a visit to England in 1788 and found preaching invitations on every side. He was almost famous. Back in Massachusetts, the widowed Murray remarried, and well. His wife was an accomplished writer from a wealthy and prominent family. Slowly Murray moved into high social and intellectual circles. He resisted strong lures, from Benjamin Rush and others, to move to Philadelphia to minister to its large Universalist Society. On a visit to Philadelphia he met President George Washington and addressed the first Universalist convention, an association of Universalists in the Middle Atlantic region. In 1793 he could not resist a call from an unorganized group of Universalists in Boston, a group to whom he had already served as de facto pastor. He agreed to become their settled minister (for the first time he accepted a salary), but only if he could preach once a month in his beloved Gloucester. He remained in Boston until his death in 1815, after an extended period of illness. His First Universalist Church became, because of the Boston location, an informal center of American Universalism. In his last years Murray was an honored citizen of Boston, welcome in liberal pulpits and a friend to all its famous men and women. By his death the Universalist movement had already moved far from Murray's doctrines, which seemed to change little during his ministry.

THE WAXING AND WANING OF AMERICAN UNIVERSALISM

While the new Unitarian movement conquered Boston, the Universalist movement seemed, all too briefly, destined to conquer America. Its organizational looseness did not prevent rapid but somewhat chaotic growth. The movement had no coherent theology, no doctrinal consensus beyond the general concept of universal salvation. Next to Murray, the ablest early Universalist leader in America, Elhanan Winchester, at least worked out a consistent conception of last things. He reflected what probably remained the majority view among Universalists, that sinners would suffer long ages of punishment after death before their restoration to holiness. Opposed to this "restorationist" view was the more irenic position of Caleb Rich that all suffering for sin occurred in this life, without any future purgation. Gradually, an able young man and soon the preeminent spokesman for a very irenic version of Universalism, Hosea Ballou, capitulated to this position and came close to shifting the whole movement in this direction.

Early Universalists had no national organization. Local congregations, in the Baptist pattern, often formed regional associations, but they were very informal. In Philadelphia in 1790 delegates from various congregations, most in the Philadelphia area, formed what they hoped would be a national convention, with a carefully developed form of congregational government. This Philadelphia convention never became truly national and expired early in the new century. It never really involved the majority of Universalists in New England, who formed their own regional convention in 1792, ostensibly as a branch of the convention in Philadelphia. It remained the dominant organization until 1833, when it became the United States Convention, an organization that was supposed to represent all American Universalists but in fact had little contact with congregations in the South. One of the continuing weaknesses of the Universalist movement in America was its inability to build strong, central organizations. It remained anarchic until 1870, and by then a tighter organization could not arrest its decline.

In 1803 the Universalists tried to define a minimal confession. The New England convention, meeting in Winchester, New Hampshire, adopted a quite general doctrinal platform. This Winchester Profession had only three paragraphs. It acknowledged the Holy Scriptures as the revelation of God, so worded references to the three persons of the Trinity as to accommodate traditional trinitarians and unitarians, and of course proclaimed the eventual restoration of all people to holiness and happiness. It did not commit itself on the question of punishment after death but emphasized the inseparable tie between holiness and happiness and recommended order and good works. An appended statement left it up to local societies or associations to adopt more detailed articles of faith (later referred to as the liberty clause).

In its origins Universalism was radical and shocking only because of its one distinctive doctrine. With Hosea Ballou it moved far toward the radical theological position of the Unitarians. Of plebeian background, a rebel against his New Hampshire Baptist training, Ballou converted to Universalism through his own biblical study and possibly from reading the rustic New England deist Ethan Allen. Ballou began lay preaching in 1791 and remained a minister until his death in 1852, by which time the venerable old man had long since been known as "Father Ballou." By the turn of the century Ballou had moved to a doctrinal stance very close to that of the later Channing. He rejected the traditional Trinity. He believed Jesus was subordinate to God but was more than a mere man. He was glad to let the emerging Unitarians fight this battle against orthodoxy, while he fought the battle for universal salvation, a doctrine that elicited all manner of calumny and persecution, while the elite Unitarians believed in the doctrine but would not profess it or fight the battle in the bastions of evangelical orthodoxy. What distinguished Ballou was the depth of his conviction that God was a God of love, never one of punishment. The Christ came to lead humans to such love, to suffer for humans. Ballou rejected any vicarious atonement. Jesus died not to appease God, not as a cause of human salvation, but because this was an expression of God's love. He most disturbed traditional Universalists by his eventual denial of any future punishment, a view even more optimistic than that held by any identified Unitarians.

The Universalist movement expanded rapidly. From 22 congregations in 1800, it grew to over 200 by 1820. By 1840, the apex of its period of most rapid growth, it reported 853 societies (probably somewhat exaggerated, or inclusive of very small fellowships), 512 clergy, and up to 500,000 members. By 1850 its number of congregations exceeded 1,000, and on the basis of poor statistics and some optimistic guesses, the leadership claimed a membership of 600,000, making it the fifth or sixth largest denomination in America. In the climactic decade of the 1840s it counted as many as 12 state conventions and 55 local associations. Its greatest strength remained in New England and New York, with up to 200 societies in both New York and Massachusetts. Universalist missionaries penetrated the West and South, founding several small societies even in Georgia, Mississippi, and Alabama. By 1850 its period of growth was over. As a proportion of the total population, it began to decline, and after the Civil War it suffered a gradual and sad decrease in the number of societies and in membership.

In reality the mushroomlike growth of Universalism led to no stable denominational center and little denominational loyalty among most converts. The total number of active members at any one time probably never exceeded 300,000. Reports of new congregations diverted attention from the almost equal number of churches that disbanded each year. In most states the Universalists adopted the old parish system of New England and formed societies made up of all local people interested in Universalism, and then recruited as many of them as possible as communicants. In most cases less than half of society members became communicants, and this meant that a reliable count of members was almost impossible.

Why did this denomination, so heretical to evangelicals, seem to grow so rapidly? It appealed primarily because of its one distinctive doctrine. People did not like hell. In the very midst of evangelical revivals and the terrible crisis of conversion, Universalism offered a refuge for those who deplored revivalistic religion and who could not accept either Calvinist or Wesleyan doctrines. Why Universalism and not Unitarianism? The clue was class differences. Universalism, in its heyday, was a mass movement with broad popular appeal. It began in cities and small New England towns. Contrary to many stereotypes, it was never a distinctively rural denomination, but its congregations did reflect the national population and thus outside New England were most often in villages or rural areas, unlike the strongly urban concentration of Unitarians. It had a broad appeal, most often among ordinary farmers, artisans, or early factory workers. It in no sense represented an elite, as did Unitarianism. Most of its ministers, like Murray and Ballou, were self-taught. Almost none had seminary training before 1850. They excelled in commonsense scriptural exegesis, much as the early leaders of the Restoration churches. In fact, one reason for

Universalist decline after 1850 was the appeal of other non-elite and non-evangelical faiths, such as the growing Disciples and Christians, or forms of non-Christian spiritualism (mediums and contact with spirits), which had an unusual and unexplained appeal to Universalist ministers and members.

Growth could not conceal internal fissures, which led to controversy and one brief apostasy. The most divisive controversy began in about 1817, although its roots went back to the eighteenth century. An extended debate between Ballou and Edward Turner, a more conservative Universalist minister, led to a public airing of the punishment issue. The debates also helped push Ballou to a fully nonrestorationist view. By bringing the more irenic view into the open, Ballou stimulated a powerful counterattack by those who insisted on future punishment. Note that Universalists who accepted a future and extended period of suffering for sins seemed much closer to evangelicals and faced little of the odium heaped on Ballou or others on moral as well as scriptural grounds. The debate, carried out in Universalist periodicals, reached a climax in the 1820s. The personal feelings ran deep, with the language often abusive. Implicit in the debate were other issues—particularly the degree to which Universalists would retain most of the traditional doctrines of the church rather than flirt with Unitarianism or other heresies or even deny the full authority of scripture. In 1827 a new convention, made up largely of restorationists, formed in Rhode Island. Because of the response from the New England convention, in 1832 a small group of ministers in this convention separated and formed a new sect called Universal Restorationists, a small schismatic movement that lasted only a decade.

The vast majority of restorationists remained in the larger fellowship. The separatists either rejoined the main denomination or gravitated to the Unitarians, who finally began openly to advocate a restorationist version of Universalism. One schismatic, Adin Ballou, not only converted to Unitarianism but formed the Hopedale Colony in Massachusetts. After 1850 the controversies subsided as the issue became less focal and divisive. Most nineteenth-century Universalists affirmed some version of restorationism, but even this position became more fuzzy or contested by the end of the century. Behind the controversies was an array of very subtle and complex doctrines about last things.

By the 1840s other doctrinal issues divided Universalists, cleavages that lasted into the twentieth century. One was the status of the Bible. The movement began with a ringing affirmation that Universalism was the only correct scriptural position. Murray and many of his successors were masters of proof texts. But slippage on this issue was apparent by 1840. This disturbed older ministers, including even the venerable Hosea Ballou. In

1847, in response to these fears, a New York convention made all prospective ministers subscribe to a statement that the Bible was a special and sufficient revelation from God, the rule of faith and practice. When the prestigious Boston convention tried to adopt the same measure, it met resistance. Eight younger ministers were unwilling to subscribe to the biblical account of Jesus, thereby placing themselves in unity with some of their Transcendentalist counterparts within Unitarianism. Two or three resigned their pulpits, but most Universalists still supported a fully Christian movement and did so until the twentieth century.

In one area of innovation—leadership roles for women—Universalists matched the Christian Connection. As a whole, new religious movements in America were first to accept females as evangelists, exhorters, or even ordained ministers. For the Universalists it was the very lack of any strong central authority that helped women locally take on new roles. As early as 1810 a woman served as a Universalist evangelist, and by 1868 the movement listed seven women as ministers. All the early Universalist academies and colleges, except for Tufts, were coeducational. In 1860 the Canton Seminary, part of St. Lawrence College, admitted the first woman to its regular ministerial course of study. This was a precedent, and the young woman, Olympia Brown, a recent graduate of Antioch College (the former Christian Connection school), not only completed her degree but received ordination in 1863. She then served as pastor of several congregations. She was inspired by Antoinette Blackwell, who was ordained by an individual Congregationalist church in 1853 but without any denominational support. It was not easy for Brown. The seminary accepted her reluctantly, and she suffered much hazing in the training and faced ridicule and resentment as a minister.

In 1870, or only five years after the Unitarians formed a national organization, the beleaguered and declining Universalists met in a centennial convention (100 years after Murray landed in New Jersey). They endorsed a new Universalist general convention that seemed, on paper, to have the same authority as major Baptist conventions. It had the power to fund and promote mission work, to secure uniform rules for ordination, and to exert some disciplinary control over local conventions and associations. Envisioned were commissions or boards at the center that would finally make Universalism a loosely centralized denomination. The need seemed great. The number of congregations, and membership, was clearly in decline. Earlier coordinated efforts had largely failed. The earlier convention had indeed made commitments, but a lack of funds had hindered home mission efforts, had provided very meager support for a few Universalist colleges (Tufts, St. Lawrence, and Lombard) and attached seminaries, and had offered almost no funding for publications (these, in most cases, were private and entrepreneurial). Organizations for women and youth had little national support. Even the new convention did not help much; it had dreams aplenty but no money. And, unanticipated in 1870, the constitution of the new convention produced almost as much conflict as had the constitution of the National Unitarian Conference of 1865.

In 1870 the Universalists came closer than ever to adopting a creed. They incorporated the venerable Winchester Profession in the new constitution and made assent to it a test of fellowship. They removed the liberty clause—the right of local societies to fill out the details of the profession. In 1872 a local convention, and then the National Convention, denied fellowship to a minister who rather clearly preached doctrines contrary to the profession. This led to a prolonged controversy muted only in 1899 after years of heated debate, when the convention approved a new statement that commended the Winchester Profession but did not make it a condition of membership. By then a small but vocal liberal minority had repudiated any creeds at all, and a few had begun to challenge the fully Christian identity of the denomination, although such radical dissent trailed far behind that in Unitarianism. In a final revision in 1935 the new statement of faith still incorporated the Winchester Profession, but as a testimony and not a test, and shifted the emphasis from final salvation to a commitment to building the kingdom for which Jesus lived and died, a clear movement toward a social gospel and away from the eschatological themes that earlier gave identity to Universalism.

After 1870 Universalist visions always outpaced achievement. Small, cyclical spurts of growth only documented a long-term pattern of decline. In 1870 the United States Census listed only 719 Universalist congregations. The denomination, after careful screening for inactive congregations, reduced even this estimate in 1871. The membership had shrunk to around 50,000 (of course, children and attending nonmembers meant up to three times this many people involved with Universalist churches) and remained reasonably stable into the new century. By then the Universalists, who had once outnumbered the Unitarians by at least four to one, were now fewer (Unitarians numbered at least 60,000). By the 1920s the shrinkage had accelerated, with the Census Bureau listing only 498 congregations in 1926. Many in the denomination predicted the early extinction of the movement. Studies, commissions, and desperate efforts to regroup or build new institutions all failed to arrest the decline. By 1947 only 258 congregations were active. The announced membership remained over 40,000, but the active membership was less than half of that. When the Universalists finally merged with the Unitarians in 1961, the official, and again overly optimistic, count was 36,864 members in 244 societies.

The story was not always a sad one. Universalists were able to sustain an active mission in Japan until after World War II, and briefer missions in Scotland and Cuba. They at least kept alive two colleges and seminaries. Gradually, Universalist membership became more urban and more affluent, thus erasing some of the differences with Unitarians. Increasingly, Universalist ministers had seminary training. Despite doctrinal revisions and a much broader and more inclusive standard for membership, the denomination insisted, until the merger, on its Christian identity. But by the mid-twentieth century it had gradually modified the very meaning of the word "universal." It no longer referred so much to salvation as to a worldwide fellowship, as Universalists joined in several efforts to create international associations of liberal religious organizations. In its last independent years as a denomination, the Universalist Church of America (so renamed in 1942) tried to keep a distinctive Christian voice in such ecumenical efforts.

THE MERGER

Space does not permit an extended history of Unitarian-Universalist relations. Efforts at cooperation and union short of merger began in the nineteenth century and revived in cyclical patterns until success in 1961. By 1850 few doctrinal issues separated the two denominations. By then almost all trinitarians had died among Universalists, and the vast majority had followed Ballou into a form of unitarianism. Meanwhile, without public profession, a probable majority of Unitarians had rejected any form of eternal torment. Thus, both denominations were unitarian and universalist in doctrine. In the American context both seemed radical to the orthodox. But in a pattern reversed in the twentieth century, the Universalists seemed most radical and most dangerous. They evangelized successfully, unlike the aloof Unitarians, and did not have the wealth and status to compensate for heresy. One only has to survey any holding by a major library to appreciate the outpouring of anti-Universalist polemics. Yet, by the twentieth century, as Unitarians moved beyond Christianity or accepted forms of humanism, most Universalists kept their Christian identity and in fact often seemed little different from liberal Methodists or Presbyterians who no longer believed in a literal hell.

Despite the seeming affinities and some movement of ministers back and forth, the two denominations retained deep suspicions of each other. As rival siblings, they quarreled all the time. Cooperation was usually closer and easier outside New England. In broad terms the Unitarians professed a greater willingness to cooperate or even merge, but often in what seemed a patronizing way to Universalists. Until after the Civil War, Universalists did very well on their own and had few reasons to join the smaller Unitarian movement. After the war, as they declined, Universalists became very sensitive to differences and very concerned to retain their distinctive identity. Class was a major issue, as both sides often stressed at the time. The educated and affluent Unitarians had a hard time accepting Universalists as equals. Universalists, at times with some degree of paranoia, accused Unitarians of snobbery. By 1900 another issue had become even more decisive. Universalists, despite liberalizing changes, refused to follow Unitarians outside Christianity. They continued their witness against humanism until the very eve of the merger.

In 1899, in behalf of closer cooperation, the AUA suggested a joint committee of the two denominations. Journalists predicted an early merger. Against some determined resistance by a few Universalist ministers, the committee formed and met for about seven years, but with little achievement. Such direct links did not revive until after World War I, but locally some congregations cooperated or even in a few cases merged their worship. By the 1920s, Universalist decline had made some form of merger very appealing, but the first serious negotiations were with the Congregationalists, a denomination that was, in many ways, closer to their theological outlook than Unitarians. By 1927 some form of union, short of merger, seemed almost inevitable. Universalists and Congregationalists approved a joint statement that seemed to mean a unified fellowship but a continued separate identity. In the crunch, Universalists revealed a fear of complete merger, while a new courtship by Unitarians possibly helped defer and eventually defeat such a merger. By 1930, Universalists were willing to enter a long and often tense courtship with Unitarians and gradually gave up on any merger with Congregationalists.

Informal talks between the two denominations were continuous by the 1930s. Humanist or creedless Unitarians feared the Christian emphasis of Universalists, while Universalists feared the radicalism of the AUA. In 1931 the AUA formally proposed merger. Instead the Universalists agreed only to a federative relationship in a free church fellowship open to other sects but, except for a few Quakers, almost entirely composed of Unitarians and Universalists. It even took four years of debate to approve a declaration of principles for the fellowship, a declaration that avoided theological issues. Almost as soon as it began functioning, the fellowship expired from an almost complete lack of support from individual congregations. But in 1937 the two denominations did issue a common hymnal, and earlier the Unitarians had absorbed the Universalist seminary tied to Lombard College. Already in 1933 the impoverished Universalists had moved their national headquarters to Beacon Street offices in Boston, offices just vacated by the more prosperous Unitarians, who moved to 25 Beacon Street.

One spur to postwar merger was the rejection of Universalist membership in the Federal Council of Churches. Another was the weakness of the church, despite a small postwar revival under General Superintendent Robert Cummings. At least a minority of Universalists followed a humanistic minister, Kenneth Patton, in trying to make of Universalism a type of eclectic world religion, with symbols borrowed from all religious traditions. Thus, by 1949 Cummings was finally willing to join Eliot of the Unitarians in serious steps toward merger. The process was tedious and began with a joint commission on church union, which first led not to merger but to another federation in 1953, the Council of Liberal Churches, with its headquarters at 25 Beacon. Under the auspices of this council, some, but not all, of the agencies and boards of the two churches merged, while a separate denominational identity remained. By then it was hard to envision a fully separate Universalist church, such was its financial and organizational weaknesses. In 1955 the Universalists recommended a full merger and approved a joint merger commission, which worked out the final details. This was difficult, and the old theological issues, particularly the issue of Christian identity, still plagued the hard work. In 1960 the members of both denominations voted on merger, with 49 of 183 Universalist congregations opposing, while 555 of 651 Unitarians approved. The name of the new fellowship was the strictly alphabetically ordered Unitarian Universalist Association. A joint annual meeting in 1961 approved the bylaws of the new denomination.

In a sense, the Unitarians did swallow up a small and declining sect. This saddened many Universalists, and several of the dissenting churches rejected merger for years, meeting as independent congregations. Theologically, Universalists had to accept a creedless church with no formal Christian commitment. But the Unitarians were as magnanimous as possible. In name and in acknowledged history, the Universalists have been at least almost equal. Perhaps the greatest disappointment for Universalists was that they had to give up their two seminaries, not because of Unitarian hegemony, but because of necessary, hardheaded decisions by the new UUA board. Since the merger, the dominant trends in the denomination have been those already affecting Unitarians. But impressionistic evidence suggests that a much greater proportion of former Universalists are part of the dwindling minority of avowed Christians in the merged denomination. They are the holdouts in a complex religious movement that led from a very humanized form of Christianity to a type of humanism without Christianity. No other new religious movement in America has moved so far beyond it origins.

READING GUIDE

Of all American originals, the Unitarians have cultivated the most scholarship. This simply reflects the eminence of members, the intensive self-consciousness of ex-Puritans, and the role of major educational institutions. Unlike the internal perspectives of scholars within most other new denominations, the work of Unitarian historians has not been apologetic or defensive, even if at times smug and self-confident.

Because of the eminence of so many Unitarians, particularly in the pre-1860 period, the biographical literature is much too extensive to list. The work on Emerson alone is mind boggling. Denominational history is more limited. The almost definitive work on unitarianism as a doctrinal tradition, and in Europe, resulted from years of labor by a West Coast Unitarian minister, Earl Morse Wilbur, and was published in two related volumes: *A History of Unitarianism: Socinianism and Its Antecedents* (Cambridge: Harvard University Press, 1945) and *A History of Unitarianism in Transylvania, England, and America* (Cambridge: Harvard University Press, 1952). Next to Wilbur, the most influential modern historian of the movement was Charles Conrad Wright. A student of Perry Miller at Harvard, he wrote the almost definitive history of the Arminian or liberal progenitors of Unitarianism in New England, *The Beginnings of Unitarianism in America* (Boston: Beacon Press, 1955), and subsequent to this several essays on Unitarian history, including *The Liberal Christians: Essays on American Unitarian History* (Boston: Beacon Press, 1970). The prominence of Unitarians in the middle period is documented in an excellent work by Daniel Walker Howe, *The Unitarian Conscience: Harvard Moral Philosophy, 1805–1861* (Cambridge: Harvard University Press, 1970). Sydney E. Ahlstrom and Jonathan S. Carey edited an excellent anthology of early Unitarian essays and sermons, *An American Reformation: A Documentary History of Unitarian Christianity* (Middletown, Conn.: Wesleyan University Press, 1985), while Conrad Edick Wright edited a collection of scholarly essays, *American Unitarianism: 1805–1865* (Boston: Northeastern University Press, 1989).

The modern historians of Universalism have reflected sadness rather than smugness. They wrote about a denomination that declined for over a century until its merger with Unitarians in 1961. The definitive history of American Universalism resulted from years of conscientious if rather plodding labor by Russell E. Miller, *The Larger Hope: The First Century of the Universalist Church in America, 1770–1870* (Boston: UUA, 1979) and *The Larger Hope: The Second Century of the Universalist Church in America, 1870– 1970* (Boston: UUA, 1985). Also after the merger, Elmo Arnold Robinson wrote a brief, highly personal and impressionistic survey of Universalism, *American Universalism: Its Origins, Organization, and Heritage* (New York: Exposition Press, 1970). The most recent biography of Hosea Ballou is by Ernest Cassara, *Hosea Ballou: The Challenge of Orthodoxy* (Boston: Beacon Press, 1961). Cassara has also edited *Universalism in America: A Documentary History* (Boston: Beacon Press, 1970). David Robinson, in *The Unitarians and the Universalists* (Westport, Conn.: Greenwood Press, 1985), has written, for a series, the standard history of the merged denomination.

3

APOCALYPTIC **CHRISTIANITY**

Adventists

and

Jehovah's

Witnesses

As Christianity developed in the Roman Empire, it moved ever farther from its beginnings among a few disciples of Jesus in Galilee and Judea. The skimpy sources will never allow us to grasp the full flavor of the earliest, Jewish versions of Christianity. But the writers of the New Testament books, although a generation or more removed from the beginnings of the church, provide some windows into those beginnings. From the synoptic gospels, from the Book of Acts, and from Paul's letters to the Jewish-Gentile congregation he had founded at Thessalonica, we can infer some of the characteristics and the doctrines of these early Christians.

The disciples of Jesus in Jerusalem remained part of the Jewish tradition. They still observed the law of Moses. They still gathered at the temple. They honored the Sabbath and probably worshiped on it. They believed that Jesus was the promised Messiah, that he came to prepare the way for a new kingdom. He had suffered, died, risen again, and ascended into the heavens, but he promised to come back shortly, before most of his followers died, and then complete his work. As the promised Son of Man, he would deliver his faithful followers from a doomed and chaotic world and then found a great new kingdom for his saints, as foreseen by several Jewish apocalyptic writers.

These first Christians already believed in a resurrection of the righteous. Thus, they were consoled that, even should they die before Jesus returned, they could live again in the kingdom. It was, in part, to reassure converts in Thessalonica of this promise that either Paul or a disciple (this remains a disputed point among New Testament scholars) wrote 2 Thessalonians. For these earliest Christians the one great hope, the central meaning of salvation, was a birthright in the kingdom Jesus would shortly establish. This means that the early Christians were, above all, Adventists, waiting and watching for Jesus' return.

APOCALYPTIC AND ADVENTIST CHRISTIANITY

The advent hope became one of the more central or essential doctrines within Christianity. In some sense almost all Christians affirm the return of Jesus to earth, for this belief is too interwoven with the teachings of Jesus and with the hopes of the early Church for Christians to reject it. Some later Christians would try to "spiritualize" this return, to see it as a type of inward revelation to individual Christians, as did Swedenborgians and Christian Scientists. For many Christians the doctrine slowly lost its early centrality and became subordinate to salvation doctrines that had little to do with the literal return of Jesus to earth. Thus, in time, those Christians who kept the centrality of the advent; who continued to view salvation in terms of citizenship in a quite literal, earthly kingdom that would either follow the return of the Christ or began at the end of a millennium; who watched eagerly for signs of the advent; and who believed it would follow an apocalyptic cleansing of the present corrupt order became distinctive within Christianity, at least in their emphases and priorities. In time, a cluster of related beliefs joined hopes of the advent to define a distinctive branch of Christianity. In America several denominations have embraced this complex of beliefs, most notably Seventh-day Adventists, Jehovah's Witnesses, Mormons, and several small sects such as the Christadelphians and the Worldwide Church of God. Because the Mormons have so many distinctive doctrines of their own, their adventism is only one of their distinguishing traits.

All Adventists especially value the apocalyptic portions of the Bible, the very scriptures most often least valued by Roman Catholics and mainstream Protestants. In this selective perspective, Adventists not only join early Jewish Christians but Jesus and his immediate disciples, who seem to have been much influenced by apocalyptic literature and by Jewish sects that embraced apocalyptic hopes. In the backwaters of Judaism, such as Galilee, and among the common folk, the apocalyptic writers had a large following, even as this literature remained suspect among the learned rabbis or Pharisees.

The word "apocalypse," like the later word "utopia," often stands for both a literary genre and a historical event. Thus, people often refer to an apocalypse as a detailed description of hidden or concealed events that an author believes will take place in the future. Others speak of the apocalypse, meaning the actual occurrence of such events. As a Jewish and early Christian literary genre, an apocalypse was always a book of revelation. Apocalyptic writers usually remained anonymous but attributed their supernatural insights to earlier sages or prophets, such as Enoch, Moses, Daniel, or Ezra. Through dreams, visions, or angelic instructions they were able to penetrate the highest mysteries of the cosmos and read the ultimate purpose of its creator. By such insight they could decipher the ultimate significance of contemporary events, see in them the portents of a coming end of the present social order or world, and glimpse beyond that a new age.

For apocalyptic writers, last things were always central in their concern. Apocalyptic literature flowered in the Hellenistic age, a time of turmoil and suffering, of chastened hopes and deep anxieties. Such a literature reflected a deep pessimism about the present or the near future, a certainty of the ascendancy of evil or of demonic forces, apprehensions about inevitable cosmic convolutions and terrors and terrible sufferings in the near future, and assurance of divine vengeance, all of which had to precede a new age. Such a consciousness of entrenched evil suggested the need for a cosmic deliverer and made some type of resurrection necessary for the achievement of ultimate justice. Such themes so magnified the contrast between the present age and the one to come as to cancel any normal sense of historical evolution. Change would be catastrophic, beyond human control, and dependent on direct divine intervention, usually through the promised Messiah. Such emphases also invited an appropriate language of allegory and obscure symbolism.

Few of these apocalyptic themes were completely new to Hellenistic Jews. Apocalyptic language goes back to Ezekiel and the Babylonian exiles. The later prophets, such as Zachariah, emphasized a great historical break and a special divine intervention at the time of the restored kingdom and related this to images of a coming Messiah. By the Persian period Jews routinely believed in demons and angels and other divine messengers. The apocalyptic writers expressed or expanded on such late prophetic themes as an omnipotent and cosmic deity who catered not just to the Jews but to the righteous in all nations. In fact, apocalyptic writers introduced a more general vocabulary into their theology and typically turned to nature and all its wonders to illustrate God's power. If possible, apocalyptic authors demanded a higher standard of moral purity than the earlier prophets. But having acknowledged these continuities, one still feels oneself in a quite different intellectual universe when one turns from the first Isaiah and Jeremiah to the apocalypse of Daniel (Daniel 7–12). Yahweh, the god of Israel, now seems an inappropriate and overly parochial reference for a cosmic deity who presides over the starry heavens and works his will through horrible natural catastrophes, who plays not only with empires and nations but with the orbits of suns and moons. The governmental deity of ancient Israel, the god who above all issued commands and asked for dutiful obedience, seems out of place. So does the older prophetic expectation that a penitent and righteous Israel could move in a normal historical process toward a golden age presided over by a descendant of David.

The last six chapters of Daniel make up the only fully developed apocalypse present alike in Jewish, Roman Catholic, and Protestant scriptures. It may well have been the earliest expression of this new genre; in any case it well illustrates the type. An unknown author wrote it, most likely at the time of the Hasmonean or Maccabean revolt (approximately 165 B.C.E.), or at least this is the judgment of most biblical scholars. But this dating was unfamiliar to ordinary Christians early in the nineteenth century and is still not accepted by conservative Christians today. They still believe that Daniel wrote during the Babylonian captivity and that his accounts of world history are prophetic in the sense of foretelling future events. In fact, Adventist cosmologies and eschatologies in the nineteenth century almost always rested, at least to some extent, on a Babylonian Daniel.

The occult atmosphere of Ezekiel's prophecy, which indeed dates from the captivity, completely dominates the apocalyptic parts of Daniel. All is dreams and visions, so rich with obscure symbolism that even Daniel requires divine help to gain his opaque interpretations. His visions purportedly reveal the future destiny of Israel, or of a righteous people Daniel refers to as the Saints of the Most High, during a succession of violent clashes among great empires. Daniel's language allows, in fact invites, quite varied readings and has over the centuries led people to correlate his predictions with later world history, as did almost all American Adventists. Actually he seemed to write a history of Persian and Greek kingdoms up to the Hasmonean rebellion. The last great empire, headed by the most evil or satanic king imaginable (Antiochus IV), would come closest to destroying the Saints and would add the grossest religious blasphemies to cruel persecutions and wars. But this awful time was a prelude to an all but instantaneous destruction of such abominations. Daniel looked forward to a sudden, violent, dramatic transformation through the direct intervention of the Most High, or to what amounted to the abrupt ending of the present historical epoch, to what he called the time of the end.

After this godly intervention all wars end, sin no longer prevails, and everlasting right reigns supreme. A new heaven and a new earth replace the old ones. This upheaval involves the direct intervention of a special divine person to effect the deliverance and to rule over the new kingdom. Daniel refers to one like a man, coming on the clouds of heaven and establishing everlasting sovereignty over all people and all nations. Finally, Daniel announces that, at the great moment of deliverance, many already asleep in the dust of the earth would come back to life, some to everlasting life and others to the reproach of eternal abhorrence. His themes— a great cataclysmic event, a godlike deliverer or messiah, and the resurrection of the dead—did not win universal acceptance among Jews, as witness the Sadducees at the time of Jesus. But for the majority who clearly accepted them, Judaism now moved a bit closer to Greek mystery cults that promised not just a transformed life in this world but salvation in a world to come.

The apocalyptic sections of Daniel are tame compared with what followed. Fragments of at least six or seven Jewish apocalypses have survived. It is impossible to gauge the breadth and depth of their impact on Jews. None save Daniel gained scriptural status among Jews, not even in the more inclusive Septuagint or Greek versions of Jewish sacred writings. What is clear is that at least two Jewish apocalypses circulated widely among early Christians. Through the receptivity of early Christian communities, and because of the later choice of Jerome, one of these (2 Esdras in the Apocrypha) made it into the Roman Catholic version of the Old Testament as 4 Esdras or Esra. The even older Book of Enoch may have had as much influence on Christians, but the whole of it survived only in an Ethiopic version.

Early Christian writers continued the genre. In a sense they changed it little. Jesus was, for these writers, the promised Son of Man (his most frequent title for himself in the canonical gospels), but he delayed his kingdom. Apostasies and corruption still haunted the earth, awaiting his return and the final time of the end, the full cleansing of the old order. But as the new faith spread to the Gentiles, the apocalyptic style became widely suspect. During the first three centuries of the Church, as the Fathers tried to isolate a body of authoritative Christian writings, four or five apocalypses (some known only by references, not by surviving texts) competed for acceptance. Only the apocalypse of John survived this screening process, and it faced more extended doubts than any of the selected books. As late as the sixth century the Syrian Church still did not accept its canonical status, and throughout the history of Christianity it has probably been the least valued book in the New Testament, save possibly the Book of James among some Protestants.

In many ways Revelation is a sequel to Daniel. Adventist Christians have usually so perceived it. It has had a perennial appeal to those people most alienated in their existing society, those most sure that their own civilization was marred by a terrible apostasy, by new and dangerous beliefs, and by every conceivable form of moral evil. Thus, the appropriate response is a righteous repudiation of the existing society, a pronouncement of God's impending wrath, and an attempt to rally a saving remnant of faithful and righteous saints. They inevitably suffer only persecution and martyrdom in the corrupted present, but by perseverance and faithfulness they can inherit all the wonders of a coming kingdom of righteousness inaugurated not by human effort, not by political reforms, not by the leadership of an ordinary mortal, but only by direct divine intervention, by a total overthrow of the existing order by a savior who will return from the heavens to rescue his saints.

Apocalyptic Christians reflect the mood of such Jewish sectaries as the Essenes and advocate a version of Christianity least affected by Gentile religions and philosophies. In this sense they are extreme restorationists. Several characteristics mark such an Adventist form of Christianity. One is the self-conscious continuities with the Jewish past and the continued relevance of Jewish laws, history, and heroes. Although the corruptions of a present age require an apocalyptic event such as the intervention of a divine savior, the coming kingdom will be, in every sense, a literal, worldly kingdom, a polity presided over by Jesus. It will involve a literal resurrection. People will come back to life again. This invites, and among almost all American Adventists led to, a repudiation of any belief in a separable mind or soul, any "spiritual" conception of the kingdom, and any continuation of the human person after death and before the resurrection (a doctrine often called soul sleep).

This rejection of Greek immaterialism has remained a distinctive mark of Adventists, and correlative to this has been a rejection of any concept of unending torment. The wages of sin are death, extinction in the eternal pit, for without some ethereal soul, some disembodied spirit, nothing remains to suffer torment. This corporealist perspective is alien to most orthodox trinitarian formulas, which almost always involve beliefs about a separable mind or spirit or the possibilities of the incarnation of spirit in matter. The literal hope for a resurrected life in a perfected earthly kingdom supports a very moralistic religion that stresses a very high level of moral purity. Faith may save, but it always joins with an obligation to observe the commandments. This concept of salvation is thus very governmental. In one sense Adventists are very supernatural, for they continuously emphasize the special providence of God, most of all at the time of the end. But they also narrow the distinction between this world and other worlds, including a tangible, physical heavenly kingdom in which reside Jehovah and his son. The final kingdom will be a perfected version of this earth, with real, bodily people doing the things they now do but without corruption or the prospect of sickness and death.

It is this complex of beliefs and attitudes, not just hope for the advent, that distinguishes apocalyptic Christianity in America. As for the advent hope, the distinction is only one of degree. Interest in and focus on Jesus' return have varied from one Christian sect to another and from age to age. In the mainstream of the Reformation, in Lutheran and Reformed denominations, and in puritan and pietist sects that sprang from them, the advent was always an important doctrine and one that often became more central or focal at times of revival or renewal. In both Catholicism and Protestantism the doctrine of the resurrection remained. Given the New Testament and the history of the early Church, no one could get rid of this doctrine. But the belief in immortality, in the survival of the human spirit or mind after the death of the body, lessened the centrality of the resurrection hope. Most Protestants believe that, in some sense, the souls of people after death immediately experience bliss or suffer torment. For Catholics, the life of spirits after death and before the resurrection allows a paradise for the worthy, a purgating experience for the redeemed but unworthy, and awful agonies for those who reject Christianity. Such beliefs diverted attention from the scriptural account of last things as provided in detail only in John's apocalypse, from emphasis on the resurrection and the process of judgment that follows, and from the particulars of life in a quite literal political kingdom here on a new earth.

A corporealist, kingdom-oriented, and apocalyptic version of Christianity has a distinguished heritage. These views apparently prevailed among Jewish Christians for two or three centuries. Such moralistic and freewill heretics as Pelagius moved back close to these Jewish progenitors. American Adventists like to claim the Waldensians as early Adventists. Extremely chiliastic sects, some with corporealist beliefs, flourished briefly in the wake of the Reformation. John Calvin wrote extensively to refute them. Thomas Hobbes, the English philosopher, developed a very detailed corporealist, kingdom-oriented version of Christian doctrine in his *Leviathan* and used it to lambast the ethereal natural-rights arguments of his political opponents. In fact, Hobbes could serve well as the theologian of most modern forms of adventism. Isaac Newton not only moved from the delights of physics to the serious matter of biblical prophecy in his last years, but both he and several of his disciples accepted a corporealist or materialistic theology. Joseph Priestley, the English chemist and Unitarian, used a rigorous, almost reductionist materialist theology to attack the two great pagan corruptions of the early, simple, Jewish Christian faith—a belief in immaterial spirits and the Trinity formula. He also attended carefully to the apocalyptic books, although not with the detailed chronological interests of Newton. Thomas Jefferson enthusiastically endorsed Priestley's Unitarianism and rejoiced in a simple, believable form of Christianity purged of all Platonic essences and immaterial spirits.

In the late eighteenth and early nineteenth centuries several Protestant ministers and scholars in several European countries wrote extensively on the apocalypse of John. In Britain Edward Irving, a university graduate and a scholar in his own right, launched an Adventist movement just before William Miller began preaching his advent message in America in 1832. The Irvinites set precedents for Americans in perfecting para-church institutions, such as prophecy conferences. One of Irving's disciples even anticipated Miller's identification of the likely date of the advent—1843. But the prevalence of undisciplined visions and prophecies and glossolalia in his own congregation considerably embarrassed Irving and his movement in Britain.

THE MILLERITES

Although many Americans, particularly in the midst of religious revivals, had felt confident that the advent was near, few made preparation for the advent the core of their preaching. Because William Miller did just that, he has gained the distinction of being America's first Adventist. He was not (Samuel Hopkins, the disciple of Jonathan Edwards, was in every sense an Adventist and confidently expected the advent around the year 2000), but Miller alone gained wide attention for a target year. Beyond this, he never accepted all the characteristic apocalyptic doctrines, such as soul sleep.

Unlike most European Adventist leaders, who were often scholars, Miller was an untutored farmer. Born in 1782 in Massachusetts, he lived most of his life in two villages on the borders of Vermont (Poultney) and New York (Low Hampton). He fought in the War of 1812 and later confessed that, in those years, he was a deist (this is such a common claim in conversion narratives that one has to have doubts or at least questions about his definition of deism). After conversion in 1816 he joined a small Calvinist Baptist congregation and began an intensive study of the Bible (also a frequent claim of converts). He was largely self-taught, and all the pity, for he was often credulous. Like so many evangelical Christians, he struggled with the two apocalyptic books but assumed that they, like all the Bible, had a story to tell that was accessible to ordinary people like himself. Possibly influenced by the speculations of Adventists in England (this is not clear), he tried to unearth the hidden secrets of some of the more obscure passages in Daniel, supplementing these whenever possible by passages in Revelation or by the apocalyptic interludes in the Gospels and even in Paul's letters. His early concern was the promised second advent of the Christ, and behind his labors was his own sense, based on biblical signs fulfilled or perhaps on his own sense of the awful apostasies of the modern age, that the time was very near.

As early as 1818 Miller had tentatively determined that the advent would probably occur in or about 1843. This was not in itself a startling conclusion, for dozens of other Bible students had already speculated about the same date, based on the same scriptures. Miller did not present his views in a public lecture until 1831 or publish them until 1832, when he was fifty years old and already afflicted with Parkinson's disease. It is not easy today to explain his prediction, for one can only, with great difficulty, move into his cultural universe. His key was Daniel 8:14, a verse that had long tantalized and confused Christians. In this verse Daniel notes that an evil ruler will suppress or trod down the Holy Place for 2,300 evenings and mornings (most Adventists believe this means 2,300 days, although it could mean only 1,150), and then God will restore or purify or cleanse it (translations vary, but the authorized version has the telling phrase "then shall the Sanctuary be cleansed"). Elsewhere, Daniel also refers to 490, 1,290, and 1,335 days. The easiest interpretation of these time intervals is that the author of the apocalypse, writing in the midst of the early Maccabean revolt against the Syrian overlords, simply used a somewhat obscure language to record events that had already occurred. Thus, the 2,300 days was simply the time during which Antiochus IV defiled the Jewish temple before Judas (Maccabee) liberated it and then cleansed and rededicated it (leading to the festival of lights, or Hanukkah, in modern Judaism). But Miller came to these obscure numbers with two assumptions: that Daniel really lived during the Babylonian captivity and that in his prophecy he used a day to represent a year (this day-year interpretation was commonplace among almost all English Protestants who attempted to make sense of Daniel). Thus, to Miller, the veiled references to future kingdoms, which make best sense as a retrospective account of events in Palestine from the Babylonian captivity to Antiochus IV, included an account of the earth's future until the end time. Thus, the cleansing of the sanctuary meant the cleansing of the earth by a returning messiah.

Given these assumptions, it was simple to calculate the date of the advent if one could determine when the 2,300 days began. Miller decided, on the basis of his commonsense reading of the total biblical text, that this was the time when the Persian emperor Artaxerxes issued the final order, to Ezra, to complete the rebuilding of the temple. The key to this interpretation was another reference in Daniel to seven times seventy weeks, or 490 days, which if interpreted as years was the approximate lapsed time between Artaxerxes' order and the birth of Jesus. Other references to days in Daniel and Revelation seemed, with a great deal of interpretive leeway, to correlate with the ascendancy of the Antichrist (the papacy), with the suppression of the Ottoman Empire, and with Napoleon's crushing of the secular power of the pope in 1798. Thus from Daniel and Revelation Miller worked out a complete chart of world history. It came to an end around 1843, although he never tried to predict the day of the advent. It was most likely, he believed, during the Jewish liturgical year that best corresponded to 1843 (March 1843 to March 1844).

Miller was a kind, good man, pudgy and unpretentious. No one who knew him ever doubted his sincerity. He reflected some of the resentments of small farmers in his region. He, like fellow Baptists, was firmly committed to the separation of church and state and took part in numerous local revivals. In almost all respects he was a typical, rural evangelical Christian, never involved in narrow doctrinal interpretations. His advent doctrine seemed so important that Miller wanted to share it with all evangelical Christians and use it to bridge doctrinal differences such as those separating Calvinists and Arminians. Thus he was very ecumenical in approach. He was also a creature of place, of backcountry New England. By moral commitment he was a staunch opponent of slavery, an abolitionist, and helped blacks make their way to Canada on the Underground Railroad. One result was that his views never really penetrated or influenced the South and remained strongest in the New England–New York area. He supported most evangelical reforms of his day, but as so many of his early followers he reflected the attitudes of lowly people, those horrified by the riches and luxuries of the cites, and was quick to condemn the apostasies of modern, fashionable churches.

With some trepidation Miller began lecturing on the advent in 1831. Within two years he accepted a license to preach from his little Baptist congregation. A mild man, he simply shared with anyone who would listen his calculations and thus his confidence in the early advent. The early date gave urgency to his message, but he did not make the date central to his message. Locally his interpretations attracted intense scrutiny, as people flocked to hear his undramatic but logical lectures or sermons. He published several of his lectures in a book in 1836, but even this did not gain him much attention outside the cities and towns around Low Hampton. Miller never considered forming a new denomination and circulated freely among Baptist, Methodist, Christian Connection, and Presbyterian congregations, and in some of his lectures he tried to broaden his appeal to encompass even Roman Catholics. He thought his message should inform all Christians. His rather specific prediction drew early criticism and ridicule, but even his opponents, if they heard Miller, conceded his goodwill and at first apparently saw no great harm in his message, since he was not dogmatic about the date. Besides, in the late 1830s, as the fervent and widespread revivals (some triggered by Charles Finney) of the mid-1830s began to abate, Miller's message seemed to be one of the few triggers for local revivals. Many ministers, totally unconvinced by his predictions, still liked to have him preach in their pulpits. His emphasis on the advent, always a favorite convicting device in evangelical preaching, took on special urgency because he was so confident of his reading of biblical prophesies. In the first decade Miller did not organize any Adventist institutions. Presumably, various Christians were to some extent persuaded by his message.

Miller's adventism became an organized movement in 1840, largely through the effective promotional labors of Joshua V. Himes. Miller first met Himes at a convention of the Christian Connection churches in New Hampshire in 1839. Himes, at thirty-nine, was much younger than Miller and was almost immediately persuaded of the correctness of Miller's calculations. Himes proved a godsend to Miller. He was pastor of the second Christian congregation in Boston, which he had helped organize, and had been a very effective preacher and reformer. An abolitionist associate of William Lloyd Garrison, Himes had been an effective advocate of peace (he was a pacifist, as were most subsequent Adventists), temperance, and women's rights. He had a broad network of friends and, most critical, exceptional editorial and publishing skills. In 1840 he began the first Millerite periodical, *Signs of the Times,* and planned lecture tours for Miller outside rural New England, including New York City.

Himes helped convene the first General Conference of Advent Believers in the fall of 1840, or what was the beginnings of a para-church movement. He, with Miller and a growing number of sympathetic ministers, began conducting revivals at any place they were welcome. At another conference in 1842 the ministers made a fateful decision to emphasize the likely year of the advent, a decision never accepted by some of the cooperating ministers and one that Miller had resisted. Consistent with this emphasis, several Millerite ministers began circulating elaborate charts showing the divine order of history, all demonstrating the end of the world in 1843. Beginning in 1842, with Himes again most responsible, the emerging Adventist sect began conducting summer camp meetings organized around the advent message. The movement gained national publicity when Himes and others contracted the largest tent ever constructed in America, which held an audience of 4,000 to 5,000. Himes also helped build a tabernacle in Boston. In November 1842 Himes made permanent what had been one of many local and temporary newspapers launched to support local revivals, *The Midnight Cry*. By 1843 a growing network of committed ministers, including Joseph Bates and James White, two of the founders of the later Seventh-day Adventists, were spreading the message to Ohio and south as far as Washington, D.C. By the spring of 1844, the terminal time of the advent as predicted by Miller, the Adventists were on the way to becoming a separate body within their traditional denominations (the largest number were from a Methodist background, followed by Baptists and other evangelical denominations, but with a goodly share of ministers from the Christian Connection). The number of people fully convinced of Miller's predictions is impossible to calculate, but he later estimated at least 50,000. Others believed the numbers were much higher.

The passing of the target year led to disappointment. Miller confessed his mistake, although he remained confident that the advent was near. Several natural signs helped reinforce his confidence. But this failed prediction did not have a devastating impact on the movement. The conferences continued. Miller had only offered a broad target, not any one date. Some ministers had refused to predict even the correct year.

Then something unanticipated changed the whole course of American Adventism. At a New Hampshire camp meeting in August 1844, a woman interrupted the minister, Joseph Bates, by noting a new calculation. This was a position that Samuel Snow had first publicized earlier in the year. Miller had briefly considered it in 1843. This was a belief that the time of the advent might be in the seventh month, not the first month, of the Jewish liturgical calendar. Snow, by reference to the fulfillment of other Old Testament types by Jesus—those matching the spring holidays—argued with some logic that the advent would come during the antitypes of the fall festivals, particularly the Day of Atonement. He therefore believed the 2,300 years in Daniel began in the fall of 457 B.C.E., the time when the Jews actually began to rebuild Jerusalem, or, in accordance with another biblical passage, on the tenth day of the seventh month (Yom Kippur), which meant that the advent would be on October 22, 1844. To establish this late date (Yom Kippur occurred in September according to the calendar used by modern Jews), he accepted the calendar of a small Jewish sect, the Karaites, who tried strictly to adhere to the Jewish scriptures and who refused to accept any Jewish calendar based, even in part, on oral tradition.

Neither Miller nor Himes was at first persuaded of this new date. But Adventists, after months of doubt and even desolation, were primed for such a message. They accepted it with great enthusiasm. This began the last, fervent, continuous Millerite revival, which lasted for only two months. The date quickly became a self-fulfilling prophecy. Its impact was so great and the fervor of the new revival so irresistible that Himes and Miller finally capitulated in early October, under conviction that the Holy Spirit had to be behind such wonderful effects (some of which were not wonderful, including several examples of fanaticism). Already the very success of the Millerites had helped split congregations, and by 1844 many Adventists had left parent churches to found new congregations. This separatism accelerated in the frenzied late summer of 1844, in effect leading to a new, Millerite denomination, although one not organized as such. By this time many Millerite leaders were urging congregations to separate if persecuted by the orthodox.

Jesus did not return as predicted on October 22. At least if he did, no one recognized him, and none of the predicted events of Revelation 20 took place. The righteous dead did not come back to life, and the righteous on earth did not rise to greet the savior as he came down from the clouds of heaven. Worldly evils continued or multiplied. What had been a restrained adventism before the spring of 1844 had become a great, all-involving cause by the end of the summer. The faithful had really believed the message. Thus, many closed businesses, stopped their harvest, or otherwise prepared for the advent. Himes announced the last issue of *Midnight Cry*. Thousands gathered for worship. A few may have gathered on hillsides or even donned robes, although most such reports were exaggerated. Such was the expectancy that many were literally crushed when nothing happened. Embarrassment and widespread ridicule added to their disappointment, and many scarcely had any motivation to go on living. So critical was this date that, from then on, Adventists have referred to it as the Great Disappointment.

Confusion followed the disappointment. In a sense the Millerite movement ended in 1844. Miller, now ill, lived for five more years, confident that his calculations had been close to the mark, although obviously erroneous. His own Low Hampton congregation denied him fellowship. Many of the separating congregations, most without meetinghouses, survived, becoming the nucleus of at least several ephemeral Adventist denominations and at least four that still survive. In particular, those Millerites who left their earlier congregations could not go home again, and thus six years later up to 50,000 people still considered themselves Adventists. By then they were divided by a dozen different doctrines. Although unified briefly by the advent hope, the movement had attracted people from several denominations and with some widely divergent doctrines. Now the differences could flower, along with imaginative new interpretations of the apocalyptic literature. New cults and sects multiplied (twenty-five by one count in 1855).

Himes, only belatedly persuaded of the October 22 date, tried to play a constructive role. Within a week he resumed his two periodicals (dwindling numbers of subscriptions eventually doomed them) and began collecting aid for the destitute (those who had given away all their property). He, with Miller, still believed the advent was near but gave up on setting any date. In a sense he wanted to reassemble the advent movement of 1840–42, when the leaders had chosen not to place much emphasis on a particular date. Working carefully with Miller, he was able to convene a special unity conference of Adventists at Albany in late April 1845. It seemed to take the first steps toward creating a new Adventist denomination. It endorsed a ten-point doctrinal platform, ordained five ministers, and planned additional conferences. In its platform it denounced a growing number of former Millerites who still wanted to keep faith with October 22 and who, in almost all cases, argued that God had shut the door of salvation on that date. Yet the vast majority were still open-door Adventists, and the promise of unity among them briefly seemed realistic. It was not to be. Other doctrinal issues soon divided open-door Adventists, most particularly the corporealist doctrines of conditional immortality (soul rest) and annihilationism.

In 1843 one of the leading Millerite ministers, George Storrs, had begun agitating the corporealist position. In January 1844 he converted Charles Fitch, who, next to Miller, Himes, and Josiah Litch, was the most prominent Millerite preacher. Few other leading Millerites were persuaded. Miller and Himes condemned this nonorthodox doctrine. This budding schism within the Millerite movement was obscured, even temporarily forgotten, in the excitement leading up to October 22. After the disappointment, Storrs won more former Millerites to his side, effectively dividing the open-door Adventists. Thus, Himes's dreams of a united denomination floundered over this issue, leading eventually to two separate denominations. In 1858 the noncorporealists formed the American Evangelical Adventist Conference. Despite the antiorganizational views of most of the corporealists, they almost had to unite in opposition to the evangelicals and thus in two steps in 1860 created the loosely congregational Advent Christian Association. Himes eventually joined this denomination, then left after a struggle over publishing and a scandal. Late in life he returned to the faith of his childhood, the Episcopal Church (he lived to age ninety). In time the Evangelical Adventist Conference faded away, in part because its doctrines were scarcely distinguishable from the growing dispensationalist premillennialist movement within the conservative factions of the mainline denominations. The Advent Christian Association (today the Advent Christian Church) grew rapidly only in the immediate aftermath of its founding. By 1900 it had over 25,000 members but was already in relative decline (it has about the same number today). It is now minute in comparison with the Seventh-day Adventists, or the largest product of post-1844 shut-door Adventism.

Ordinarily, the shut-door doctrine would be a fascinating footnote in American religious history. It is more than that because of its place in Seventh-day Adventist history and its complicated relationship to Ellen G. White, the prophetess of the denomination. Miller, as most orthodox Christians, had always believed that all opportunities for salvation would end with the advent. In the immediate aftermath of the disappointment, he briefly found attractive some shut-door theories; at least he ceased all evangelical activities. But increasing fanaticism among some shut-door advocates led him firmly into the Himes faction. Others, such as the original leader of the seventh-month interpretation, Samuel Snow, would not give up on the October 22 date. Something cosmic had to have happened on that date in fulfillment of the Daniel prophecy. But what? Some, like Snow, believed that the Christ had come to earth spiritually on that day and would soon come in the flesh. In this short interval the doors of salvation were closed. Such a "spiritualized" interpretation was usually combined with a certainty that the visible advent was near. Some projected new dates, all doomed to failure. Each of these shut-door advocates established periodicals and gained at least a local following. Some were cultlike and probed new forms of enthusiasm and fanaticism. Dreams and visions were commonplace. Most such cults proved ephemeral, with no surviving denominations. Some of the more extreme spiritualists found a home among the Shakers, a few at the communal colony at Oneida, New York. But from the shut-door Adventists came the founders of the Seventh-day Adventist church.

SABBATARIAN ADVENTISM

Four or five individuals who had been devoted disciples of Miller early adopted a Sabbatarian form of Adventism. These Sabbatarian Adventists were soon distinguished by four characteristics: special interpretations of Miller's prophecy (the sanctuary doctrine), seventh-day or Sabbath observance, corporealist views of reality and thus the doctrine of soul sleep, and acceptance of modern spiritual gifts, most importantly the gift of prophecy. Apart from these distinctive affirmations, these embryonic Seventh-day Adventists were close to Methodists in their belief in free will and complete atonement; evangelical in the sense of requiring a crisislike conversion, in emphasizing a high level of spiritual zeal, and in demanding puritanical moral standards; and close to Freewill Baptists in their baptismal practice (immersion), in the ordinance of feet washing, and in their insistence on a complete separation of church and state.

The Sabbatarian Adventists emerged from the shut-door faction and kept faith with the seventh-month chronology. It was not clear at the time, but in a sense a new religious movement began on the day after the Great Disappointment. Young Hiram Edson, a distressed Millerite, according to his later confession had a visionary experience while walking through a field. He saw that Miller has mistakenly assumed that the cleansing of the sanctuary referred to the advent and the cleansing of the earth (the sanctuary of humans). Not so, he now learned, for the sanctuary in Daniel 8:14 referred to a heavenly sanctuary that had the same position in the new Christian dispensation as the sanctuary of the Ark and then the temple had under the Abrahamic covenant.

Edson was not a theologian, although he would be a dutiful preacher in the Adventist cause. It was two of his colleagues, O. R. L. Crosier and F. B. Hahn, who in the next few months helped work out a rather elaborate theory about this heavenly sanctuary. Drawing from several New Testament sources, and particularly from the images of a heavenly high priest in the Book of Hebrews, they now understood that Jesus, in the interim before October 22, 1844, had assumed the role of a high priest in the sanctuary of the new covenant in the heavenly kingdom and was there continuously pleading the case of redeemed sinners before Jehovah from an altar in the outer chamber of this temple or sanctuary. This was a ministry of forgiveness. It paralleled the work of priests in the outer chamber of the Jewish temple. This work by Jesus assumed a new form on October 22, when he had moved from the outer chamber into the Holy of Holies (on Yom Kippur). Since the cleansing of the Holy of Holies occurred only once a year, the time was brief compared with the ministrations over 364 days in the outer temple. This meant an early advent, but one at a time unknown to humans, which after all was what the scriptures taught. In the Holy of Holies Jesus would actually blot out the sins of all believers and thus in a sense fulfill or complete the atoning work of his crucifixion. They believed that Jesus, in this brief time in the Holy of Holies, would complete a type of preadvent investigative judgment, a necessary prelude to his return to earth.

Not only Edson but abler colleagues such as Joseph Bates further developed this sanctuary doctrine over the next decade. It became a central theme for later Seventh-day Adventists, one that provided needed continuity with the Millerite movement. It seemed to justify a new chronology of human history correlated with the messages of the first three angels in Revelation 14. But before this full correlation, they had to discover Sabbatarianism.

As is clear from labels, the most critical, distinguishing doctrines of the later Seventh-day Adventists involved the early advent and the Sabbath. Some of the Millerites, in areas where they interacted with Seventh-day Baptists, were persuaded that no scriptural justification existed for Sunday worship. One Millerite congregation in Washington, New Hampshire, began Sabbath worship before the Great Disappointment. But the three most active founders of the Seventh-day Adventist Church not only adopted Sabbath worship but soon buttressed this practice with such a complex array of doctrines that Sabbath observance became, in effect, the most important identifying mark of a remnant of faithful Christians. It was not a new doctrine. A small group of Sabbatarian Anabaptists, led by Oswald Glait, had moved to America in the eighteenth century and indirectly influenced American Adventists. Of the three most influential Seventh-day Adventist founders—Joseph Bates, James V. White, and Ellen Gould Harmon White—Bates was the first to embrace the Sabbath. No one ever proselytized more earnestly in behalf of one doctrine.

Joseph Bates hailed from New Bedford, Massachusetts, and from a seagoing family. As a young sailor in Liverpool, he was impressed into the British navy and then spent the war years (1812–15) as a prisoner of war in England. Back home he rose, by hard work, to captain of a merchant ship and accumulated considerable wealth before retiring to a farm and to profitable land speculation. Just before giving up the sea, he converted in 1831 in a Christian Connection congregation, choosing this denomination because of its baptismal doctrines and Arian views about the Trinity. As a prominent citizen he became very active in antislavery and temperance reform before capitulating to the Millerite views of Joseph Himes, a close personal friend, in 1839. Bates, typical of his personality, poured all his energy and soon all his accumulated wealth into the advent cause. He became a lay preacher. Almost alone among the Millerites he dared pitch a revival tent in slave country, on the eastern shore of Maryland. Just before October 22, 1844, he sold his home and most of his real estate. The Great Disappointment left him impoverished but still committed.

In the troubled aftermath of the Disappointment Bates read an 1845 tract on Sabbath worship by another Millerite minister and was quickly persuaded. At a conference he met Hiram Edson, was persuaded by Edson's sanctuary doctrine, and in turn persuaded Edson to accept Sabbath worship. By 1846 the Sabbath doctrine had become the core of Bates's message, making him seem to critics a one-issue Christian. He traveled to New Hampshire in 1846 to meet the Sabbatarian Adventists there and in the same year met with James White and Ellen G. Harmon, just after their marriage. After some resistance, he converted them to the Sabbath doctrine. By 1847 the three had become a triumvirate committed to winning converts to their increasingly coherent interpretation of biblical truths. At the time they had no buildings, no publications, and only a handful of disciples. It soon became clear that each would play a very different role in transforming this tiny nucleus into a growing denomination. Bates became the itinerant evangelist, always on the road, carrying the message west to Michigan and beyond. James White was the organizer and publisher. Ellen G. White became the seer or prophet, using her visions to confirm, reinforce, or in some cases extend the developing doctrines of the movement. It was she who eventually gave special authority to the Sabbatarian cause.

Bates and others combined the sanctuary doctrine with Sabbath worship. In particular they used the account of three angels in Revelation 14 to certify a new eschatology. They saw the Millerite movement as a fulfillment of the warning of the first angel, who announced an early judgment on the earth. The second angel, who announced the fall of Babylon, became a message of doom to all existing, Sunday-worshiping Christians, Protestants as well as Roman Catholics (most Protestants had considered the Church of Rome to be the modern Babylon). It was the third angel's message that became central to the sanctuary doctrine. This angel referred to those who kept the commandments of God as opposed to those who worshiped the beast and had its mark on their forehead. The Sabbatarians interpreted this mark as standing for a denial of the Sabbath, and thus of contempt for God's commandments. In the brief interval before the advent, the remnant of Sabbath worshipers had the duty to carry this third angel's message to as many former Millerites as possible and to persuade them to honor all the commandments. These Sabbatarians could only rejoice that they were among the 144,000 who, by the promise of the first verse of Revelation 14, would be ransomed at the time Jesus returned to earth.

At first the emerging handful of Sabbatarian and sanctuary advocates believed that the door remained closed, that salvation was impossible for those who had rejected the Millerite message. Jesus, when he entered the heavenly Holy of Holies, had ended his period of judgment in the outer temple and had closed its door. But after 1850, aided by clarifying prophetic visions received by Ellen G. White, the Sabbatarians revised this view. They believed that a new era had begun in 1844, one that was beyond the time of the end of Daniel. Jesus, although he had closed the door to the outer temple, had opened a new door—to the inner temple. This meant promise, not foreclosed opportunities. The ranks of the 144,000 saints of Revelation 14 were not yet full, perhaps because of continued apostasy on earth. The present age was, in fact, a time for special mission activity, driven by the urgency of little time and a last chance. From an early nucleus that repudiated further mission activity, the emerging sect eventually became the most dedicated to missions of any Protestant body and, in the wide reaches of the world, was one of the most successful. To-day Seventh-day Adventists have a higher percentage of membership abroad than any other major American-based denomination (over 90 percent).

The opening of the door of salvation reflected a predictable response to the passing of time after 1844 without the expected advent. In many re-spects the shut door was an artifact of the confused and despairing after-math of the Great Disappointment. It not only offended most Christians but most Adventists, since it suggested a small elite of genuine saints. It is still impossible to trace the exact evolution of a new open-door stance among emerging Seventh-day Adventists. The records are not complete. More important, perhaps, this shift has bared a sore point among Ad-ventists. It is clear that for four or five years Ellen G. White accepted the closed door. Later she embraced the open door. At stake in this issue is her prophetic status. Could a true prophet change her mind about such a crit-ical doctrine? In any case, by around 1851 Bates and the two Whites began to preach the open-door position and to do so, at least in part, because of the pressure of new converts and some prophetic insights by Ellen G. White.

Ellen Gould Harmon, born in Gorham, Maine, in 1827, grew up in Portland. As a child she suffered a broken nose and extensive nasal block-age because of a stone thrown by a playmate. The physical effects joined with a type of psychological withdrawal, and a very sensitive Ellen grew up at home while her twin sister attended school. As an adolescent Ellen heard William Miller preach in Portland in 1840. Her family became Millerites, but the predicted advent threw Ellen into deeper depression. In time she experienced a religious conversion and joined a Methodist congregation (it expelled her and her family in 1844 because of their Adventism). Ellen was particularly devastated by the Great Disappointment. But in its after-math she experienced the first of what eventually became hundreds of vi-sions (she already had experienced religiously significant dreams). During a trance, she was consoled by a sight of advent people traveling toward the city of God. After a subsequent vision led her to share her insights with others, seventeen-year-old Ellen used this first prophetic revelation to comfort Adventists in Portland. She thus began her unique ministry of visions, interpretations of them, and the use of these revelations for the instruction of others. Just after she began to have frequent visions, she met and married James White in the summer of 1846. She also met Joseph Bates and became persuaded of the correctness of the Sabbath doctrine. Just after this she had a special vision, possibly the most important in her long life because it provided special, supernatural authority for the Sabbath.

In her vision, White was privileged to view the inside of the heavenly sanctuary and to look upon the two tablets of stone within. As she looked at the ten commandments, she saw the fourth, the one on the Sabbath, bathed in a halo of light. This made clear not only that all humans were obligated to obey all ten commandments, but that the obligation to honor the Sabbath had a special status among the ten, for it was a direct memorial to creation. It above all commandments established God's authority and drew the distinction between God and his creatures. From this insight came a rather complex body of Adventist doctrines. First-day worship represented the major apostasy of Christian history. Adventists soon used apocalyptic symbolism to express this. The great apostasy began in the Church of Rome, which first endorsed Sunday worship. Adventists often referred to those who shared this apostasy as bearing the mark of the beast, and in their early preaching they made clear that Sunday worshipers, once they were aware of God's demands, jeopardized their salvation. Those who reembraced the Sabbath, who fully adhered to God's commandments, made up a saving minority in these last days, for they alone had the "seal" of Sabbatarian obedience and fulfilled the demands of the third angel of Revelation. Bates was particularly harsh on Sunday worshipers and in early sermons denied that they could be saved. This extreme emphasis on Sabbath observance, this degree of exclusiveness, added to an often radical anti-Catholicism, alienated other Christians, and led to at least mild forms of informal persecution.

The actual observance of the Sabbath in America created more problems for Adventists than the special doctrines that supported it. They tried to adhere to the Jewish restrictions. They would do no work from sunset on Friday to sunset on Saturday. They would do nothing to honor Sunday and eventually fought legal battles in many states against Sunday, or blue, laws. They were at times a beleaguered minority, frustrated by their efforts to gain a full separation of church and state. Religious freedom became one of their most cherished ideals. Like Jews, they went against the grain of popular culture and became increasingly alienated from the larger society and from government. Their sabbatarianism eventually joined support for a type of pacifism (most of their young men accepted only noncombat duty in the Civil War), Arian views of the Trinity, and dietary rules to set them apart and to make them objects of popular ridicule. But such opposition only reinforced their sense of being a saving remnant and their belief that almost all the world around them was lost in a horrible apostasy.

A third doctrine soon distinguished Sabbatarian Adventists, although it too had been a small undercurrent among Millerites. This was a doctrine relating to last things, often referred to by Adventists as conditional immortality. It was a doctrine with a long history, but among the Millerites only George Storrs preached it before 1844. Privately Ellen G. White had already accepted it. It so happened that this doctrine appealed to Bates and James White and of course won divine sanction from the inspired teachings of Ellen G. White. For Bates and James White, an openness to the doctrine probably reflected their background in the Christian Connection, since the two founders of the Christian movement in New England, Elias Smith and Abner Jones, had at least briefly affirmed a corporealist view. It quickly became pervasive among early Sabbatarian Adventists, along with a subordinationist or Arian understanding of the Trinity (also out of the Christian Connection). Strategically, the denial of any separable mind or soul, and thus any survival after death (the soul slept until the resurrection), provided the strongest possible ammunition against the great spiritualist movement that peaked in the 1850s. At the heart of spiritualism, which was usually non-Christian and by claim scientific, was communion with the spirits of the dead, usually through a medium. Adventists saw this as a dangerous and unscriptural form of superstition. Since Adventists denied the survival of any soul, the claims of mediums had to be bogus. Their denial of immaterial substance and their emphasis on a holistic conception of personality (what immaterialists conceived of as a separable soul, Adventists saw as the animating breath of life that came directly from God) underwrote their rejection of any eternal torment, a doctrine predicated on spiritual survival. In the popular mind, Adventists had rejected hell. In time their doctrine that the wages of sin were simply death (annihilationism) had broad appeal. Ellen G. White, with her humane and irenic bent, emphasized that God could not be so cruel as to assign any person to permanent torment, let alone gain any glory from such suffering.

The label "conditional immortality," as used by Adventists, simply meant that humans are born as mortals, with death as the normal end of their life. But faithful and obedient Christians have the promise of a new life at the resurrection and from that point on are immortal. Thus immortality is an added gift, a product of God's grace. Sabbatarian Adventists believed in a universal resurrection, but the unsaved live only for a time, suffer divine judgment and a punishment proportionate to their sins, and then experience a final and complete death. Other versions of conditional immortality have some currency among contemporary evangelical theologians, but many of these non-Adventists do not believe in any resurrection for the wicked. Others affirm the survival of a soul after death but still expect an extinction of the wicked after divine judgment. Despite the orthodox belief in immortality and a separable soul, Adventists argued quite persuasively that a preponderance of biblical references endorsed a final exclusion and destruction of the wicked, not endless torment.

Corporealism, tied to an emphasis on strict obedience of the commandments, seemed inconsistent with a religion that affirmed the visions of Ellen G. White. And tensions did exist in the early sect, as they still do in modern Adventism. The announced scriptural basis for Ellen G. White's visions was the gift of prophecy, as itemized by Paul in his list of the gifts of the Spirit. Thus those Sabbatarian Adventists who accepted the authority of White's visions had to spend much time defending at least the gift of prophecy (and, by implication if not overtly, all gifts listed by Paul) and even offered monetary rewards for anyone able to prove that any part of the New Testament either repealed the Sabbath as the proper day of worship or canceled the role of the gifts enumerated by Paul.

The early Adventist movement matured in an intense revival atmosphere. Adventist revivals were perhaps more ecstatic than Methodist ones, with shouts, moaning, and frequent swooning. They also involved gifts such as glossolalia and inspired exhortations based on visions and dreams, or what some saw as a vivid illustration of the prophetic gift. No orthodox Christian could eliminate the spiritual gifts from the Bible, although they often disagreed on what they meant in the modern age. Ellen G. White, as many early Adventists, believed herself healed through prayer and joined in the healing of other people. After all, healing was another undeniable gift of the Spirit as listed by Paul in 1 Corinthians. Yet some ministers continued to distrust White's visions. Because of this, for five years in the early 1850s her husband tried to limit publicity about them. The divisions over Ellen G. White and over the status of her voluminous writings continued into the twentieth century.

Prophecy posed enormous dangers for any new sect. Could anyone prophesy? What if the visions contradicted one another? How could one judge the claims of divine influence? How could Adventists preserve order in a church if everyone could gain direct insights from God? Such visionary Christianity was a form of religious enthusiasm, as defined and condemned by the orthodox, who insisted that the Bible remained the only source of authority for Christians, at least after the development of the New Testament canon. Yet despite the dangers of religious anarchy, any religion needs the flexibility to interpret doctrines to fit new problems, and whether authorized or not, or tied to prophetic claims or not, the custodians of religions do just that. What seems most useful is a source of authoritative judgment that is singular and constrained, even guided, by the larger religious community or its leaders. The pope has gained such a restrained, responsive, and revelatory role in Roman Catholicism, and so has the president of the Council of Apostles within Mormonism. One of the most fascinating themes in Seventh-day Adventism is how this movement used Ellen G. White to serve the ends of a religion that came to symbolize obedience and good order, not enthusiasm and ecstasy. I can only hint at some of that story here.

Very early, the leaders of the church stressed that all Adventist doctrines rested on the authority of scripture, not revelations given by Ellen G. White. Of course her visions, which were indeed largely pastoral, served over and over again to settle major conflicts about what the scriptures meant. In effect White certified and confirmed doctrines that she rarely originated, at least in the early, formative years. In this sense she was very convenient so long as the dominant ministers were able to control her. They did not always control her. She quickly developed a popular constituency in the movement and in her later years, after the death of her husband, took plenty of initiatives on her own, not without opposition and controversy. But in the critical early years her husband exerted a powerful, constraining role over Ellen G. White, not just in helping shape her beliefs but, as a publisher, in the way he chose to announce her visions and in the literary form they took. In a sense she functioned as an Adventist pope, at least for those who accepted her prophetic claim. Her writings eventually gained enormous status within Seventh-day Adventism. Her initiating role was most significant in areas such as hygiene and health, but even here she had the guidance of a group of able physicians and health reformers and drew her ideas from the broader literature of health reform available to her.

In most respects Ellen G. White reflected a needed restraint. Unlike Joseph Smith and Mary Baker Eddy, she did not write any new scriptures. She did lend special authority to her gloss or interpretation of key biblical texts. Other biblical commentators had no compelling reason to accept her interpretation, and here is where her claim to divine direction was critical. Seventh-day Adventists thus have something close to a divine sanction for what many outsiders see as highly speculative interpretations of biblical texts, particularly in Daniel and Revelation. One of White's weaknesses was her propensity to assume the prophetic role too often. Her detailed visions in one of a series of books she wrote on the Bible, *Patriarchs and Prophets*, added a personal gloss to the Genesis account of origins. She defended seven quite literal days of creation, which was consistent with her Sabbatarian emphasis. She also accounted for present geological formations on the basis of the destruction wrought by Noah's flood and by the erosive effects of a great wind that followed it. This gloss, if accepted as inspired, committed Seventh-day Adventists to one form of flood geology, or a position that so filled out scriptural accounts as to leave modern Adventists with almost no interpretive space. Thus Adventists led the way in endorsing a young earth, a literal six-day creation, and a major role for Noah's flood, or the creationism of the twentieth century. Her continuing prophecies, some full of questionable historical judgments and some clearly copied from unacknowledged sources (perhaps innocently), also meant in time a lowered respect for purportedly inspired "testimonies," which eventually filled nine volumes. Like constitutions, prophetic teachings work best if they remain relatively brief and focus on critical issues.

Exclusivity is critical to the conservative use of prophecy. Adventists, without any formal decisions, soon moved to a clear consensus. On issues affecting the church as a whole, Ellen G. White spoke with special authority. Adventists chose not to institutionalize her role (unlike the Mormons), and thus she was the first and only seer of the movement. This did not mean—could not mean—that only Ellen G. White could enjoy the gift of prophecy. After all, Hiram Edson gained the sanctuary doctrine through a vision, and other people in the movement claimed visions of their own. But the few men who dominated the movement were quick to deny authority to some young women who later claimed prophetic powers like those of Ellen G. White. Of course, individuals could have visions, learn from them, or apply their lessons to their own lives. But they could not instruct the church as a whole. No one wrote this down, but it early became a working agreement within the movement. In time the gifts of the Spirit became less and less central to the life of the sect. That is, healing, glossolalia, and prophecy declined as an aspect of personal devotion or public worship, until today they are extremely rare, although, being scriptural, no church can condemn them completely. According to its latest statement of belief (1980), the Seventh-day Adventist Church still affirms the gifts of the Spirit as enumerated by Paul, but it stresses only prophecy, attests to its role in the ministry of Ellen G. White, and does not even mention tongues or healing.

The final body of distinctive Seventh-day Adventist doctrines involves hygiene and health. But they developed slowly and became central to the movement only after the embryonic Sabbatarian Adventist movement had matured into an organized denomination.

THE SEVENTH-DAY ADVENTIST CHURCH

James V. White contributed most to the organization of a new denomination. White hailed from Maine, where he became a schoolteacher. He was one of the better-educated early Adventists. At age fifteen he experienced conversion and joined a Christian (Connection) congregation, further demonstrating the critical importance of this restoration sect in the development of American Adventism. His family helped woo him to Adventism by 1841. Very quickly he decided to commit his life to the cause and had become an effective preacher by 1843, accepting ordination in his own Christian church. He suffered through the Great Disappointment but remained committed to the advent cause. When he married Ellen G. Harmon in 1846, he was almost penniless, and she was often ill. Despite this and the burden of several children, the two became an inseparable ministerial team.

As late as 1850 the Sabbatarian Adventists probably numbered no more than 300. The expansion then began, as Bates and the Whites stepped up their active evangelism, not just among former Millerites (as suggested by the shut-door doctrine), but among all Christians. In 1850 they did not have a single meetinghouse. This meant, for a few years, a rather unique ministry based on widespread travels to meet with friendly folk or to hold outdoor meetings or services in rented or borrowed buildings, joined with an early and active publishing effort. Institutionally the Seventh-day Adventist Church began largely as a small publishing empire, which matured into a denomination.

James White began his editorial career with a single leaflet in 1846 but followed this with a pamphlet in 1847. In 1848 a few Sabbatarian Adventists, meeting in informal conferences, agreed to sponsor a periodical, led as usual to such a decision by a timely vision from Ellen G. White. James White agreed to edit it and published the first number of *Present Truth* in Connecticut in 1849 (the periodical subsequently moved frequently with the Whites). It became the primary contact with scattered Adventists of like mind, who sent letters, and the major medium for bringing the Sabbatarian message to those already sympathetic with Adventism. As a deliberate policy, for the next several years James White used only scripture, not the visions of his wife, to support the movement's doctrines. Meanwhile he published tracts and, in 1849, the first hymnbook.

In 1850, in Maine, James White launched a second journal, *Second Advent Review and Sabbath Herald*. This became the most important publication in the movement and has continued to the present, although in 1851 it became *The Advent Review and Sabbath Herald*, with subsequent shifts in the exact title. In 1852 White purchased a printing press for what became the nucleus of a central headquarters in Rochester, New York. With this asset White expanded his repertoire of tracts, pamphlets, and small books and began selling his publications to help pay costs. By 1852 at least fifteen ministers were at work, most as itinerants. Some very talented young men had joined the founding triumvirate, most critically John Nevin Andrews and Uriah Smith. Slowly the strength of the movement had shifted to the Midwest. Thus in 1855, after earlier visits, the Whites moved to Battle Creek, Michigan, the new capital of Adventism and later the center of a booming cereal industry that originated in Adventist health beliefs. Local supporters provided a permanent home for the presses and Adventists built their first meetinghouse. Within a few years the growing publishing house was the largest employer in Battle Creek and, for most believers, the only institutional manifestation of the church.

After the relocation to Battle Creek, the movement grew slowly each year, with perhaps 3,000 members by the Civil War. But it remained a somewhat ephemeral movement with no formal organization. James White, at the center and in desperate need of financial support, worked consistently for some type of denominational structure and for some way of licensing or certifying ministers. He faced immense resistance, for many of the ministers identified denominational organizations and their associated wealth and luxury with the great apostasy. Thus a loosely organized group of ministers slowly backed into a denominational structure. In 1859 they voted for a new plan of support (not quite a tithe, but systematic giving) to support ministers. In 1860 a general conference approved an incorporated publishing house and, in the debates over it, chose a name for their movement, the Seventh-day Adventist Publishing Association. In 1861 the Michigan congregations (the most numerous of all) formed a state conference and in a sense began certifying acceptable member congregations and ministers. It in turn issued a call for a general conference, which met in 1863 with delegates from six states. It approved a short constitution for a continuing organization, or what amounted to a republican or presbyterian plan for a denomination. It was the only ex-Millerite denomination to adopt such a degree of centralized control and direction.

By the time of this formal organization, the movement was deeply involved in issues of health and hygiene. In a sense Adventism was a daughter of abstemious living. Bates had been a leading temperance reformer in New England. Alcoholic beverages were anathema for Adventists from the beginning, and even in the struggling 1850s Sabbatarian Adventists, guided by a prophecy from Ellen G. White, launched a crusade against tobacco. She had also gained new insights about diet and dress but did not as yet make these a test of fellowship. She used a popular water therapy to treat her own children. Her developing ideas came to a head during the Civil War. Ellen read extensively in the vast and diverse literature on diet and hygiene. Theories competed, and various reformers had their prescriptions for health. From these influences and from a continuing series of visions, particularly one in 1863, she worked out her own regimen and began a series of health publications.

White condemned meats (the stricture had little effect on many Adventists, and she herself did not always follow it), coffee and tea, and excessive amounts of food (she recommended only two meals a day). But her work ranged far beyond restrictions and encompassed rules for child care and dress reform (she tried to get Adventist women to accept simple and unrestrictive clothing, with pants or bloomers under a modest skirt), guidelines for cleanliness, an early crusade against all the purported evils of masturbation, and above all a type of hydropathic therapy (water cures that involved no drugs). After 1868 even the opening of carefully planned Adventist camp meetings in part reflected her beliefs in the healthful benefits of the open air. In 1864, when James White suffered an apparent stroke, he and his wife visited, for the first of two times, the famous health institute in Danville, New York, directed by James Caleb Jackson, who made famous a type of water therapy. Here they gained inspiration for similar efforts to cure disease and found reinforcement for their distrust of most contemporary physicians and their medications.

In 1866 Ellen G. White persuaded the General Conference to establish the first institution for the "rational" treatment of sickness, the Western Health Reform Institute. This attracted to Battle Creek a growing number of committed but often poorly trained Adventist health care workers. Early "physicians," including one woman, either trained with Jackson in Danville or eventually gained an M.D. from one of the many inadequate medical schools that existed all over the country. The first well-trained and innovative physician was John Harvey Kellogg, who at age twenty-four became head of the institute in 1876, after the Whites helped him gain his M.D. from demanding medical schools. Kellogg was one of several members of his family who were leaders in early Adventism in Michigan, but he later broke with the church leadership in 1907. John Harvey Kellogg helped perfect a method of turning cooked grains into dry flakes but for a time opposed any commercial exploitation of such cereals. Not so his entrepreneurial brother, Will Keith Kellogg, who eventually built a cereal empire in Battle Creek, as did C. W. Post, one of the patients at John Harvey's famous sanatorium. After completing his degree in orthodox medicine, John Harvey Kellogg helped expand the early institute into a huge

Adventist sanatorium, one of the largest and most influential in the United States, and treated what seemed like practically every famous American. In 1895 he began a medical missionary college in Chicago to train Adventist physicians. When Kellogg left the church in 1907, taking with him the college, the General Conference decided to build a new medical college in Loma Linda, California. Eventually the church assembled a national system of hospitals. In time Adventist water cures blended with more orthodox medicine, but even to this day Adventist health care workers of all types retain a special dedication to proper diet and a commitment to preventive medicine (most remain vegetarians and exclude coffee and tobacco). In this sense they retain some of the earlier flavor of White and Kellogg.

By 1880 all Adventist doctrines and practices were in place. The denomination had an enduring identity. From its Battle Creek headquarters it was able to expand rapidly. The great organizer and builder James White died in 1881. In a sense this freed Ellen G. White for a more active leadership role, but one more often challenged and controversial. In 1888 she published the final version of her most important book, in a sense the great epic of Adventism, *The Great Controversy*. It reflected the mature, somewhat systematized doctrines of her church and placed these in the context of a vast history, stretching from the fall of Jerusalem in 70 C.E. to the end of the millennial age and the restoration of a new Jerusalem on a cleansed earth. Her role and her books helped make White one of the three most influential prophets in American religious history (joined by Joseph Smith and Mary Baker Eddy). She died in California in 1915 at age eighty-eight.

White remains, for the historian, a puzzling person. Except for substantiated examples of plagiarism, she was never involved in the types of scandals that plagued Joseph Smith and Mary Baker Eddy. Few have challenged her character or integrity, although she developed plenty of enemies within the church, some of whom found her dictatorial or high-handed. Her writings reveal a becoming tenderness or softness. Even when most apocalyptic or most harsh in her judgments of the apostasies and the moral lapses of the modern age, she still emphasized a God of love and at times was much more generous than her colleagues in her overtures to other Christians. In fact, one largely devotional book, *Steps to Christ* (1892), the one best used by the church in its outreach to evangelicals, is mediational and inspiring and assumes a generalized, Arminian scheme of salvation that seems very close in spirit to the outlook of John Wesley.

After the death of her husband, Ellen G. White demonstrated considerable political skills. She very much missed his writing and editorial skills, which had helped shape her earlier publications. In a personal sense, one of her sons eventually assumed some of the roles of her husband. In her later years she turned to younger assistants to help her in her writing. They were responsible for the final literary form taken by her testimonies and books. Some of the most extensive copying of passages from other texts dates from these later publications. She had, if anything, even more influence in these later years. At times of controversy in the church or of difficult new decisions, her will generally prevailed. Yet she never tried to gain the type of direct control exercised by Smith and Eddy. For years she worked dutifully in the mission field and only occasionally intervened, when she had to, in the management of the American church. In a sense, she became a captive to her prophetic role. Adventists found inspiration in her most casual writings, and she was burdened to defend the authority of almost all her testimonies, even those that ranged broadly into topics on which she was ill informed or naive. She freely borrowed ideas and in fact almost had to in order to write on some topics. She did not have the originality of Eddy, even as she had little of her megalomania. She left her church a mixed legacy. Its members are, today, still involved in the task of sorting out their understanding of her role. Some Adventists read her writings as if they were scripture. Others try to distinguish the gems of inspired wisdom from the clearly personal and fallible. Some want to honor her contributions but deny to her any divine inspiration.

Long before White's death in 1915, the church suffered major divisions or tensions, some of which remain today and some of which involved her own prophetic role. Space does not permit a clarification of all these conflicts, such as that between an avowedly noncreedal church but one with a quite detailed statement of belief; between a voluntaristic sect and yet one with a very powerful central bureaucracy; between a church with certain radical commitments (vegetarianism, pacifism, a complete separation of church and state) and a well-ordered and conservative leadership; between a nominally charismatic church (tied to the visions of Ellen G. White) and one, in fact, very much committed to good order and to what often seemed a near-legalistic approach to salvation; between a church with a strong separatist heritage (reflected in its large system of parochial schools and colleges and universities) and yet a church with its network of modern hospitals and with one of the largest and most sophisticated publication and broadcast empires in the world; between a church still largely financed and governed by Americans, but one in which 90 percent of membership is outside the United States, most in the third world (images of religious colonialism).

One tension that has been most basic and enduring involves Seventh-day Adventist identity. The movement had its roots in Millerism and thus in early nineteenth-century evangelism (a commitment to a crisis rebirth, to an affecting spiritual life, to moral purity, and to mission outreach). These evangelical characteristics remained a part of Adventism and are most evident in its worship services, in its modes of baptism and celebration of the Lord's Supper, and in the format of its Sabbath schools. Yet, by the 1880s the church had established its quite distinctive doctrines and had struggled to defend them against all other Christians. For most Protestants its sanctuary doctrine was speculative and strained, its corporealism dangerous, its sabbatarianism quirky and scripturally unjustified, its health regime attractive but legalistic and divisive, and the special role attributed to Ellen G. White blasphemous. Taken collectively, these "strange" beliefs seemed to set it apart radically from mainstream evangelicalism. As a minority fighting to establish its legitimacy, it is no wonder that most of the effort of Adventist ministers had been devoted to the defense of these special doctrines. Its Jewish continuities and its emphasis on obedience to all the commandments seemed to bespeak a very legalistic form of Christianity in which faith and grace were secondary. Ellen G. White sensed this in 1888 and gave her support to younger ministers who wished to emphasize salvation as a gift, with faith taking precedence over works (a position they called "righteousness by faith").

To the extent that this emphasis on faith prevailed, and it has had a recurrent restatement within the denomination, Adventists moved closer to conservative Methodists and Baptists. In its present statement of beliefs, the Seventh-day Adventist Church affirms a rather unexceptional but Arminian plan of salvation. Other evangelicals have to accept its members as authentic, born-again Christians, for all its distinctive doctrines involve practices and expectations, not salvation itself. Some Adventists have even been influenced by the holiness movement and have tried to incorporate some type of second-step sanctification into the movement. Such trends have led to a greater consciousness of overlap and commonality with conservative Protestantism, or in the twentieth century have provided links to, and some instructive dialogue with, the leaders of fundamentalist and evangelical sects. This convergence was furthered by the decision of Ellen G. White and by later denominational leaders to repudiate the early and openly Arian view of the Trinity. The very active Adventist opposition to Darwinism, and the key role of Adventist George McCready Price in the twentieth-century creationist movement, also helped build bridges to fundamentalists. Yet, convergent trends seemed to threaten Adventist identity and usually produced countermovements in behalf of such distinctive and offsetting doctrines as that of the sanctuary, which has remained an internal source of criticism or revision.

The tensions did not necessarily impede growth. They allowed various people to find what they wanted in Adventism. So far, the leadership of the denomination has been able to avoid significant schisms. The only one that led to an enduring sect came early; in 1858 some Sabbatarian Adventists who denied the prophetic role of Ellen G. White formed a separate but still tiny denomination, the Church of God (Seventh Day). In 1937 Herbert W. Armstrong, a successful radio minister within this small sect, embraced the idea that Anglo-Saxons made up the lost tribes of Israel and formed a new sect, the Worldwide Church of God. It was Sabbatarian and supported more Jewish continuities than Seventh-day Adventists. After Armstrong's death in 1986, his successor led this denomination back toward evangelical orthodoxy. But as it repudiated most of Armstrong's distinctive doctrines, such as Anglo-Israelism and a Mormon-like conception of plural deities, it lost a majority of its members to two splinter factions.

Until 1900 the Seventh-day Adventist Church remained a small sect, with only 63,000 members in the United States. But it was already more strongly committed to missions than any other American denomination. In the years after 1865 it first devoted its limited resources to westward expansion and soon had strong churches in California and Washington. Today the Pacific Coast has the largest membership of any region in the United States. By the 1870s, Adventists were very successful in converting recent midwestern immigrants from Scandinavia and Germany. This led to ethnic congregations and new, European-language periodicals. In turn these ethnic converts carried the faith back to Europe. By its own initiative, a small Swiss congregation had affiliated with American Adventists in the 1880s and subsequently provided a mission base for converts in Germany and other countries. In 1885 the General Conference decided to launch a mission to Australia and New Zealand. It proved very successful, and as missionaries traveled down under, they successfully proselytized the islands of the South Pacific. They converted the entire population of Pitcairn Island and in 1890 launched a mission ship, the *Pitcairn*, to win Polynesian converts. Today, Seventh-day Adventism joins Mormonism as the strongest American-based denomination in the islands and possibly also in Australia and New Zealand. The General Conference first sent missionaries to South America in 1887, to Hong Kong and China in 1888, to Turkey in 1889, to blacks in the American South in 1893, and to black Africa in 1894.

The missions were costly. The denomination at times faced bankruptcy and had to depend on various money-raising schemes as well as a highly sanctioned tithe by members. Although growth was slow at first, the church gradually learned how to expand successfully, and it made the needed commitment. Early missionaries held tent or camp revivals, began a publishing operation, set up schools and eventually colleges, recruited native leaders, and in time established sanatoriums and hospitals. The top leadership actively supported the missions; Ellen G. White spent much of two years in Europe and nine years in Australia and New Zealand. Several presidents of the General Conference had mission experience, which in turn helped create a quite cosmopolitan hierarchy by 1920. By 1926 its foreign membership exceeded that in North America, and today its African membership exceeds that on any other continent. Since 1960 the growth rate has been low in Europe and Australia, as well as in America, but high in most third world countries. Seventh-day Adventist congregations exist in almost every member country of the United Nations.

In the 1890s the church faced more than its share of crises, which continued into the new century and for a decade retarded its growth. Doctrinal controversies, particularly over faith righteousness, ballooned and for a time threatened schism. The main publishing plant in Battle Creek had to do contract work to help fund its operations, and then it burned in 1902. Earlier in the same year the huge, famous Kellogg sanatorium burned. By most accounts the qualifications of ministers were falling, and few received much training. To the despair of Ellen G. White and others, the church was overly clannish, with too many members clustering around strong churches in Battle Creek or Los Angeles (White lived in California). One senses that a small group of leaders, most with extensive foreign experience, were increasingly embarrassed by their home congregations. Their efforts at reform were early intimations of a sect that was ready to assume the role of a conservative church. It did this over the next thirty years.

Ellen G. White returned from Australia in 1901. She supported a major reorganization of the church bureaucracy and in 1903 helped encourage the move of the main denominational facilities. The church had already supported a few missions in large cities, some tied to health outreach, and thus sought an urban location for its headquarters. It almost selected a site near New York City but eventually chose a location largely in Takoma Park, Maryland, but on the border of the District of Columbia. Here, after 1903 and as soon as it could make the move, it established a new sanatorium, a new college (Columbia Union), and just over the district line its General Conference headquarters and a new publishing house.

This move coincided with the most publicized controversy in denominational history, between White and loyal denominational leaders on one side, and John Harvey Kellogg and his supporters on the other. Kellogg had built a medical empire largely under his control. After the fire in 1902 he rebuilt the Battle Creek sanatorium, even as Ellen G. White wanted to replace one large institution with a group of small sanatoriums all around the country (most of these, in time, became hospitals). In 1901 a new General Conference president (the most influential in the denomination's history), Arthur Daniells, was determined to bring the health institutions completely under the control of the church, and this meant an inevitable power struggle with Kellogg. Daniells was a personal friend of White and had served with her in Australia. Kellogg was not only suspect because of his independence but because he had accepted and tried to publish some theological views that bordered on pantheism. In the midst of his struggles with Daniells, he turned against many of the clergy, openly questioned the inspiration of many of White's testimonies, and created a crisis. Daniells won, brought the medical institutions under direct church control, and left an infuriated Kellogg in rebellion. His congregation in Battle Creek expelled him in 1907, but well before this he led a dissident faction, including many of the ablest Adventist physicians, that challenged the church at every opportunity over the next decade. In many ways this was a sad divorce, because Kellogg, more than anyone else, had created the medical assets of the denomination and had been an early and close associate of the Whites. As one effect of this battle, those in the church who had most valued Ellen G. White's prophetic teaching were now in the ascendancy. This so enhanced her status and role as to make acceptance of her testimonies almost a condition of fellowship.

Adventism is unique among American denominations because of the role of its medical institutions and thus because of the legacy of Kellogg and other early reformers. Today many of its hospitals in a network of 148 (43 in the United States) are in financial trouble because of intense competition and, in the United States, new federal regulations. Many may not survive, and others already reflect less overt ties to the denomination. Most Adventist physicians and nurses resemble those outside the church, and physicians attached to the hospitals maintain a private practice. The old sanatoriums have gone, replaced by special efforts in health education. Hospital chaplains, almost alone, attend to the avowed spiritual mission of such institutions.

By World War I the tightly organized church was well primed for its period of most rapid growth. The tensions remained, as they remain today. But the church had the institutional strength to control them. In the 1910s the worldwide membership of the church increased dramatically, from 104,000 to 185,000. The centralization of power in the growing bureaucracy at conference headquarters led to new controversies in the 1920s and to the apostasy of some able ministers. Efforts to define conclusively the role of Ellen G. White failed, leaving that issue unresolved, as it remains unresolved today. In a sense the White legacy became institutionalized in the Ellen G. White Estate, with its special archives and a growing hagiography, yet with an increasing body of able Adventist scholars who have forced even the most loyal White supporters to admit some faults or mistakes on her part. These controversies, which continue, also illustrated the inevitable effect of academic success as Adventist colleges sought and gained regional accreditation, as the church became home to a much larger circle of intellectuals, and as more ministers completed training at the denominational seminary (at first at Takoma Park and now at Andrews University in Berrien Springs, Michigan). Still a very conservative denomination, highly resistant to certain forms of critical biblical scholarship and to Darwinism, it nonetheless has clear liberal and conservative factions. In most respects it now faces the same problems as mainline churches.

The role of women best illustrates developing tensions. Women have increasingly demanded leadership roles, particularly in North America and in Europe. In 1881 the General Conference approved the ordination of women, which was only consistent with the growing role of Ellen G. White. But apparently no one ever implemented this vote, and White never assumed the status of an ordained minister. The issue of ordination first came before the modern General Conference in 1968, with a request from Finland for the right to ordain a woman minister. In 1984 the General Conference gave to the eleven world divisions permission to ordain women as elders if a division so chose (it was clear that the demand came primarily from North America and Europe). Over 1,000 women now serve as elders in the North American division. In 1990 the General Conference voted to allow divisions to dedicate women as commissioned ministers, able to perform all the duties of pastors, but without ordination. In North America and Scandinavia several such women serve as pastors of congregations. Finally, in 1995, in a widely publicized action, a congregation located next to the world headquarters in Maryland ordained a woman minister but without any legal authority to do so from the General Conference.

The issue of women's ordination almost dominated the General Conference in the Netherlands in July 1995. This large conference, or world congress, carefully organized with the aid of the latest computer networks, had to decide on a resolution from the North American division, asking that each world division have the right, if it so desired, to ordain women. The most determined opposition came from third world divisions. In a tense meeting a former dean of the theological seminary at Andrews University defended the resolution, and a present professor marshaled strong biblical opposition based primarily on the New Testament epistles attributed to Paul. Hundreds lined up at the pro and con microphones, but time allowed only a small percentage to speak. Never before had so many delegates tried to participate. The vote was 673 for the resolution, 1,481 opposed, or only a slightly smaller percentage opposed than for a closely related vote in 1990. This vote is unlikely to settle the controversy. But in what seemed a deliberate gesture to the losers in the vote, the same conference passed strong resolutions on women's rights, committed new efforts to gaining literacy for third world women, and passed a very strong resolution on the equality of all people. Within the last few years an increasing number of women have moved into divisional committees or into higher administrative positions.

Throughout its history the one constant in Adventism has been growth, but today that is occurring primarily in the third world. In the United States, membership is around 850,000 and almost stable, but this joins an estimated 7.8 million abroad (as of late 1995). The Church has enjoyed an increase of over 1 million new members since 1992. It is outwardly prosperous. It was able, after the dislocations of World War II, to regain organizational control, except in China, but still faces enormous challenges in fully empowering its third world members as well as females, who do not have anything close to proportionate representation in the central offices of the church. It is worth noting that no other American-based denomination has ever attempted to transform itself so fully into a worldwide fellowship. No other American-based denomination has turned so fully to modern communications technology, including the use of the Internet.

After such a cursory institutional history, a return to doctrine is in order. This is where it all started, and in their distinctive beliefs Seventh-day Adventists have remained firm. In spite of 150 years of waiting since 1844, they still look forward to the early advent of Jesus. Perhaps the hope, among many, is less central and vital. How could it be otherwise? But officially they affirm the scenario of last things sketched in Revelation 20–21, possibly the most important part of the Bible for them. Not that the scenario is completely clear or that all Adventists agree on exact details. They all look to the second coming, to the resurrection of the righteous at that time to join Jesus in a heavenly kingdom and to help him in his subsequent judgment of the rest of humankind. They have had problems with the 144,000 living saints mentioned in Revelation 14, problems that became more acute when their membership soared into the millions. Yet, some conservative Adventists still believe that only 144,000 saints will join Jesus at his return. Unlike almost all other Christians, they believe that the saints will live in a heavenly kingdom during the thousand years. At the advent, Jesus will destroy the ungodly, leaving the earth desolate and unpopulated, except for Satan and his demons, who will, in a sense, remain in captivity on this savaged planet.

At the end of this heavenly millennium, Jesus and the saints will indeed return to this earth to establish an enduring kingdom. The New Jerusalem will descend from the heavens to be the new world capital, and Jesus will be king. At this point the remaining dead will come back to life to face a final judgment. Since they are among the unrighteous, and doomed, the judgment of them involves proportionate punishment for the sins of their life on earth. At the end of the thousand years, Satan is again free to pursue his rebellion, and from the newly resurrected he gathers an army to do battle with Jesus and the saints. His forces lay siege to the New Jerusalem. But the glory of Jesus on his throne immobilizes the army, and a divine fire consumes Satan, his angels, and his army of rebellious humans, even as it cleans and purifies the earth. This is the final death of the unjust. The saints live forever on this perfected earth, in a divine utopia. Faithful Seventh-day Adventists still nourish this vision of last things and are confident that they will rise to meet Jesus, should he come before they die, or be among those who experience the first resurrection, should they die before the advent. They know that they are worthy of this if they are children of faith and obedient to God's commandments, with Sabbath observance a critical witness of such faith. In this set of beliefs they seem very close to the Christians Paul addressed in Thessalonica in the early days of Christianity, and close to the apocalyptic expectations of Jesus and his disciples.

CHARLES TAZE RUSSELL'S BIBLE STUDENT MOVEMENT

Even as the young Seventh-day Adventist Church struggled to establish its own identity, another related but completely separate apocalyptic movement had its beginnings. The present-day Jehovah's Witnesses now claim to be the second largest apocalyptic sect in America (behind the Mormons). By their own careful and strict assessment of membership, they are domestically slightly larger than the Seventh-day Adventists, with over 800,000 members in the United States (they have fewer non-American members, but still an impressive 4 million). In some Latin American countries they probably make up the largest non-Catholic denomination; their most successful proselytizing has been in preponderantly Roman Catholic areas of the world (40 percent of all Jehovah's Witnesses today). They have won converts among Buddhists in Japan, but very few in Islamic and Hindu countries. In parts of Africa they are the largest Christian sect.

The first phase of what became the modern Jehovah's Witnesses lasted from around 1870 to World War I. This was the period dominated by the founding prophet, Charles Taze Russell. Since 1916 the movement has continued to affirm most, but not all, of his unique biblical teachings and in most respects has become more sectarian, more separatist, and culturally more isolated. This pattern reverses that of Seventh-day Adventists.

Russell, the founding prophet, was born in Pittsburgh in 1852 and grew up as a Presbyterian. As a teenager he first heard the advent message in an Advent Christian congregation. The deep dark secrets of biblical prophecy immediately absorbed him and led him into intensive biblical study (compare with William Miller). He was blessed with wealth, derived from a family dry goods company, and devoted all of his worldly goods to what soon became his unique advent ministry. Not a trained scholar, he yet read widely and became a rather knowledgeable consumer of biblical scholarship (much more sophisticated than William Miller), including some of the most daring criticism of the nineteenth century.

As he developed his own distinctive beliefs, Russell borrowed widely from Adventist sources. He honored Miller for what he attempted but faulted his scholarship and thus his chronology. He knew about the English Irvinites and adopted several beliefs that paralleled those of John Nelson Darby, the English dispensationalist and founder of the Plymouth Brethren. He first learned the doctrine of soul rest from the same Adventist who taught Joseph Bates, or George Storrs, who in the post–Civil War years remained a leader in a very small, post-Millerite sect, the Life and Advent Union (it had only four remaining congregations in 1950). Storrs eventually left this denomination because of his developing belief in a second chance of salvation for all resurrected people during the millennium, or what became a key doctrine of Russell's. Notably, Russell was never greatly influenced by the Seventh-day Adventists. He did not adopt their Sabbath worship, sanctuary doctrine, or health theories (he did condemn tobacco but not meat or moderate amounts of alcoholic beverages).

Russell, while still a teenager, began in 1870 to gather friends for intensive Bible study. Within a few years such local study groups became, in effect, an emergent new denomination. In 1875 Russell published his first prophetic book (on the manner of Jesus' return to earth). In 1876 he briefly joined forces with another Adventist, Nelson H. Barbour, who had already established a periodical to expound his earlier views that Jesus would return in 1874, but which Barbour subsequently interpreted to be an invisible presence. This doctrine would inform and in many ways complicate doctrinal developments within Russell's emergent movement. From Barbour, Russell gained a way of understanding the three great periods of world history and the ages within each. This method involved a parallelism between the life and ministry of the Christ and the various ages of the gospel dispensation that followed. This led Barbour and Russell to conclude that the spiritual presence of 1874 would lead in 1878 to the final rapture of the living saints and the beginning of a millennial age. The two published a book with these prophecies, but after disappointment in 1878 they parted, with Russell working out another ingenious explanation of what had happened in 1878.

To promote his interpretations Russell founded a new periodical in 1879, *Zion's Watch Tower and Herald of Christ's Presence* (today *The Watchtower*). Within eight years he was publishing over 4 million copies of this magazine every two weeks. In 1884 at his home in Allegheny, Pennsylvania, he incorporated a publishing society, the Zion's Watch Tower Bible and Tract Society (he soon dropped the word "Zion"), or what remained throughout Russell's life the only formal organization of his new sect. Just after 1900 he moved the publishing aspects of this society to the present denominational home, on the East River in Brooklyn, and incorporated a printing and publishing corporation under New York law, but with the same title.

By 1886 Russell was ready to announce his doctrines to the world and did so in the first of what eventually became a six-volume work, *Studies in the Scriptures*. In his first volume, called *The Plan of the Ages*, he presented what remain his most distinctive doctrines and an outline of world history. Without exploring the nuances or the complexities of his chronology, it is possible to summarize some of his major beliefs. Most of them still guide contemporary Jehovah's Witnesses, and in total they constitute what might be called an apocalyptic form of unitarianism and universalism.

Russell affirmed the central doctrines of American Adventists: corporealism and soul sleep; the literal resurrection of people to live in a new earthly kingdom; death, not eternal torment, as the wage of sin (no hell); and the early return of the Christ to establish his kingdom during a millennial age. To this, Russell added an Arian conception of Christ as Logos (he was God's first creation, known as the archangel Michael before his incarnation, and higher in the order of creation than the rebellious archangel Lucifer). This Logos chose to become a human; Jesus was in all ways a man and not a god (thus Russell affirmed the traditional unitarian belief in a fully unitary god and in a human Jesus). The Holy Spirit was not a person but the power and energy of God.

Russell was equally distinctive among Adventists for his near universalism. He was an irenic man, sure of the apostasy of most conventional Christianity but never harsh in his evaluations of other Christians. He rejected Calvinism because of its perceived harshness and always proclaimed a god of love. He always accepted the Arminian belief that Jesus died for all, that his atonement was complete, a ransom for all people. He argued that such a god would not condemn people to a final death after the resurrection without giving them a final, and fairer, chance to love and obey him. This was particularly necessary if God was to deal justly with the billions of people who never had a chance to hear the gospel.

Russell wrote at great length about the millennial age, a thousand years when Jesus would rule directly on earth after he had crushed the existing

Gentile nations. During this thousand-year period various people in their graves would awaken to new life, with the most deserving awakening first (among the first would be the great men of Israel). After the awakening, these humans would have a long period in which to inform themselves about the truth, to repent of sins, and to become humble and obedient. As he described the process of careful education of former sinners, often by members of their beloved family, it seems hard to believe any would reject the Christ, making Russell's position very close to that of Universalist restorationists. Only those humans who, after all the enlightening instruction, still rejected Jesus would suffer extinction or a second and final death (Russell's extreme freewill beliefs required that everyone retain the power to reject the Christ, although it is difficult to comprehend why any would have the will). After 1916, Jehovah's Witnesses would at times qualify this irenic universalism, but the second-chance doctrine is still normative among Witnesses. They may vary in their expectations about who and how many will enjoy a resurrection during the millennium, or how many of these will accept the Christ during this age (Russell's successor at times seemed to suggest that most of the clergy in the existing churches and the great rulers of the world would continue their rebellion), but all will at least have another chance.

The other distinctive doctrines of Russell either involved his attempts to chart future events or his unique beliefs concerning the church. In a sense, and in ways he perhaps could never admit, his early involvement with Barbour and his commitments to 1874 and 1878 as special times that began the millennium placed Russell in a bind. He never formally rejected the significance of these invisible events. Using Jesus' ministry as a guide, Russell interpreted 1874 as the beginning of Jesus' second ministration to the world (he was invisibly present) and 1878 as the time of his final judgment on the world (parallel to his earlier crucifixion). Russell further believed that in 1881 the gathered church was complete (144,000 called members from the time of Jesus to the present), but the door for membership was not finally closed because of the likely apostasy of church members living at that time. Finally, based on the time between the resurrection and the fall of the temple, Russell believed that the work of Jesus in his warfare against the powers of the world (Babylon) would be complete by 1914, and in that year, or close to it, the millennial age ruled by Jesus in the flesh would begin. This scenario was not inflexible, and in time Russell shifted some of his emphases. After his death the movement all but ignored the three early dates, but it could not evade the prediction about 1914, which became almost as important to Bible Students as had Miller's prediction about 1843.

Interwoven with the ever-more-elaborate chronology and the increasing complexity of events that inaugurated the millennium was Russell's concept of the church. Long before his death this led him to affirm what amounted to two classes of Christians. Like many other earlier Adventists, he interpreted references in Revelation to mean that the Body of Christ, the Church, would be made up of only 144,000 saints. Saints already dead would arise and join Jesus in the heavens at the opening of the millennial age. Those still alive would, perhaps after the completion of their natural life, also immediately enjoy a spiritual resurrection. All 144,000 would then join the Christ in the instruction and eventual judgment of the rest of humankind (those who were alive when the millennium began, or all those dead who would progressively awaken to a new life). This 144,000 was a very special class of spirit-filled (or spiritually baptized) and obedient saints, fully consecrated by God not only to be his church but to gain a type of spiritual immortality that virtually incorporated them into the Christ. These saints thus had a special status in being, a status denied all other humans, including Moses, Elijah, and other ancients. The labels for this elite varied, from "elect class" to "little flock" to "bridal class." After baptism they alone were worthy to participate in what Russell called a memorial communion service, celebrated by his Students each year at the time of Passover (still the most sacred annual event for Jehovah's Witnesses and their only festival or holy day).

The small number of early Students (not more than 12,000 by 1914) meant no problem with the 144,000 limit. But Russell's belief that the 144,000 was complete by 1881 did raise perplexing problems for new converts. From then on, Russell admitted that converts, however faithful they were, might not be able to be among the 144,000. Thus, implicit in Russell's movement almost from the beginning was a dual system of rewards: a select group who alone experienced the first resurrection and an angelic status, and the great company or crowd of other reasonably faithful but spiritually unbaptized Christians, including an incalculable number of Russell's own followers. Here was the basis of a continuing and, for some, disturbing doctrine.

By his death in 1916 Russell had clarified as well as he could the two classes of Christians. It has always been tempting for Adventists, who uniformly take a moralistic, freewill, and governmental approach to salvation, and who believe in a literal earthly kingdom ruled over by Jesus, to think of both rewards and punishments in graded terms. This, among the Mormons, would lead to several gradations of rewards in a coming kingdom. For the Seventh-day Adventists it led to a concept of proportionate punishment immediately after the second resurrection. For Russellites it meant that the dead would reawaken in an order tied to their faithfulness. The awakened humans would in turn truly repent and offer full loyalty to their king at different points, with those most obedient on earth almost immediately rendering full obedience. Since only the 144,000 ever gained the full spiritual status entailed by being the Body of Christ, the great company of people, including even faithful Christians, could only gain lesser rewards. If dead, they had to await the time of their awakening sometime during the millennium, although they could expect it early. If alive at the beginning of the millennium, they did not gain the spiritual status and assured immortality of the 144,000, but instead had to live as natural humans in the new kingdom and thus were still at risk of losing their salvation by willful disobedience or by joining Satan in his final battle against the new Israel at the end of the thousand years. But for devout Bible Students this possibility of a fall from grace seemed a remote possibility, and Russell, as he matured his doctrines in the years before his death, tried to offer all possible assurance to these second-class Christians. Their rewards would be great even if short of those enjoyed by the saints fully in the Church. It is also evident from participation in communion that most of Russell's converts believed themselves to be among the 144,000. New converts could hope that they were replacements for those after 1881 who rebelled and left the church. The great memorial communions in these years involved most faithful Students.

This preponderance of the bridal class changed dramatically in the years after 1916. Eventually the sheer number of Jehovah's Witnesses made clear that only a minority could be among the 144,000. In the 1930s the leadership began to stress the great company, the majority of Witnesses who could not claim to be in the elite class. Since then the leaders have set such high standards and expectations as effectively to discourage converts from claiming spiritual baptism and from taking communion. Today in some local memorial communions no one may dare come to the table. Perhaps no more than 9,000 commune in the whole church (this includes the leadership at the top, but not necessarily elders in local congregations). Thus the doctrine of 144,000 eventually led to a church most of whose members had to accept a second-class salvation. It led to the celebration of the society's most important sacrament by a small minority, or a practice reminiscent of the medieval Eucharist performed by a few priests before a large but non-participating audience.

One other emphasis of Russell's was critical. As most Adventists, he stressed the continuity with the Jewish religion and believed the biblical promise that Jews would be first in the kingdom. Thus, when the Christ begins building his millennial kingdom on earth, it will first take the form of a restored Israel, with Jerusalem its capital. All the 144,000, plus all others who yield full obedience during the millennium, will in effect become Jews, dutiful citizens of the new Israel. In time the glory of this new Israel will attract the people of other nations, and they will capitulate to or ally with Israel and thus become a part of the messianic kingdom. These doctrines allied Russell with some early Jewish Zionists and led him, in the two years before his death and during World War I, to believe that the Jews would soon return to their homeland as a prelude to a restored Israel.

This completes the doctrinal survey. Around these doctrines Russell slowly built a new denomination quite different from other churches. His first congregations were really Bible study circles, led originally by him and then, as they spread, by loyal disciples. These were fully autonomous congregations, which eventually elected deacons and, from among their most dedicated male teachers, elders. Russell did not control the societies, but he tried to guide them through the publications of the Watch Tower Society. To this day Jehovah's Witnesses is a movement that has two basic motifs: the continuous, intensive, question-and-answer study of the Bible as guided by the Watch Tower literature, and the distribution and sale of this literature as a form of evangelism. From the earliest study circles, Russell emphasized that this was not a conventional church. It had no separate class of ministers (all Christians were ministers of the gospel). It had no creed. Legally it was an incorporated society, the only central government being the directors of the Watch Tower Bible and Tract Society, with Russell as chairman or president. In a sense the denomination was only a vast publishing operation. Local congregations varied somewhat, but the most faithful worked to distribute the literature. In Russell's time, members did not agree to specific hourly assignments, but the most obedient served as colporteurs or pilgrims, traveling locally or even at a distance to sell (or give away) the Watch Tower periodicals and tracts and Russell's many sermons and books. It was this unique evangelism plus the magnetic role of Russell (he syndicated newspaper columns) that won a trickle of converts to the Bible Student movement.

Russell died in 1916, a crisis period for his Bible Students. His carefully hedged predictions of the beginning millennial kingdom in 1914 seemed mistaken, even though the outbreak of World War I just before the October deadline led Adventists to the conclusion that Armageddon was at hand. In the disillusionment, many Bible Students defected. Russell's death led to a leadership crisis among the directors and other officers at the Brooklyn headquarters (called Bethel). After a power struggle, the directors of the society in 1917 elected a tall, forceful, at times tyrannical Missouri lawyer, Joseph F. Rutherford, as president. He slowly turned the Bible Student movement into the modern Jehovah's Witnesses.

JEHOVAH'S WITNESSES

Rutherford had scarcely set about reforming the Bible Student movement when the United States entered World War I. Under Russell the Bible

Students had joined other Adventists in a pacifist stance, and almost all the young men among them refused induction into the military. Already the Students had rejected oaths of allegiance, salutes to the flag, and even standing for the national anthem. This meant problems after 1917. Locally, mobs attacked Students. Several conscientious objectors went to jail. Finally, because Students distributed literature (written before the war) that allegedly encouraged young men to resist, and published strong antiwar statements in the Watch Tower periodicals, Federal officials arrested eight directors, led by Rutherford, under authority of the Sedition Act of 1918, and the federal courts sentenced all but one to twenty-year terms (they served nine months before they won a retrial on appeal, and the government then dropped charges). This is the only time in American history when almost all the leaders of a denomination were in jail. The imprisonment won some sympathy, as did the evident courage of Bible Students around the country, but the internal conflict, the external persecution, the imprisonment of the leadership, and the destruction of all their Brooklyn printing equipment practically destroyed the Students, with perhaps no more than 4,000 still active by 1919.

Meanwhile, those most loyal to Russell and most resistant to the soon dictatorial leadership of Rutherford, gradually left the movement during the 1920s. Out of the defectors came some surviving Russellite sects, the largest being the Dawn Bible Students Association. These small sects have retained the more irenic outlook of Russell, have kept friendly contacts with other conservative sects, and continued the loose, congregational polity of the early Bible Study societies. Today these are the only true Russellites, for out of the chaos of 1919 Rutherford built a very different religious movement, one he eventually renamed Jehovah's Witnesses.

Rutherford launched a new era with a great convention in 1919 in Los Angeles, or the first of what became a trademark of the movement. By the end of 1919, after a temporary use of presses in Pittsburgh, the leaders had begun to rebuild the Brooklyn printing facilities. Rutherford launched a second major periodical, *The Golden Age* (now *Awake*), began to emphasize home evangelism by each Student, and adopted the beguiling slogan "Millions now living will never die." He referred to the movement as the New World Society, even as he began to organize and systematize the evangelism and to push foreign missions. He organized a monitoring system for all "publishers" (a name still used for faithful Witnesses who carry out the door-to-door evangelism), which required weekly reports from each one. In time, Witnesses had to accept a weekly quota of hours (the expectation today is at least ten to twelve hours per month) spent in house-to-house work, and those who met certain standards became pioneers (about ninety hours of witnessing per month), or a level of service almost necessary for leadership roles in the society. In each region the societies worked out territorial assignments that, along with careful reports of each visit, ensured full coverage. In theory almost everyone in the world will eventually receive a visit by a Witness.

Organizationally Rutherford gradually gained central control over each congregation (they called their small, modest buildings Kingdom Halls). He abolished the elected elders, set up what amounted to district overseers, and guided the choice of leaders locally. He had trouble at first with a leader in England but soon took charge of all foreign missions, with eighteen foreign offices by 1921.

At first no major doctrines changed. In time many did, at least in importance and emphasis. Russell became less focal in the memory and respect of Witnesses. Without any formal decision the purported events of 1874 and 1878 dropped from the chronology. Even before he died, Russell offered an explanation of the seeming disappointment of 1914. Once again, invisible events took place. Jesus completed his final judgment on the Gentile nations, and World War I reflected the first result of his vengeance. As Rutherford later interpreted this climax, a great battle in the heavenly kingdom led to the expulsion of Satan and his angels to the earth, there briefly to effect all manner of mischief. Satan helped create the great new Babylon, often allied with the Vatican, which Rutherford identified as the League of Nations; after 1945 the leadership placed the same stigma on the United Nations. Thus 1914 marked the beginning of the millennial age, for at that point the dead members of the Church of 144,000 came back to life (they joined Jesus in the heavenly kingdom for the brief time before his return to earth). Jehovah's Witnesses still honor this doctrine, and many continue to believe that Jesus will return to earth finally to defeat worldly powers before the death of at least some Witnesses alive in 1914 (the leadership began to amend the meaning of generation by 1994, as if to prepare members for the death of the last survivors of 1914). Unfortunately, Rutherford tried his hand at biblical interpretation and made some influential but hedged predictions that 1925 would be the Armageddon year, leading to some enthusiasm, a flood of new converts, but another disappointment and a momentary drop in membership (there were no more than 10,000 publisher members in the United States at that time).

Under Rutherford the Bible Students became more separate, angry, and defensive. He was a class-conscious populist who hated finance capitalism, the existing churches, and above all the clergy (their attacks had helped send him to jail). Gone was the irenic stance of Russell and the last interchange between Students and even other Adventists. This small sect defiantly stood against the world. Among other consequences, it was continually caught up in legal battles. Of over forty cases concerning Jehovah's Witnesses to come before the Supreme Court, the Witnesses eventually won most, thereby expanding the personal freedoms of all Americans. In the two most famous cases, involving schoolchildren who refused to salute the flag, the denomination first lost in 1940 (*Minersville School District v. Gobitus*) but then won on the same issue (*Barnette v. West Virginia State Board of Education*) in 1943. More than any other sect, the Jehovah's Witnesses forced Americans to confront the full meaning of freedom of worship and separation of church and state and gradually won the right to evangelize door to door, to distribute or sell literature in public places even on Sunday and without a license, and to reject all symbols of allegiance to worldly powers. Later they struggled, sometimes losing, sometime winning, over the issue of blood transfusions, a procedure denounced by the society in the Rutherford era (based on a biblical prohibition of eating blood) and still a continuous source of conflict, particularly when parents refuse to allow children to have blood needed to save their lives. Fortunately the society eventually dropped early condemnations of vaccinations and of the use of aluminum pans.

In 1931, after careful consideration at the Brooklyn headquarters, Rutherford announced a name change. The awkward Bible Students would now carry a more catchy, appealing, and distinguishing label, Jehovah's Witnesses. This title soon took on doctrinal significance. Witnesses insist that they worship a specific god, not a god in general. His name is Jehovah (the English rendering of the four consonants in the Hebrew Bible, VHWH), and they even argue that the Christ died not just as a ransom for humans but as a way of vindicating the name of Jehovah. In the modern era, Witnesses have so emphasized Jehovah as to reduce the status or importance that most Christians give to Jesus.

Rutherford died in January 1942, which brought the second change of leaders at the beginning of a great world war. He had by then established a highly centralized religious organization, or what he and others in the movement referred to as a theocracy. Rutherford's strong personality may have served well to revive the movement after World War I and to keep it alive in the depression years. Yet the organization did not grow rapidly and at his death had only about 30,000 active Witnesses or publishers in the United States, but the work abroad had been increasingly successful. The extent of Witness influence was clear in the 115,000 who attended the St. Louis convention of 1942 (as in all such assemblies, many were in Witness families but not publishers). Rutherford had his own personal problems, including too much drinking, a separation from his wife tied to an almost pathological animus toward any leadership role by women, and a taste for luxury. Unlike Russell and all later leaders, Rutherford lived in mansions and drove luxury automobiles. He died in a large home in San Diego constructed with society funds under the ruse that it was to be the dwelling place of the ancient heroes of Israel, who, according to a doctrine developed by Rutherford, would be resurrected before Armageddon in order to lend their political skills to the building of the new Israel.

World War II inaugurated a great period of growth for Jehovah's Witnesses. In fact they proudly claimed, with some justification, to be the fastest-growing religious organization in the world. They grew worldwide from 115,000 in 1942 to 884,000 in 1961 and more than 1.65 million in 1972 (they claim over 5 million today). In one sense the war was a disaster. The Jehovah's Witnesses in Germany and in Nazi-occupied areas became special targets of the Nazis, as resented as Jews and Gypsies. Unfortunately the church leadership in Germany at first tried to appease the Nazis and used their World War I imprisonment to ingratiate themselves to Hitler. Nothing worked. Almost all professed Witnesses ended up in concentration camps, with most executed before the end of the war. But their plight and an increased public sympathy for the Witnesses slowly abated the worst persecution in the United States. The *Gobitus* case plus the tensions as war approached had led to a flurry of local persecutions of Witnesses in 1940 and 1941 and even local governmental efforts to suppress their church (Canada did ban it during the war years). But unlike in World War I, the attorney general tried to moderate such populistic repression, while the American Civil Liberties Union helped the Witnesses win case after case in the federal courts. At least thoughtful Americans appreciated the irony of American schools forcing little Jehovah's Witnesses to salute the flag even as hundreds of Witnesses died in German concentration camps because they refused to say "Heil Hitler."

In World War II, Witnesses who wanted to could benefit from a much more sympathetic Selective Service system. They could qualify as conscientious objectors. Most Witnesses did not want to take this option and, when so classified, refused to do alternate service. They stressed that they were not pacifists, for they would fight in Jehovah's army, and thus asked the same exemption as enjoyed by other clergy. Most local draft boards rejected this argument, at least for all but those Witnesses who had been working full time for the church, and the courts upheld them. Around 4,500 Witness youths went to jail for draft violations and often rejoiced in the opportunity to continue their witnessing to other prisoners.

At Rutherford's death the Watch Tower Society elected as president a much more mild-mannered successor, Nathan Homer Knorr. He was an organizational man, personally modest and able to work effectively with a growing staff at the Brooklyn Bethel. From a cult of personality the movement adopted something closer to a collective or bureaucratic leadership. Knorr was not a prophet or a writer and soon provided that all society publications be anonymous, meaning that a few authors at Bethel began writing the growing stream of books and periodicals, or what had become one of the largest and most efficient publishing efforts in the world (in 1983 over 53 million books and Bibles and more than 460 million periodicals, with some books still selling for only one dollar). Above all else, Knorr tried to strengthen the growing army of evangelists in its main work—witnessing along the roads and streets of America. He set up a ministry or missionary school near Ithaca, New York (later moved to Brooklyn); required each Kingdom Hall to have weekly training courses for publishers (one of five mandatory weekly services); developed an even tighter control over publishing work; required strict discipline at the congregational level (judicial committees tried and excommunicated disobedient, rebellious, or immoral Witnesses and required remaining members to ostracize those banned); and at least moderated Rutherford's outspoken hatred of other Christian denominations. In many respects he created an almost perfectly disciplined salvation army.

Knorr also inaugurated a series of great world assemblies, with 80,000 attending the first in Cleveland in 1946. These quickly expanded, with over 100,000 meeting in Nuremburg in 1955 at the site of Hitler's earlier parades and reviews. After over 250,000 people attended an assembly in New York City in 1958 (at both Yankee Stadium and the Polo Grounds), the society had to substitute smaller national or regional assemblies, dozens of which now take place each year, some with a great deal of local publicity. The Witnesses, who early owned a radio station and leased time on over 400 others, used blaring speaker systems on automobiles, and for a time even lugged around phonographs, eventually had to give up on all electronic media, in part because their virulent attacks on other Christian denominations, particularly Roman Catholics, led to FCC investigations and a voluntary withdrawal from the airwaves by Rutherford in 1937.

Knorr, in his last years, fell into the trap of his two predecessors. He came to the conclusion that Armageddon would begin in 1975. His predictions were tentative. But local Witnesses leaped at the prospect, and many made plans for life in the new kingdom. With this prophecy came a temporary relaxation of centralized control. In 1971 Knorr established an eleven-member governing body for the society (its cardinals), with a rotating chair and less power in the presidency. He also restored the old system of local elders that Rutherford had disbanded and set up a rotation among the overseers at the district and zonal level (these in effect were the synods and presbyteries of the movement). Briefly, Knorr relaxed the requirements of door-to-door witnessing, allowing more of the teaching and supportive work to take place within the congregation. But this liberalizing trend, if it was such, ended after the disappointment of 1975 and Knorr's death in 1977. His successor, Frederick W. Franz, had been a colleague and vice-president. Franz had served under Rutherford and was an eighty-four-year-old man when he assumed the presidency. He had three years of college training, had some knowledge of Hebrew, and had already taken the lead in developing a new translation of the Bible (the New World Translation, completed in 1960) that reflected Witness doctrines (they changed all references to "God" in the New Testament to "Jehovah"). Franz lived into his nineties, meaning that until Michael Henschel replaced him in 1994, the society had only four presidents in 120 years. Franz tightened the centralized control. This led to a continuous loss of members, particularly those with the most education. Converts, particularly in the third world, more than made up for defections, but since 1975 the domestic growth of the society has been modest.

Today Jehovah's Witnesses make up the most visible and most sectarian wing of apocalyptic and Adventist Christianity. Both Mormons and Seventh-day Adventists have taken a more accommodating path and today are much closer to the mainstream, in style and practices if not doctrine, than are the Witnesses. Under Franz and a conservative and aging leadership in Brooklyn, the movement resisted innovations of any type. In most of the world, as in the United States, its membership ranges from the middle to lower social and economic classes. It has almost no members from the top of society, although in some African countries Jehovah's Witnesses often rise to the top professionally. The society's demands on its publishers in developed countries are so great that many career opportunities are almost foreclosed. The hours of witnessing each week and the lengthy training and Bible study at the halls mean a high degree of isolation for Witnesses. Most social contacts are within the church. Members have no time and no inclination for involvements in the larger society. They have no social action committees, rarely become involved in charity or relief, have no political role (they do not vote or hold office), and join no secular organizations. They resist most forms of entertainment, and the leadership has even discouraged young people from attending colleges (almost none do, meaning that most college graduates and professional people in the society have been converts). When parents or young people reject this advice, most end up leaving the movement. Today the turnover is high, and the number of dissidents or defectors is growing. A few celebrities (movie stars, professional athletes, and even rock star Michael Jackson) have been Witnesses, but they have not usually remained orthodox and in good standing.

The lives of Witnesses revolve around their unique evangelism. Their time in Kingdom Hall is devoted almost entirely to preparing for this ministry. Week after week they study the same literature they must distribute and sell (approximately 3,178 pages of obligatory reading each year). Why do they do it? They have motives other than winning converts. It is their obligation, the key to obedience to God, to do this witnessing. They gain an assurance of an early resurrection in the kingdom and of eternal salvation. More than the leadership wants, some still testify to a spiritual baptism and thus claim to be in the 144,000. But whether of the elite or only the great company, they know they will share in God's work, not just converting people but in the separating and judging that is to be part of the millennium.

The growth of the movement is only half tied to the outdoor evangelism (the other half is recruitment by friends or family members), and it is quite inefficient. The society keeps meticulous records. Officials each year can calculate with great accuracy the exact return from the public proselytizing. For example, in 1983 Witnesses worldwide devoted exactly 436,720,991 hours to witnessing. They helped gain 155,408 converts, or a return of one convert for each two years of witnessing. Not much. But if they can get a targeted individual or family to agree to follow-up home Bible study sessions, then the returns approach 50 percent. They are able gradually to instruct and woo such interested people into participation at a hall and eventually to baptism (by immersion) and assumption of the door-to-door work. The goal of publishers is to gain converts who will become clones of themselves, performing the exact same ministry.

A Witness gives of himself or herself (women are equal in the ministry but still hold no leadership roles and do not teach males), but not in monetary contributions. The society benefits from gifts and bequests and makes money on concessions at its large conventions or assemblies. But at the national level the largest source of income is the publications. Each Kingdom Hall, even each individual publisher, has an assigned quota of literature to distribute. The Bethel publishing empire in Brooklyn (a type of monastery, with several hundred mostly young and very devoted Witnesses living in the compound or nearby residential buildings and doing all the work for room, board, and small allowances) literally sells its publications to the local congregations. The price is set to cover all costs except gifts. Individual publishers have to "buy" the literature they distribute. Thus the Witnesses have a compelling motive to do the work effectively and to get the needed contributions from those whom they visit. Any "profits" help fund the local congregation. In a sense, non-Witnesses who are kind to the missionaries that come to their door (most are not kind; some are rude or even abusive) and who pay for the periodicals largely fund the movement.

Despite their cultural isolation the Witnesses have not developed the institutions needed to cultivate loyalty across generations. A very high percentage of membership is always recent converts. Unlike the Seventh-day Adventists, they have not created separate schools and have no colleges. Unlike Mormons, they have not created a rich diversity of clubs and activities for all age groups. They do very little for youth, who have to sit through the boring Bible study sessions week after week. They do not even have Sunday schools. They work in the larger society, do not wear distinctive clothes, and have few effective institutional barriers against the inroads of a secular culture. What they do have is a disciplined system of training and indoctrination, a close monitoring of members, and warm and close communal support within the local congregations. They also have been unusually open not only to the poor and rejected but to blacks and Hispanics, although only recently have blacks achieved higher leadership roles. Some estimates place black membership in America at 30 percent, and the local congregations have achieved a degree of racial balance and interaction unique among Christians.

The Witnesses rely almost entirely on their salvation doctrines to recruit and retain members. They offer little else except a warm welcome. Their biblical interpretations may sway the innocent, but today these are not only highly selective in focus but arbitrary in interpretation. The daring and stimulating speculations of Russell have given way to repetition and a defensive orthodoxy. Thus one becomes a Witness and devotes such a large share of one's life to selling Witness publications because one believes the prophetic message. Salvation is at stake. The future hope is what it is all about. The kingdom is indeed near, as close as next week. And one must be ready and fulfill one's obligation to take the message to the whole world. God commands it.

READING GUIDE

The scholarly literature on Seventh-day Adventism is extensive and growing rapidly. The scholarship on Jehovah's Witnesses is thin, both within the denomination and without. Most of the best scholarship on Adventism has been by Seventh-day Adventists, or at least those who grew up in the church.

The Millerite movement has long fascinated historians. In 1924 Clara Endicott Sears published *Days of Delusion: A Strange Bit of History* (Boston: Houghton, Mifflin), which established some enduring myths about the movement. Francis D. Nichols used his book, *The Midnight Cry* (Washington, D.C.: Review and Herald, 1944) to defend the sanity of the movement and to debunk most of the apocryphal stories about the Great Disappointment. Clyde E. Hewitt, in *Midnight and Morning* (Charlotte, N.C.: Venture Books, 1983), offers a balanced study and an introduction to Advent Christian history. A brief, informed survey by George R. Knight, *Millennial Fever and the End of the World: A Study of Millerite Adventism* (Boise, Idaho: Pacific Press, 1993), reflects the views of a very sophisticated Adventist scholar.

Seventh-day Adventists have carefully cultivated their own history. Even though most of their own history is partisan, it includes an enormous range of details. This literature includes a large number of Ph.D. dissertations. The great background study is by LeRoy Edwin Froom, *The Prophetic Faith of Our Fathers: The Historical Development of Prophetic Interpretation*, 4 vols. (Washington, D.C.: Review and Herald, 1954). The most detailed but celebratory history of the Seventh-day Adventist Church is by Arthur W. Spalding, *Origin and History of Seventh-day Adventists*, 4 vols. (Washington, D.C.: Review and Herald, 1961–62). Richard W. Schwarz abridges this into a one-volume text, *Lightbearers to the Remnant* (Mountain View, Calif.: Pacific Press, 1979). George R. Knight provides a brief but very informed survey, *Anticipating the Advent: A Brief History of the Seventh-day Adventists* (Boise, Idaho: Pacific Press, 1993).

Notably, all these histories are by Adventists with different levels of scholarly sophistication. I do not know of any general history of the Seventh-day Adventist Church written by a non-Adventist. In 1974 Edwin S. Gaustad edited an anthology, *The Rise of Adventism: Religion and Society in Mid-Nineteenth-Century America* (New York: Harper and Row), that contains essays by several non-Adventist scholars and an all but definitive bibliography. Yet the essays as a whole provide a setting but add few new details about the church. The best illustration of the sophistication of contemporary Adventist scholars is in an excellent anthology edited by Gary Land, *Adventism in America: A History* (Grand Rapids, Mich.: Eerdmans, 1986).

Adventists have written biographies of the important founders, although some of these remain unpublished dissertations. The most controversial of these founders was Ellen G. White. Her books are mostly still in print and are sold at low prices by her church. Her vast body of unpublished manuscripts will soon be online. The definitive official biography is by Arthur L. White, *Ellen G. White*, 6 vols (Washington, D.C.: Review and Herald, 1982–86). The best-known book about White, and particularly her health reforms, is Ronald Numbers, *Prophetess of Health: A Study of Ellen G. White* (New York: Harper and Row, 1976). Numbers, from an Adventist family,

presents an ambivalent view of White that is mixed with continued vener-
ation and at the same time great disappointments at her personal weaknesses and her widespread borrowing of ideas and even text from other
writers. The book led to a storm of criticism within Adventist circles.

I am not happy with the available literature on Jehovah's Witnesses. The
most detailed and on most issues the most reliable book is by a disillusioned
ex-Witness, M. James Penton, *Apocalypse Delayed: The Story of Jehovah's
Witnesses* (Toronto: University of Toronto Press, 1985). This book is rich
in detail, usually helpful on doctrines, and most revealing on organization,
evangelism, and local issues. A. H. Macmillan, *Faith on the March* (Englewood Cliffs, N.J.: Prentice Hall, 1957), is a memoir by a former Witness
leader imprisoned in 1918. It is defensive but provides a good internal perspective and is helpful on doctrine. William J. Whalen, *Armageddon around
the Corner: A Report on Jehovah's Witnesses* (New York: John Day, 1962),
offers a breezy, unscholarly Roman Catholic perspective. Chandler W.
Sterling, *The Witnesses: One God, One Victory* (Chicago: Henry Regnery,
1975), is thin, fair in the characterization of Russell, but mistaken on many
details. William Kaplan, *State and Salvation: The Jehovah's Witnesses and
Their Fight for Civil Rights* (Toronto: University of Toronto Press, 1989),
provides a detailed history of Witness involvement in civil liberties issues in
Canada. David R. Manwaring, *Render unto Caesar: The Flag Salute Controversy* (Chicago: University of Chicago Press, 1962), offers a perspective on
the most important legal cases in the United States.

Charles T. Russell, *The Plan of the Ages*, vol. 1, *Studies in the Scriptures*
(Allegheny, Pa., Watch Tower Bible and Tact Society, 1886), offers the first,
full survey of key doctrines. David Horowitz, *Pastor Charles Taze Russell:
An Early American Christian Zionist* (New York: Philosophical Library,
1986), offers a Zionist perspective but is otherwise not helpful. Stan
Thomas, *Jehovah's Witnesses and What They Believe* (Grand Rapids, Mich.:
Zondervan Publishing House, 1967), is another rather naive book by a disillusioned ex-Witness who is now a part of the Evangelical movement.
Timothy White, *A People for His Name: A History of Jehovah's Witnesses and
an Evaluation* (New York: Vantage Press, 1968), is a standard history, now
dated but abundant in details. Raymond Franz, *Crisis of Conscience* (Atlanta:
Commentary Press, 1983), is a sad book by the son of a church president
personally committed to an open church, but who was dropped from the
leadership in the last major internal fight.

4

MORMON **CHRISTIANITY**

The

Church

of Jesus

Christ of

Latter-day

Saints

The Church of Jesus Christ of Latter-day Saints (LDS) is the largest apocalyptic denomination in the United States. It has more than 4 million members, is growing each year, and has an estimated 9 million members worldwide. It is now the sixth largest denomination in America, larger than traditional mainstream bodies such as Presbyterians, Episcopalians, and Congregationalists. In doctrines it reflects the basic beliefs of other apocalyptic Christians (an early advent, corporealism, Jewish continuities, and a sense of the apostasy of orthodox churches), but it has so many distinctive doctrines and stands so far apart from all other Christian denominations as to constitute a completely new religious tradition. Some scholars, rather than classifying it as a Christian denomination, see it as a distinct and separate world religion.

The story of these latter-day saints, or Mormons, has become an American epic. It is a story of belated success. A small, cultlike sect, much persecuted and reviled, matured into a large, international religion in only one century. It is a story of courage in the midst of deviance from normative beliefs and practices. It is a story of acculturation, as the LDS rose from the most hated and stigmatized sect in America to one of the most respected denominations. It is a story of worldly success, as a small, semicommunal, radical sect grew into a socially conservative church marked by worldly success and wealth. This is the external story. What is less well known are the very distinctive doctrines and practices that still set Mormons apart from all other Christians. To do justice to the Mormons, a historian has to enter rather deeply into both the epic of the church and its doctrines.

JOSEPH SMITH AND THE BOOK OF MORMON

It all began with Joseph Smith. Much more than Ellen G. White for the Seventh-day Adventists, Smith was the founder of Mormonism. Joseph Smith Jr., the prophet, was born in 1805 in Sharon, Vermont, in a downwardly mobile family. His father farmed, taught schools, lost everything in a speculative venture, and became, for much of his life, a tenant who moved frequently. He desperately sought ways of redeeming the family fortune, including searches and digging for precious metals or for money (purportedly buried by pirates). Smith's father and mother also remained at the fringe of organized religion, perhaps in part because of their frequent moves, which brought the family to Palmyra, New York, in 1816. Within two years they saved enough money from running a small restaurant and peddling various items to buy, on credit, a farm in Manchester, New York, beginning a reasonably stable period, although they never gained a secure title to the farm.

One can say with some assurance that Joseph Jr. was a bit of loner as a youth. He was sporadically involved with organized religion (some neighbors remember his participation at a Methodist revival) and was fascinated with occult phenomena. As a young man he found three different seer stones, small, colored rocks believed to have magical properties. He used them to find underground water or lost items and apparently hired out his services to those who sought buried treasures. Thus, as a youth he gained a reputation as a seer, in a culture and an age in which large multitudes believed in and relied on such special gifts (his father had frequent visions).

In 1825 Smith moved to an area around Colesville (in Chenango County), not far from the Pennsylvania border. There he worked for two entrepreneurs who sought an ancient Spanish mine, purportedly with buried coins, across the border in northeastern Pennsylvania. They wanted young Smith to use his supernatural powers to locate it for them, which indicates that he sometimes sold his advice. While in the area of the mine, at the small village of Harmony, Pennsylvania (in northeastern Susquehanna County), he met his future wife, Emma Hale. Apparently because of his involvement with treasure seekers and what some believed was his intent to deceive innocent people, Smith was arrested in Colesville, tried, and apparently convicted on charges of disorderly conduct in 1826 (he escaped, perhaps by the intent of the authorities, who probably wanted him out of the area).

According to Smith's later memory, even before he found his first magical stone or undertook his venture in southern New York, he had his first religious vision. This apparently occurred in 1820, when he was only fourteen. As he reported it much later, this vision, which became critical for the Mormon religion, occurred in the midst of local religious revivals that intensified the usual competition among sects. The Smith family could not avoid the religious excitement or the persuasive appeals directed at them. Joseph's mother and some of his siblings joined a local Presbyterian church. His father held back and apparently so did Joseph Jr. According to Smith's memory in 1838, God and Jesus, both fully distinct and physical, appeared to him out of a pillar of light, blessed him, bemoaned the sins and corruptions of the world, and promised a new revelation that would soon come. But above all, as Smith interpreted the meaning of this revelation, God made clear the apostasy of all the competing Christian sects of the day and told Smith that he must not join any of them. This became, for Mormons, the vindication for Smith's lack of early church membership, the first testimony to the great apostasy of modern Christianity, and the background for a new revelation that God would soon share with Smith.

By Smith's memory, his next great vision came three years later at the fall equinox in 1823. An angel, later identified as Moroni, and who had once lived as a human on the American continent, told Smith about a history written on gold plates—a record of earlier inhabitants of America—which Moroni had helped complete and which he had deposited in its resting place. This history contained the fullness of the Gospel as Jesus had revealed it to ancient American inhabitants. With the gold plates was a breastplate containing two interpreters or seer stones (later identified by Smith and by Mormons as the legendary Urim and Thummim of the Old Testament). Moroni also revealed that Jesus would soon return to earth and that Smith was to prepare for that return. Moroni did not show Smith the plates but revealed where he had hidden them.

This account has become part of a story believed and esteemed by all Mormons. Of course, being entirely private and based on a supernatural experience, it is beyond any historical vindication. Skeptics later interpreted the visions, if they even occurred, quite differently. Desperate money diggers, like the father and son, leaped at the opportunity opened by these visions, for the hill (named Cumorah by Smith) on which the tablets rested was only three miles from the Smith residence (close to Manchester). To critics this was simply the beginning of another great and successful nineteenth-century scam, one that eventually paid off, if not in wealth at least in fame and power as well as eventual martyrdom for Joseph Smith and in a type of reflected eminence for the whole Smith family.

According to Smith, he first uncovered the plates after the first vision, or in September 1823, but he could not remove them. In successive Septembers (fall equinoxes), he went to the hill as instructed and checked on the plates, but only in 1827, after some periods of temptation and repentance and after his escapades in southern New York, was he able to take them from their chamber. Smith was then not quite twenty-two years old. No precise description of these plates remains, even by witnesses who testified to their existence. The witnesses later estimated that the stack of gold leaves, which seemed to make up a metallic book, weighed up to fifty pounds. Only with difficulty, because of fears that enemies would steal them, were Smith and his family able to hide them at various sites until Smith began the work of translation at his wife's home village in Pennsylvania. The plates, as he described them, were covered with hieroglyphics, in an Egyptian-like script, but apparently the script recorded a text written in a form of the ancient Hebrew language. The key to interpretation was purportedly the two stones, mounted in something resembling the frames of eyeglasses. In fact those who observed him at the work of translation often referred to a single seer stone, which he looked at with his face covered by his hat. He did not look directly at the plates when translating and in some cases apparently translated without the plates being present in the same room.

His wife, Emma, transcribed the first "translations." Then a New York neighbor of the Smith family, Martin Harris, came to Pennsylvania and took over the transcription while Smith, concealed behind a blanket, translated with the aid of his stone (or stones). Harris was in a sense the first convert outside the immediate Smith family. But this first effort was doomed to failure, even if one sees it as a great scam. Harris first offered proof to skeptical neighbors back at Palmyra after Joseph and Emma "traced" on paper a page of characters and symbols. Apparently at Smith's request, Harris sought two Orientalists, one at Rutgers and one at Columbia College, to verify the characters and Smith's translation of them.

What happened at Columbia College has occasioned unending controversy. The later, accepted Mormon version is that Harris presented the documents to Professor Charles Anthon sometime in 1828. According to Harris, Anthon certified that these were indeed ancient characters, Egyptian or otherwise, and that Smith had correctly translated them. Anthon even gave him a certificate to confirm this judgment. But when Anthon found out about the nature of the plates and the purported source of the transcription, he took back the certificate, tore it up, and said that he could not read a sacred book. Harris came back convinced that Smith was indeed a prophet and that he, unlearned, could do translations that baffled a great scholar, fulfilling a prophecy in Isaiah. Subsequently Anthon completely denied this version, denied that the document contained Egyptian characters, and denied that Smith or anyone else could translate the strange figures. He argued that he saw the whole episode as part of a hoax and that he had so warned Harris.

After this, Harris almost sabotaged the planned book. He persuaded Smith to allow him to show the translated material (161 scribbled pages) to his doubting wife back in Palmyra. Disobeying Smith, he apparently also showed it to many curious neighbors. Somehow he lost the manuscript. According to one story, Harris's skeptical wife burned it. The story accepted by Mormons is that someone stole it. This presented dilemmas. Smith reported that Moroni temporarily took back the plates and interpreter's stones to punish Smith for releasing the manuscript. The lost section, as he and Harris described it, covered the first 400 years of the history of an ancient Jewish people in America and was the opening part of a history written by someone named Mormon (thus the *Book of Mormon*). But since the first translation was in enemy hands, Smith was afraid to do this part over for fear that critics would find discrepancies between the two versions or would so alter the first as to ensure such discrepancies. Thus, he never retranslated these plates as written by Mormon but instead, guided as always by another vision, translated some plates (called small plates) of Nephi, an earlier book that covered the same events as recorded later by Mormon, who had derived his account from the large plates of Nephi, which were not available to Smith. These events considerably confuse the background to the *Book of Mormon*, which turned out to be more than the actual writings of Mormon. They also make very confusing what the plates contained. Instead of one metallic book, the cache apparently contained at least three different sets of plates, as the story will later make clear. Also, the recourse to the original plates of Nephi seemed to critics an overly clever way out of a dilemma by a cagey Smith. Since they believed he made up the stories from whole cloth, then he simply announced a change of plates anytime it suited his purpose.

After losing the opening section of the story, Smith eventually, after a period of repentance, resumed his translation of the rest of Mormon's writings. Even this did not fully exhaust his labors. At the end, he translated an abridgment of another set of plates much older than even the Nephi plates and that recounted the history of the first settlers of America (more on this later). The loss of the first translation did not immediately end Harris's role as transcriber. He and Emma both did further transcriptions but soon surrendered this role to Oliver Cowdery, a twenty-two-year-old school-teacher, psychic, and Joseph's distant cousin, who came to Smith to find out more about the now well-publicized plates. During the spring and into the summer of 1829 Smith and Cowdery rushed the manuscript toward completion, finishing the work not at Smith's home in Pennsylvania but at the home of a friend, John Whitmer, in Fayette, New York (twenty-five miles southeast of Palmyra), where they had protected privacy. Thus another family became involved in the work, and most members of the Whitmer family later joined the Mormon Church.

David Whitmer, the son of John, became so involved that Smith, as always guided by divine revelation, chose him, along with Cowdery and a forgiven Martin Harris, to witness the plates. Their witness occurred after prayer and meditation and in a supernatural atmosphere. Smith did not show them the plates, but rather the angel Moroni revealed the plates to each of the three witnesses, making this closer to a vision than to an ordinary inspection. But this special divine atmosphere, for Mormons, gave authority to these first three witnesses, who signed a statement in which they testified to what they saw. Smith included their statement in the first edition of the *Book of Mormon*. Later, according to all the accounts and the recorded testimony of those involved, four sons and one son-in-law of David Whitmer and three of Smith's brothers also saw the stack of gold plates, again in a supernatural context. Their witness would have been more believable to outsiders had they not all been members of the two families who had the most compelling reasons to uphold the credibility of Joseph Smith. For those who take a cynical view, the three witnesses, in a carefully contrived and suggestive environment, only had a supernatural vision, while the eight simply joined in a great scam. Despite numerous cases of apostasy, none of the witnesses ever repudiated their testimony, a point much stressed by Mormons but not hard to comprehend, since their credibility was at stake and since, in all probability, they did participate in a supernatural experience.

A Palmyra printer finally agreed to publish the *Book of Mormon*, but only after Martin Harris mortgaged his farm to provide the needed security. Fearful of mob action or a theft of the manuscript, Cowdery carried it to the printer in small segments. Cowdery also helped the printer add the needed punctuation marks to the raw manuscript (this first edition still had many grammatical mistakes). At least locally, the story of the gold plates and speculations about the content of the forthcoming book created great interest. Already, neighbors ridiculed Smith and called him the prophet but in so doing only increased interest in his book. The completed *Book of*

Mormon went on sale in March 1830 (Moroni took back the plates) and despite the widespread interest did not sell well at first. But Smith was a nationally known figure because of the extensive newspaper coverage of the publication. He was notorious, not respected, because almost everyone saw the book as a gigantic hoax, while orthodox Christians also saw it as blasphemous.

In fact, the *Book of Mormon* was a rather innocuous book, at least from a religious perspective. In almost all respects it supported a very eclectic, Arminian, evangelical, Pentecostal, and Adventist form of Christianity and on almost all issues was in agreement with, although supplemental to, the Christian Bible. The most distinctive Mormon doctrines came not from this book but from a series of visions and revelations later experienced by Smith, some of which were not clearly consistent with the *Book of Mormon*. That the book did not sell well among Smith's neighbors is easily explained by the text. The style (King James Old Testament), the redundancy, and the internal complexity of some of the stories make it a very difficult book to read. But, in a sense, the book is rather simple; it is a series of narratives that include moral teachings. It would have much broader appeal today, and lose nothing in content, if Mormons were willing to tighten up the prose (it could be half as long) and convert it to contemporary English. At the time, the book was most important not for the details within but for the overall claim that it made about the ancient history of America and for the fact that a poorly educated Joseph Smith was either able to recover and translate such a book (the Mormon claim) or able to spin such a fantastic story from his own fertile imagination or by borrowing ideas from others (the view of most non-Mormons).

The overall story in the *Book of Mormon* is complex. It purports to be three different translations: first, the small plates of Nephi; second, the later parts of a book composed by Mormon; and finally, appended to the end, an abridgment of the ancient plates of Ether, an abridgment made not by Mormon but by his surviving son, Moroni. Since this appended book (called the Book of Ether) begins the complicated history contained in the total, but in part misnamed, *Book of Mormon*, its explication should come first. This book tells, briefly, the story of an ancient people, the Jaredites. They were not Jews but a pre-Hebraic population with their own language. Jared, the founder, was present at the Tower of Babel. Jehovah informed Jared that he and his people were to migrate to a distant land, and thus they made preparations, moved to the sea, and used special submarine-like barges to travel to a promised land in America, where they established a kingdom similar to the later Hebrew kingdom. There they experienced cycles of obedience and disobedience to Jehovah, heeding and then ignoring a series of prophets until Jehovah wreaked a final vengeance on the Jaredites, destroying them in fratricidal wars (some Mormons now believe a few scattered Jaredites survived). Ether was the last prophet of the Jaredites and thus wrote the plates that Moroni abridged. He began with a brief summary of biblical events from the creation to the Tower and then recounted the history of the Jaredite people. The Book of Ether, doctrinally, is one of the most significant in the *Book of Mormon*. It documents the physicality of God and of Jesus, makes clear that the promised city of Zion will be on the American continent, and in several allusions seems to refer to the later work of Joseph Smith.

The main part of the *Book of Mormon*, purportedly translated from the Nephi plates and the Mormon plates, is a complex history of a Jewish people who left Palestine and traveled to America. These were the children of Lehi, with two sons, Nephi and Laman, playing the most important role. From the tribe of Manasseh, this family was not part of the earlier ten lost tribes of Israel (which were somewhere else on earth). This people left Jerusalem about 600 B.C.E., or just before the fall of Jerusalem to the Babylonians, and then seemingly crossed the Indian and Pacific Oceans in a ship (they had journeyed to the east from Jerusalem) to arrive at the promised land (America, which was the site of the original Garden of Eden). The story of this growing tribe in America contains several references to another migrating offshoot of Israel, the sons of Mulek, who came to America about ten years after Lehi and his sons and generally lived to the north of them. The Mulekites are only marginally significant in the story because they did not bring any of the Jewish scriptures and thus had no religious message to leave behind for future Gentiles. Even before arriving in America, Nephi and Laman quarreled and became the progenitors of competing tribes or nations. At first Nephi and his descendants (confusingly, some of Nephi's obedient descendants assumed his name, meaning that the *Book of Mormon* abounds in Nephis) tried to follow the Mosaic law and thus were the righteous descendants of Lehi, while Laman and his descendants generally disobeyed God and persecuted the righteous. For their apostasy they received a curse (dark skins), but not the curse of Cain or a later Ham, which Mormons long used to justify an exclusion of Negroes (not all black people and not all Africans) from their all-male priesthood (an exclusion removed in 1978). The American Indians are the descendants of Laman. But this oversimplifies the story. At times the Nephites were as sinful as the Lamanites, and at times various Lamanite groups converted and excelled the Nephites in their obedience. When Jesus visited both peoples in America, all the Nephites and Lamanites followed his teachings (some Mormons believed that Lamanites, if they repented and became faithful, would regain white skin). But, over time, it was clear that the Nephites were the chosen people of God, with more expected of them as a result.

The main body of the *Book of Mormon* reads like the historical and prophetic books of the Jewish scriptures. The historical narrative (repetitious and detailed) alternates with moralistic teachings or prophecy. Long sections are from the Jewish scriptures, including extended quotations from Isaiah. In this mass of detail a brief section (III Nephi 11–28) recounts the visit of Jesus to the Jews of America. As the promised Messiah, he could not neglect them (he also appeared before the lost tribes, but this appearance is only noted, not described). Even before Jesus appeared in America, the Nephites experienced natural wonders at his birth as well as terrible storms and earthquakes at his crucifixion. Within a year of his resurrection he came, as the righteous Nephites had long anticipated, to America to instruct his people, first meeting them at their temple in the city of Bountiful (many Mormons believe this was in Central America). The record covers only his three-day visit. On the second day he taught in greatest detail, but the record is close to a copy of the sermon on the mount as given in Matthew. Except on a few issues (the proper method and purpose of baptism, including the baptism of the Holy Spirit, and several references to the future of certain Gentiles in America who would by repentance and proper baptism join themselves to all the promises of the covenant and thus help build in America the new Zion), Jesus did not reveal any dramatic new insights in this American appearance. But he did found a church in America, something that he did not do in his Palestinian ministry. He also duplicated his ministry in Palestine, even to the appointment of twelve American disciples, and instituted the Lord's Supper by a sacramental meal before his ascension.

After the appearance of the Christ, the story of the Nephites and Lamanites was most often a sad one. A final, cruel war between the Lamanites and the Nephites led, in 384 C.E., to the virtual extinction of the Nephites. From the Hill Cumorah (some Mormon scholars believe this was not the hill in New York to which Joseph Smith gave the name), only twenty-four survivors surveyed thousands of their fallen comrades. The last great Nephite leader and prophet, Mormon, wrote on plates the accumulated history of his people and addressed the resulting plates or book to the surviving Lamanites to win them, if possible, back to the gospel of the Christ. In about 420 C.E., Moroni, the surviving son of Mormon and the lone remaining Nephite, began the writings that supplemented the story as told by Mormon. He noted that the writing was in Egyptian characters, and he foretold the coming age when the church would be lost in apostasy, when Christians would be mired in sin and corruption, and when God would disclose the *Book of Mormon* to an unbelieving generation. After abridging the Book of Ether, the lonely Moroni, hiding from the warring Lamanites, wrote a final postscript that is doctrinally significant to Mormons because of details about baptism, the Lord's Supper, and the priesthood. At this time, about 420 C.E., Moroni finally deposited the plates on the hill in New York where Joseph Smith recovered them.

This is the narrative structure of the *Book of Mormon*. It may be unfair or beside the point to subject the book to critical analysis. As most writings deemed sacred by religious people, including the Christian Bible, it has problems. At a hundred points it confirms or expands the stories contained in the canonical Jewish scriptures. The sons of Lehi purportedly carried with them plates containing all the Jewish scriptures that dated to the time before the exile. In addition to this, the Nephite prophets anticipated much that came later in both Jewish and Christian history. The first book, I Nephi, gives a vivid account of the future Messiah, even to the approximate time of his birth; details the apostasy of the church; and describes the future restoration of a true church (it does not name Joseph Smith). Thus, in a sense, the whole Bible, read literally and often quoted in words that duplicate or approximate the King James translation (presumably this was a result of the transcription, not the actual language on the plates), provides a backdrop for the book. The *Book of Mormon* gives special support to the foreshortened chronology of the Jewish calendar; to the historicity of the creation myths and Adam and Eve (Adam is very much a hero in Mormon hagiography); to the accuracy of the stories about the long-lived patriarchs (Enoch, in particular, has great importance to Mormons); and, of course, to the historicity of the Tower of Babel from which the Jaredites departed. The Mormons, more than any other Christian sect, have a living sense of these beginnings, for through the Nephites they identify with almost all this ancient tradition. This literalism later created a special affinity between Mormons and other conservative Christians who believe the Bible does not err even in its historical or scientific claims.

Because of outside critics, Mormons have had to work hard at defending the *Book of Mormon*. The defense has become more difficult through time because of new scholarship and new scientific understanding, problems that Mormons share with other conservative Christians or with orthodox Jews. The scholarly problems had little impact on the early history of the Mormon Church but created dilemmas for later Mormon intellectuals. The understanding of the Bible reflected in the book (and in a Mormon perspective by the ancient authors of the plates) was that of most ordinary Christians in 1830.

The issues that have most challenged later Mormon apologists, and at times those most eagerly affirmed by Mormon apostates, have involved alleged anachronisms. Since the sons of Lehi in America had no subsequent contact with their brethren back in Palestine, their knowledge of precaptivity Jewish history had to depend on the completed scriptures they brought with them to America. Today few biblical scholars believe that more than small components of the later Jewish canon had been collected or even written before the captivity. In one case it seems impossible that Mormon, writing in America, could have had available some of the passages he quoted from the Book of Isaiah. This book, as later collected and included in the Jewish canon, includes material from more than one prophet. The Isaiah who advised King Hezekiah (before 600) and whose teachings make up all, or a major part, of the first thirty-nine chapters of the later compilation could not have written chapters forty to fifty-five, for this second Isaiah celebrates Cyrus and the liberation of the children of Israel from their captivity in Babylon (events that occurred more than fifty years after Lehi traveled to America). A less complex charge of anachronism involves the Old World livestock and planted crops that are part of the story of the Nephites in America, despite the lack of any archaeological evidence of such in pre-Columbian America. Mormons have tried to vindicate through archaeological research not only these seeming anachronisms but the complex history of civilizations in America as recorded in the *Book of Mormon*. Despite their efforts, Mormon archaeologists have failed to persuade experts in the field on any significant point, although in the process some Mormons have completed useful field research. Even the story of the Jaredites does not begin to account for ancient human populations in the Americas or for people here thousands of years before the date Mormons give to the Tower of Babel. Almost no physical or linguistic evidence links present Native Americans to the ancient Hebrews, although for two centuries before Joseph Smith such theories about Hebraic origins had been widely popular.

Clearly, the *Book of Mormon* was much more believable in 1831, before a whole series of findings in several fields by scholars and scientists, than it is today. Several portions of the Christian Bible were also more believable then. At the time, Joseph Smith's new scriptures had considerable appeal not so much because of the details in the book but because of the overall claims that it vindicated: that in the past a people, the Nephites, had for a time lived in complete obedience to God; that they had created a purified church and a righteous society; and that they had done so here on the American continent. Smith catered to wide public interest in the ancient peoples of America and in theories about their Hebraic origin. Among some people—disinherited, unsuccessful, and frustrated—the argument that present institutions were corrupt and that all churches were lost in apostasy had great appeal. The message appealed even more to lowly people in Protestant Europe, in part because the message often joined with an opportunity to emigrate to America. The history in the *Book of Mormon* is full of strife, cruelty, and terrible apostasy, but it holds up an ideal of obedience realized by a few in heroic periods. Thus it is a prototype of the history of Israel in the Jewish Bible. Plenty of Americans and plenty of Europeans in 1830 were receptive to a new gospel, to a new, uncorrupted religion. In the same sense they were open to a new prophet. Perhaps more than anything else, the *Book of Mormon* lent credibility to Joseph Smith and to a series of revelations that he used to found a new religion.

THE EARLY MORMON CHURCH

One can date the beginnings of a new Church of Jesus Christ to the spring of 1829, while Smith and Cowdery completed their manuscript. Guided by an angel who identified himself as John the Baptist, Smith and Cowdery baptized each other in the Susquehanna River, by immersion and for the remission of sins. The angel identified Smith as first elder of a new church and Cowdery as second elder, titles the two subsequently used. Of course, all accounts of these baptisms came later and probably reflected doctrines not yet developed. But as Smith later understood it, this baptism bestowed on the two men the priesthood of Aaron. This is, in the dual-priesthood system of the Mormons, the lower of two orders, but it bestows the authority to administer all the ordinances of the church, including baptism. Promised at this time, according to the later explanation of Smith, was a higher priesthood, that of Melchizedek (the somewhat mysterious king of Salem who as the priest of God Most High blessed Abraham and received his tithes). This priesthood would bring with it the power, through the laying on of hands, of bestowing the gift of the Holy Spirit. Even at this first baptism the two men were caught up in ecstasy and enjoyed the gift of prophecy. Within the next few weeks Smith began baptizing his brothers, creating what might be identified as the first Mormons.

A formal church organization came only after the publication of the *Book of Mormon*. Guided by a divine revelation, Joseph Smith selected April 6, 1830, as the time for founding a church. A small group of about fifty, including most of the Smith and Whitmer families, gathered, probably at the Smith household in Manchester, although later Mormon historians have usually located the event at David Whitmer's home in Fayette. Smith and Cowdery mutually ordained each other as elders and officiated at a communion service. For legal purposes, four other men listed their names as founding elders. In the following weeks Smith, Cowdery, or other elders ordained in these first few months baptized all converts to the new faith and began ordaining men as elders, priests, or teachers, labels that as yet did not denote any particular rank.

The first phase in the history of the new church primarily involved three New York villages—Manchester, Fayette, and Colesville—where Smith had developed friends or disciples. The New York phase was very brief. In a January 1831 conference almost all the New York Mormons decided to move to Kirtland, Ohio. They did this, in part, to escape persecution in New York but also in obedience to two different revelations to Joseph Smith. Most of the 200 or so members of a church without meetinghouses moved to Ohio over the next year, leaving only a few Mormons in New York.

The move to Kirtland involved adventitious circumstances. In August 1830 Parley Pratt, a member of a Disciples of Christ congregation (formerly Reformed Baptists) from near Kirtland, inquired about the new Mormon religion and was quickly converted, baptized, and ordained an elder. In the fall of 1830 the elders of the new movement decided on a momentous mission to the Lamanites (Indians). The first mission team, led by Cowdery but including Pratt, stopped in Kirtland and interested the local and by now schismatic Campbellite minister and colleague of Pratt, Sidney Rigdon, in the new religion. Perhaps more important, they converted several local Disciples. After study and a religious vision of his own, Rigdon converted and accepted baptism. Shortly thereafter he visited Joseph Smith in New York. He was the most eminent convert thus far to the new Mormon sect, and he helped bring even more Kirtland-area Disciples into the movement. Rigdon had already broken with Alexander Campbell over a community of goods, which he believed necessary to have a fully restored New Testament church, and thus he had created at Kirtland a semicommunal congregation. This made possible a coherent and clustered Mormon community.

Although with few members, this embryonic Church of Christ already displayed several distinctive features. It was closer to mainline evangelical Christianity than it would ever be again. One early peculiarity proved enduring: the family-based nature of the church. Within the first few months a vast majority of Mormons represented only five families, some of them distantly related. It was a clanlike church. Sixty early Mormon converts were from these five families, including the Smith and Whitmer families. From then on, new converts accepted, as a first responsibility, the conversion of family members. The leadership of the church remained in the same families generation after generation. Such a family orientation soon had doctrinal justification.

In organization the early church was patriarchal with a democratic tinge. In a sense it was theocratic, for God continued to guide the church through direct revelations, given to all elders before September 1830 and then, as decided in a crucial but tense general conference, on critical points of doctrine or issues concerning the church as a whole only through the first elder or apostle or seer, meaning Joseph Smith. But early, as in the enunciation of the first summary of principles and practices in 1830, the Book of Commandments (this later became the authoritative *Doctrine and Covenants*), some of the revelations offered by authority of Smith reflected the collegial judgment of several elders. Thus, God made the critical decisions, the first elder received these decisions and enunciated them, and scribes wrote them down (Joseph was not a fluent writer and would never be a very effective preacher). The other elders made up a small, confirming oligarchy. Finally, the small oligarchy eventually presented all new policies or doctrines to the gathered membership at general conferences, which met semiannually from 1840 on. At these conferences the leadership (later called the general authorities) asked for a confirming vote (always forthcoming). Since all innovations came with a seal of divine authority, it was simply inconceivable that conference delegates would ever vote "no" on any important issue. In modern times these two-day conferences are as carefully organized as political conventions and are broadcast via television from the tabernacle in Salt Lake City to Mormons around the world.

The fullest priesthood dated from late 1830. By Smith's later understanding, this followed severe local resistance to the Mormons in Colesville and his arrest and exoneration on a charge involving exorcism. At this time the two senior elders (Smith was only twenty-five) received, in a special vision, a visit from Peter, James, and John, who ordained Smith and Cowdery as apostles and thus to what they later denominated the priesthood of Melchizedek. This gave them the authority to bestow the gift of the Holy Spirit after baptism through the laying on of hands, but it was only later that the church developed its elaborate dual priesthood. In 1831, in Kirtland, Smith first announced this new priesthood.

The early Mormon movement seemed, to converts, an Adventist sect otherwise quite similar to the Methodists and the Disciples, the sources of the largest number of early converts. Guided by revelations as well as the *Book of Mormon*, Smith became a complete Arminian. He rejected the whole array of Calvinist doctrines. Humans were not completely depraved but in the image of God, essentially minor deities even though in rebellion against God (Adam is not the devil but a hero who helped place the burden of mortality on humans but who also opened the prospect of salvation and a higher glory for those who attain a high standard). The grace of God was free, offered to all. Each person was free to accept or reject it, even as converts could backslide and lose the promise of salvation. In this sense as well as many others, Smith lowered the distance between God and humans and stressed the benevolence of God. This led him, through an early revelation, to reject eternal damnation for all except the worst sinners (sons of perdition, usually meaning apostates). He was not a universalist but learned from God that punishment, for most, would terminate and that God fitted the punishment to the crime. This joined with a later doctrine that certified three realms of heavenly bliss, with these further divided into numerous gradations.

With a vengeance Smith was a restorationist. The LDS was a purified church, the only one consistent with the true gospel and the only one organized correctly because of the latter-day revelation in the *Book of Mormon*. Smith seemed to be much influenced by Alexander Campbell and the Disciples. At least he agreed with them at several points. He made baptism for the remission of sins obligatory for Christians, insisted on adult baptism (age eight or above) by immersion, required rebaptism for all converts, and celebrated communion weekly. He tied faith to simple belief in witnesses and stressed obedience to God's word as the primary requirement of faith.

Smith did not stop with such a restorationist goal. His church was Pentecostal in the sense that it emphasized all the gifts of the Spirit. Prophecy was most critical in the early church, for many of its doctrines rested on prophetic inspiration or direct revelation. Visions and visits by angels were frequent among the early priests. Smith and other elders frequently healed and exorcised, while ecstatic speech or glossolalia was common. Perhaps influenced by frequent interaction with ecstatic Shakers, many of the elders became proficient in tongue speaking, apparently with a beautiful, songlike delivery. The diaries of early Mormons are full of references to ecstatic gatherings and to both tongue speaking and interpretations of non-syntactical speech. At every important juncture in the beleaguered early history of the church, through the early settlements in Utah, spiritual gifts marked every celebrated success and consoled in times of adversity.

Finally, the early Mormons were Adventists, millenarians, and corporealists. In this they were close to the Seventh-day Adventists but with some unique twists. The early converts and Smith himself were positive they lived in the very last days and that Jesus would shortly return to establish his millennial kingdom, a quite literal kingdom here on earth and the home for all resurrected saints. The rediscovery of the *Book of Mormon* and the gathering of the new and beleaguered Mormon saints prefigured awful persecutions and sufferings (a prophecy realized for the Mormons) that were to precede the advent. Lacking so far was the gathering of far-flung Jews, who were to return to Israel before the advent. Mormons, therefore, took a special responsibility for the conversion of America's Jews (the Indians). This accounted for their mission west in late 1830. Cowdery wanted not only to convert Indians but to locate the site of the New Jerusalem as foretold in the Book of Ether. It was to be in America, the site of the Garden of Eden, and on the borders of the Lamanites, which he and Smith interpreted as somewhere in western Missouri. It was in America, not Palestine, because here the latter-day saints, the ones who alone followed the true gospel, would gather. But other prophecies made clear that, even before the heavenly Jerusalem descended, the saints in the last days should build their own city of Zion, a prototype of the future New Jerusalem, as a refuge for those saints suffering intense persecution. Cowdery and Smith subsequently located the exact site at Independence, Missouri, and for a while this area of Missouri became the prescribed gathering place for all Mormons.

These early doctrines were eclectic, but most had precedents among sectarian Protestants. They proved only a departure point for the church later centered in Utah but remained very close to the continuing beliefs of the Reorganized Church of Jesus Christ of Latter Day Saints (RLDS). The most original and distinctive beliefs and ordinances came later, most in the three years before the death of Joseph Smith. In the twentieth century these early beliefs, which Smith summarized in the still-official Articles of Faith, have provided a modern bridge to conservative evangelicals. The articles are orthodox or conventional on most issues (theology, emphasis on free will, baptism and communion, and the gifts of the Spirit).

Soon after the move to Kirtland, Smith began building on these early Mormon doctrines and practices. In 1832 he first began sending out missionaries in twos, a continuing tradition. The first Mormons to move to Independence, Missouri (Zion), began in 1832 to lay in provisions in storehouses, the basis of a semicommunal welfare system. Smith first endorsed tithing in 1833, and even earlier had proclaimed a law of consecration. This set what turned out to be an unachievably high standard for even the most devout Mormons—that they dedicate all private property to the welfare of all the saints and receive in return a promise of economic security in a communal system (called the Order of Enoch when Brigham Young tried, with limited success, to move back to such communalism in Utah).

Smith used revelations as a guide to the gradual development of a complex priesthood. In 1833 he formed the first presidency, with himself as president and with two appointed counselors. By 1836 he had named all the priestly offices, but for most of the rest of his life the exact authority and rank of various ordained offices remained confused or in flux. Only under Brigham Young would the priesthood take its modern form. The lowest, or Aaronic priesthood, went back to the first ordinations in 1830. Until after Smith's martyrdom, the three Aaronic orders were adult priest-hoods, selectively bestowed on deserving men. In the modern church these three ascending orders are largely youth organizations. The Aaronic priest-hood includes, in ascending rank, deacons (most boys now gain this office at age twelve), teachers (also held by boys fourteen and older), and priests (sixteen and older). Deacons and teachers largely assist in worship. Priests (usually late teenagers) often officiate on sacramental occasions. Today, for girls and young women, functionally similar organizations lack only the priestly titles and roles.

The Melchizedek priesthood is more difficult to describe, since the di-visions are as much of function as of rank. The broad base of this priest-hood contains elders and high priests, offices clarified by Smith as early as 1832. Today, devout young men, as they enter adult roles or prepare for missionary work, usually move up to this higher priesthood as elders. The next advance, for those who are both devout and talented, will usually be to the highly selective office of high priest (the spiritual office of most of the Mormon men who, in effect, serve as pastors of modern congregations or wards). At the top of this Melchizedek or spiritual priesthood are seven-ties and apostles. By 1835 Smith had ordained men to both these priest-hoods, but their early role was quite different from that later in Utah. Smith first ordained a council of twelve apostles in 1835. The apostles were not tied to the presidency and at first had largely mission assignments, meaning that they were often traveling around the United States or in Eu-rope. In effect, they had full authority over all Mormons outside the home base and could ordain priests in these outlying areas. They also had au-thority over a new mission priesthood, the seventies, ordained later in 1835. Smith selected seventy men to take the gospel to Gentiles around the world. The governing body of these seventy would be a first council, made up of seven presidents each of whom presided over smaller quorums. Even-tually the first council of the seventies would have authority just below that of the twelve apostles. Both councils, along with the presidency and certain administrative officers or bishops, make up the present general authorities of the church.

More confusing are two other offices in the church, patriarchs and bish-ops. Even before he ordained the council of apostles, Smith had selected his father as the first presiding patriarch of the church (an office discontin-ued in 1979 by the Utah church but still accepted by the RLDS). It is difficult to know what he intended for this office. At first the patriarch gave special blessings primarily to youth, often those without a father. But Joseph Smith often so described the position as to make it at least equal to that of apostle, or even that of counselor within the presidency. The office was to be in some sense hereditary, bestowed on older men in the priestly line, like the patriarchs of ancient Israel. Eventually, with the organization of stakes and wards, other elderly men gained ordination as local or stake patriarchs or evangelists. The position was additive to the two priesthoods. In time the patriarchs would have a standard ritualistic role, one with hints of prophetic power. They would give once to every willing young person a special blessing, involving not only promises of a righteous future but a naming of their tribal identity (one of the tribes of Israel).

From the beginnings of the church, Smith appointed bishops. The title has always been a bit confusing. It is not a spiritual title and is not equivalent to the Aaronic and Melchizedek orders. It has always reflected a governmental or administrative role. In the early days, when the church was not organized into stakes or wards, the local bishop had responsibility for the economic affairs of the church and was responsible for supervising the Aaronic priests. By the time the saints gathered at Nauvoo, Smith had appointed more than one local or general bishop as well as regional or stake bishops. In Nauvoo the bishops gained supervisory authority over sections of the city, a suggestion of later ward bishops. From the bishops at the center, or general bishops, has derived the presiding bishopric of the church, the officials at Salt Lake City who supervise the various administrative and business affairs of the church. With a fully developed stake and ward system, each regional stake had its own presidency and high council. The individual congregations or wards are governed, if that is the right word, by a bishop, normally a high priest in the Melchizedek order. The bishop and his counselors supervise the Aaronic or youth priesthoods, have charge of Sunday worship, exercise church discipline, and in the early Utah days closely supervised the taxlike tithing system. For local Mormons the bishop is the main representative of the church hierarchy, much as a priest is in a Catholic parish.

The office held by Joseph Smith has continued in the presidency of the church, but with major changes after his death. In the succession crisis following Smith's assassination the council of twelve apostles made a largely successful but contested bid to inherit the powers of the presidency. In the three years before his death, Smith had begun to elevate the role of the apostles but had never given them governmental power over organized stakes. Under the leadership of Brigham Young, the council claimed the right of succession, but at first only as a collectivity. Young was president of the council, not president of the church, although the distinction soon began to blur. For an interim the church had no presidency. Only during the move to Utah did Young get council approval for a reconstituted presidency, with himself as president and with two counselors drawn from the apostles. Unlike the pattern under Smith, the presidency was now a creature of the council. Young happened to be, barely, the oldest member of the council, although his leadership did not depend on this almost incidental fact. But his seniority set an enduring, although extralegal, precedent. From his presidency on, the council of twelve has always elected the senior apostle to the office (today always a very old man). The president remains the symbolic head of the church, and he alone can receive revelations respecting its basic doctrines. Thus, although an apostle in the order of the priesthood, the president is also a seer. The president, working through the presiding bishopric, also heads what is now the vast bureaucracy of the church—the Mormon welfare and relief system and extensive business and publishing enterprises.

One of the most distinctive aspects of Mormonism is this complex priesthood. In the early years it was in every sense a lay priesthood. Every white or Native American male was eligible to serve in one of the priestly offices. Priests as such received no pay (later, the general authorities of necessity became paid, full-time bureaucrats), and most had no special education. In a sense this has remained a very democratic priesthood, for today every eligible boy, if obedient, moves almost automatically into the order of deacons at age twelve. In the early, as later, LDS almost all adult males could become priests, with lofty titles and with ceremonies to mark their successive ordinations as they moved up the hierarchy.

Women have never enjoyed any priestly authority in this patriarchal church, except briefly and temporarily during the trek to Utah. Only in 1842 at Nauvoo did Smith organize the Masonic-like Female Relief Society, with his wife as its first president, the first leadership role open to women. This society has continued as the most important organization for women and in time would allow some women very important leadership roles. In an informal way it has developed functional female equivalents for the priesthood quorums. Smith intended the women to work out degrees or orders within the society. Also, with the temple endowments introduced at Nauvoo, women gained a type of incorporation into the two priestly orders but have never had any governmental role.

In 1833 Smith revealed that the proper center of worship for the saints would be a temple, as it had been for the Jews and the Nephites. Thus, the Mormons began construction of their first temple in Kirtland (they did not yet have meetinghouses or tabernacles). In 1836 they dedicated this first small temple and soon began a second (never completed) in Far West, Missouri. The first temple housed administrative offices on the attic third floor, a school for elders on the second floor, and a public meeting area on the first floor. This was elaborate, with special pulpits for each order of priests and movable veils that could divide the sanctuary into smaller rooms. The dedication produced ecstatic outpourings from the factional- ized membership. Special baths and anointings with oil, part of special en- dowments for the higher priestly quorums, anticipated later ceremonies open to all Mormons. At the dedication Smith promised new keys and mysteries but had to postpone these to the temple later built in Nauvoo, Illinois. The Kirtland temple, primarily a meetinghouse, was midway be- tween a church building and the later Mormon temples, which feature special, secret rituals performed nowhere else. Only in Utah would the Mormons be able to supplement their temples with local or ward meeting- houses or chapels for worship and instruction. Before this they worshiped in homes, barns, and schoolhouses, or outdoors.

The temple was only the most tangible symbol of the close identification of Mormons with Jews. Their subsequent jurisdictional divisions (regional stakes of Zion and local wards) had a Jewish flavor (these were stakes of the great tent that was the church, or images borrowed from the history of Israel). Mormons considered themselves the rightful successors of the Nephites, adoptive Jews, latter-day children of the covenant, and have al- ways referred to non-Mormons as Gentiles. Thus, more than in any other branch of Christianity, including Seventh-day Adventists, the Mormons have rejected any radical break between two dispensations and easily blend Old and New Testament institutions, language, and rituals. The most conspicuous departure from this sense of continuity was their rejection of sabbatarianism.

Smith was never as much of a health reformer as Ellen G. White. But in early 1833 he offered his Word of Wisdom (Section 89 of *Doctrine and Covenants*) on diet and health. This became, much later, one of the three or four most significant and authoritative revelations by Smith, although its dietary guidelines long remained optional (or largely ignored throughout most of the nineteenth century). Only in the twentieth century have these become near-absolute rules, often enforced as a condition of admission to temples. In the Word, Smith condemned tobacco and all forms of alcohol plus hot drinks such as tea and coffee (Mormons eventually substituted wa- ter for wine in their communion services). He recommended a sparing amount of meat and celebrated seasonal herbs, fruits, vegetables, and grains. After Mormons recanted polygamy, these dietary constraints became per- haps the most visible sign of their religious distinctiveness. Such asceticism now helps Mormons to nurture a sense of identity and to maintain bound- aries between themselves and Gentiles in a period when they no longer can separate themselves geographically or institutionally from the Gentile world. Whereas in the nineteenth century Mormons saw dietary rules as a form of renunciation of the world, in the twentieth century they have often proudly noted the healthful benefits and rejoiced in the longevity of faithful Mormons. It is clear that few Mormon men in the early church followed this Word of Wisdom. Many were rough, often crude men, with chewing tobacco and whiskey omnipresent even among church leaders. Joseph Smith imbibed and at times was clearly drunk.

One of the appeals of Smith's new church was its eclectic body of doctrines and practices. These overlapped at points with other Christian confessions. Added to this was the appeal of early Gnostic sects and non-Christian forms of occult religion or popular supernaturalism. The church literally had something that appealed to almost everyone. Of course, this mix meant that it had something to offend every orthodox Christian, in whatever confessional tradition. It was corporealist, superstitious, and enthusiastic (in time the ecstatic elements, particularly speaking in tongues, became more infrequent or lapsed all together). Smith's later doctrinal additions made it seem much worse to other Christians, particularly a polytheistic and materialistic theology, new temple ceremonies, and as part of those, the doctrine of plural marriage. But even before these additions, the early Mormon sect faced intense opposition.

By 1837 the saints faced adversity everywhere. An illegal Mormon savings bank (when it failed to get a state charter, Smith called it an antibanking company) failed in Kirtland in 1837. In effect, it defrauded hundreds of people of their savings. Factions seemed to arise every year to undermine Smith's authority, and the panic of 1837 increased pressures against the Missouri brethren. Facing arrest because of what Gentiles and many dissident Mormons saw as his banking scam, Smith had to flee Ohio in early 1838. By then, such were the divisions at Kirtland that Smith and Rigdon had few options except moving Mormon headquarters to Far West. Dissenting Mormons now had control of Kirtland and of the temple. Half the early leadership was in apostasy, at least from the perspective of Smith. The only relief from gloom was the astonishing success of a British mission effort led by Heber Kimball and other apostles. Converts there were able to form a priesthood and meet in conferences. Subsequent missions to Scandinavia, particularly Denmark, were equally successful.

After 1840, when most Mormons lived in Nauvoo, Illinois, Smith completed the doctrinal development of Mormonism. Before he had the time and opportunity for such innovations, he had to deal with a series of threats to Mormon survival. By June 1831 the Mormons at Kirtland had decided to move, as soon as possible, to the site of the new Zion in western Missouri and there prepare for the early advent. On his first visit to Missouri

Smith had staked out the exact spot for a temple, and Rigdon subsequently platted a great temple complex. But such great hopes for Zion in Missouri soon fell apart because of mob action against the Mormons. First driven from Jackson County (around Independence) in 1833, after one short skirmish with Gentiles, the Mormons settled in Clay and other nearby counties and then most intensively in a new county, Caldwell, created as a refuge for Mormons (Far West became its seat). Of special importance in later Mormon history, Smith helped organize a group of about 200 young men to march to Missouri in 1834 to try to save the first Mormon settlement in Jackson County. Called Zion's Camp, this little army fell into all manner of problems, suffered from a cholera epidemic, and arrived too late to effect events in Jackson County, which it never entered. But Zion's Camp contained a large share of later Mormon leaders.

From 1834 to 1837 the Mormons in counties north of Kansas City enjoyed relative peace, with tense but usually nonviolent relationships with neighboring Gentiles. As so often in the early history of the church, internal factionalism led, once again, to external repression. The new era of conflict, which lasted only six months, began when Smith and Rigdon moved permanently to Missouri in the spring of 1838. They tried to regain full control over the local church, which had its own, less authoritarian leadership. Smith, as so often in his career, indulged some grandiose schemes, began a new temple in Far West, and at least briefly believed he could both purify the local church and effectively defend Mormons against outside enemies. At least half of the local Mormon leaders rejected his authoritarian methods and faced excommunication when they openly protested his decisions. Smith even excommunicated Oliver Cowdery. Smith and Rigdon tried to form a new communal order, in part, it seems, to improve their own fortunes. The issues were complex, but in a sense the Missouri Mormons fell into an embittering civil war. In this context Smith and Rigdon tacitly approved secret vigilante groups, sometimes called Danite bands, which helped drive most of the dissidents from the Mormon settlements. More threatening to Gentiles was an incendiary speech by Rigdon, a new militancy on the part of Smith, and the formation of Mormon military units that, in retaliatory raids, burned some Gentile homes. Opposition to the Mormons rested less on religious concerns about Mormon doctrines and more on a fear that Mormons would complete compact settlements, and in a sense displace or exclude Gentiles.

In the fall of 1838, at election time, a statewide effort to expel the Mormons from Missouri as a whole gained wide public support. The governor capitulated to mob pressure and allowed the expulsion. The story is much too complex for any short account. In one skirmish, some Mormon troops shot at an unrecognized state militia unit. Such active resistance gave the governor an excuse to order the militia to drive from the state up to 8,000 Mormons. In one massacre, at the Mormon settlement of Haun's Mill, a mob brutally killed approximately seventeen Mormons, some of whom were children. The informal war ended when an army surrounded Far West and demanded its surrender. In effect the Mormon leaders capitulated, agreed that all Mormons would leave the state under protection, and themselves became prisoners of the state to await trial for various alleged crimes. Smith and some associates were almost shot by order of a militia commander. As the elders awaited trial, the Mormon families moved as quickly as they could to Illinois during the winter of 1838–39, leaving behind most of their property. From November 1838 to April 1839 Smith and his fellow elders languished in Missouri jails, awaiting proper charges and a trial. While on the move to a new jail in April, they escaped, seemingly by design of the Missouri authorities, and joined the exiled Mormons at Quincy, Illinois.

In Illinois the Mormons briefly found safety and succor. People felt sorry for them and provided as much relief as possible for destitute families. Local politicians also solicited their votes. Committees of Mormons thus sought land. After Smith escaped, he affirmed earlier plans of Rigdon to buy from a speculator several plots of land at Commerce, Illinois, upriver from Quincy and at a site that he hoped would become a new gathering place for all the saints. They conveyed titles to land back in Missouri in partial payment and never fully discharged all their debts (the church was, in effect, on the verge of bankruptcy during the Nauvoo years). Of course, many Mormon families made their own arrangements. Unscrupulous land agents cheated some, but throughout 1839 a majority of the faithful settled at Commerce or just across the Mississippi at Montrose in southeast Iowa (a territory at that time). As the Mormons bought up most of the land around Commerce, they in effect took control of the little village and soon renamed it Nauvoo ("beautiful place"). In October the church organized two stakes, one in Nauvoo and one in Iowa. Within a year 3,000 Mormons had settled in Nauvoo, and within two years it was the largest town in the state. In December 1840 the state granted a charter to the now-incorporated city, giving it virtual autonomy in all matters of local government, including full control over a local militia (the Nauvoo Legion).

The Mormons enjoyed only two or three calm years in Nauvoo. But briefly they were safe from outside persecution. Joseph Smith was able to evade several efforts by Missouri authorities to bring him back for trial, and he soon had such control over the Nauvoo militia and local courts as to frustrate most legal actions against him. He built and operated a general store and used the upstairs for all manner of church meetings (this was the Mormon Upper Room). This interlude of peace allowed another wave of institutional and doctrinal development. The mission enterprise climaxed, with the twelve apostles all taking mission journeys to Europe in 1839. They held a council meeting in England in 1840, convened a general conference, and launched a British hymnal and periodical. By the end of the year, the British saints numbered 4,000, and the first shipload of emigrants sailed for America and for Nauvoo.

NEW GODS AND NEW ORDINANCES

In what turned out to be a momentous decision in October 1840, Joseph Smith gave the command of God that the Mormons erect a temple in Nauvoo. This was to be a complete and perfect temple, which the one at Kirtland was not. Smith did everything possible to get Mormons, in Europe as well as America, to contribute to what turned out to be a very elaborate and expensive building. It required an enormous sacrifice by faithful Mormons, who at times practically did without food in order to contribute money or labor. In conjunction with the building, Smith developed new doctrines for the church, most related to ceremonies and promised blessings that would mark the rituals of the new temple.

By then he had matured a new theology and from 1842 to 1844 began to clarify its details. But he did not have the time, and perhaps did not have the skills, to develop a systematic or entirely clear Mormon cosmology. This meant plenty of room for further elaboration by his more able theological peers and successors, particularly by Parley and Orson Pratt; but these elaborations would not be of a piece, and most did not please Brigham Young. Thus, nothing is more difficult and more treacherous than any attempt, in either a brief or an extended essay, to clarify these crucial doctrines, which in many respects provided a backdrop for the new temple ordinances.

In the early Articles of Faith and in the *Book of Mormon* Smith's references to a god were quite orthodox. The singular, capitalized generic term, "God," dominated. Such a singular reference remains most common among Mormons today. But as Mormons know and as evangelical critics point out all the time, there is much more than this in Mormon theology. Soon after the founding of his church Smith made clear his acceptance of a corporealist conception of reality, which joined him to other apocalyptic or Adventist Christians. He never had any taste for some purely spiritual realm or for some ethereal mind or soul. Later, Mormons would ridicule the airy abstractions voiced by the Gentile clergy and note how such corrupt priests used such verbal nonsense to dupe ordinary people.

Smith used new translations, and thus new scriptures, to broach new metaphysical issues. He included these insights in the Book of Abraham, which he claimed to be a translation from funerary papyri (these accompanied some Egyptian mummies that Smith purchased). This, along with his translation of certain early but missing parts of the Bible (the Book of Moses), make up the brief *Pearl of Great Price*, which Mormons honor as scripture. Modern scholars have identified the Egyptian papyri as typical funerary records from the Book of the Dead. The story in Abraham involves what seems to be a higher or governing deity working with other, unnamed gods, and also the sons of this ruling deity, Jesus and Lucifer. They all live on a glorious, transparent planet—the Kingdom of Heaven— which is near the most magnificent star, Kolob. These gods, collectively, came down and formed the earth and all that is on it (a recapitulation of the Genesis story of creation). In this story the god who instructed Abraham clarified the eternality of intelligence and made clear that humans, such as Abraham, had a prior existence as spirits before their birth in the flesh. One son, Jesus, happily agreed to come and help in the great work of creation. The other, Lucifer, angry at not being first chosen, refused to help and led other spirits into rebellion.

In his endowment ritual and in a funeral oration only three months before his martyrdom (the King Follett discourse), Smith plunged even further into metaphysical speculations. It is impossible to locate a fully coherent theology in these suggestive nuggets. Thus, even today, Mormons have no fully normative theology and no creed or confessions that contain such. In a sense, out of the suggestions offered by Smith, they create their own theological insights. For reasons that should become clear, the theological game is a very exciting one among contemporary Mormons.

Smith, although in no sense a theologian or a philosopher, brought a certain perspective to his most cosmic speculations. For him, reality (all that exists) makes up an ultimate ground, eternal and thus noncreated. He called this matter. He distinguished two forms of matter, one coarse or physical and the other fine and equivalent to intelligence. He often used the word "spirit" for intelligent beings without a fully physical body but emphasized that such spirits had a spirit body composed of fine matter. Smith was not in the materialistic tradition of Newton or Joseph Priestley. His world was not fully lawful or unified or determinant. It was complex, at times messy, full of mysteries and of magic, often guided by occult forces, and peopled by various spirits, but at the same time it was conducive to ecstatic experience. Contemporary Mormons no longer believe in the magic and no longer experience the ecstasy.

In this ontological context one can understand what Joseph Smith meant by the word "god." A god is a complete person, with mind and body. A human is a near-god or an incipient god but is not yet god because of mortality, of having a corruptible body. Gods have incorruptible bodies and are very wise or very powerful. Angels are spirits without a physical body. They are thus incomplete, lower in the order of being than gods, and often servants of gods. Gods have flesh and blood, are gendered, and are in process, always changing. It is their physicality, even their sexuality, and above all their power to form and shape the world about them that makes them Olympian-like gods, gods that are so like humans as to be approachable and comprehensible. Such gods necessarily live someplace and act at some time. Since gods are male and female, they marry and copulate and have children (Jesus is a son). They are finite but partake of the eternal being that is matter. Once gods come into being, they are immortal. What Smith did not do, as far as I can tell, is provide an explanation or even a mythic story about how discrete gods, those with a distinct personality, emerged from primordial matter. Intelligence is eternal, but it is not clear that gods have always existed. Since they are evolving individuals, the great gods of the present were not always so. They were as we now are. In time we can become as they now are. Note that this version of theism can be very congenial to theories about organic evolution and at least suggests interesting congruences with modern physical theory, although such uses were far from the concerns of Smith.

This approach to gods is reasonably clear. What is confusing is the cosmic history—the numbers, the names, the ranks, and the roles of the gods that control our world. Smith named only a few gods: Elohim, the greatest god; Jehovah, a seeming near-equal of Elohim; and Michael, who becomes Adam, the father of humans. Elohim has two sons, Jesus and Lucifer. Each of these five named gods has one or more wives, but except for Eve they are unnamed. For Mormon feminists, here is the wonderful opening for a truly androgynous theology, and some have tried without success to get the all-male hierarchy of the church to recognize and honor a heavenly queen or mother. At times it seems that Elohim, Jehovah, and Michael make up a Mormon trinity, but at points Smith seemed to so elevate Jesus as to make him almost synonymous with Elohim. Jesus then seems the highest god. Michael not only joined the other gods in forming the earth but then agreed to assume a mortal body and become Adam. His mortal body was formed from the dust of earth, and Eve's mortal body came from his rib. But Michael-Adam remained a god and, after his mortal death, returned to his prior status in the heavenly kingdom. Presumably, so also did Eve. Jesus, the son of Elohim and fully dutiful in all things, consented to take on a mortal body in order to redeem obedient humans. With his ascension he also regained his incorruptible body in the heavenly kingdom. He will retain it when he returns to earth to govern those saints who are entitled to exchange their corruptible bodies for incorruptible ones. Not only do multiple gods have a tie to this earth, but other gods govern other worlds, worlds almost without end. The most divisive theological controversy in the early church involved theories about Michael-Adam. Brigham Young believed that Adam was the supreme god of this world, or really Elohim. The church did not accept his theory.

Humans are a vital part of this cosmic history. In the heavenly kingdom they were conceived and born as spirits, with the status of angels. This meant incompleteness, for they had no physical bodies. Who conceived these spirits? The answer is not entirely clear. It was either the gods, considered collectively, or possibly all were the offspring of Michael-Adam and one or many wives. In any case, Adam, in the delightful Garden of Eden, gave in to the enticements of Eve and ate the forbidden fruit. He suffered the ills of the flesh as a consequence and faced the death of his physical body. But his transgression of the command of Elohim had a noble, even sacrificial purpose, for this so-called fall really began the process of physical procreation and thus allowed more human spirits to gain mortal bodies. With such bodies, humans have the fullness of being, the ontological status, of gods and because of the redeeming work of the Christ can, through faithful obedience in his church, gain incorruptible bodies and become gods in the future celestial kingdom.

Mormons have always believed the advent near. Several have believed it may come around 2000, the beginning of the seventh millennium in Mormon chronology. Their eschatology is close to that of many other Adventists. Jesus will come to the earth for a thousand-year millennium. While Satan is chained, humans will live in a perfected world, still working and procreating but without former temptations and afflictions and with physical death marking only a transition to a higher, incorruptible status. At the time of the advent the righteous dead regain perfected bodies in a first resurrection and have a special juridical role during the millennium. Among those who enjoy this resurrection will be many righteous people who lived before the restoration of the true church, but during the millennium they will be able to convert to the true faith (very close to the second-chance doctrines of later Jehovah's Witnesses). Only very evil people experience death at the time of the advent, with their tortured spirits suffering through the millennium. At the end of the millennium, all faithful saints move onto a new and purified earth and into a new kingdom with three levels of rewards. The faithful Mormon saints, including the converts during the millennium, plus all their willing progenitors sealed by vicarious baptisms, endowments, and marriages, can move immediately to the highest level of glory, the celestial kingdom, and become kings and queens or even gods in their own right, able to govern or even form and shape new worlds. At the end of the millennium, Satan breaks free, gathers an army of the damned, and besieges the saints. But he is defeated, and he and his followers are forever expelled from the earth. In Mormon beliefs it seems that those who suffer a final banishment with Lucifer will be few in number. Most humans will at least gain membership in the two lower kingdoms, the telestial and the terrestrial.

This theology is unique and unlike that of any other religion in the world. In it lay concealed the heady promise of Smith's late doctrines. He offered Mormons the opportunity to become gods. He provided them the means to move more quickly to this status in his new temple ordinances—baptisms for the dead, endowments, and marriages for eternity. For living Mormons, endowments and temple marriages are climactic moments (they have already received their own baptism locally, at age eight or when converted). After their own endowment or marriage, Mormons continue to perform the three ordinances for their progenitors (or in some cases for other than progenitors), in periodic visits to their regional temple. Critics saw in these new ordinances and the promises that went with them a deliberate strategy for Smith to get funds for the temple and to gain more power for himself. Later, a minority of Mormons, who joined several small splinter sects or became members of the RLDS, rejected these doctrines.

In January 1841 in conjunction with launching the temple, Smith announced two of the new ordinances: "washings and anointings," later called endowments, and baptisms for the dead (Section 124 of *Doctrine and Covenants*). As he later claimed, he also received at this time revelations concerning celestial marriage but did not disclose these mysteries to the council of twelve until 1843. These three ordinances provided the authority for very sacred and secret temple rites. The doctrinal background to these new ordinances was complex. In Moroni's first visit to Joseph Smith he revealed that Smith would later receive an understanding from Elijah of a special priesthood that would become active again in the last days. The visit by Elijah was promised in the last verses of the Old Testament, Malachi 4:5–6, a critical part of the Bible for Mormons and one quoted by Jesus in his visit to America. In 1836 at the temple in Kirtland, Elijah appeared to Smith and Cowdery and announced that at this time the keys to a new dispensation were committed to their hands and that they could, by this fact, know that the advent was near. In 1841 Smith interpreted this to mean that with a new and correct temple the keys were to open three new, sealing ordinances for the living and for the dead.

The first ordinance widely practiced at Nauvoo was the baptism of the dead. The doctrine is simple and is based on Paul's reference to the baptism of the dead at Corinth in 1 Corinthians 15:29 (the only explicit reference to such a practice in the New Testament). The practice also has some similarity to purgatory doctrines among Roman Catholics, particularly the medieval use of special masses to aid souls in purgatory. According to Smith, progenitors of faithful Mormons, or people who had not had a chance to hear the latter-day message but who would most likely have accepted it had they heard it, could now receive the benefits of such acceptance vicariously (Mormons have baptized over 200 million people and have, by far, the richest genealogical data in the world). Any Mormon in good standing in the church and eligible to enter the temple (with a temple "Recommend," verified by a card issued by a ward bishop and approved by a stake president) could accept baptism in behalf of a dead ancestor. This baptism, Smith affirmed in 1841, had to be in a special font in the new Nauvoo temple, although for a year God allowed the Mormons to celebrate such baptisms in the Mississippi River. But as soon as they could complete a baptismal font (a pool supported by twelve stone oxen, representing the twelve tribes of Israel) in the basement of the uncompleted temple in late 1841, they began this special temple rite. Smith not only legitimized such proxy baptisms but made them a special obligation of Mormons, a test of their faith and commitment. Thus, Mormons after 1840 had a compelling reason to identify progenitors, eventually for all three ordinances. Such proxy baptisms helped create a special sense of a vast extended family, encouraged an almost Jewish sense of a covenantal bonding over the centuries, and promised a special family relationship in the coming kingdom. Ancestors were free to accept or reject the benefits of such a baptism (these, when conjoined with the two other vicarious ordinances, admitted one directly to the celestial kingdom).

Temple baptisms are simple and, because of the heavy temple traffic, today are almost always hurried. Proxy candidates take seats around the font and, when their names are called, move into the font for separate immersions in the name of each candidate they have on their list (each immersion in the water takes only a few seconds). Following this water baptism another priest lays on hands to mark the baptism of the spirit or a type of confirmation. Males may also receive a proxy ordination into the Melchizedek priesthood. In a few cases individuals submit to such baptisms for hundreds of names. Since baptism for the dead, alone among temple ordinances, does not require the proxy to have had his or her endowment, parents often introduce youth to the temple ceremonies by having them serve as proxy. The church has tried to restrict the names to identified progenitors, but in some cases the temple workers have accepted the names of celebrities or, in a much-advertised case, the identified names of Jewish victims of the Holocaust (the church subsequently agreed to remove these names from the list of baptized). Today the church tries to keep a careful record of those so baptized but in the past could not prevent some duplicate baptisms. Widely distributed Family History Centers, linked to the huge genealogical archives maintained by the church in Utah, provide the names of ancestors to Mormons who request such assistance and offer to the broader public the most extensive genealogical resources in the world.

Of the other two ordinances, Smith first announced what became endowments. The word "endowment" has a special meaning to Mormons. Already, at the Kirtland temple, those admitted to the higher priesthood had received endowments, meaning certain blessings and promises that were part of a washing and anointing ritual. But this came before a perfect temple and the fullest revelation of formerly sealed ordinances. Thus, in 1841 Smith promised that all the saints (women as well as men) could receive "washings and anointments" in the new temple but not until its completion. He actually allowed sixty-six people, elders and their wives, to gain their endowment before his death in 1844, and thus before the opening of the designated rooms in the attic of the temple. Smith used canvas partitions above his store to create pale approximations of the later temple rooms. These who gained this early endowment constituted a special, secret elite, including some who had also contracted secret polygamous marriages. The endowed elite met frequently in an anointed quorum.

In the midst of these early endowments and a developing civil war among the Mormons in Nauvoo, Smith added an additional ceremony, called a second endowment or anointing, leading to the "fullness of the priesthood." Unlike the first endowment, it involved a simple or short ceremony, but it promised heady returns for those who gained it. In Smith's words, it moved them up the spiritual hierarchy to the status of kings (queens) or gods. It meant an immediate and higher level of exaltation than that gained through the regular endowment ceremony. From the beginning this second endowment was by invitation of the president or, later, of a few additional priests selected by the president. It was thus a bestowed honor. Smith clearly used it as a tool to maintain the loyalty of able associates in Nauvoo and particularly as a reward for those who accepted plural marriage. He also included wives in this special anointing (usually husbands and wives joined in the short ceremony) and in this case clearly used the elevated promises to help secure the loyalty and the silence of women who had to accept additional wives in their own households. Brigham Young continued this special anointing and also allowed such anointings for the dead, but he discontinued the attendance of women at anointed quorums. In the twentieth century this second endowment gradually became a less important ritual and one with a somewhat different meaning. By 1940 almost all such special endowments had ended, and today they are few and fully confidential and function as an honor or recognition for elderly and faithful Mormon couples. Few contemporary Mormons even know about this ritual, and no one now seems to interpret it as an automatic pathway to special, even monarchical, powers in the coming kingdom.

Of the three ordinary temple ordinances, the endowment ritual was and is by far the most time consuming. Except for the climax, it is, by necessity, a group experience, even today almost an assembly-line production in overcrowded temples. Today most participants have already gained their own endowment and go through the rituals in behalf of progenitors. In his announcement of this new ordinance, Smith referred only to anointing and washing. The background included rites of purity or cleanliness, with baths and special robes, performed in the ancient Jewish temple. Also influential, and in some details controlling, were the Masonic initiation rites, which were very familiar to Smith since he had become a Mason in 1842 (just before he carried out the first endowments) and a member of a new Nauvoo lodge (the largest in Illinois). Mormons who receive their own endowment or additional endowments in behalf of their progenitors are sworn to secrecy about the rituals, with originally very bloody and harsh, Masonic-derived penalties (throat cutting, disembowelment) for any violation of this oath. In fact, apostates soon revealed the details to the world and, as far as the records reveal, without any violent reprisals by the church. In the twentieth century, critics or apostates have recorded and published the entire endowment ceremony (versions of it are even available on the Internet). It may soon be politically desirable for the church to do away with the secrecy.

The endowment rituals involve both dramatic enactments and initiation rites. The endowment, for the living, normally occurs when young adults take on full responsibility in the church and is a requirement for males who enter the Melchizedek priesthood or assume missionary assignments (yet today a majority of Mormons do not go through the endowment, either by choice or because they cannot meet the morally rigorous requirements for a temple Recommend). For some it is one of the most important events of a lifetime. This is because the endowment rituals are directly related to the achievement of celestial glory or a type of heavenly divinity. The performance of the vicarious ritual is also a mark of devotion for obedient Mormons, meaning that some Mormons, in a lifetime, may repeat the ritual hundreds of times.

The details of the rite stimulated curiosity on the part of Gentiles and led to false rumors of erotic content. Without violating the Mormon desire for secrecy, it is fair to point out that the endowment ceremony does involve an opening preparation for separate groups of males and females: a ceremonial bath and anointing with oil, the assumption of a new heavenly name (whispered by a temple worker), and the donning of a special undergarment (the cut and fabrics have varied through time, but not the four Masonic-like symbols). Faithful Mormons wear this undergarment for the rest of their lives. After the washing and anointing, the patrons begin their dramatic journey toward the celestial kingdom. In the early temples actors performed the dramatic roles, as participants moved through separate temple rooms (creation, the Garden of Eden, and the lone and dreary world). Today the dramatic reenactments are on film, and much of the instruction is on tape. Mormons who go through each endowment ceremony view a dramatic and extended enactment of cosmological beginnings, with heavenly characters, including Lucifer, and details about the creation of the earth and the fall of Adam and Eve. For many Mormons this is their most vivid contact with the special cosmology of their church. What follows was directly influenced by the Masonic initiation (Joseph Smith claimed that he perfected a corrupted ceremony that went back to Solomon). In groups the candidates, like pilgrims, move at least symbolically through the two lower realms of the kingdom and at four stations, two for the Aaronic priesthood and two for the Melchizedek, receive special instructions that, if learned and retained and joined with obedience, will gain them admission to the celestial kingdom. At each of the four stations they learn the tokens of that priesthood, which involves passwords, a recited covenant, and signs and penalties symbolized by special hand grips or movements. In the course of such instruction they don and shift from one shoulder to another a special robe and with it put on over their white clothing an apron, sash, hat, and even special slippers. Significantly, the Melchizedek covenants involve a commitment to chastity and to the early Mormon law of consecration. The climax comes at the end, as the pilgrims symbolically approach the celestial kingdom. A sermon and a prayer circle prepare everyone for the climax. One by one the candidates, on cue and with help if needed, repeat the signs and passwords before a veil that conceals a usually luxurious room that represents the celestial kingdom. An actor behind the veil (which contains the four symbols on the special garment) plays the part of Elohim and, after hand grips through holes in the veil and a final embrace through the veil, offers admission to the kingdom.

The endowment ritual has changed through time. In fact, no one knows the exact ritual as Smith first used it in the rooms over his store. Insofar as possible, temple workers followed his precedents when they were able to give endowments in the new temple. Only in Utah did Brigham Young finally commit the ritual to writing, and minor changes have been frequent. The most recent changes came in 1990. New wording replaced the gory penalties for violating secrecy and eliminated from the early drama the heavily caricatured character of an apostate clergyman, full of spiritualistic and pompous mysteries, who was actually in the service of Lucifer. Perhaps more significantly, the revision did not contain some former words that committed wives to abject obedience of husbands. The last change seemed to reflect the council's increased sensitivity to the concerns of women. The church had been embarrassed by the enormous publicity that surrounded its excommunication of Sonia Johnson in 1979 after she helped mobilize Mormon women in support of the equal rights amendment and in opposition to the well-organized church effort to ensure its defeat. Note that Mormon women, if they choose, can appeal to the early endowment under Smith, to the second endowment ceremony, and to the anointed quorum to claim that he had, at this point, inaugurated a fuller and higher priesthood fully open to women.

For Mormons who faithfully do their temple work, the endowment ritual takes much time. Usually the baptismal ritual precedes the endowment, and if genealogists have been able to identify the names of both a wife and a husband, it is followed by the marriage ceremony or, in some cases, by the sealing of children to parents. Several ornate sealing rooms in each temple have altars, and in these a woman and man (vicariously representing the named ancestors) go through the brief marriage ceremony, thus uniting the earlier couple for eternity. With this step the temple rites are complete. Note that, for a few in each group, the rituals are for themselves and thus have an even deeper significance. Gaining one's endowment is even more significant for Mormons than the first communion is for Roman Catholics. For those eligible, temple marriages are likewise a high moment. In the temple the presiding priest usually adds instruction to the still relatively brief ceremony, and family and friends, if they have a temple Recommend, are able to attend this ceremony.

Today the temple ceremonies face problems within Mormonism, particularly outside the United States. In a sense, faithful attendance at temple rituals identifies a special elite, for even the gaining of temple Recommends requires a high level of commitment and obedience. Increasingly, according to the testimony of those who have left the church, the endowment ceremony is strange, for some shocking, and not very coherent with the rest of their Mormon experience. Even the idea of secret initiations, strange hand clasps, and secret words is as out of fashion or seems as childish as Masonic or other fraternal initiations, while the theological content of the ceremony features the very doctrines that most distinguish Mormons from other Christians.

It is not easy to describe the doctrine of plural marriage, which was a complement to temple marriages. By Smith's claim, his fullest understanding of marriage was complete by 1841, at the time he revealed the other two new temple ordinances. But he knew how explosive the marriage doctrines were, how hard it would be for Mormons to accept them, and how much outside ridicule and condemnation they would invite. Of course no one can prove that Smith received any revelation in 1841. Maybe the doctrine was a clever rationalization of his own sexual indulgence. A still-youthful, magnetic, and even charismatic individual, Smith became virtual king of Nauvoo. He had enormous power over the 15,000 Mormons who had gathered in that area by 1844. At age thirty-five he was still very attractive to women. Maybe his power and the sexual opportunities went to his head and he succumbed to temptation and then sought ways to vindicate his own behavior. Maybe. The possibilities are almost endless, and one can only speculate about motives.

The records of the church reveal that on April 5, 1841, one day before the cornerstone ceremonies for the new temple, Smith was groom in a special wedding, marrying for eternity a second wife. Records for the next three years include the names of eight other new wives. But this is only a small part of a complex and only partly known series of events. By most non-Mormon estimates, Smith married as many as forty additional wives. His escapades with women stretched back to his early Kirtland years and in one case involved a conspicuous liaison (he was caught in the act) that helped alienate several of his friends, including Cowdery. He later married the women with whom he had these early affairs, and he may have fathered children by some of them. It is possible that even in Kirtland he had begun to develop his later marriage doctrines. In any case, he performed some illegal bigamous marriages in Kirtland between Mormon men and women converts who had left their non-Mormon but still living husbands. But it was only in 1841 that Smith revealed his new marriage doctrines to a few elders and began sealing a few of them (possibly as many as twenty) in marriage to more than one wife. Apparently some did it as a religious obligation, reluctantly. These early exemplifications of the new doctrine remained more or less secret. He did not announce them to the Mormon community as a whole, but as early as 1842 an enemy of Smith openly accused him of polygamy. From then on accusations and rumors of sexual deviance fed the internal opposition to Smith and, even more, the external hostility to Smith and to the Mormons as a whole. Thus the doctrine of plural marriage underlay and affected the events that led to the murder of Smith and the subsequent expulsion of the Mormons from Illinois.

Smith's conduct from 1841 until the fall of 1843, when he seemingly stopped contracting plural marriages, has remained the most troubling cloud over the complex career of the Mormon prophet. Smith seemed, in the perspective of critics, to let sexual lust take control of his life. Even his friends and loyal supporters were perplexed and confused by his behavior. Not only did he contract marriage with young "virgins" but in a few cases with married women (including the troubled wife of Orson Hyde, an apostle away on a mission trip to Palestine). The victims were the women he approached. His prophetic status and his claims of divine approval led many to succumb, with what degree of guilt or self-hatred we will never know. Other young women rejected his offers despite intense pressure and then suffered harassment and character assassination, particularly if they dared inform others about the offer. One such strong-willed victim was the daughter of Sidney Rigdon, whose rejection of Smith led to much personal pain and to a long period of tension between Smith and his first counselor. The small circle of men who, despite public denials, took additional wives soon constituted a self-protective little oligarchy, with enough elements of conspiracy and wife sharing to risk accusations of free love. The pre-temple endowments, and particularly second endowments, were compromised because such initiations into divinity may have helped buy the silence of wives who resented second marriages by husbands. But the second endowments did gain for a few women a status and power never before, or perhaps since, enjoyed in the Mormon religion. It is even conceivable that women would not have gained the right to the later, normal endowments if it had not been for the complex relationships between plural marriage and endowments from 1841 to 1844. Even the creation of the female relief society may have helped soothe the hurt feelings of Emma. Finally, the actual initiation of such marriages may have helped shape the details of the new marriage doctrine, which Smith formalized only in 1843.

In 1843 Smith communicated the doctrine of celestial marriage to the council of apostles. Not until 1852 in Utah did Brigham Young reveal it to the membership. Smith began his revelation with the question of how God justified multiple wives and concubines for Abraham, Isaac, Jacob, Moses,

David, and the other heroes of Israel. To clarify this, God revealed to him a new and everlasting covenant that, when understood, became obligatory for anyone who would gain the highest celestial glory. Only those vows, contracts, or obligations entered into and sealed by "the Holy Spirit of promise" by him who was anointed (Smith or presidents of the church who followed him) last beyond this life. Thus, ordinary marriages end at death. At the resurrection, such couples are not man and wife and cannot then marry (this is based on the New Testament). They live their later life singly and as angels who are mere servants of those who are worthy of a much higher level of glory. They can never become gods. But those who are sealed and anointed in marriage by the head of the church or his representatives are married for eternity, participate in the first resurrection (at the beginning of the millennial age), and later attain the highest levels of celestial glory ("then they shall be gods" and shall "pass by the angels, and the gods, which are set there, to their exaltation and glory in all things"). Such marriages are properly sealed only in the temple, but obviously Smith and a few elders had a special dispensation to contract such marriages before the temple was ready for the ceremonies.

Note that this doctrine places an obligation on Mormons to marry. It is a divinely appointed duty of humans, in their earthly assignment, to marry, to form families, and to conceive children. The procreative ends and the blessings of family life always had the highest place in Mormon justifications of their marriage doctrines, but the sensual side was important. The Mormons were never abstentious in their approach to sex, only rigid in placing it within narrow bounds. They believed marriage and sexual union to be natural and ordained by God. Although the practice of multiple marriages while on earth was discontinued by the church after 1890, the doctrine of celestial marriage remains one of the most important in Mormonism, even as the temple marriage ritual is a climactic event in the life of many Mormons (Mormons who are ineligible for a temple marriage or who choose not to have one contract ordinary marriages, which are not for eternity). Since Mormons married before the enunciation of this doctrine did not have the promises it contained, over 2,000 married Mormons flocked to the new temple in Nauvoo to receive this new seal before they left for Utah.

One implication of such temple marriages was that some Mormon men, even when monogamous, would have more than one wife in the coming kingdom, so long as they contracted another temple marriage after the death of a first wife (women could not be sealed to more than one husband). Given marriage for eternity, then a plurality of wives was obviously acceptable to God, else widowers could not remarry in the temple. In his revelation from God (Section 132 in *Doctrine and Covenants*), Smith set down the terms for plural marriages here on earth. The taking of a second wife or concubine, as in the case of Abraham in the Old Testament, was accounted righteousness, for Hagar enabled Abraham to have children and to begin a whole tribe of people (thus the procreative goal, particularly for righteous patriarchs likely to father exemplary children, or a mild eugenics goal). The restriction was also clear: one could take additional wives only when it was God's will. Since in the *Book of Mormon* God had specifically condemned marriage to more than one wife (Jacob 2:27), Smith had to stress that God had commanded such an exception to his own rules in order to fulfill certain purposes in the brief period before the advent, even as he had made exceptions for the Jewish patriarchs of old. In Nauvoo this meant that only God's agent on earth, or the president and prophet of the true church, could approve multiple marriages. One further condition qualified such additional marriages. If a man espoused a second virgin for a wife, then the first wife had to give her consent (this later entailed her participation in the temple ceremony).

Even the revelation contained some troubling personal information. Speaking in the name of God, Joseph Smith had a special warning for his first wife, Emma. God commanded her to receive the additional wives, to cleave to his servant Joseph, and not to accept an offer of property apparently made to her by Joseph in the way of appeasement. Emma had been very distressed and angry because of his earlier affairs with women, particularly those involving clear romantic involvements. In 1842 and 1843 she fought back and used every opportunity to deny the new doctrines or to condemn those involving plural marriages. Even participation in a first and then second endowment did not appease Emma. After Joseph's death, Emma apparently burned the original transcript of his marriage revelation. For the rest of her life she denied that Joseph had ever married additional wives or promulgated the doctrine of plural marriage. Yet those loyal to Joseph always claimed that she not only knew about the marriages but helped select some of the brides. The records indicate that she participated in at least two of his marriages, involving household servants. It is possible that she believed, at least for a time, that these were spiritual (unconsummated) marriages, but she soon had proof that this was not so. Joseph's early death foreclosed a continuing and nasty battle in his own household. On the other hand, Emma's knowledge of the nasty truth about Joseph's sex life gave her enormous power. She needed only to speak out publicly to sabotage his already precarious leadership in the church.

By 1843 the prophetic phase of Mormonism was over. The fullest doctrinal developments were in place. In Nauvoo it had become a very different religion from what it had been at its beginnings in Palmyra. The new temple rituals and the distinctive theology almost supplanted the earlier evangelical themes (grace and atonement). In a sense, the new Mormonism was much more a religion of works or obedience than one of faith. At the very least, the temple ordinances were necessary conditions for the highest level of celestial glory, and the priests, as much as or more than in ancient Judaism or in medieval Roman Catholicism, held the keys to such an earned form of redemption. Yet, like Seventh-day Adventists, Mormons retained a tension between faith and works and through the decades have tried to resolve these. In the twentieth century, Mormons have not repudiated the centrality of the temple work. In some respects, they have placed even greater emphasis on it. Yet, they have often moved back toward the more evangelical themes of their beginnings. They have generally denied that any sealings in the temple guarantee later glory, for the saints can still sin and lose this promise. Such a freewill interpretation has allowed a degree of convergence with conservative Protestants. But in ways the anti-Catholic Mormons would never admit, the rich temple ordinances added a final eclectic element to their religion, one comparable to the rich liturgies of Roman Catholicism or of the Greek Orthodox churches.

It is important to note that Mormons at any distance from Nauvoo were not involved in the early temple rituals. Although nearby Mormons rushed to the temple in late 1845 and early 1846 for endowments and marriages, the temple ceremonies effectively ended for an extended period after the move to Utah and the closing of the Nauvoo temple. All the leadership in Utah had participated in the temple ceremonies, and most had received their second endowment. They did not forget or repudiate the rituals or the supporting doctrines, but they could not practice them. What is unclear is how many outlying or European Mormons knew about or valued these rituals and the doctrines that justified them. It would be a decade before Young resumed the temple ceremonies in a special Endowment House in Salt Lake City, and yet another decade before he resumed second endowments. At Nauvoo and then at first in Utah, the endowments and marriages were almost always for the living and not for the dead. The modern pattern (most for the dead) developed only after completion of a temple in St. George, Utah, in 1877 and, finally, in Salt Lake City in 1893.

A description of distinctive Mormon doctrines and temple rituals does not do justice to the Mormon religion or fully explain its broad appeal. Perhaps a majority of Mormons have never understood the subtleties of the Mormon cosmology, and many have not experienced the temple rites. What are closer to Mormons everywhere are the weekly services at the ward level. Here, Mormon instruction and worship, as formalized in the twentieth century, is close to the free Protestant model. It developed slowly out of a somewhat anarchic or regionally variable pattern of worship even as late as the Civil War and from a widespread neglect of worship or other formal gatherings by a majority of early Utah Mormons. Eventually, organized Sunday schools and new ward chapels helped standardize worship.

Twentieth-century Mormons gather for teaching and worship on Sunday. All required corporate activities take place during approximately three hours on Sunday morning. Young children attend Sunday school classes. Boys and young men meet in Aaronic priesthood quorums, which are the equivalent of Sunday school classes for older youth. Girls meet in functionally similar classes. Adult men meet in their Melchizedek priesthood quorums; adult women, in equivalent classes of their relief society. After such classes, all gather for worship, which Mormons often refer to as the sacrament meeting. Their worship is very close to that of the early Disciples movement. The ward bishop usually presides, makes announcements, and welcomes guests. But he is not primarily a preacher. A Mormon hymn and a prayer begin the service, possibly with special music or choral performances. The communion usually follows. After a prayer the bishop breaks the bread. Deacons pass it to the audience. They repeat this with the water. Instead of a formal sermon, appointed members may come to the pulpit for brief, often assigned talks, giving an informal, lay orientation to the service. The bishop may conclude the talks. A hymn and prayer usually conclude the service. It is not secret, but the communion is for members only. On the first Sunday, or fast Sunday, impromptu testimonials replace assigned speakers and faithful members skip two meals and, in an old tradition, give money for the needy. Testimonies are vital to Mormonism, and individuals often talk of gaining or losing their testimony, meaning both a type of vital religious experience and a deep personal commitment.

The Sunday services, however central and basic, join with many other activities, such as social or recreational meetings during the week. Most parents have a family night for both religious discussions and enjoyable activities on Monday of each week. In most cities the church provides daily educational programs for both high school and college students. Every devout Mormon has a "calling," some assigned office or work within the church.

For devout young men, and increasingly also for young women, the highest and most visible calling is to mission work. Carefully planned indoctrination and, if needed, language instruction precede this service. For Mormon young men in the United States from reasonably affluent and very devout families, the normal pathway to church leadership includes four years at Brigham Young University and then two more years of mission work (financed by the family). In many ways this tour is like military service. The basic training comes in the intensive indoctrination of the training course. The active duty involves daily proselytizing, often in third world countries, with plenty of hazards at least to one's health (or to one's life, since two Mormon missionaries were gunned down by nationalist terrorists in Bolivia in 1989). It is most often from mission veterans that the church recruits its ward bishops and general authorities.

The Mormon religion is governmental and humanistic and, in its own terms, sensual and joyful. People have a divine heritage in a previous life and are born into the world not resentfully, not as a curse or because of any depravity (a very alien doctrine to Mormons), but as a challenge and an opportunity. The snares are many. One can so easily mess it all up and, instead of growing spiritually, can so regress into sinfulness as to deserve only damnation. Life on earth is a period of trial and testing. One is on probation or, perhaps better, on an assignment. In the great test one has to obey the divine governor and the authorities within the church, be a faithful servant, and do one's duty. The rewards are not ephemeral or mystical, but a richer and fuller life—good food, good companionship, domestic love, and increased power and authority. One becomes more like a god and in effect, after the resurrection, can join Jesus in ruling and judging and creating. Life on earth may be hard. Suffering is part of life, as it is part of any basic training. One must bear up under the burdens and thus gain the later glory.

Mormon communal life is very supportive, not at all ascetic. Mormons, from the beginning, loved sports, games, theater, and dancing (today the dances are carefully chaperoned). They still love good clean fun and have artful ways of achieving it at their frequent socials. Back in Nauvoo, after the struggle and sacrifice to complete the temple and after the sleepless days and nights that the leadership spent getting participants through the ceremonies, the tired workers finally relaxed in the evening, enjoying food and a spirited and joyous dance within the holy spaces of their new temple. In Salt Lake City a despairing Brigham Young once protested that almost no one attended worship services, while everyone came to the dances that often lasted all night.

MARTYRDOM AND DIVISION

Even as Smith completed the doctrinal development of Mormonism, it faced a decade of adversity. From 1841 to 1844 Nauvoo was racked with internal factionalism, which only reinforced external hostility. In the background of almost all the turmoil were the now widely aired charges of polygamy, which Smith and the council consistently but duplicitously denied (they did not consider plural marriage a form of polygamy). The old enemies in Missouri still hoped to arrest Smith and bring him to trial or set him up for a lynching, particularly after one of Smith's bodyguards attempted to assassinate an ex-governor of Missouri. Smith faced increased opposition within the church. He prevailed, but not without the loss of able lieutenants. The church excommunicated several elders, while the first counselor, Rigdon, was often away from Nauvoo. Dr. John C. Bennett, Smith's ablest early political ally in Nauvoo and an early mayor of the city, either misinterpreted the new doctrine of plural marriages or deliberately used it to rationalize several sexual escapades. As a result of severe church discipline and then excommunication, Bennett became a bitter enemy of Smith. He wrote a damning book about both the doctrines and the political authoritarianism of Mormonism, plotted with Smith's enemies in Missouri, and urged Illinois legislators to repeal the Nauvoo charter (they did this in 1845, after Smith's death). For a time Smith had used Mormon bloc voting as a political weapon, since the Mormon vote could tip the balance in the state, but he lost this leverage in January 1844 when he renounced both political parties and convened a local convention to nominate himself as a candidate for president of the United States.

Even as he became a candidate and ostensibly sent the twelve apostles east to campaign for him (and also to seek converts), he formed a new council of fifty. This council has invited much scholarly controversy. Even today it is impossible to assess its exact role. At the time it seemed to be an adjunct to Smith's new political ambitions. It included most, but not all, of the twelve apostles. It was an advisory body, not a church agency. It included the ablest Mormons clearly loyal to Smith, in the midst of the deep divisions or even civil war under way in Nauvoo, but also included three friendly Gentiles. In the two months before Smith's martyrdom this council seemed to spend most of its time discussing a possible move of the Mormons to a site in the Rocky Mountains, where they could find the desired isolation and be able to set up a Mormon polity to parallel the priestly organization within the church. At times Smith and others referred to this as the Kingdom of God, a premillennial kingdom that would nonetheless prefigure the type of order that would follow the return of Jesus and the formation of his kingdom on earth, with capital cities at both Zion in Missouri and Jerusalem in Palestine.

All along—and this was what most frightened nearby Gentile neighbors—the Mormons had clustered much as communal colonies. Smith had consistently demanded that all Mormons who could possibly do so gather at one place, first in Kirtland, then in Missouri, and finally in Nauvoo. In each case, troubles had beset the effort and led Smith to contemplate a final move to the West. Consistent with the council of fifty, and possibly with his own grandiose political ambitions, was Smith's sense that God was on the side of the saints and that God might, at any time, weaken or destroy the Gentile governments that surrounded and so often threatened them. Thus he occasionally talked about a time in the near future when the Mormons would expand to the boundaries of the whole nation, or even the whole world, and be able to set up their own anticipatory kingdom. By this line of speculation, Smith added one final theme to his religion: a postmillenarian optimism, a dream of an earthly, Mormondominated kingdom that would prepare the way for the return of Jesus. In such moments of illusioned expectancy, Smith dreamed of being king of the United States or even of the whole world.

Nauvoo was an incipient but flawed and beleaguered kingdom of the saints. By the spring of 1844 it was about to explode internally, even as outside enemies prepared to invade Nauvoo, "free" its citizens from Smith's dictatorship, and possibly expel all his Mormon supporters from Illinois. Meanwhile, there were other Mormons, with their own complex story, one usually ignored by historians. This story involves not only the converts in Europe but numerous scattered Mormons in various parts of the United States. Some could not move to Nauvoo, at least not quickly. Others chose not to do so. The new temple rituals were all but meaningless to them, even when they knew about them. These Mormons met in small clusters for worship in homes and, in time, in their own meetinghouses. They apparently faced little hostility from their neighbors and blended into the religious mosaic of America. Yet many of them later made their way to Utah and became part of the largest and most durable kingdom of the saints, joining on the way west a steady stream of Mormon immigrants from Europe. Not all came to Utah. But if they did not, they remained stigmatized, for they could not, until the twentieth century and a complete change of policy on the part of the general authorities of the church, gain local temples and become fully integrated into the church. Many such scattered Mormon congregations, particularly throughout the Midwest, later moved into the reorganized church. Notably, these congregations never assimilated the new doctrines and rituals that Smith developed in Nauvoo.

Back in Nauvoo, events came to a final and violent climax in 1844. The personality of Smith, as much or more than unique Mormon beliefs or Mormon exclusivity, lay behind the final conflict. Smith was still young, charming in some contexts, but very unpredictable. He overused his prophetic claims with revelations about trivial or very personal issues. Some individuals believed power had gone to his head. The very situation of Nauvoo was contradictory in America—a church with full political control, or something close to a theocracy. The spread of rumors about the new temple rites posed grave risks for the church. The rites were secret, privileged (only dutiful Mormons could participate in them), abetted tremendously the power of the higher priesthood, and departed much farther than any earlier Mormon practices from orthodox Christianity and even from the most direct reading of the *Book of Mormon*. At the same time, the temple rites reinforced the urgent need for all Mormons to gather at one site. The legal risks occasioned by plural marriages among the higher priesthood bound them even closer in a cultlike relationship to their prophet.

Joseph Smith's kingdom fell in the spring of 1844. The demise began with the most broad-based rebellion ever within the church hierarchy, for several apostles and even one counselor (William Law) conspired to depose Smith. They feared his volatility, condemned his high-handed dictatorship, resented recent revelations, and refused to accept polygamy. Given the position of Smith, his immediate access to God, his control of all local newspapers, and his control of the local government and the 3,000 troops in the Nauvoo Legion (he was the commander and a lieutenant general and was often addressed by this title), they had no easy way to proceed, no democratic procedures to follow. Thus they plotted in secrecy and realized that they might have to join outside conspirators who wanted nothing less than the death of Smith. Inevitably Smith learned of the plots, used his authority to excommunicate the leaders of the revolt, and then tried to ride out the local shock waves.

Smith then made what turned out to be a fatal mistake. He either deliberately risked or even sought martyrdom or was seduced by illusions of personal invulnerability. When the plotters set up an anti-Smith newspaper, the *Nauvoo Expositor*, and published in its first number vicious attacks on Smith's dictatorial pretensions and his new doctrines, Smith commanded the civil authorities in Nauvoo (he was mayor and controlled the city council) to break into the building, remove the presses, and destroy all remaining copies of the first number. This illegal action gave the anti-Mormons in the area, particularly those in the Hancock County seat of Carthage, the needed excuse to launch a broad legal and political attack on Smith and Nauvoo. To escape arrest, he at first fled across the river to Iowa but returned when the governor threatened a siege of the city. Finally, on a promise of protection from the governor, he came with his brother Hyrum and a few others to Carthage, where he was arrested for treason.

The governor reneged on promises of protection, and at the Carthage jail a mob gunned down a resisting Smith and his brother on June 27, 1844. Hyrum died when shot in his jail cell. Joseph pulled a concealed pistol, shot to death two men in the assaulting mob, received a bullet while at the window, fell wounded to the street below, and there died after a barrage of additional shots. He was buried at Nauvoo on June 29. In these last days many friends reported a dispirited Smith who talked about giving up the new marriage doctrine.

The martyrdom of Smith did not have the effect expected by his enemies. The Mormon religion continued and in a sense gained new zeal. Smith's martyrdom identified him, in the eyes of his defenders, with Jesus. In retrospect it seems that Smith's death aided the growth of his church and perhaps was even necessary for the survival of the form of Mormonism that he had created over the previous three years. A charismatic and prophetic figure was necessary to launch such a bold new religion. But increasingly Smith had become a liability. He had frequently violated civil laws, had tried to create a separate Mormon nation, and just before his death had contemplated an independent empire somewhere in the West. He was sure to incite even more dissent and opposition in the future. The Mormons needed stable leaders with greater political skills, even as they needed to consolidate and assimilate the new doctrines.

Yet Smith's murder did pose a very serious leadership crisis for the church. Even as late as 1844 the Mormon religion still had cultlike features, particularly in Nauvoo but less so in the more far-flung congregations (some overly optimistic Mormons estimated a worldwide membership of 100,000, while less than 20,000 lived in the Nauvoo area). Smith had not clearly identified a successor or, perhaps more accurately, had at different times seemed to anoint varied successors. The presidency temporarily ended with Smith's death, although one of his two counselors, Sidney Rigdon, claimed the right of succession. Had Hyrum Smith not been killed, he would have had almost irrefutable claims, but this was true for no one else. Most were willing to concede a future role to Smith's oldest son and namesake, Joseph Smith III, but he was only eleven in 1844, and his mother, Emma, did not want to push his claim because she feared another assassination. In any case, someone would have had to serve as his regent or adviser and by this gain the full power of the office. Thus Emma supported the president of the Nauvoo stake, William Marks. He had as much claim as did the twelve apostles, since their jurisdiction so far had involved those Mormons not in organized stakes. At least eight other people advanced their own claims, including Joseph's erratic and sexually undisciplined brother William, who did become patriarch only to abuse that office. Thus, in Nauvoo the main battle soon involved either Marks or Rigdon on one side and Brigham Young and the council on the other.

The stakes in this succession conflict were very high. Emma knew that Marks opposed polygamy and that he would end the practice if he gained the presidency. Since Marks soon deferred to Rigdon, it was also clear that

Rigdon would reject plural marriage and possibly all the new temple ordinances. On the other hand, Brigham Young and the council he presided over were clearly committed to all the recent innovations and thus to preserving the new Mormonism that Smith had only recently announced, and which most church members, even in Nauvoo, did not yet know about in fullest details. In this sense the resolution of the succession crisis would determine the nature of Mormonism in the future. Had Marks or Rigdon succeeded, the church would have reverted to the pattern before 1841 and would have closely resembled the later and unneeded RLDS.

For the only time in its history a church conference had the power to determine vital issues. In outdoor meetings first Rigdon, then Young appealed for support. Rigdon had been volatile, at times at odds with Joseph Smith, and mishandled his speech and the politics of the moment. He did not have any of the leadership skills so badly needed by the church. Young managed the meetings perfectly and won an almost unanimous vote of support for himself and the council. In fact, as some people later remembered, they sensed a miracle, as they literally saw Joseph Smith in the visage of Young (the transfiguration). His mantle had passed by God's will. Young quickly took charge of the church and retained the loyalty of most local members. Yet so many factions soon dissented that in the next four or five years possibly half of all Mormons left the church now led by Young.

Among those who rejected the leadership of Young, the rebuffed Rigdon had the best claim to preference. Locally he soon gathered a dissenting faction that included William Marks. When excommunicated, Rigdon and his closest followers moved to Pittsburgh and formed their own Church of Christ. Rigdon, long haunted by periodic depression, became more unstable with each year and soon overwhelmed his church with wild visions. By one such revelation he identified the future site of the New Jerusalem as near Greencastle, Pennsylvania, and there gathered his church in what was a quickly declining commune. When the group could not pay its debts and lost its land, most members left, some to join other dissenting Mormon sects. Rigdon did not give up but, usually from a distance, tried to lead a successor group, called the Church of Jesus Christ of the Children of Zion (by Rigdon's instructions it ordained women as priests). Its few dozen members established a commune in Iowa and then finally expired in Manitoba after Rigdon's death in 1876.

Inspired by Rigdon's doctrines, in 1862 William Bickerton formed an enduring but still tiny Church of Jesus Christ, which is still identified by the label "Bickertonites." In 1864 another Mormon, Granville Hedrick, followed a new revelation, which prompted his small sect (also named the Church of Christ) to purchase the temple lot in Independence originally dedicated by Joseph Smith; many refer to this continuing but very small sect as the Temple Lot Mormons. William Smith, brother of the prophet, pushed his hereditary claim to the presidency and did inherit the post of patriarch. Because of an early power grab he suffered excommunication. For the next two decades he tried to find a leadership role in various splinter groups but never lasted long in any, in part because of his instability and continuing sexual escapades. Survivors from Rigdon's Church of Christ formed a congregation in Kirtland from 1847 to 1849 and worshiped briefly in the old temple. This small congregation was headed by William McLellin, a former missionary and apostle, and by Martin Harris; it briefly attracted the distant support of both David Whitmer and Oliver Cowdery, thus including three of the witnesses of the golden plates. William Law, the most vocal critic of Smith in Nauvoo, briefly formed a congregation in Hampton, Illinois. Later, David Whitmer formed a small congregation in Iowa. And so it went, with some of the dissidents from Nauvoo wandering from one small sect to another for the next twenty years.

A bizarre figure in American religious history, James J. Strang, led the most successful early dissenting faction. Just after Smith's martyrdom Strang produced a convincing letter from Smith appointing Strang, a very recent convert, as successor. The letter, undoubtedly a forgery, persuaded many outlying Mormons who knew Strang, and thus he began building his own church, abundantly guided by a series of new revelations and even the translation of additional plates that he professed to find. He made his headquarters in Voree, Wisconsin, and in the early years denounced polygamy. But Strang grew more wild and eventually moved his immediate followers to Beaver Island in Lake Michigan to found a personal fiefdom. He reintroduced polygamy, named his village St. James, and pronounced himself king. He had some ability and represented the northern counties of Michigan in the legislature. But as he grew more bizarre, and before he was murdered, he lost all but a small following, leaving many of his Wisconsin and other midwestern disciples disillusioned (a few hundred Strangite Mormons survive today).

A few former followers of Strang built a new Mormon sect from 1851 to 1853. Jason W. Briggs rejected the claims of all the aspiring successors to Joseph Smith. He had his own visions and in them gained divine vindication of his belief that the seed of Joseph Smith should preside over the high priesthood. This had to mean Joseph Smith III, who in 1851 was eighteen and still living with his mother in Nauvoo. Soon a handful of Mormons in southern Wisconsin and northern Illinois agreed with Briggs and began contacting remnant Strangite congregations in the area. Above all, these unaffiliated Mormons rejected polygamy. They organized as a church in the spring of 1853, filling the various priesthoods and guided throughout by a series of visions and revelations. Briggs was the first president. The group decided that what they were about was not the formation of a church but the reorganization of the true church after a period of disorder that followed Smith's martyrdom. This small Reorganized Church of Jesus Christ of Latter Day Saints grew slowly over the next five years but still awaited its prophet.

Briggs and others, at different times, approached a reluctant Joseph Smith III in Nauvoo. In 1856 Smith rejected their offer, but by 1860 he had decided he should assume the office of president and prophet. In the meantime, Emma Smith had remarried and attended a Methodist church, as did Joseph, who by then had studied law, farmed, and engaged in a variety of business activities. He was married and for several years had had little involvement with the Mormon religion. He and his descendants lent a needed legitimacy to the RLDS (Smith headed the church until his death in 1915; three of his sons successively ruled until 1978, followed by a grandson who ended this family dynasty with his retirement in 1996). A pudgy Joseph Smith III was cautious and mediatorial, the opposite of his father.

The reorganized church grew slowly but steadily and became the major Mormon body in much of the Midwest. At first its headquarters followed its prophet, beginning in Nauvoo; then Plano, Illinois; and from 1870 to 1906 at Lamoni, Iowa, the home of the church's first college (Graceland). Only in 1906, in semi-retirement, did Smith move to new church headquarters just off the temple lot in Independence, Missouri. Through complex legal action the church gained title to the old Kirtland temple in 1880 but did not have an active temple until 1993, when it completed an impressive structure in Independence (an administrative and educational center, not the site of secret rituals). By 1900 this sect had almost 40,000 members, less than a sixth that of the Utah church, and its growth was much slower in the twentieth century (today it has are approximately 200,000 members).

The doctrines of the RLDS were those of the main body of Mormons up to about 1840, or before Smith announced his new temple doctrines. The Articles of Faith, as originally written by Smith in 1830, with their evangelical and adventist motifs, very well fit the reorganized church. Above all, the reorganized saints rejected plural marriage and with it the doctrine of celestial marriage. They also rejected the extreme physicalism and polytheism of Smith's mature theology and by 1865 had ordained black (but for a time segregated) priests. They published their own *Doctrine and Covenants*, with the major differences involving the "false" doctrines they left out, but by means of new revelations by their presidents they added new articles.

Emma joined the RLDS. Both she and her son maintained, against the abundant historical evidence, that their husband and father had not been responsible for the new and scandalous doctrines at Nauvoo (they claimed he either did not enunciate them or was used or manipulated by those under him). Thus the reorganized church claimed to be the true LDS as founded by Smith. It never tried to gather its saints to any one location and was much closer to mainstream Protestantism than the Utah branch. By dissociating itself from its parent church, it was able to escape persecution. In the twentieth century it moved in the more liberal direction of mainline churches. Because of recent, more critical perspectives on Joseph Smith, more questioning studies of the Bible and the *Book of Mormon*, various ecumenical overtures to other denominations, and a 1984 revelation that led to the ordination of women, a fundamentalist faction led by Richard Price has very recently formed a schismatic, independent branch of this denomination.

The smaller splinters had limited impact on the main body of Mormons. Utah and reorganized Mormons maintained contact and tried to debate their various differences. In Utah, unwelcome RLDS missionaries gained a few converts and established at least three congregations (with only 1,000 Utah members by 1900). Joseph Smith III visited and preached in Salt Lake City on four mission trips and at least maintained cordial relationships with his many cousins. Only after the Utah church repudiated polygamy did the two groups at least begin more open discussions and contacts. To the reorganized church, the great devil was Brigham Young. But he became, next to Joseph Smith, the greatest hero of the regular Mormons, and for good reason. Although major theological differences and the temple rites still separate the two largest of nearly fifty Mormon or Mormon-related denominations, the trends within the larger church have converged toward the RLDS in one sense—a more evangelical emphasis—but have diverged in others—a much greater resistance to biblical criticism, to ecumenical outreach, and to humanitarian reforms.

Young was a leader, not a prophet. Eventually, when he moved up from council president to a restored presidency in 1847, he had the power that Smith had, but he did not use it to change any of the major doctrines of the church (some of his views on Adam as the god of this world purported to be revelations, but the church subsequently rejected these teachings). His immediate problems were political and practical, issues for which he was much better qualified than Smith. The hostility toward Mormons in Illinois abated only briefly at the death of Smith. For years Smith had contemplated moving the saints to the more distant West, to somewhere in the Rocky Mountains or in Oregon or California. Just before his murder he had organized a group of men to explore sites in the far West, and one elder formed a small colony in Texas. These plans were publicly known and led Mormon opponents in Illinois to join in meetings and in written proposals that the Mormons peacefully leave the state. With surprising speed Young and the council agreed in September 1845 that most Mormons would move out of Illinois in the spring of 1846, provided they received help and fair treatment in disposing of land and property and in acquiring the needed supplies for a massive migration. This brought only a brief peace to Nauvoo but allowed a winter of feverish preparatory work. Meanwhile the Mormons rushed to complete the temple. By its formal dedication in May 1846, Nauvoo was a virtual ghost town, for by then a majority of the saints had moved into Iowa.

By the spring of 1846, Young and his elders had chosen a destination: the valley of the Great Salt Lake. Recent explorations had opened a trail to the site, and its isolation, not its farming potential, made it more appealing to Mormons that either Oregon or Washington. In 1846 it was in Mexican territory, and some Mormons clearly wanted to escape the boundaries of the United States, although by the time of settlement it was clear that the area would become a part of the United States.

The move out of Nauvoo reflected an unusual level of devotion and a willingness to sacrifice worldly wealth. Mormons had to sell their land and houses, sometimes at a fraction of their cost. Some did not sell and remained in Nauvoo, along with disaffected or dissenting Mormons, most of whom left the church. Although in their bitterness the migrating Mormons blamed their financial losses on the government and people of Illinois, such losses were an inevitable result of so many houses going on the market at one time. Demand was lacking, and even many who purchased city lots would not occupy the houses, leaving much of the city deserted. Nauvoo survived, but barely. Since some Mormons remained in the city until the summer of 1846, and other Mormon officials returned to dispose of property, a mob of anti-Mormons besieged the city in September 1846. Both Mormons and new non-Mormon residents built barricades and tried to defend their city. A battle, which included artillery shelling, ensued, fortunately with more physical than human destruction. After six days Nauvoo surrendered. The governor had to come to help restore calm to an occupied city. In 1848 someone set fire to the new temple, destroying all but its walls. In 1849 Etienne Cabet purchased much of the deserted city as a home for an Icarian communal colony. Before the colonists could restore the temple building, a tornado leveled it. Through time people carried away its large stones for other construction, leaving only the foundations. Members of the two larger Mormon denominations have recovered and restored many of the larger homes and commercial buildings of Joseph Smith's Nauvoo.

THE GATHERING OF ZION IN THE
VALLEY OF THE GREAT SALT LAKE

For the fleeing Mormons the great hegira to the Utah Mecca came next. It became almost as much a part of Mormon identity, even as central to the religion, as the *Book of Mormon*. The Mormons of Nauvoo began crossing the Mississippi River in February 1846, utilizing winter ice. Young and other leaders were forced to cross earlier than intended because their enemies were able to indict them for counterfeiting (such unproven charges had been a continuous aspect of the factionalism, on both sides, and reflected the evils of a decentralized state banknote system in which up to half the circulating currency was bogus). The fleeing Mormons established their first winter camp a few miles from the river, in an area of prior Mormon settlements. After some early confusion Young was able to organize the families into tightly disciplined camps under what amounted to military rule. During the next three years, more than at any other time in Mormon history the faithful shared their goods, fulfilling the earlier law of consecration. They pooled what they had in order that every Mormon who wished to, however poor, could move west. But one must not envision a whole population, 15,000 strong, moving across the plains. It never happened that way. By choice many Mormons outside Nauvoo moved to Utah, as did a growing stream of European converts.

The Mormon move to Utah resembled modern assaults on Mount Everest. A series of base camps allowed each advance, with only a part of the total group moving to the next camp. In the spring of 1846 Young established a major summer camp, which soon became a small town, at Garden Grove in central Iowa in time to grow bountiful crops in the deep virgin soil during the summer. Some Mormon families remained there for several years. Between there and the Missouri River at Council Bluffs the Mormons established other camp-farms and in 1848 helped form a county in extreme western Iowa. In 1846 Young decided not to push on to the mountains until the next spring, in part because he committed the Mormons to supplying 500 men, or what became the Mormon Battalion, for the Mexican War. The battalion was famous not for battles fought but for a successful and ill-provisioned march all the way through what is now New Mexico to California. These men were vital to their Mormon families, but they won some goodwill and income for the much-resented Mormons and perhaps reflected Young's hope of creating Mormon colonies in California (the battalion was there early, and its discharged members made up a good share of those involved in the early gold rush). Young's advance party spent the winter at the present site of Omaha, with some inevitable suffering but still disciplined work for the great efforts in the coming year. The worst hardships and the highest mortality marked the first very difficult year in Iowa, not the more romantic later crossings of the plains and mountains to Utah.

In the late winter of 1847 Young formed a pioneer camp of about 150 for the final advance beyond the mountains. These celebrated pioneers took the easiest possible route—through Fort Laramie, over the south pass, and then across what is now southwest Wyoming into the valley of the Great Salt Lake. They created a new trail (soon worn by Mormon travelers) from Council Bluffs to Laramie and then departed the Oregon Trail for their descent into the valley (on modern maps the whole is identified as the Mormon Trail). The advance party only entered the valley on July 21, too late to plant food crops. An ill Brigham Young arrived two days later. By July 24 the whole camp was on the site of what became Salt Lake City and had dedicated the land. In the exultation of the moment the saints renewed their covenant and rebaptized one another (such rebaptisms were later ended by the church). Even in this first, foreshortened summer the saints built a fort, named streams, explored several sites for villages, and began building small dams and irrigation canals, ensuring crops in 1848. Young and others helped plat the city (using some designs earlier drafted by Joseph Smith), with broad streets, large rectilinear blocks, and a choice location for the future temple. Small bands of Mormons came from California, including some of the Mormon Battalion joined by Mormons from Mississippi who had taken a ship to California. By the fall almost 1,500 had crossed in wagons from winter camp, making over 2,000 in the valley by the end of the year. But Young and many of the original pioneers hurried back east to lead the great migration in 1848.

In 1848 most Mormons in western Iowa moved to Utah in a series of camps, a migration that continued year after year for the next decade. Only in one case, that of several handcart companies that tried crossing in 1856, did the migration come close to disaster. A few Mormons decided not to go on to Utah in spite of admonitions from Young, and one Mormon missionary to the Indians, Alpheus Cutler, formed a small schismatic group (Culterites) in Iowa that still survives. In most cases the camps were disciplined and well organized, with better than normal relationships with the Indians. After 1848 an increasing proportion of the migrants were European immigrants, who came at the request of Young to the gathering place for all the saints. European converts had another role: as much as their resources permitted, they collected funds to help finance this huge migration.

Back at Salt Lake City, the early residents were able to plant their irrigated grain crops in 1848, only to have the fields threatened by a cyclical grasshopper explosion (these are now called Mormon crickets). It seemed a miracle, an omen, when seagulls appeared and ate most of the "crickets," another, often exaggerated part of the great Mormon epic. The grain harvest was still limited but the pioneers celebrated it by a festival in the fall. The massive arrival in 1848 led to the expansion of settlement throughout the larger valley and the formation of new towns. By 1849 the church had divided the settlements into stakes and wards. It also set up a permanent emigration fund to help both American and European members cross the plains. The dire poverty and short food supplies of 1848 yielded to some prosperity in 1849, as Mormons were in a perfect position to outfit those flocking to the new goldfields of California. Young Mormon men, some from the Mormon Battalion, remained in the minefields of California, sent a growing supply of gold to Salt Lake City, and provided the basis of a short-lived mint established there by Brigham Young.

At first, church and state were virtually one in Utah. The Mormons realized the old dream of Smith for a Mormon Kingdom of God. By petition the Mormons were able to get permission to organize a territorial government for what they wanted to call Deseret, but which opponents insisted on naming Utah in the organizing act of 1850. President Millard Fillmore appointed Brigham Young first governor. The Mormons clearly controlled the area, established the first newspaper, built the first schools (for the next fifty years the public schools in the territory were, in effect, Mormon parochial schools), and enjoyed a cultural monopoly. Most important, the elders platted the new towns, helped fund a very tight system of colonization, and retained full control over local governments. The council of fifty re-formed in Utah and, whatever its governmental role, at least supplied almost all the political leaders for the next fifty years. In Salt Lake City in 1853 the assembled Mormons laid the cornerstone of what would be their long-delayed but greatest temple. Non-Mormon officials felt resented and excluded and soon began their complaints back to Washington, D.C. In 1852 Young publicly announced the doctrine of plural marriage, and by then several other Mormon elders were living openly with multiple wives. This created both a local and a national scandal. Thus, almost from the beginning, the new Mormon kingdom was locked in combat with the rest of the United States. Even the desert offered no escape, no peace.

The first period of tension preceded the Civil War. Once again, part of the problem derived from the joint civil and religious role of Young, who duplicated Smith's mistake in Nauvoo. By 1856 Young was involved in a bitter personal conflict with the appointed federal judges in the territory, who accused Young of destroying court records and clearly favoring Mormons over Gentiles in several of his decisions and appointments. Soon they judged him rebellious and asked President James Buchanan to remove him from office and send troops to the territory. For once the Mormons did not yield. They decided to defend themselves whatever the cost. Army troops, ordered to Utah from Fort Leavenworth in 1857, did not make it to the valley largely because of effective guerrilla action by the Nauvoo Legion (under Governor Young's control, it burned all the Mormon forts and provisions along their trail). Helpful mediation before the summer of 1858 prevented an open war, but fears had led most Mormons to flee Salt Lake City. The troops eventually established camp outside the city and remained in uneasy barracks duty until the Civil War.

In the midst of the mounting tensions in the fall of 1857, Mormon settlers and Paiute Indians in extreme southwest Utah massacred all the adults in a wagon train made up of migrating families from Arkansas and Missouri. The Mormons, possibly provoked by verbal ridicule from Gentiles, inflamed by bitter memories of how the Mormons had suffered in Missouri, at first only detained the wagons. Brigham Young sent a letter asking for the release of these migrants, but it arrived too late. After negotiating the terms for safe passage and disarming the settlers, both Indians and Mormons ambushed the wagon train at a place called Mountain Meadows. They spared only children too young to report the slaughter. Exact details of the atrocity remained unclear in its immediate aftermath. Local Mormons blamed the massacre on Indians. This was the explanation offered by Brigham Young. One of his close friends, John D. Lee, was among the attacking Mormons and subsequently briefed Young about what happened, possibly lying about Mormon involvement. In the succeeding years, as more details of the massacre became known, this horrible event added further embarrassment for a church already under siege because of polygamy. Finally, in 1875, Lee, alone among the guilty, stood trial for murder. After two trials, an all-Mormon jury, with the clear support of the church, convicted him. In 1877, twenty years after the slaughter, he chose death by a firing squad. In the end he was full of bitterness. He believed that Young and the church as a whole had made him a scapegoat in order, finally, to exorcise bitter memories of Mountain Meadows.

These incidents of violence have left some of the most intractable problems in Mormon scholarship. Early perspectives by minority Gentiles clash with the memories of later Mormons, including those who became able academic historians. Two questions are central: did ordinary Mormons live under an authoritarian or even totalitarian regime, and did Mormons organize secret vigilante groups (Danite bands) and, at times, use a purported doctrine called blood atonement to justify the murder of apostates or enemies?

Clearly, most of the Mormons who flocked to Utah accepted the leadership of the council and usually deferred to the layers of authority within the priesthood. In most elections Mormons voted as a block, as instructed by their leaders. This assured a one-party system until effective apostate and Gentile opposition slowly created a two-party system by 1890. Most Mormons so internalized beliefs and values as to support a very exclusive and, for dissidents or outsiders, a quite repressive social order. Mormon villages resembled Puritan towns, in which formal participation was very high yet tolerance for deviance very low. No doubt apostates suffered ostracism and at times violence. Those who supported the most effective Mormon schism in the postwar years, the Godbeites, fought for a more open, pluralistic society and, incidentally, for one more receptive to private entrepreneurship.

Whether Mormon authorities sanctioned blood atonement in any official way is not clear, despite all the rumors and charges by Gentiles. Blood atonement is not an official Mormon doctrine. It never was. Yet both Joseph Smith, in his last two years in Nauvoo, and Brigham Young, in the early Utah years, did refer to apostates or outside enemies whose crimes were so horrible that their only chance for salvation required their death, or the shedding of blood. No clear evidence exists that they or later presidents of the church ever turned this belief into an excuse for murder, particularly by Danite bands. No doubt Mormons in outlying villages did resort to extralegal forms of repression. Less clear is whether they organized secret, quasi-legal military units similar to reported bands formed by a few modern, extremist polygamous sects.

The Civil War abated the direct confrontations with Gentiles, but nothing in it gave the Mormons reason to hope for any regained autonomy in the future. They were beleaguered in their own empire. This abetted the institutional development of the Mormons in the West. Later descriptions of Mormon communalism were misplaced. From the beginning they held land privately, with the elders quite self-consciously scouting out some of the best lots when they first arrived. Young and other elders became wealthy. They did not always carefully distinguish what they owned personally from what they held for the church. The church offered cooperative support for private effort by controlling the irrigation works and supervising the marketing and storing of goods. The church also did all it could to encourage tithing and used its own wealth to create needed social services. The church also owned the newspaper and, eventually, other enterprises. This meant that the church, despite great disparities of wealth, could provide at least a minimal safety net for all members (yet plenty of visitors to Utah described large Mormon families just above the level of destitution).

PLURAL MARRIAGES AND FEDERAL SUPPRESSION

After the Civil War the Mormons were never strong enough or foolish enough to contemplate military action against the United States. The tension took other, often legal forms but did not abate. Behind the resentment were two familiar problems. One was the degree of political control enjoyed by the church hierarchy and, along with that, what Gentiles saw as the dictatorial rule of Young and his closest advisers. The second was the strange religious practices of the Mormons, but increasingly one Mormon religious institution: plural marriage, or what Gentiles always referred to as polygamy.

Given the almost universal outside condemnation, this Mormon marriage doctrine became much more important to Mormon identity than it might have without opposition. What can be stated with some confidence is the following: plural marriage occurred throughout the western Mormon settlements (rarely in the eastern United States or in Mormon communities in Europe). Acceptance and defense of the doctrine became a mark of Mormon identity, although most men remained monogamous. Estimates vary, but probably no more than 10,000 to 15,000 Mormons (fewer than 10 percent) ever lived in polygamous families. But these low ratios are misleading, in the same sense as the low ratio of large slave owners to white men in the Old South. Those who gained the highest positions in the Mormon priesthood almost always married more than one wife, and those who were both wealthy and high in the priesthood (the two correlated significantly) almost had to marry more than once, for reasons of doctrine and peer pressure. For a very devout Mormon male, a plurality of wives was both a privilege and a responsibility—a privilege when it permitted older men to indulge sexual yearnings for younger or more attractive wives, and a responsibility when men were sealed in marriage with older or unattractive or sexually inactive women as a social or familial duty.

It is almost impossible for most people today to understand plural marriages. In the forty years such marriages retained the official support of the church perhaps it was also impossible for Mormons fully to assimilate the practice, since they could not be immune to the ideas of romantic love so pervasive in the larger society. The institution entailed a patriarchal family structure, with the father as king and progenitor. The values, to the extent assimilated, made the fathering of many children a high obligation. Theological motifs supported this goal, for one aspect of this critically important assignment to life on earth was to provide opportunities for the spirits who lived in a heavenly kingdom to take on mortal bodies and move a first step toward the goal of celestial glory, which was impossible for one who did not live for a time in a physical body and impossible for one not sealed in marriage for eternity. The duty to marry and the duty to conceive children were conjoined. Birth control remained anathema to Mormons. Marriage involved many benefits, not least the righteous fulfillment of sexual desires, but progeny was its greatest justification. And as Joseph Smith stressed, the most righteous were in the best position to rear a righteous progeny. Better they have the most children.

Most polygamous husbands had only two or three wives. They could not afford more, or refused more. Only a few men of great wealth had well-publicized harems, such as that of Brigham Young (fifty-five wives). In the lower priesthood, individuals could reject the option of plural wives. But as they moved up, they faced increased social pressure to take additional wives. In fact, at the top of the hierarchy, in the church and in Mormon society, the number of wives became a mark of status and righteousness. Contrary to many apologies for plural marriage, a surplus of women had nothing to do with the enunciation of the doctrine or its practice in Utah. In fact, the sexes were nearly equal from the beginning, in itself a testimony to Mormon success in winning female converts, for the West as a whole long had an overabundance of men.

What about the women? Given the tremendous religious sanction for temple marriages, some women, particularly unattractive and poor women, gained increased chances of celestial glory because of polygamy. In this limited sense the doctrine had egalitarian implications; almost any woman who wanted marriage might obtain it. Otherwise, it had elitist implications. Wealthy men, or those of high standing in the church, could exploit their position to marry the most appealing brides, including impoverished girls just arrived from Europe, leaving poorer young men with few attractive marriage partners.

Young women never had to succumb to any marriage offer, at least not according to the official rules. But young women from poor families were under pressure to accept marriage proposals from well-placed men, however much older. Such marriages rested on criteria not at all tied to romantic feelings or to mutual affection, but to various economic and religious interests. Young women who accepted the status of a second or later wife calculated their advantages by standards hard to accept or even to comprehend today. A bride might cohabit rarely with her husband, and that might have been as she wanted it. Plenty of evidence suggests that Mormon males did succumb to the temptation of viewing women as commodities (their religion condemned this), of thinking of them as good workers or good lovers, and in some cases of offering them very little sustaining affection. If lucky, each wife had separate quarters or at least a separate room, but in theory all worked under the supervision of the first wife, meaning that some late wives became, in effect, servants. When young, a wife was doomed to perpetual pregnancy, but her religious values may have helped establish motherhood as a vocation much above that of wife. In any case, all evidence shows that a vast majority of Mormon women, both in and out of plural marriages, affirmed the system. This may largely reflect the extent to which they had internalized the values of their religion and how much religious goals overrode all others. What historians search for today are the types of fulfillment that lay behind this loyalty (feminists seek it in the extended, almost entirely female households, or in the bonding between women).

In any case, the system attracted unending scrutiny. People came to Utah to observe it and write about it. Young's harem became a tourist attraction. Journalists (including Mark Twain) cut their teeth on stories from Utah. Preachers all over America made the sinful Mormons object lessons in their sermons. Clearly, the strange institution titillated and amused. One had to profess moral outrage, and this became a competitive game for politicians. Polygamy prevented Utah from gaining statehood for forty years. In 1862 Congress passed the first antibigamy law but did not at first do much to enforce it. As at Nauvoo, internal factions within the church led to apostate cooperation with increasing numbers of anti-Mormon Gentiles (the transcontinental railroad opened Utah to the world in 1869), who abetted outside efforts to discipline the Mormons. Measures to curtail the local government in Utah joined with a series of tougher antibigamy bills before Congress. The Mormons had a hard time fighting back. They circled their wagons, developed their own separate institutions, and even tried to set up their own mercantile cooperative and boycott Gentile merchants. But about their only real recourse was the federal courts. They were confident that the first amendment protected their marriage practices, since these were so central and vital to their religion.

Mormon hopes proved illusionary, as the pressures against them built almost yearly. For years federal authorities had been hesitant to enforce the 1862 law. This changed in the 1870s, largely because of mounting pressure from Washington. The prosecutors chose not to make an elderly Young the test case, although at one point a judge sentenced him to one day in jail for contempt. Instead, in 1874 federal prosecutors charged Young's friend and private secretary, George Reynolds, with bigamy in what everyone perceived as the critical test case. The local courts convicted and assessed a one-year jail sentence plus fines. The territorial supreme court overturned this verdict on a technicality. The second trial, in 1875, led not only to a guilty verdict but to a harsher penalty—two years at hard labor. The territorial court upheld this decision, and the church appealed to the Supreme Court of the United States. Brigham Young was spared the final bitter result; he died in August 1877. In January 1879 the Court unanimously upheld the conviction of Reynolds, removing the last legal hopes of Mormons. A subsequent appeal removed the hard labor from the penalty, and Reynolds spent a rather benign eighteen months teaching school within a Utah prison. But practically every official in the church was subject to felony prosecution and long prison sentences. Subsequent prosecutions involved more embarrassing cases, particularly those in which wives or ex-wives brought charges against polygamous husbands. For the next decade the church leadership practically went underground, as harsher legislation further imperiled it. The Mormon celebration of the Year of Jubilee (fifty years from the founding of the church) in 1880 and an elaborate Pioneer Day Celebration had a bittersweet quality for the approximate 125,000 Mormons then in Utah and immediately surrounding territories.

The climactic anti-Mormon legislation came in two bills. The first, the Edmunds Act of 1882, so amended the bill of 1862 as to make illegal not only bigamous marriages but polygamous living or "unlawful cohabitation." The bill allowed the president of the United States to grant amnesty to those who entered such marriages before January 1, 1883, and made legitimate all children of plural marriages born before that date. Much more threatening, the bill denied anyone involved in a plural marriage, as husband or wife, the right of franchise and office holding. In a near-repeat of reconstruction enforcement for the South, federal commissioners moved into Utah, set up registrars, and administered a test oath to adult Mormons. From a Mormon perspective this disfranchisement accompanied a virtual reign of terror, as federal agents and courts tried to stamp out plural marriages. Since it was possible to prosecute Mormons for successive violations of the Edmunds law, then the maximum fine of five years could increase to a life in prison. This drove many Mormon families into hiding.

A new law in 1887—the Edmunds-Tucker Act—drove the church into exile. It disincorporated the church, dissolved its emigration fund and gave the assets to the public schools of Utah, abolished female suffrage in the territory (antipolygamists had resented instructed or bloc voting by

Mormon women), and began proceedings to strip the church of all property except that directly used for worship. Under legal proceedings an appointed receiver took charge of all church properties, even renting space to church officials for the tithing and historical offices. In 1887 the president and successor of Young, John Taylor, an adamant defender of plural marriage, went into hiding to avoid arrest and died during the summer of that sad year for Mormons.

The next president of the church, Wilford Woodruff, was in an impossible bind. The church had for three decades argued the centrality of its marriage doctrines and could not suddenly repudiate them. The members would be disillusioned, with grave risk to the church. Opponents would gloat and charge hypocrisy. Yet the church was in grave peril. In the modern world plural marriages were as much against enlightened opinion as human slavery. It is as difficult to envision the LDS in the twentieth century with plural marriage as it is to envision the South with a continuation of black slavery. Woodruff soon decided that he could only save the church by concessions. In 1890 in a short and rather strained declaration addressed to "whom it may concern," he announced the termination of plural marriages within the church, made clear the illegality of a reported and recent marriage of this type, and announced his intention to submit to the laws of Congress and to use his influence to have members of his church do likewise. He specifically advised all members of LDS to refrain from contracting such illegal marriages. At the next general conference the assembled church approved the declaration. Much later the church interpreted this declaration, developed as a purely political concession, as a revelation given by the authority of God and thus included it in its *Doctrine and Covenants*.

This backhanded capitulation became a milestone in the church, the most important turning point in its history. It was not clear at the time that it would be so. Woodruff repudiated no doctrines. Yet thousands of Mormons felt betrayed. Practices did not change quickly. Many Mormon priests continued to sanction or even perform plural marriages, and apostles of the church continued to live in plural families for at least another decade. As late as 1899 President Lorenzo Snow secretly approved such marriages. This near-duplicity began to change in 1904. The church had assured the election by the Utah legislature of one of its apostles, Reed Smoot, as United States senator. Since he formerly had plural wives, his election led to extensive challenges to his seating and to extended hearings in Washington (he eventually won). These hearings embarrassed the LDS leadership. Even the new president of the church, Joseph Smith (Hyrum's son), admitted under oath to continued cohabitation with plural wives after 1890. But these hearings produced sincere commitments to end all evasions of the law, and Joseph Smith began, after 1904, active but never fully effective efforts to root out polygamy. Only in the 1920s did the church begin extensive excommunications of those recalcitrant priests or fundamentalists who adhered to the marriage doctrines defended by the church before 1890. Such were the external pressures and the strength of its desire for respectability that the church had no alternative.

Despite official repression, a sizable subgroup of Mormons surreptitiously continued plural marriages. These polygamous Mormons (some would eventually adopt new names, such as Apostolic United Brethren) soon developed a special subculture scattered in small towns all over Mormon country. The two most important leaders, Joseph W. Musser and Dr. Rulon Allred, were competent and quite sincere in their loyalty to the old church, but after World War II their dissident group experienced numerous internal divisions and schisms, leading to several small sects. By some possibly exaggerated estimates, up to 50,000 people now adhere to these polygamous sects (the number of plural marriages today may exceed the number at any time before 1890). Massive arrests and imprisonments of polygamous priests in Arizona and Utah at the end of World War II created so many human costs among wives and children and led to such high social welfare costs for the states that a policy of official blindness has become the norm, except for a few exceptionally notorious cult leaders who resorted to violence.

The declaration by Woodruff did not appease popular hostility toward Mormons. But it did clear the way for Utah statehood in 1896, with female suffrage. Since almost all the anti-Mormon sentiment had centered on plural marriages, the end of the practice slowly defused hostility. In a religiously pluralistic society, the peculiar doctrines of Mormons no longer seemed threatening, and in the new century Mormons became experts at building bridges with conservative Christians at points of overlap, and in deemphasizing Mormon distinctiveness. Equally important, the church gave up its earlier refuge identity and its effort to achieve a semisovereign, relatively isolated Mormon kingdom, and thus no longer asked all saints, if possible, to gather in Zion (Utah). The council of fifty had already disbanded. In a major new policy, the church asked new converts to build new Mormon communities where they were and soon began constructing temples around the world (after a rather long delay, it finally began translating the temple rites into non-English languages). By the mid-twentieth century the church had learned the art of public relations and used its radio broadcasts, its wonderful Tabernacle choir, its well-displayed museums, and its genealogical resources to gain widespread respect. Its great trek to Utah became a national epic. In the 1930s in particular, its purported economic self-sufficiency (almost always exaggerated) and its techniques of community cooperation became famous among social scientists and agricultural reformers. The Mormons now stand for traditional and conventional moral values, for political conservatism and patriotism, and for healthy living and longevity, characteristics that make them seem anything but radical and threatening.

The gradual repudiation of polygamy reflected a pattern in Mormon history, a reluctant and defensive accommodation with the outside world whenever the survival or success of the church was at stake. In 1978 the announcement by President Spencer W. Kimball that the church would henceforth admit Africans to the priesthood reflected the same willingness to compromise with new realities. The exclusion of Negro males from the priesthood had never, technically, excluded Africans from church membership and thus salvation, but few joined a church that clearly stigmatized them. The exclusion rested on the Mormon view of history, including a purported lack of zeal during the pre-earthly period by those who became Negroes, and subsequent curses for either Cain or Ham (in Joseph Smith's Book of Abraham, God denied the priesthood to Egyptians, who were purported descendants of Ham and by Mormon understanding the progenitors of Africans). Note that the church admitted, as equals, people of color, not only Lamanites but people from the South Pacific. The stigma was tied to racial descent, and thus to anyone with any admixture of Negro blood (when genealogical research disclosed Negro progenitors, males had had to resign their priestly offices). Until 1978 the increasingly beleaguered church had defended the exclusion. It suffered increasing condemnation; even its athletic teams at Brigham Young University faced boycotts and the possible loss of conference membership. The civil rights movement and the rapid shift in views about race had by then isolated the church almost as much as polygamy. Then, without any exploration of past doctrines or any elaborate justification, the president, in effect, told Mormons to forget about the past and to embrace a new future, one that permitted effective mission efforts in Africa and among African Americans. The church even retranslated one word in the *Book of Mormon*, a word that gave preference to white skin.

Despite such efforts to reconcile themselves with the outside world, Mormons have retained a distinctive subculture. To replace the geographical isolation of the nineteenth century and the isolation created for them by outside hostility, Mormons have developed institutions that allow them to maintain a cultural isolation even in the midst of an urban, pluralistic American society. Unlike the Anabaptist sects, which preserve their separate identity through distinctive speech, dress, and occupational clustering,

Mormons blend into the larger society and excel in all occupations and professions (their educational attainment is above average, their incomes just below). This integration into the larger culture has its dangers. Mormons have their share of lukewarm members, many who do not practice their faith (up to one-half the listed membership), and some open apostates (the church, more than any other large denomination in America, still disciplines its members and, when necessary, excommunicates). But such is the effectiveness of home training, of church-sponsored education, and of a whole spectrum of church societies and organizations for all age groups, that most young people assimilate or internalize, perhaps to an unrivaled degree, the belief system of their church.

Mormons as a whole reflect an unrivaled confidence in their basic beliefs and perplex outsiders by what seems their almost reflexive acceptance of "strange" scriptures and doctrines. Clearly they find what they need, and what they want, within the received religion. This involves a great deal more than appealing beliefs. It involves warm and supportive communities. Even in large cities, Mormons still limit their primary social relationships to the church community, and young people still marry within the faith. However close the working relationship of Gentiles to Mormons, however extensive the shared interests, and however fulfilling the human contacts, there is always a limit, a boundary beyond which outsiders cannot move and are not welcome. This is only to certify that Mormons have found effective means to pass on their culture, to educate or indoctrinate their youth, and to maintain a special way of life.

READING GUIDE

Mormon studies are booming. In a few more years the extent of Mormon scholarship may rival that on seventeenth-century New England Puritanism. The books appear at the rate of five or more per year, and at least three scholarly journals feature Mormon research. The complexity of Mormonism, its distance from most other forms of Christianity, the scholarly controversies that surround it, and the wealth of manuscript resources about it have helped maintain academic interest.

In spite of the range of topical studies, I still have not found a single book on Mormonism as a whole that I can wholeheartedly recommend. This results, in part, from the limitations of even the best scholarship by Mormons and from the very selective perspective of most non-Mormon historians. The standard introduction to Mormonism remains an outdated *The Mormons* (Chicago: University of Chicago Press, 1957), by Thomas F. Odea. Much more informative is the most scholarly survey by Mormon historians, *The Mormon Experience: A History of the Latter-day Saints*, 2nd ed. (Urbana: University of Illinois Press, 1992), by Leonard J. Arrington and Davis Bitton. It has many strengths, including insights into the Mormon experience in the West and an excellent phenomenological introduction to the life of Mormons. It is not a work in apologetics, a virtue not present among Mormon historians before the extensive scholarship of the church's most influential historian, Arrington. But this book is least perceptive on theological and doctrinal issues, and it subtly assumes a Mormon stance on many issues.

Arrington, more than anyone else, has given credibility to Mormon historical studies, combining good scholarship with the advantage of access to the LDS archives. He began in the familiar area of western economic history with his published dissertation, *Great Basin Kingdom: An Economic History of the Latter-day Saints* (Cambridge: Harvard University Press, 1958). He also trained several historians at Brigham Young, and these younger scholars have edited major series of LDS manuscripts, organized Mormon archives, and published monographs on several Mormon topics, all reflecting scholarly criteria within a context of confessional commitment. But even Arrington, a faithful Mormon, faced opposition from the general authorities when he served as the first professionally trained church historian and had to accept a transfer to Brigham Young, where he did not speak as directly for the church. There he completed, in 1985, a prize-winning biography, *Brigham Young: American Moses* (New York: Knopf). Another Mormon, Richard L. Bushman, who is an eminent colonial historian, has written a relatively brief but careful history of the founding of Mormonism: *Joseph Smith and the Beginnings of Mormonism* (Urbana: University of Illinois Press, 1984).

The experience of Mormons who wrote on the history of their own church has not always been pleasant. In some ways the most tragic story involved Fawn McKay Brodie, a daughter of a member of the presidency, whose readable, complex, psychologically informed biography, *No Man Knows My History: The Life of Joseph Smith* (New York: Knopf, 1945), remains the most popular book on Joseph Smith, but one that is highly speculative. Her title was prophetic and taken from a statement Smith made about himself. He remains an elusive subject for biographers. This book, which reveals a complex Smith who was in some ways a self-persuading impostor, led to Brodie's excommunication on charges of apostasy.

Klaus J. Hansen, a Mormon, wrote *Quest for Empire: The Political Kingdom of God and the Council of Fifty in Mormon History* (Lansing: Michigan State University Press, 1967), another pathbreaking book that displeased the church hierarchy. Hansen touched on some of the most sensitive issues among Mormons and in no way was deferential toward Mormon traditions or church authority. Subsequent to this book, D. Michael Quinn, who has become the most notable historian of Mormonism short of Arrington, explored almost every detail of church governance, including the succession crisis and the development of the priesthood. His most recent book is almost definitive in detail and meticulous in research: *The Mormon Hierarchy: Origins of Power* (Salt Lake City: Signature Books, 1994).

At least for Gentiles, the most challenging aspects of Mormonism are its unique doctrines and practices. In 1985 Jan Shipps published *Mormonism: The Story of a New Religious Tradition* (Urbana: University of Illinois Press), in which she emphasized the uniqueness of Mormonism, or its discontinuities in doctrine from Christianity, yet noted interesting parallels in its historical development. Shipps was the first non-Mormon historian to assume a fully sympathetic approach and to try to get inside a religious movement. Except for a good bit of attention in theological journals, the cosmology that Joseph Smith developed toward the end of his life has attracted too little attention, although the hermetic or occult aspects of this cosmology are featured in a highly speculative book by John L. Brooke, *The Refiner's Fire: The Making of Mormon Cosmology, 1644–1844* (New York: Cambridge University Press, 1994). The most recent and by far the most informative introduction to Mormon temple rites is in *The Mysteries of Godliness: A History of Mormon Temple Worship* (San Francisco: Smith Research Associates, 1994), by David John Buerger. The best introduction to contemporary Mormon society and particularly to the experience of missionaries, women, and blacks was edited by Marie Cornwall, Tim B. Heaton, and Lawrence A. Young, *Contemporary Mormonism: Social Science Perspectives* (Urbana: University of Illinois Press, 1994).

Although it was not my purpose to write a detailed story of the RLDS, I was disappointed in my search for any recent history of that church. Several official histories exist, and an excellent recent biography of its first president is *Joseph Smith III: Pragmatic Prophet* (Urbana: University of Illinois Press, 1988), by Roger D. Launius, who has also, with Linda Thatcher, edited a series of vignettes on Mormon dissenters: *Differing Visions: Dissenters in Mormon History* (Urbana: University of Illinois Press, 1994).

5

SPIRITUAL **CHRISTIANITY**

Christian

Science

and

Unity

The Church of Christ, Scientist, presents more problems for the historian of Christianity in America than any other denomination. Its beliefs are very elusive. Its records are secret. The scholarship about it is deeply polarized between the apologists within the church and the critics without. It seemed to reach the apex of its growth and influence around 1950 and is now declining in membership. Above all, almost every critical judgment about its prophet and founder, Mary Baker Eddy, remains controversial. Today it seems that a related and in part derivative religious movement, Unity, will eventually surpass Christian Science in membership and influence.

In no other enduring Christian sect has the founder been more central than in Christian Science. Even Joseph Smith never had as much of a formative influence or so dominated the development of a new religion as did Eddy. Neither did his *Book of Mormon* so shape a religious movement as did *Science and Health*, arguably the best example of an American scripture. In one sense the comparison of Mormonism and Christian Science is apt, for both have shared a prophetic and charismatic founder, both have a tightly centralized system of church government, both have moved very far from any traditional form of Christian orthodoxy, and both supplement the Jewish-Christian Bible with their own authoritative revelations. Yet no two forms of Christianity could be farther apart than a corporealist, practical, and very ritualistic Mormonism and an ultraspiritualist, nonsacramental, and transcendentalist Christian Science. Here are the two poles of American Christianity.

MARY BAKER GLOVER, 1821–1875

The childhood and youth of Mary Baker is only slightly more accessible than that of Jesus. The evidence is fragmentary and often opaque in what it suggests. Not that biographers have not sought every artifact and mined each for its possible revelations. In a three-volume work of love and apology, Robert Peel has examined all the evidence and provided as much of a day-by-day biography as the sources allow. Fortunately, even for his purposes, early critics of Mary Baker Eddy began, long before her death, to conduct interviews and search for published and unpublished documents that related in any way to her youth. From this effort has come a rather clear, uncontested outline of external events.

Mary Baker was born in 1821 on a farm near Bow, New Hampshire, in the Merrimack valley south of Concord. The last of six children, she spent the first fourteen, largely undocumented years of her life there. Her father, Mark Baker, was a reasonably prosperous farmer, a dedicated member of the Congregational Church, and a demanding but loving parent. Later, Mary repudiated what she remembered as his harsh Calvinism, but like most of the newly emancipated she never gave any clear definition of Calvinism. Her father held family devotions twice a day, affirmed standard evangelical doctrines, and tried to encourage high moral standards in his children. In a sense, Mary later rebelled against this childhood religion, or at least the rather crude caricatures of it she later featured in her reminiscences. By her memory she joined the Congregational Church at age twelve; church records indicate that it was at age seventeen. She also remembered that she did so only after repudiating predestination; but the word is a treacherous one, almost defying clear definitions, and her memories are suspect on this issue. In short, the fragmentary evidence of childhood does not suggest any but a rather conventional New England religious experience.

Because of frequent illness, Mary had limited schooling. It is impossible to fill in the exact periods of attendance. Yet she was early literate, at least in the sense of reading and writing, albeit with a lifetime propensity for poor spelling and awkward grammar. By age twelve she was composing romantic and pious verse, and even as a teenager she developed aspirations as a writer. Already as a youth she had a burning ambition to achieve greatness, to make something of herself. She put on "airs," in the language of neighbors, and was always concerned about her appearance. She was impeccable in dress and always as fashionable as resources permitted.

Mary's illness remains the great puzzle not only of her childhood but of her whole life. A persuasive historical diagnosis has eluded all her biographers. She seemed at most times a vivacious, fun-loving child much involved with siblings and close friends. But periodically she collapsed in what some called hysteria. At times relatives referred to "fits," or behavior that suggests, wrongly one suspects, epileptic seizures. Her whole life was beset by a periodic illness, with varying symptoms, that seemed both mental (from nervous prostration to depression and even clinical paranoia) and physical (acute back pains, digestive problems, debility, and weakness). Her life involved a vain search for good health and thus a preoccupation with illness and wellness that helped shape her later religious beliefs. At times, both as a child and as an adult, Mary used her illness as a means of controlling other people and for receiving attention and help. This led some people to believe she at times faked illness for manipulative purposes, a charge unproved and perhaps unprovable.

In 1835 Mark Baker bought a new farm in a town called Sanbornton Bridge (later Tilton), north of Concord. From age fourteen this would be the family home of Mary Baker. Clearly, the Baker family prospered in this new location. Except for an ailing Mary, the Baker children thrived socially and occupationally. Mary's sister Abigail married Alexander Tilton, the wealthiest man in the village and the owner of a growing textile mill. A brother, George, later entered a partnership with him. Mary's sister Martha married affluent Luther Pilsbury and lived permanently in nearby Concord, providing an enduring Baker family presence in the state capital. Mary's favorite brother, Albert, graduated from Dartmouth, taught school, became a successful lawyer and politician, served in the New Hampshire legislature, headed the state Democratic Party, and became a close friend and adviser to Franklin Pierce in the years before he became president of the United States. Beset by consumption and driven by ambition, Albert died in 1841 from a kidney infection. His loss was a terrible blow for Mary, who had been close to him and who gained much of her literary skills and her scattering of knowledge about many subjects under his tutelage.

Two years after Albert's death, Mary married George Washington Glover. He was eleven years her senior and tied to her by the much earlier marriage of his sister to her oldest, least successful, and least emotionally supportive brother, Samuel. Seemingly a very successful builder, Glover had moved to Charleston, South Carolina, and became engaged to Mary on a trip back home. Information about him and about Mary in these years is sparse. She had been almost continuously ill in the preceding two years, adding an element of uncertainty to the engagement and marriage. Just twenty-two, Mary was, if not beautiful, at least compellingly vivacious and attractive. After the marriage the couple returned to Charleston only briefly and then moved temporarily to Wilmington, North Carolina. After five months, Glover died there in a yellow fever epidemic, just after he had lost many of his building supplies in a fire. He had been planning a major project in Haiti. In this brief six months, Mary became pregnant, resumed her occasional writing for newspapers, and apparently quickly established herself as a socialite. Throughout her life, at times of exciting new challenges her health temporarily improved, and this may have been true in her brief career in the American South. But this interlude was a prelude to two turbulent, miserable, sickly decades.

After her husband's death, Mary had no alternative but to return to the family farm in Sanbornton in July 1844. She gained no significant inheritance from her husband. In September she gave birth to a son, the only child she ever bore. Of course she gave it her husband's name. But the birth was difficult, and the aftermath was worse. Always frail and beset with nervous illnesses, Mary fell into months of incapacity, probably involving, at least in part, what we now refer to as postpartum depression. She was incapable of caring for young George, who appears to have been hyperactive from birth, and she never had a normal mother-son relationship with him. A neighboring woman nursed him; a maid and friend, Mahala Sanborn, cared for him and soon became his substitute mother. Illness or emotional detachment or circumstances conspired to separate Mary from her son. Later her relationship to little George became one of the several controverted issues about her life. Christian Scientists would stress her desire to be a mother and the evidence of love and concern on her part but would attribute the separation to circumstances beyond her control. Critics would see in her willingness to give up George a defect of character, or at least the effect of an overpowering emotional or mental illness. The evidence is insufficient to verify either point of view.

In these years of widowhood and renewed economic dependency, Mary on occasion rose above her illness and tried to build a career. She wrote poems (some later became hymns in her church) and newspaper articles and often identified herself as an author, an identity that matched her high estimation of the academic and literary culture she lacked. She briefly headed an infant school and taught temporarily in a local academy, but she never had the physical stamina or emotional stability to keep such positions. In 1849, as her parents planned to move from the farm into the village of Sanbornton, Mary's mother died, a loss comparable to the death of Albert. In the village Mary had new social prospects and entertained suitors, one of whom died after moving to California in the gold rush. For long periods she was abed with her vague illnesses, under the inexpert care of nearby physicians and probably already attracted to the increasing number of popular therapies that competed for attention in those years (at one point she tried the Graham diet). Despite all the work of biographers, it is not possible to find much in her letters or sentimental and romantic newspaper essays that suggests her later religious views.

When her father remarried in 1850, she felt increasingly alienated in the Baker household. According to some speculations, Mary's new stepmother resented six-year old, rambunctious little George, leading Mark Baker to ask that he leave the household. The evidence does not prove this, but such pressure may help explain or justify Mary's decision to place George with his long-term caretaker, Mahala Sanborn, who married Russell Cheney and moved to a farm forty miles away in the lee of the White Mountains. For Mary this meant infrequent contact with her son and even more illness, most suffered after she moved to the household of her sister Abigail. After two years with Abigail, Mary Glover decided to marry again. She chose Daniel Patterson, a dentist. It turned out to be a poor choice for both of them. He saw her vivacious, gay side before marriage and was ill prepared for her debilitating illnesses. She saw a handsome and apparently successful suitor but not his recklessness, impulsiveness, and proclivity to womanizing.

The newly married couple moved frequently. In 1855 they bought land and moved close to New Groton, where Mahala lived with young George, but this did not lead to a resumption of Mary's role of mother. Why is unclear. Her apologetic biographers attribute it to Patterson's refusal to accept the unruly eleven-year-old, who was still unschooled and illiterate. Within a year Mahala and her husband moved to Minnesota, and George moved with them, apparently with Mary's permission (she later talked of a conspiracy by her father and husband to steal her son from her). She did not see him again until 1879, when as a bearded and still near-illiterate mining prospector from Lead, South Dakota, he visited his mother in Boston. They had almost nothing in common. Meanwhile, Mary's marriage with Patterson was soon jeopardized. Patterson eventually lost his farm in 1859 when Mary's sister had to foreclose on a mortgage. The couple had to sell most of their furniture, and from this time on they lived together only intermittently, at times in boardinghouses. Mary was almost continuously ill. She had tried homeopathy, with what seemed early but soon dwindling effects. Her husband even added this practice to his work as a dentist (the minute quantities of medications used in this popular therapy enabled one with little training to open a practice). She, as almost everyone in the

1850s, dabbled with spiritualism and later, at rare intervals, assumed the role of a medium. In this time of confusion the nation moved toward civil war, which in a sense helped Mary escape temporarily from an increasingly impossible marriage.

In Minnesota young George Glover, aged seventeen, suffered the death of the only real mother he ever had, Mahala Cheney, and rushed off to volunteer in an infantry unit. Pathetically, a fellow private had to write letters for him to Mary Patterson in distant New Hampshire. Meanwhile Daniel Patterson, on an assignment from the governor to carry funds to southern sympathizers, was captured while touring the site of the battle of Bull Run and placed in a Confederate prison. Typically, Mary rose to the new challenge, wrote letters to secure his release, and seemed to thrive on the new responsibilities. She was also free to seek cures for her illnesses. She first tried a hydropathic institute (water cures were then very popular) but probably gained more from the supportive talks with the physician than from the baths. At this point she decided to visit Phineas P. Quimby in Portland, Maine. Her husband had first corresponded with him about Mary in 1861 and received a pamphlet about his methods. Mary resumed this correspondence while Patterson was in a North Carolina prison, and she tried to get Quimby to visit her in Sanbornton. When he could not do this, she resolved to travel to Portland, and after scrounging to get the money, she did so in October 1862. This extended visit changed her life and launched her on the path that led to Christian Science.

Quimby was a remarkably successful healer. He was also a kind and generous person. It is easy, in retrospect, to attribute his success as a healer to personality, not to any theories or methods. Early in his practice Quimby had used hypnosis, or what many referred to as mesmerism. According to the theories of the time, this involved passing a type of animal magnetism from one person to another and usually required direct physical contact. From this early practice Quimby retained a type of manipulation. Mary Patterson at first followed the same techniques but later repudiated them. Quimby had, by the time he moved his practice to Portland in 1859, already repudiated mesmerism or any hypnotic influence over his patients. This left him with largely a form of oral therapy, along with some massaging. Later, such nonhypnotic therapy gained the general label of mind-cure and led to a considerable movement in post–Civil War America.

Quimby had to develop some explanation for his success with patients. To do this he drew on the various strands of spiritualism so popular in the pre–Civil War decades. He argued that disease resulted from erroneous beliefs, which led to physical maladies. Thus, the way out of illness involved new beliefs and the repudiation of error, and then the body would,

in a sense, recover its natural state of health. His sessions involved suggestions of this type to patients. He had a strong and soothing personal approach and communicated confidence to his patients. They believed in
him and believed he could help them cure themselves. For many patients
the effect seemed almost miraculous. So it did for Mary Patterson.

The influence of Quimby over Mary Patterson has become the single
most aggravating issue in Christian Science historiography. In the fall of
1862 Mary believed herself almost miraculously cured and for some
months suffered none of the effects of illness. Obviously she had nothing
but praise for Quimby, wrote effusive letters about him to a local newspaper, and tried to learn what she could about his theories and methods.
For a few years she clearly considered herself a loyal disciple and soon tried
to use his method in healings of her own. Even much later, with the organization of her first classes and the beginnings of Christian Science, she still
followed Quimby in most respects, including the use of hands in her treatments. Later she repudiated his methods, largely dismissed his influence,
and tried in every possible way to disassociate Christian Science from
Quimby. To many outside her movement this seemed nothing less than
rank ingratitude and historical distortion. Even today many list Quimby as
the founder of Christian Science and Mary Patterson Eddy as his pupil and
successor. Historians within the movement, without exception, have gone
out of their way to minimize the influence of Quimby or to prove that his
approach was little more than a modified form of mesmerism. Thus they
emphasize his use of manipulation, quote his more mesmerish statements,
and deny much religious, let alone Christian, content in his theories.

The truth lies somewhere between these polar interpretations. It is unfair to Mary Glover to attribute much of the content of her *Science and
Health* to Quimby. It is equally unfair to Quimby to identify him with
much of her teachings. His ability as a healer far exceeded that of Glover.
He was most attuned to what worked. He had some rather coherent theories about the role of mind in health, generally believed that mind or spirit
represented the truest and highest reality, and often identified his methods
with those of Jesus, even as he expressed strong anticlerical sentiments. In a
few cases he referred to his method of healing as Christian and at least
twice as Christian Science (not a new phrase), although his usual term was
"Spiritual Science." His explanations were much more simple and much
more coherent than those developed later by Mary Baker Glover Eddy.
Also, his theories, so directly attuned to effective healing, were less overtly
Christian than those of Eddy. Thus, as Mary Glover began trying to formulate a philosophy to support her own healing and teaching, she soon
wandered far from Quimby, but in eclectic and philosophically confused

directions. Quimby probably would not have claimed parentage and might have been distressed at some of the directions taken by one of his prized pupils. Yet his methods and theories provided a beginning point for Mary Glover, and thus it is almost inconceivable that she would have developed her therapy and her religion without the enormous impact of Quimby. In this sense he was the grandfather of Christian Science.

For Mary Glover, Quimby's cure lasted longer than most, but for less than a year. Until she died, she continued to suffer bouts of illness. Her own therapies were no more successful. She was a physician never able to cure herself. But briefly she had the illusion of a cure. She remained in Portland for two happy months, became friends with some of Quimby's patients, and resumed her active writing, now in defense of her great physician. She persuaded Quimby that she, perhaps more than any of his patients, understood his theories. In December her husband joined her after escaping from his Confederate prison. They returned to Sanbornton, where Mary lived with Abigail, and Daniel roamed about New England seeking a way to make a living. These moves helped retrigger Mary's illness. She vainly sought relief in correspondence with Quimby and in the summer of 1863 returned for one final bout of therapy. She gained enough good health to write regularly for the Portland newspapers. By early 1864 in Portland she was able to give her first public lecture, in which she celebrated Quimby's cures and tried to provide a philosophical explanation for his success. Perhaps for the first time in public she aired some of the opaque metaphysical views that later dominated *Science and Health*. They seemed confusing to her audience. The book later confused most readers.

Mary left Portland in March 1864. She never saw Quimby again but immediately began lecturing about him. The next two years were critical in her life and career. They were hectic years. Her husband set up a practice in Lynn, Massachusetts, but was away on trips as frequently as he was at home. In these two years the marriage, in effect, ended (the actual divorce came in 1873). He was unfaithful and deserted her for months at a time. When together, they moved from house to house. For a period Mary fled to one of Quimby's disciples. In 1865, just after the death of Mary's father, Quimby died. Mary wrote a moving poem–obituary and felt more alone than ever.

In February 1866 Mary fell to the ice on a Lynn street corner. She seemed badly hurt. In a nearby house she was attended by a homeopathic physician and comforted with morphine. Her always weak spine seemed affected, and according to Mary's later memory the physician feared that she would either die or never walk again. His notes do not document such dire predictions. In any case, she was carried, under sedation, to her home,

and there she seemed to linger close to death. By Sunday her Congregationalist clergyman prayed with her, as if administering last rites. Yet during the night she recovered almost completely, to the extent of walking
across a room. As before with Quimby, the cure did not last. But according to her later memory, she had gained a miraculous cure and with it insight into the true causes of illness. She attributed the insight, in part, to
Bible reading and thus identified it with Christianity. In her own mind, in
the mythology of a later Christian Science this was her Damascus road experience and, incidentally, an experience that, by her understanding, decisively distanced her subsequent healings from those of Quimby.

Later, Mary Baker Eddy identified almost all of her developed theories
with this 1866 experience. She deceived herself, although probably not in-
tentionally. By the time she published *Science and Health*, nine years later,
she had finally achieved an identity of her own. By then she desperately
wanted to be recognized for her contributions and needed to get out from
under the haunting shadow of Quimby. The miracle of 1866 was a needed
and useful tool for achieving these goals. To so interpret the accident is not
to deny the crucial importance of 1866 for Mary. In that year her marriage
finally failed. She was cast adrift, forty-five years old, with no achievement
of note. She had no Quimby to turn to and in fact tried desperately, just after the accident, to get healing help from Julius Dresser, a disciple of
Quimby and the one who saved his papers. By the fall of 1866 she had begun an unfocused pilgrimage that lasted for the next nine years. She had
no place of her own, was increasingly alienated from Abigail, and literally
moved about New England, finding temporary room and board wherever
she could, usually for short periods of time. Her ego, her ill health, and at
times her paranoia seemed to alienate most of her best friends, and thus
some asked her to leave their homes. But in these awful years she tentatively began a new career as a healer and teacher and, as often as she could
in these exile years, worked on what she expected to become a book. As
early as 1870 she had a rough manuscript. This eventually became *Science
and Health*.

From 1866 on, stories circulated about miraculous healings by Mary,
who soon assumed her former name, Mary Baker Glover. One beneficiary
was a niece. As for all such reports, the details remain rather vague and the
exact illness unspecific. Many of the memories date from years afterward,
when Mary Baker Eddy was a famous woman. Before the end of 1866 she
also had her first student, a shoemaker named Hiram Crafts. She moved
into his home, and after about five months he felt qualified to advertise his
skills as a healer, thus becoming in a sense the first Christian Science practitioner. He soon had satisfied patients; but his wife distrusted Mary, and

Crafts soon withdrew from his adventure as a "doctor." It is unclear what methods Crafts used (he later said he did not manipulate) or what type of theoretical understanding he gained from Mary Glover.

Mary Glover first advertised for students in a spiritualist journal in 1868, without immediate success. By then she was steadily working on a simple manual or text on her method of healing. At the time she still considered herself a disciple of Quimby and utilized a small list of questions and answers that she had copied from Quimby. But it is clear that she now had a new and compelling mission in life: to clarify a science of healing tied more closely to the Bible and to Christian themes than that of Quimby or the hundreds of other freelance healers who thrived in post–Civil War America. The manuscript she worked on, then called "Science of Man," became a practical guide to healing and, after numerous revisions, remained as a chapter of *Science and Health*, titled "Teaching Christian Science."

During 1869 Glover met and became a close friend of Richard Kennedy, an engaging young man who was fascinated with her approach to healing. He played a complex role in her subsequent career. It is probable that Glover became infatuated with Kennedy, both as a surrogate son and as someone who brought a hint of romance to her lonely life. She always seemed to need a man in her life, and for a time Kennedy was such. She considered him her skilled student. In February 1870 she and Kennedy signed an unusual contract. He agreed to pay her a total of $1,000 over two years for her instruction. Shortly thereafter Sarah Bagley, a spinster who had hosted and befriended Glover for over two years, also decided to practice healing and did well. She at first agreed to pay Glover 25 percent of her earnings, an agreement that was later canceled. So in 1870 Mary Baker Glover had finally, in middle age, discovered a way to make a living.

In May 1870 Kennedy and Glover moved back to Lynn, where she and Patterson had spent their last unhappy months of marriage. This would be the first center of Christian Science. They rented the second story of a house, and Kennedy immediately launched a very successful practice. He was gifted in this type of healing and had a long career in what was then a highly competitive profession. Before the later improvements in medical education, such healers often had more success than trained physicians. While Kennedy practiced, Glover tried to gather a group of paying students. She had gained experience with Bagley and Kennedy and had a completed manual to use as a text. Above all, she had an intense conviction and an almost hypnotic manner of presentation, and thus would have an enormous impact on those who accepted her approach.

Glover advertised her first class in the Lynn newspaper and had an almost immediate response. This class, now famous in Christian Science hagiography, had six students. It set enduring precedents. The classes met for only three intense weeks, with the instruction in the evening. The fee, originally $100, she later raised to $300. This seemed prohibitively high, for it took months of low-skilled labor for working people to save so much money. But the rewards could be very high if the graduates were successful in their practice. Kennedy was a living demonstration of the possibilities. For many young men and women, such expensive instruction offered the prospect of social mobility and, particularly for women, a way to move quickly from being artisans or homemakers to a professional career. In addition to her fee, Glover required her graduates to pay her 10 percent of all future earnings from their practice, which seemed a way of establishing a large, lifetime income for herself. After years of dependence and of living on the hospitality of others, she craved financial security and for the rest of her life took special pains to maximize her income and wealth. Her craving for money was obvious to her students, but the school was also a good business venture for them.

The partnership with Kennedy lasted only two years. The separation turned ugly. Kennedy soon became, according to Glover, a sinister and malignant enemy who tried to use telepathy to harm her. Kennedy, more stable and more successful, did not take the rupture quite so seriously and never entertained any paranoid suspicions about his teacher and first partner. He continued a successful healing practice for much of the rest of his life. The breakup is not easily explained. Once again it has occasioned controversy among biographers. Glover was not easy to live with. She was sensitive, manipulative, and jealous of rivals. One of her students, who had set up practice in Knoxville, turned against his mentor and published several nasty criticisms of her semi-mesmeric methods. Other students rushed to her defense, but in response to this hostile exchange, the first of dozens over the next thirty years, Glover decided to reject the hands-on-the-head method that had been part of her healing and her teaching, and which was basic to Kennedy's practice. Kennedy would not submit on this issue and continued manipulation as part of his treatment of patients. This change in methods also marked a move away from Quimby, even though her last effusive evaluations of Quimby date from this period. With the separation from Kennedy, she had to give up their quarters and suspend her classes for the next three years.

Once again Glover wandered from one house or apartment to another. In the midst of illness, which she now increasingly attributed to the evil thoughts of Kennedy, she worked at a new book. Her "Science of Man" had been a teaching guide. Now, pressed to defend the originality and the foundational principles of her therapy and training, she turned to what she called metaphysics. She also turned, much more clearly than before, to religion, to her own reading and reinterpretation of the scriptures that had been familiar to her since childhood. In a sense, Christian Science would be an amalgam of a highly ethereal Christianity and a form of therapy. The end product of this writing would be all but the last chapter of *Science and Health*. The manuscript was complete by 1873, copyrighted in 1874, and published through a subsidy contributed by students in late 1875. The title was in part accidental, chosen when the publisher informed her that her preferred title, *The Science of Life*, was already taken by someone else.

SCIENCE AND HEALTH

Mary Glover did not waste her years of exile, struggle, and painful composition. *Science and Health* would, in time, ensure her fame and fortune. It became one of the most influential religious books ever written by an American. It helped shape a new religious denomination. Despite its flaws, and they were many, Glover had a central insight that burned within her and gave the book its passion and power. The insight is not easily grasped, never quite yielded to the confinements of English words, and never had the coherent explication that careful readers wanted.

Of course, *Science and Health* never remained static. It was an ever-developing book. Mary revised the book at least once every year (it went through nearly 400 editions in her lifetime, but most were essentially reprintings) and basically recast its chapters at least three times, with the last major changes in 1907. At points in this book and in other writings she freely but probably innocently borrowed unacknowledged sentences or phrases from other authors, leading to later charges of plagiarism. The first editions suffered from awkward language and poor spelling and grammar. But the arguments were about as clear as they would ever be, and the style was effective. This fact later led Mark Twain to deny that Glover could have written even this first edition, since he found all her other writing so different in style—childish, effusive, and syntactically confused. He identified no author but probably believed it was Quimby. Twain's literary judgment, although based on a careful analysis of texts, has persuaded few biographers and is completely untenable today. What is conceivable is some literary help from students.

The complex history of the various editions of *Science and Health* reveals little about her religious beliefs but much more about her personal biography. None of the textual shifts changed the central message of the 1875 original. The philosophical foundation remained the same. This does not mean the central insights were clear or that she was able to develop them coherently. But they were about as clear in 1875 as in 1910.

It is almost pointless, and unhelpful, to try to trace the sources of Mary Glover's key insights. Most scholars have tried to unearth them, at least in part. The guesses have ranged from Hindu and Buddhist scriptures to the work of Emmanuel Swedenborg to Emersonian Transcendentalism to Hegelianism. Echoes of each are present in *Science and Health* but not basic to it. Once again, as in assessing her indebtedness to Quimby, claims of dependence turn out to be challengeable in a double sense, not only because they are unfair to the originality of Glover, but they are also equally unfair to the more coherent systems developed by other thinkers.

Science and Health is one of the most repetitious books ever written. One basic claim appears hundreds of times. This is a seemingly simple claim, but one with all manner of difficulties and almost innumerable implications. Simply put, it is the claim that reality (not only ultimate reality but all that is real) is one unified whole, and in all senses perfect. Glover had difficulty naming this reality. The generic term, God, drawn from Christianity, was not quite adequate, for she repudiated all anthropomorphic or personal images of a god. Always intensely aware of the limitations of the words that she used, inexactly, to communicate a central insight, Glover made do with an often intimidating array of suggestive synonyms. Thus, in addition to the word "God," she used at least a dozen other "ultimate" and capitalized terms, but most frequently seven others: Mind, Spirit, Soul, Principle, Life, Truth, and Love. For her, these were all synonyms but in various contexts suggested different qualities present in reality. In Glover's writings, Spirit and Mind appeared most frequently, often with one or the other paired with her references to God, a god whom she usually identified, consistent with literary convention, by male pronouns, but misleadingly so. She always stressed that the divine Spirit transcended gender distinctions and included in itself the best qualities associated with both masculinity and femininity.

Her language suggested some form of philosophical idealism or transcendentalism. The use of multiple synonyms to suggest reality was reminiscent of Ralph Waldo Emerson. Yet, even though she frequently drew on the language of nineteenth-century idealism, her views were much more complex and contestable than any system of philosophical idealism. The difference lay in her attempt to deal with what people referred to by such words as "physical," "mortal," or "material." All philosophical idealists profess monism; only one substance is real, and this is mind or ideas. But they at least accept the proposition that certain ideas (of solidity, resistance, and extension) are real, in the sense that a mind thinks these ideas and that such ideas may have an internal coherence and directly influence human sensibility. The so-called physical universe, although not made up of some substance called matter, as we humans so easily but mistakenly assume, is nonetheless real, even though in substance ideal. Glover was unique in denying even such an ideal status to the world of sensuous experience and the conceptualized physical world humans construct on the basis of this experience.

Her reality was, in effect, beyond any human description. Yet, by her understanding, each human was an individuated reflection of the divine Spirit, at one with it in essence. She never was able to find the words or to achieve the clarity needed to distinguish a unified whole from what seemed, in some sense, various persons or spirits with identities of their own. In her vocabulary, completely unitary images of reality mix with references to a differentiated universe of spirits. But her central claim is clear: in their true realities, each spirit or person is fully unified in substance with God, and thus is perfect. Each spirit is implicated in the eternality of Being, and thus is in no sense mortal. Spirits are not born and do not die. Thus, people are in fact immortal and spiritual beings, and as such are beyond any error or limitation or pain or suffering or death. Unfortunately most humans do not know and acknowledge this fact. They mistakenly assume that they are part of a material world, and in this false assumption lie all the evils and suffering of human existence. What mortals call matter does not exist, is not real, but is only a product of their own erroneous beliefs, a type of dream or fantasy world. This nonreal world of matter is without spirit or mind or intelligence. It cannot suffer, feel, or will. It cannot, by its very unreality, be the home of spirit or mind.

This bold claim lay behind all of Glover's religious thought and also anchored her beliefs about health. For her disciples, this claim was mind shaking, the basis of a new religion. For her critics, it was a bundle of sophistries. Most people mocked her denial of even a secondary or derivative reality to the body, to the senses, or to the world that seemed to lie all about. Since she did not even accept the idealistic claim that ideas of solidity and extension are quite real, and so experienced, even when not in themselves substantial, she could never frame an apology for her claims of nonreality that even made sense to most people. In the end she could only confess the inadequacy of the English language and suggest that a type of intuition, even a type of conversion, was necessary to grasp her key insights. If one ignores her metaphysics (she used this label for her ontology or "science" of reality), then Glover offered a familiar, even Neoplatonic version of human captivity in the world of matter. She offered counsel on how humans could recognize this captivity, see themselves as maneuvering among the mere shadows of a real world, and work toward some type of enlightenment that would loosen its hold over them (shades of Buddhism). In such transcendence one could escape all error and disease. But such a view still assigns some level of reality to matter, even as it may demonize the material world. It also places human spirits in a world of matter, in some sense interacting with it, and thus involves a type of dualism, all of which horrified Glover. Thus, for the rest of her career she clung tenaciously to her claims of nonreality, but by so doing she had to find some verbal conventions to deal with present human beliefs and experiences. Only her disciples believed she solved this problem.

Glover could deny the ontological implications of a language of things, yet she had no alternative but to speak it. Thus her ordinary language, the language she used daily and in her homilies, seemed to betray her extreme monistic philosophy. After all, she was personally beset with an illness that seemed very real in her experience. Her way of dealing with ignorance and evil involved some novel inventions of her own, the most important being what she called mortal mind. By mortal mind she seemed to mean a captive mind, one seduced by the world of things. Indeed, a mortal mind was a mind that believed matter real, believed that mind or spirit had its home in matter, and that mind was variously influenced by matter. But what is such a mind? Is it real? Not in Glover's estimate. It partakes of the world of matter and is, in a sense, brain bound. Since mortal mind does think, it has some of the characteristics of Mind or Spirit; it may suggest such a reality, but it is not one with Spirit, and thus is nonreal. But all humans are, to some extent, captive to mortal mind. Even Jesus, the most complete image of God, voluntarily bound himself to some of the afflictions of mortal mind and thought, because such a bondage, and the suffering it entailed, was necessary if he were to lead humans toward spiritual emancipation.

In the concept of mortal mind Glover had her substitute, in a Christian perspective, for the idea of an Adamic fall. Indeed, she saw in the mythic story of Adam the original symbol of human error and disease. He fell into all the illusions that haunt mortal minds. Glover saw in Eve not the temptress but the human who first perceived a redemptive pathway out of such illusions. Thus, Eve pointed toward a Jesus who would bruise the heel of the serpent (materialism), who first lived a life of perfect spirituality and healed people by his understanding of their real selves. Perhaps Eve also anticipated Mary Baker Glover Eddy, who after centuries of neglect revived Jesus' methods of Christian healing as the prime evidence for the solitary reality of spirit.

What is missing in all versions of *Science and Health* is any overall cosmology that might explain the fact (not the existence) of mortal minds and all their illusions. In a sense, Mary Glover's whole system involved a theodicy, a complete denial of substantive evil of any sort. Yet she had to deal with the troubling fact of human error and human sin. In most orthodox versions of Christianity, the Christian God willed the whole scenario of human fall and redemption, purportedly for his greater glory. Glover never affirmed such a willful God and was always horrified at a god who would will human suffering. Thus she always exempted her infinite Mind or Spirit from any possible involvement with sin. God willed neither mortal mind nor the illusions, such as matter, imagined by mortal minds. Thus, in a sense, no one willed evil. Yet humans have to deal with "it" all the time, even if "it" is unreal or has no ontological status (here the language problem is acute). At times Glover even intimated that the fact of evil and disease was indeed a mystery, one that resisted any solution according to human (and thus flawed) understanding. But the human plight had indeed led to all types of mythical answers to the dilemma, most involving anthropomorphic gods or devils. Such myths only further documented, rather than explained, the illusions entertained by mortal minds.

All humans are to some extent lost in the illusions of materiality, whatever its origins. But they can move toward their true self, come closer to a recognition of their inherent spirituality and perfectibility. The role of religious insight is to facilitate this growth toward authenticity. With such growth, the illusions—the dreams—of mortal mind give way, at least in part, to the truth of one's immortal (and real) mind, which is in reality a sharing in the perfect mind of God. With the realization that the material world and all its lures and enticements ard unreal, a human gained more and more spiritual insight. Such insight banished illusions or erroneous thought and also banished sinfulness or unrighteousness. When this occurred, the awful products of mortal mind, including sickness and death, also dissipated. Thus the road to health was a road to enlightenment, a banishing of false beliefs. All products of mortal mind, including a belief in diseases, were illusions that had to be banished in order to gain health and happiness, even of the attenuated forms that are possible short of complete enlightenment.

Mary Glover never claimed that one could, in this life, completely transcend the errors of mortal mind. Should one do this, then all the tokens of mortality would disappear, and one would realize complete spirituality. She saw this as the eventual but not yet realized attainment of humanity. In a sense such enlightenment, although attained briefly and incompletely during mortal life (this is a type of heaven), would mark the end of mortality. For the emancipated it would mean a fullness of life, but a life lived on a plane that had no contact with the illusionary worlds created by mortal mind.

This overall philosophy was difficult to communicate and never seemed to critics to be coherent. But it did allow Glover, quite persuasively, to distinguish her religion from that of others. She was best at defining what she did not believe. She rejected all orthodox versions of Christianity, for these affirmed a personlike and masculine god who created a material world and who was, in some sense, responsible for the evil in it. She repudiated any version of pantheism, for such involved a god who permeated or was imminent in a material world. She repudiated all forms of spiritualism, some of which had earlier enticed her and clearly influenced her religious development, because any spirits that in any way appeared to mortals were infected with materiality, as were spirits that controlled a medium or rapped. Above all, she repudiated mesmerism, or all attempts by mortals to influence or control the thought of others. Implicit in this hatred, or her nearest approach to a type of demonology, was her belief that mortal minds could influence others, even at a distance, in what amounted to a type of telepathy. As one approached true spirituality, one would renounce such mind control. When people realized their true spirituality, their oneness and unity with God, no basis or opportunity remained for such willful control over others.

When Glover wrote the first edition of *Science and Health* she had not yet created a new religion and perhaps did not envision a Christian Science church. She intended the philosophical or theological content of the book to serve as a foundation for her courses on healing and as a more extensive guide to her students than the small text she had heretofore used. By 1875 she had repudiated some of her early healing techniques, such as the use of hands on the head, and was determined to distinguish her healing from that of Quimby. *Science and Health* placed her healing in a broad religious context, purportedly based its principles on an informed reading of the Bible, made Jesus the founder and authority for such healing, and made parallel the problems of illness and sinfulness. In the book, religion and therapy blended, with neither purpose clearly predominant, but Glover believed the success of her method of healing was the empirical proof of the correctness of her philosophy. Just as Freud did later, she based a complex system of beliefs or theory on clinical evidence.

Therapies abounded in 1875 and for the next quarter-century. Until then, professional and increasingly licensed physicians were not notably more successful than other practitioners. The failures of what would soon be touted as scientific medicine left an opening for people like Mary Glover and her often quite successful students. Yet Glover did not want to be identified with the various competing therapies, whether involving water cures, radically attenuated uses of medications, hypnosis, elaborate types of diet and hygiene (she condemned only alcohol and tobacco), or various forms of mind cure. In all these she found elements of the occult or concealed means for therapists to exercise mental control over patients. Neither did she want to be identified with an emerging emphasis on healing among evangelistic Christians, particularly among what became the holiness and Pentecostal denominations. She rejected what she saw as their simpleminded biblical literalism, their captivity to matter or some form of metaphysical dualism, their retention of the harsh doctrines of Protestantism, and their emotionalism. No one could have been farther away in temperament and beliefs than she was from this branch of Christianity, and her appeal was to a very different constituency.

Glover endlessly used the word "science" to distance herself from either occult or conventionally Christian forms of healing. She appealed to what she believed was her correct description of an objective reality, to the laws of Mind, and thus to a type of knowledge that was, in her estimation, internally coherent and subject to empirical verification. Such an appeal to the prestige of the word "science" was not new. Quimby made the same claim and so had other therapists, while many of the leading nineteenth-century spiritualists had insisted on the scientific status of their theories. Outwardly Mary Glover did all she could to support her scientific claim. She soon formed and, by some good fortune, gained a state charter for a metaphysical college. She believed she subjected students to a rigorous form of training. She and her students assumed many of the emblems of professionalism and called themselves practitioners. Soon such practitioners formed a professional association, with a published list of official or licensed therapists, periodicals and conferences, and in some cases even advanced courses of instruction for a favored few. Nothing could have seemed more removed from the tent revivals and emotional cures of Pentecostal evangelists.

Science and Health was both a manual for self-healing and a guide to Christian Science students and practitioners. In theory those who read and understood the book could cure themselves of any disease and also rid themselves of sin and disobedience (Glover always paired error with disease, righteousness with wellness). Healing, in her system, always involved a change in beliefs, and thus she advocated one form of mind cure. Both sin, or rebellion against one's true spiritual nature, and disease, or what seemed to be various afflictions of a physical body, were rooted in illusory beliefs that matter was real and that it could suffer pain and affliction. All disease, all pain and suffering, was a product of mortal mind, not something inherent in illusory matter. Thus, because one believed in the efficacy of matter and in the possibility of disease, one became ill. At the same time, such beliefs, themselves erroneous, helped alienate people from their own spiritual nature and thus were parent to a sensuous and selfish life, or a life of sin. If one could recognize the error of such beliefs and come to understand one's own spiritual nature, then such a change in belief would cure error, disease, and sin.

After 1866 Mary Glover made frequent claims of almost instantaneous healing of other people, people who did not know and would never grasp her philosophy or religious beliefs. That is, she believed that she healed people who remained fully captive to their false beliefs about matter. This seemed to mean a type of healing that was not rooted in self-enlightenment but bestowed by another person. This seemed to be true when Jesus healed, at times gratuitously and at times with a simple request that the patient trust or believe in him. Jesus did not require a course in metaphysics or ask for a new and profound level of spiritual understanding.

Mary Glover at times claimed almost immediate cures for infants, who were not even open to any new understanding. Practitioners also claimed, at rare times, to heal animals. They had an open practice and invited everyone to come in search of healing, totally apart from any receptivity to philosophical insights. Of course, Christian Science practitioners did try to instruct clients, to persuade them of their true nature, and to get them to shift their beliefs. In this context practitioners offered an intensive type of instruction and through it allowed patients to heal themselves. Mary Glover, as she wrote about healing, often shifted from a straightforward claim—"I healed him"—to a therapeutic language in which the healing did involve a new self-understanding; might take a long period of time; might involve an intense period of stress and even worsened symptoms as a patient gave up old beliefs (a process called chemicalization by Christian Scientists and reminiscent of some aspects of Freudian theory); and might, in some cases, never be successful because of the patient's resistance to the required new beliefs. Glover even argued that the healing of an infant reflected a change of belief on the part of parents or caretakers, for it was their false beliefs, somehow communicated to the child, that led to illness.

Such ambiguities yield no full resolution. In her preparation of students who would become practitioners, Glover emphasized their degree of realized spirituality. This meant both metaphysical understanding and a reformed personal life. Presumably such right thinking by practitioners would mean a high level of health as well as moral purity on their part. In fact, Glover argued that they would lose effectiveness as healers if they themselves were not models of enlightenment, righteousness, and health-fulness. Implicit in this requirement is a power in a truly spiritual person to heal people who are not enlightened. It is as if their spiritual understanding extends outward, at least for a moment enveloping and transforming a trusting but uncomprehending patient. This fit what Jesus did. And this needed role for the practitioner—this attenuated method of healing short of the longer educational process leading to self-understanding and auto-matic wellness—provided something more than an educational role for practitioners. But the two methods were never quite distinct in Christian Science. Mary Glover taught people and let them heal themselves, but at other times she took credit for healing patients. Presumably, this quick healing did not involve any teaching. Somehow she then extended the benefits of her own spiritual insights or strength to others.

However skeptical one may be of Christian Science healing, one can-not ignore the testimony of thousands of people who experienced it, and still experience it. The same is true of other forms of religious healing. Not only patients who came to the office of a practitioner, but others who simply read *Science and Health* or attended Christian Science worship ser-vices on Sunday confronted a form of therapy leading to a type of self-understanding. It could be very effective. It could lessen anxiety, calm fears, create an atmosphere of trust and confidence, and thus help induce both mental and physical well-being. Its success depended on the receptiv-ity of the patient and on the appeal and charisma or air of authority and competence reflected by a practitioner or a Christian Science lecturer. In this context the boundary between mental and physical maladies blurred or disappeared. That some Christian Science practitioners were adept at such therapy is obvious from their results. Clinical success was proof enough. Such success does not prove that the metaphysical support for such healing was true, or that therapies based on it were more successful than others that competed for patients in the late nineteenth century. Some mind-cure or new thought healers were just as successful as any Christian Scientists, even as the most hated apostates of Mary Glover often were successful healers. What other healers did not have was as elaborate a philosophical system, or what became the foundations of a new religion and a well-organized church. In all the confusion of competing therapies, the organizational and promotional skills of Mary Glover enabled her to win overwhelmingly in the competition.

Such healing success still begs all the hard issues that Glover had to con-tend with for the rest of her life after the publication of *Science and Health*. Could Christian Science offer solutions to the problems of what she called organic maladies (tumors, broken bones) and for the greatest of all human problems, death? Most people who came to a Christian Science practitioner had what they called "functional" problems. The label no longer makes much sense, but it referred to people who seemed to have all their organs in proper repair but suffered from some disease. We would now include in this category all diseases caused by bacteria, parasites, fungi, or viruses, plus all the "nervous" ailments that do not have any clear source in pathogens or in any identifiable organic pathology. Mary Glover lived during the period when physicians recognized more and more bacteria that caused diseases, and in a few cases they used vaccines to prevent such infections. Unfortunately they were virtually helpless, except for symptomatic relief, in treating diseases caused by most pathogens. Even surgery, for clearly organic problems, remained very risky. In this context she was absolute in her claims but hedged in recommended practice. She always claimed that error lay behind all diseases, organic or functional. She claimed cures for cancer and even broken bones. But in fact she recommended that practitioners use surgeons for clearly organic problems such as broken bones and explained this, as so much else, by the unadvanced state of enlightenment, even among Christian Scientists. Someday they would be able to dispense with all such illusory or mortal types of cure. The same was true for diseases, such as smallpox, for which effective vaccines existed (she took away her earlier ban on vaccinations in 1901). Prudence suggested immunization even for Christian Scientists, particularly since their illnesses could infect others. Since she at times used morphine to control her own pain, she could do no other than commend such pain relief in our present state of unachieved spirituality. Most Christian Scientists also used dentists, wore eyeglasses, and eventually accepted treatment for infectious diseases such as diphtheria.

Glover included under the label "functional" all those diseases caused by pathogens, whether or not anyone had yet identified such pathogens. To her the germ theory of disease was at one with all the other illusions about the physical world and its claims over Life and Spirit. If one were caught up in the illusions of mortal mind, such explanations of disease, along with the fabric of physical science, might represent a more coherent or useful way of classifying illusions. In this sense it might be desirable that people fully subject to mortal mind utilize such sciences, but in the larger sense of spiritual truth all were illusory. For pathogen-caused diseases, which seemed to make up a majority of cases that came before Christian Science practitioners, Glover's therapy may have been as successful as any other, perhaps superior to all others. The teaching and the trust and confidence developed in one-to-one sessions may have done as much as anyone could to abet the spontaneous healing that long remained the only hope of such patients. By combining the popular appeal of Christian symbols and meanings with the increasing confidence inspired by the word "science," her student practitioners were in the best possible position to gain the early confidence of patients.

Very important to Glover and part of the advertised appeal of her therapy was its professed nonmanipulative intent. Her reaction to Kennedy and her paranoid aversion to mesmerism or even less intrusive methods of influencing or controlling the thought and will of another led to her constant admonitions to students: Do not try to use your thought to control or manipulate patients. Let the glow of your conviction, the power of your moral purity, and the influence of your prayers affect others, but do not impose on them. She recommended a calm understanding of a patient's beliefs and values and only a gradual and nonmanipulative introduction of Christian Science concepts into the healing relationship. Such an approach was one side of the only demonology that appeared, with different degrees of emphasis, in all editions of *Science and Health*. This involved her condemnation of malicious forms of animal magnetism, at first directly related to hypnosis but later tied to manual manipulation or even more subtle, telepathic attempts by one person to control or harm another. In almost all cases of her own illness, Glover blamed the projected evil thoughts of Kennedy and later apostates or enemies. When such evil projections were present, it took an even higher level of spiritual understanding to regain health. Glover frequently engaged her students in efforts to overcome malicious animal magnetism, which became for her a substitute for Satan in conventional Christianity. In later editions of *Science and Health* she reduced the chapter on animal magnetism and left out the more barbed even though indirect attacks on her persecutors, but it still remained central to her understanding. The one positive result of her own paranoia was an acute sensitivity in her and in her students to the autonomy of other people and to the possibly dangerous effects of too much intervention or suggestibility in dealing with patients.

Death is the ultimate human problem. To Glover it was the ultimate illusion. People, who are in reality spirits in the image of God, are immortal. They cannot die. With sufficient enlightenment they become free from their bodies, which are only creations of mortal mind. Jesus, as an immortal and perfect image of God, accepted the limitations of mortality for instructional purposes, but as soon as he had delivered his message of spiritual emancipation and demonstrated it by healing, he returned to his true or spiritual state and thus was no longer visible to mortal sight. His ascension, in Glover's typical spiritualized interpretation of biblical texts, was in reality his resumption of pure spiritual being. This will be the fate of all people in the future. When this age of full spiritual realization arrives, then one might say that everyone has died. That is, if there were a mortal left (there would be none), such a mortal would say that everyone else had died. They would no longer be within the reach of bodily senses and thus would be unheard and unseen.

But Mary Glover strongly denied that mortal death automatically led to such spiritual enlightenment. Any religion that promised salvation at death seemed as morally irresponsible as her caricatured Calvinism. She rejected most orthodox Christianity on this point, because it offered a type of salvation based not on hard discipline and moral reform, but on an unearned gift of grace. She actually rejected almost every orthodox doctrine of the historic churches, but particularly all ideas of a substitutionary atonement. In this she was the complete Arminian. Jesus had an instructional or demonstrational role, not a juristic one. Atonement meant coming to be at one with God, becoming like Jesus, in understanding and in service. Thus those who remained captive to mortal mind during their lifetime would remain subject to the same illusions after mortal death. The individual, as a spirit, would no longer be bound by a brain but would still believe the same errors, suffer the same types of affliction although without organic manifestations, and endure the same forms of revolt and disobedience. The spirit would escape only certain beliefs about the physical body. Mortal death, in itself, emancipates from nothing important, but as a theological universalist Glover believed that all such burdened spirits would still, sooner or later, gain the needed enlightenment. Glover believed in what one might call tortured spirits, still bound to false beliefs about matter and still tainted by mortal minds. Insofar as humans rightly reported contact with spirits, it would be contact with such unemancipated spirits, those still burdened by mortal mind. In short, any spirits contacted by a medium would be unenlightened spirits.

Glover's references to death remained more elusive and full of more conundrums than her much more extensive discussion of illness. She always listed death with error, sin, and disease but offered no clear therapies for death. In a sense, denial seemed sufficient, and Christian Scientists have always tended to ignore or minimize the significance of what ordinary people see as the passing of life. Many of Mary Baker Eddy's most loyal disciples speculated that she had attained such a level of spiritual enlightenment that she would never die. In old age Eddy tried to conceal her fading health and keep up, at least in public, an image of youthfulness. Perhaps at moments even she thought she could transcend the experience of death. But in the context of her teachings, her views are reasonably clear. For people—perhaps all people but Jesus—mortal death will come before complete spiritual enlightenment, before anyone, continuously, has transcended mortal mind. If this is so, then death marks a transition in one's spiritual pilgrimage. It is a positive transition, because one loses the apparitions that go with the body, loses the sensuous temptations of the body, and this can help speed one along the road toward enlightened understanding and thus a final redemption. The person does not die. The soul has nothing to do with matter and has not lived by any power in matter. Thus nothing is lost in death, for all the dimensions of a human body have been no-things all along. On the other hand, this passing of all bodily illusions is not a time for rejoicing, since this event does not emancipate the Spirit. This means a rather novel view of what most people call death—a transitional event that has nothing in itself to do with redemption or damnation, and therefore an event that is not very important. Damnation and redemption depend on how the human spirit has believed and lived both before and after the emancipation from the body. Hell is to be captive to sin, disease, and death; redemption is to transcend all of these. Each can be a part of human identity at any time.

BUILDING A CONGREGATIONAL CHURCH—1875–1890

A long road lay between the publication of *Science and Health* in 1875 and the formation of an enduring Christian Science church. It took fifteen years. The achievement, again, was almost entirely due to the effort and the unswerving commitment of Mary Baker Glover Eddy. For a while the early intimations of a church involved only her few loyal students. Since she would allow no competitors and even broke with students who had great talents or an independent turn of mind, her early movement was a cult, a religious organization that was completely under the sway of a charismatic leader. She not only retained this dominance until her death but in the *Manual* of the Church of Christ, Scientist, left such an organization and set of rules as to control the church long beyond the grave.

After writing and publishing the first edition of *Science and Health*, Mary Glover resumed her teaching, after a three-year break. The book was a dismal failure from a publishing standpoint. Few newspapers reviewed it, and those critically. Almost no one beyond her students bought it. In time, students even tried, with small success, to sell it door-to-door. But it did bring Glover some notoriety, particularly when she responded in letters or in newspapers to some of her critics. At least in Lynn, she enjoyed the status of a published author. The book did not win her a slew of new students, for only six or seven enrolled in her courses in 1876, which she taught in her own house in Lynn, a house she could afford only by letting out some of the rooms. But by 1875 the ten or so students in the area referred to their group as the Christian Scientists and for five weeks met to listen to Sunday lectures by Glover. In the next year, with two new crops of graduates (each, if able, paid $300 for the twelve three-hour sessions spread over most of three weeks), a growing nucleus of students formed the Christian Scientist Association. This organization was not a church—not primarily a religious organization—but closer to a professional organization made up of practitioners.

Before the student group could mature into a church, Mary Glover had to endure one embarrassment after another. These helped her in only one sense—for the first time she became a household name in Massachusetts. In the midst of the trials, and on New Year's Day 1877, she married a former student and loyal supporter, Asa Gilbert Eddy, who was ten years her junior. This was, by her claims, a nonsexual union. Eddy helped sustain his wife during a period when her ablest students seemed to desert her or even launch effective attacks against her character and teachings. To her old devil, Kennedy, she now added several more, including the most gifted of her new students, Daniel Spofford. He had even taken over the distribution and sale of *Science and Health*. But as so many more after him, he tried to play an originative role in the development of a Christian Science movement and soon broke with Eddy. In the series of student apostasies that marked the rest of her career, it is impossible to assign guilt or praise. Mary Eddy was hard to live with and was demanding and at times manipulative with students, from whom she expected complete loyalty and intellectual deference. She had no place for anyone who tried to interpret, expand, or even order her ideas.

Spofford became a new devil, viewed as malevolent and as much a source of malignant animal magnetism as Kennedy. Without his help, however, she had difficulty completing an abortive second edition of *Science and Health*, which rambled on for two volumes. In this case her paranoia about Spofford became public knowledge. Desperate for money and abetted by a student with legal pretensions (he too soon deserted her), she sued not only Kennedy but other ex-students for unfulfilled contracts, in what turned out to be a losing cause. In the end she won an original judgment against Kennedy but then lost when he appealed and requested a jury trial. This forced her to debate her views about healing in a public forum, with plenty of harmful publicity. Her cause suffered ridicule when one of her students asked the court, in Salem, to issue an injunction to prevent Spofford from causing her illnesses through mental mesmerism. The court ruled that it had no way to control the thought of people and dismissed the case, but not without providing a field day for newspapers, in what they called the second Salem witch trial. Finally, while the Kennedy case was before the courts in 1878, Spofford mysteriously disappeared and was assumed dead. He was really in hiding. An informant came to the police with an elaborate story of how Gilbert Eddy and another Christian Science student had hired someone to kill Spofford. They were arrested, indicted, and held over for trial. In the end it turned out that the informant had lied and someone had fabricated the whole scenario, but by then the damaging publicity had ensured that Mary Baker Eddy would lose the Kennedy case. Subsequently she lost other cases in which she sued to recover promised fees, leaving only chagrin for this brief entrée into the legal system.

In the same year, with at least more name recognition than ever before, Mary Baker Eddy began a series of lectures in Boston on divine healing. She preached on Sunday afternoon in a Baptist church, with a growing audience and some friendly newspaper coverage. This lecture series led to a continuing circle of disciples, or an embryonic congregation that met at least irregularly from this point on. Back in Lynn, in April 1879 her students voted to organize a Church of Christ. In August the group gained a charter for a Church of Christ, Scientist, with Eddy as president or pastor. It began with twenty-six members and soon had services in both Lynn and Boston. In both locations Eddy lectured or preached. The group early adopted silent rather than public prayers (save for the Lord's Prayer), a continuing Christian Science tradition. After hymns and reading from both the Bible and *Science and Health*, Eddy lectured and responded to questions. This meant a service that was halfway between worship and a continued course on healing, or a blending of therapy and religion. The Boston lectures in particular helped her recruit new students for her courses back in Lynn.

By 1879 Eddy was becoming more and more committed to her congregation in Boston, although she retained her Lynn home for two more years. She conducted the services in the Boston congregation in 1879 and into 1880 and even taught one course in Boston. She retreated to Concord, New Hampshire, to finish a third edition of *Science and Health*, which for the first time contained a vindictive attack on Kennedy and Spofford and on malicious animal magnetism. In 1880 in Boston the growing congregation had its first communion service (without sacramental elements), and Eddy published the first of her sermons. But she still returned to her house in Lynn for most of her courses, now better attended than ever. Because of the anticipated effect of a new state law requiring training for all who practiced healing, and taking advantage of a new but temporary state incorporation law, Eddy formed a board from among her former students and successfully petitioned for a charter for a metaphysical college to teach both medical subjects, such as pathology, and metaphysical ones, such as ontology, all related to healing. She received the charter in January and placed an appropriate sign on her house in Lynn. She was president and sole faculty of this new college and continued to teach her courses as before.

By 1880 the Christian Science movement was at a takeoff point. It had a nucleus of students and religiously interested disciples not only in Lynn and Boston but in several cities across the country. Students came from several states and then went home to launch a practice and, in time, teach their own students and even form local Christian Scientist associations. By then the movement was thriving but a bit anarchic in Chicago, which became the main western center for Christian Science. The Christian Scientist Association even met in Chicago in October 1881, and Eddy attended the gathering, her first trip west.

She should not have left Massachusetts. While Eddy was away, a student revolt occurred back in Lynn. This was not the last. A meeting of the Christian Scientist Association (practitioners) and the Church of Christ, with twenty present (the core or nucleus of the movement), received notice from eight former students of their withdrawal from the association and church. They cited the bad temper, love of money, and hypocrisy of Mary Baker Eddy. Others soon joined the revolt; a few repented and returned to the fold. The rebels included two of Eddy's earliest Lynn students. The reasons made sense. Eddy was often dictatorial, did have a bad temper, did jealously seek to maximize her own income, and often did not live up to the principles she taught. Those who boarded with her, who knew her in all her moods, and who often had to respond to arbitrary commands or verbal abuse, slowly lost the zeal they had gained from her lectures. This defection was a devastating blow to Eddy. Ultimately the loyalists expelled the dissenters (they did not have a right to resign) and almost immediately ordained Eddy as their pastor. But by now Gilbert and Mary Eddy were anxious to leave Lynn for good. They held the last service there at Christmas 1881. They moved briefly to Washington, D.C., for lectures and then to Philadelphia before settling in a house in Boston. From this point on, Boston was the center of Christian Science.

During the 1880s, Christian Science became a national, even an international, movement. Mary Baker Eddy moved her Metaphysical College to Boston and even briefly tried to add two sympathetic physicians as faculty members (this never worked). But her husband did not live to enjoy her growing fame. He died of heart failure in June 1882. Mary would not accept the medical verdict. She believed that he died from malicious animal magnetism, or what she called a form of mental arsenic administered tele-pathically by Kennedy and Spofford. She so charged in a Boston news-paper. Even an autopsy failed to persuade her otherwise.

After grieving on a rest trip to Vermont, Eddy returned to Boston and for the next several years concentrated on her teaching. It gradually helped her gain financial independence, for not only student fees but the unstated obligation of all students and practitioners to buy each new edition of *Science and Health* added to her annual income. She more than replaced the Lynn defectors by over fifty new students in 1882−83. In 1883 she launched the first enduring Christian Science publication, the *Journal of Christian Science*, and as its first either wrote or selected all its content. Her movement expanded rapidly but not without continued controversy. She had to defend herself against the students and descendants of Quimby, who now broke into print to deny Eddy's originative role in the founding of Christian Science. She suffered a steady stream of defectors, almost always her ablest students. In a sixth edition of *Science and Health* (new editions came at least once a year now), she added some early biblical interpreta-tions (*Key to the Scriptures*), which had occupied her for several years (some sections on Genesis preceded the writing of *Science and Health*). Later she expanded this into chapters on Genesis and Revelation, plus a glossary of terms. In each case she rather freely interpreted the Bible in spiritual terms. Her distance from Christian orthodoxy was now clear, and this biblical "tampering" gained condemnation from evangelicals. In reality Eddy had embraced almost every traditional heresy: she was a type of modern Gnos-tic, an antinomian, an Arminian, a universalist, and a unitarian. She re-jected any binding biblical authority and freely rejected parts that seemed inconsistent with her metaphysics. This included the account of creation in the second chapter of Genesis. She had read broadly in biblical criticism and arbitrarily drew on this source to bolster her idiosyncratic interpreta-tions. She even wrote and used a spiritualized version of the Lord's Prayer.

Personally, in the busy mid-1880s Eddy's health was probably better than ever. More and more, loyal disciples cared for her. Her secretary and loyal defender for the rest of her life was another man, Calvin Frye, a rather dry, taciturn individual. He became accountant and bookkeeper for her movement and at times was her chauffeur and servant. Live-in students were at her beck and call, even for manual labor and as her own spiritual physicians. But the school had many of the petty jealousies of a communal colony. Some students accepted the arbitrary and capricious regime un-der Eddy because they so deeply believed in what she taught. But those with a more critical turn of mind rarely remained loyal. Increasingly, her ablest students were women, and all along a majority of practitioners were women, although, except in leadership roles, the ratio of women was not that divergent from mainstream denominations.

The growth of Christian Science after 1880 paralleled the growth of mind-cure therapies and the philosophies that abetted them. The number of practitioners outside Christian Science far exceeded those under Eddy's control, as she often lamented. Several even used the label Christian Science, leading to confusion and unjustified criticism of Eddy's students. To counter this proliferation and near-anarchy caused by so many seemingly related movements, Eddy tried even more to impose strict discipline in her ranks. Each practitioner had to gain new certification each year, and the *Journal* listed the accredited. Eddy insisted on strict adherence to *Science and Health* and almost always condemned and tried to suppress what she saw as mistaken interpretations of her teachings. Thus students had little leeway in modifying, simplifying, or even publishing commentaries on her writings. Many, at times most, resented the dictatorial style, but it proved a necessity. None of the other New Thought groups had the cohesion, and thus the survival capacity, of Christian Science, with its one prophet and one scripture.

The cost of such discipline was high. From 1880 until Eddy's death in 1910, the Christian Science movement did not gain and retain any person of commanding originality or brilliance. Able people with considerable business or administrative skills joined and served, but in every case the disciples that had the most to give to the movement eventually broke with Eddy or suffered unilateral dismissal at her command. The one who came closest to staying the whole way was partially protected by distance, Augusta E. Stetson (a graduate of 1884), a charismatic woman and brilliant speaker who built her own little Christian Science empire in New York City. Her very influence and power and independence proved her ultimate undoing. She reflected a power center that threatened Eddy in her last years, and thus Eddy helped engineer Stetson's expulsion from the church just before Eddy's own death in 1910. At the national level her most influential student was Emma Hopkins (another 1884 graduate), who excelled Eddy in intellectuality and who briefly served as an able editor of the *Journal*. Hopkins could not accept the discipline or the narrow exclusiveness of Eddy. She left to form her own Christian Science movement in Chicago, eventually with its own institutes and journals. She was much more eclectic than Eddy and less overtly Christian. Like so many in the New Thought movement, of which she was a founder, Hopkins wanted to merge insights from several world religions and included in these Eddy's version of Christian Science. But she lacked Eddy's organizational and promotional skills.

Christian Science attracted its share of cranks. Many became students after being healed (no one seeking healing could enroll until well), and some retained very fragile personalities afterward. Many failed in practice, and some ran afoul of state laws, were embarrassed by publicized failures, or faced criminal prosecution when their patients died without other medical attendance. Almost as embarrassing as the witch trial in Salem were the trials and tribulations of Josephine Woodbury, another 1884 student. Sensuous, effective in healing, and appealing in personality, she bedded with a troubled student, became pregnant even though married to someone else, and then claimed that she conceived the child by immaculate conception. She christened the poor boy the Prince of Peace, left Christian Science to spare the movement embarrassment, and eventually died by suicide. For several years Eddy was willing to forgive Woodbury and tried to save her brilliant talents for Christian Science. When this failed, Eddy seemed to denounce her in a written address as the whore of Babylon. Woodbury sued for libel, leading to a nasty and drawn-out litigation only settled, in Eddy's favor, in 1901.

Such aberrations did not slow the accelerating growth of the movement. By 1887 Eddy taught 167 students in one year. A few able and sophisticated men, such as Edward Kimbell, relieved her of some administrative and ministerial duties. In 1886 she formed the National Christian Scientist Association, of which her Massachusetts group was only one member. The first meeting included delegates from fifteen states. In several cities growing congregations duplicated the worship of the well-established assembly in Boston. Although Eddy left most of the preaching to others, her sermons in Boston were well publicized and well attended. A few more liberal ministers defended her (most of the more orthodox or conservative excoriated her beliefs), and she had occasions to defend her views, which she did with great passion and conviction. Well before 1890 she was one of the best-known citizens of Boston.

In the midst of continuing frustrations Eddy enjoyed an increasing number of successes. Her teaching attracted all the students she could manage, and this meant a growing personal income. This enabled her to buy a new house in Boston. The Sunday services in Boston grew too large for Hawthorne hall, forcing a move to a larger auditorium. In 1884 Eddy convened her first normal class for experienced practitioners who locally offered instruction in Christian Science. In 1885, in recognition of her need to appeal to better-educated readers, she engaged James H. Wiggin, a retired

Unitarian clergyman, as editor of the sixteenth edition of *Science and Health*, the first of four major revisions of her text. He clearly improved the style and for the rest of his life helped Eddy, in a sometimes tense advisory role, with not only subsequent editions of the text but periodicals, serving for a few years as editor of the *Journal*. He respected Eddy but, with an almost supercilious detachment, never accepted her beliefs. In her personal life she formed a final alliance with a man, a forty-year-old student, Ebenezer J. Foster, whom she legally adopted as a son. His earned M.D. lent respectability to the movement, but unfortunately he later proved less than obedient. For several years Foster-Eddy played an important role in her household and gained more leadership roles in the church than his talents or integrity merited.

In 1887 Eddy enjoyed her greatest triumph in the midst of a new revolt in her own Boston congregation. She went to Chicago to attend a meeting of the National Christian Scientists Association. Her announced attendance helped attract 800 delegates (including most practitioners in America). Unknown to her, she was an announced speaker at an open meeting crowded with 4,000 people. She typically rose to the occasion, gave such a moving speech that she was virtually mobbed by cheering disciples after it ended, and by many reports helped heal many in the audience. She had more honor in Chicago than back home, and from hundreds of her disciples who had long yearned to meet her in person. Back at her hotel she was again pressed by people who wanted to see her. She was finally a celebrity.

In Boston the rebellion continued. It began when an Eddy student and practitioner was charged in court after a patient and an infant died in childbirth. The student was exonerated, since the tragedy would probably have occurred even with an attending physician. But Eddy was slow to defend her student, much to the consternation of several members of her congregation, who nourished several other grievances. As the controversy brewed, thirty-six members resigned (technically illegal) and kept control of the congregation's records. Eventually others also left. Before returning the books, they won the right to leave without formal expulsion or excommunication, and some practitioners continued their career in the Boston area. This split devastated Eddy. By early 1888 she was clearly tired and visibly old (she was sixty-seven). She almost joined her friendly supporters in Chicago and did take a long vacation in New Hampshire. Her movement seemed increasingly out of her control, even as it grew more rapidly than ever (in 1890 it had over 20 churches and over 250 licensed healers). Yet new enemies and new factions emerged each year. She increasingly felt a strong urge to retire from the battlefield, at least under the existing organizational structure. She taught large classes in 1888 and what turned out to be her last and largest regular class (seventy students) early in 1889. By then she had already reduced the number of sessions from twelve to seven. She also gave her last major public lecture, in New York, in 1889.

To the surprise and shock of her followers, in October 1889 Eddy announced the closing of her Metaphysical College (the name and charter continued, and later the church gave "degrees" in its name to graduates of normal schools). She also recommended the dissolution of the local Christian Scientist Association (it obliged). She resigned as president of the National Christian Scientists Association and three years later persuaded it to disband. She also resigned as pastor of the Boston congregation and soon forced the Boston church to dissolve as a legal entity (worship services continued). Meanwhile the church had raised money to buy land for a planned building. Eventually a member absconded with some funds of a building committee, which then could not meet payments on the mortgage. Eddy had already, in a clever if shady plan, purchased the mortgage and in the foreclosure sale gained the land for half its value. In turn she offered it for value to any former member of the congregation who had contributed to the fund. A close disciple purchased it, deeded it to her, and she in turn deeded it to three trustees on condition that they build a sanctuary when $20,000 was in hand. In a legal sense these moves ended the first Church of Christ, Scientist, leaving all local congregations adrift but, for a brief time, free to make decisions for themselves.

Of course, Eddy's motives for this revolution of 1889 remain a subject of controversy. She justified it by a need to dispense with human organizations and to recover a needed spirituality. Such language duplicated earlier rejections of any form of church organization. But more was involved. She wanted to retire from the strains of her busy life in the 1880s. More important, she wanted to start over with her church and do it better the second time. To do so, she had to clear away all the accumulated structures. She may not have envisioned, at the time, the exact means to rebuild, but when she took the necessary steps in the 1890s, she created a tightly centralized church completely under her control. This is the Church of Christ, Scientist, that survives to the present.

Eddy retired to the home country of her childhood. She leased a home in Concord, New Hampshire, and then in late 1890 bought a lovely, hillside farmhouse a mile outside the city. There, in a refurbished and much enlarged house she named Pleasant View, she lived in seclusion for all but the last three years of her life. For her, retirement was a tactic that allowed her to attend to her writing and, at a protected distance, control her movement. Her seclusion helped create an air of mystery about her and in the eyes of her disciples raised her to a near-god. Only those who attended her in her house—the ever-dutiful Calvin Frye and former students who came back to serve as virtual servants—knew about her continued health problems, her paranoia, and her desire both to control other people and to gain wealth for herself.

BUILDING A CENTRALIZED CHURCH

By 1890 the polity of Christian Science was not unusual in the American setting, except for its entanglement with healing. In almost all cases the early students of Mary Baker Eddy set up practice in a city, gained enough patients to make a living, and in time started teaching courses modeled on those of Eddy. Through such courses a practitioner built a small community of like-minded people, who soon formed a local Christian Scientist Association modeled on the one in Massachusetts. This small community might begin worship services on Sunday, with the original practitioner usually serving as a de facto minister.

The early Christian Science worship service was a typical free-form or nonliturgical service closely modeled on New England Congregationalism and Unitarianism. The service involved the same familiar elements (hymns, scripture, the Lord's Prayer, and a sermon). It was distinctive only in the silent prayer, readings from *Science and Health*, and possibly a question-and-answer period at the end. In addition to this Sunday and often also Sunday evening service, local Christian Science congregations usually followed the Boston lead and held weekly services on Wednesday evening, which they devoted to testimonies, largely by those healed. These gatherings closely duplicated prayer meetings or witness meetings in Protestant churches. No denominational board or hierarchy had any control over the local group, and until after 1890 Mary Baker Eddy issued no formal guidelines for worship. The local practitioner may have dominated such groups, but in form they were democratic and open to the input of members, if they had formal members. The core of those who attended were the students or aspiring practitioners and others who had been healed and thus developed an interest in Christian Science. One cannot be sure, but in all likelihood healing (of oneself, a family member, or a close friend) remained the main recruiting tool of Christian Science well into the twentieth century. Those who came to the services represented a broad cross section of the local population, but in time the appeal seemed to exclude the extremes. That is, the very poor and the wealthy rarely joined. But quite affluent businessmen and lawyers joined along with a preponderance of women, most homemakers but quite often from respectable or even eminent families.

Despite the congregational polity, early Christian Science congregations had more form and order than competing New Thought societies. Each congregation had its own holy book, credentialed healers as leaders, and a degree of guidance from Eddy. It had not a creed but a restrictive body of beliefs, or what already amounted to a form of orthodoxy tied to *Science and Health*. Yet the identity of most local congregations inevitably reflected the personality of local, often charismatic, practitioners, such as Augusta Stetson in New York City. In the provinces, well away from the scrutiny of Eddy, congregations varied in many details.

From 1890 to 1895 Eddy imposed on this decentralized congregational system a highly centralized directorate that soon produced uniformity across the country. Most critics saw her tactics in these years as part of a single-minded effort to gain full control. Indeed, she certainly loved to be in charge, to control everyone in her movement. But it is unlikely that she planned the steps that she took during these years or foresaw, or even recognized, the outcome. A solution to one problem led to another, and out of this came a unique organization. From 1895 on, she certainly did all possible to perfect it. It worked.

One source of what later seemed a brilliant, or malevolent, plan involved the land already held for a church building. Eddy had indeed maneuvered to gain full control over it and had placed it under loyal trustees in 1890. They began fund raising but eventually could not get an insured title. At this point Eddy resumed ownership and had these first trustees return all gifts for a building (they kept a record for future use). She then carefully formed a legally sound second trusteeship. She once again deeded the property to four completely loyal disciples, with a reservation clause if they were not able to fulfill the conditions of the gift. These conditions not only required them to build a sanctuary costing at least $50,000 in five years but also specified that they were to organize and maintain public worship in the completed building and make all needed rules to achieve these goals. Since the old charter for a Boston church had not been annulled (it was just in-active), she faced such difficulties in forming a new church corporation that she eventually decided to build her new church around the deed and the trustees. Thus the self-perpetuating trustees, called in the legal trust a board of directors, became sole owners and managers of what became the mother church in Boston. Of course the gift included several consultation or approval clauses that actually left the final power in the hands of Eddy. Thus, in a sense, she began a new church on the basis of ownership of its property and full control over every detail of its management. This meant a degree of personal authority unique in American religious history. No-tably, in her trusts or other legal arrangements she almost always turned to men, not to women. This reflected both a very conventional understanding of certain gender roles (lawyers and accountants were almost always men) and a concession to the beliefs of the larger culture.

In the summer of 1892, even as she perfected the trusteeship for the land, Eddy began reorganizing her church. She selected twelve individuals, male and female, and after deciding against a new church charter, designated them charter members of the mother church, had them elect a chair and a secretary, and asked them to approve twenty additional members, or a combined group henceforth designated First Members. She presented to them a very simple, quite general set of tenets that new members had to accept (she continued to insist that this was not a creed). These tenets were very close to a general Protestant confession and would have posed few problems to any prospective member. The tenets did not refer to *Science and Health* and had only a few phrases that suggested Eddy's distinctive theology. Subsequent bylaws, after the first publication of a church *Manual* (1895), all drafted or approved by Eddy, created a rather complicated path to membership, including an application form, a commitment to the teachings in *Science and Health*, approval by an existing church member, and acceptance by the board of directors.

In October 1892, at a called general meeting, the Boston congregation learned about the new organization. Its members were pleased, grateful to Eddy for, in effect, giving them the land for a building, now with realistic prospects of an early and successful building fund drive. As many present as were willing to accept the tenets could apply for membership, and soon most loyal members in Boston joined the mother church. What they probably did not notice is that they, as members, had no real voice in the governance of their congregation. In fact, their congregation remained unique in the new denomination, for unlike branch churches it had almost no leeway for local decision making. Eddy opened membership in this mother church to Christian Scientists anywhere in the world. This was and remains the most novel feature of Christian Science polity. New bylaws soon required that all readers, practitioners, and teachers in branch churches be members of the mother church. Not only such local officials but most dedicated Christian Scientists wanted to be members (they had to contribute only annual dues to the mother church). Within a year over 3,000 had joined.

In 1895 Eddy completed the centralized control initiated in 1892. In that year she guided a committee in drafting the original *Manual*, with a set of bylaws relating to every aspect of the mother church and, in some cases, even the branch congregations. Before Eddy's death in 1910, it went through eighty-one editions and almost every year received new bylaws from Eddy, some largely involving her own personal status in the church.

She also eliminated some bylaws that caused embarrassment, such as one prohibiting members from joining any secular organization that did not accept both sexes as members. The most important innovation was centralized control over worship. Until then, the congregations had routinely heard sermons by their pastor (usually the original practitioner and teacher in the region). In the sermon, as in their teaching, they had some room to innovate, even in the interpretation of Christian Science doctrines. They also had a means to build a local following and, as Stetson had demonstrated in New York City, to build congregations that rivaled the mother church in Boston. Eddy had already found sources of factionalism, or potential threats to her own hegemony, in some local preachers. Now she decided to abolish the sermon and with it any pastoral role.

She did this with a bylaw that eliminated ordained clergy and made the Bible and *Science and Health* the "pastor" of each congregation. Instead of a sermon, the audience was to hear only readings from these two scriptures, and the officials in Boston determined the approved readings for each week. A new publication, the *Christian Science Quarterly*, first launched in 1890 with daily guides to scriptural readings, began listing the Sunday morning readings. These involved the International Bible series used by most Protestant Sunday schools and correlated reading from *Science and Health*. Both the mother church and the branch churches would henceforth have two lay readers, but no pastors. Usually one reader was female, the other male. The Bible reading came first, but then the person listed as first reader read from *Science and Health*. The bylaw prohibited readers from making any comments about the reading or answering any questions. In time the directors would even, in a few cases, try to control elements of voice and inflection, thus eliminating any possible avenue for personal creativity by readers.

These bylaws did not abolish all leeway for extemporaneous talk. During the week the branch churches still had the Wednesday testimonial service in which people largely testified to their healing experiences. No one could control what they said. Under Eddy's guidance the church established Sunday schools for youth under twenty, and the adult teachers in such schools had to interpret the weekly scripture and readings from *Science and Health*. Beyond the requirements imposed from Boston, the local congregations were self-governing, at least in areas related to finances and business. They certainly had no leeway for doctrinal discussions, let alone innovations. All the local officials were members of the mother church and subject to its tight discipline.

In place of pastors, Eddy approved traveling lecturers (following a brief period in which the church had appointed missionaries). The directors (or really Eddy until her death) selected each year a group of approved lecturers (she preferred males) and by rules forced local congregations to pay their fees. The lecturers traveled from congregation to congregation (each congregation or local group of congregations was obligated to engage one such lecturer each year). They were by design public relations experts, able to defend the church or the reputation of Eddy. They responded to outside critics of the church and hoped to gain favorable newspaper attention locally and thus possibly help in recruiting new members. Typically the local congregations publicized the lecture, which they held in public halls. But the lecturers were not freelance speakers. They had to write lectures, mail copies for approval to the clerk of the church in Boston, and were not supposed to deviate in any way from the text.

When Eddy gave up her instruction, she left the education of practitioners to local teachers, some able, some not. They had gained their status by taking classes with Eddy. Needed was some stable and enduring structure to regulate teaching. Eddy tried to provide this with a bylaw establishing a board of education to license and supervise teachers. It had to offer a normal class every three years and hire a teacher for instruction. Since this class lasted only a week, it seemed more a mode of certifying the competence or orthodoxy of teachers than increasing their skills. Certificates from this normal class took the place of classes directly with Eddy. Back home, such certified teachers could offer a course only once a year to no more than thirty students and with no more than $100 for tuition. They could form all their students into a local association. As Eddy's students died, this method of teacher certification limited the number of training courses and, perhaps, in time helped account for a decline in practitioners.

Publishing always had a major role in Christian Science. When she had only a few students, Eddy established the *Journal*. At times she assigned ownership of it to the Christian Scientists Association; at times she recalled it to herself. The association sometimes referred to the Christian Scientists Publishing Society, but it had no clear legal status until 1898. When Eddy dissolved all the associations by 1892, she was the only owner of the growing number of periodicals, with the *Quarterly* (1890) and a weekly *Christian Science Sentinel* (1898). In that year she transferred ownership of all publications to a newly organized Christian Science Publishing Society and selected the first, self-perpetuating trustees for this soon large and most costly aspect of the church. In 1908, encouraged by a journalist friend, Eddy commanded the society to launch a daily newspaper, the *Christian Science Monitor*. In time this became one of the most prestigious and honored newspapers in America and more than any other publication gained favorable attention for the church. Eddy died before anyone could appreciate its potential.

In the bylaws, Eddy assured herself complete control over the church. She had the right to approve or veto all officers and committees and new bylaws. She could order the dismissal of any officers, including directors, on request. She could block any called meeting. Many bylaws involved her personal privileges. She mandated that her name be cited at any reading of *Science and Health*, a practice still followed ad nauseam in Christian Science worship. No member could publish extended excerpts from her writing. She could accuse anyone of mental malpractice, with her accusation sufficient proof thereof. She could unilaterally excommunicate members who reviled her or treated her with disrespect. Any member who troubled her about any subject was subject to punishment. By making a verbal complaint against any member, she could block their membership for twelve years. All officers had to comply with her written orders. No member could bring legal action affecting her property.

Most revealing was a bylaw called Opportunity of Serving. On the surface this seemed a license for peonage. If Eddy requested, through the directors, that any members of the church come to her and serve her for three years, they had to come or risk excommunication. If they came and left before the end of the three years, they would be liable for fees covering the value of the instruction they received from Eddy. In this case, the assumption was that these people would be either students or practitioners and that their role would match that of her earlier, in-house students. Another bylaw had the same requirement for household help or maidservants. It is important to note that most faithful members saw this three-year service as a type of apprenticeship, an opportunity more than a burden, and that each received room and board and a then-impressive $1,000 annual salary. In fact, those students who so served in her last years became an elite in the church, for they were in effect graduate students sitting at the feet of the master. A few bylaws seemed more self-effacing but were not so in effect. One forbade holiday or birthday gifts to the leader (she had been inundated), and another asked the board not to consult her on membership, discipline, and excommunication (despite the bylaw, she was consulted on important disciplinary matters or dismissals).

This highly centralized church grew rapidly. By 1907 it had 710 branch churches, with 58 abroad. The mother church had over 43,000 members, not including those members of branch churches who did not apply for membership in the mother church (this dual membership has always made it difficult to establish firm membership figures for the church, which according to one of Eddy's bylaws was not supposed to compile a membership count and which since 1936 has carefully concealed all membership figures). The growth in part reflected good promotion and public relations.

The *Monitor* helped. So did the reading rooms established by each branch society (these had to be open to the public and include only official church publications). Using another bylaw, Eddy established the somewhat confusingly named Committee of Publication. This one-person committee (with later assistants in the mother church) was really director of public relations, particularly in response to outside criticism. In time most branch societies also appointed such a "committee," which meant ready and often very sophisticated publicity all across the country.

When she deeded the land to her new board of directors in 1892, Eddy was able to ensure the early completion of a sanctuary. She endorsed a new fund drive, contacted affluent members, and considered donations for the building as special Christmas gifts to her. By early 1894 the directors had the needed funds and broke ground for a sanctuary that was completed and fully paid for by January 1895. Most faithful members considered it a gift to their "Mother," an endearing term they briefly used for Eddy. She accepted the completed building but then "gave" it to the directors (Mark Twain referred to it as her mosque). It included an opulent Mother's Room, which soon became a much-visited shrine by Christian Scientists touring Boston. Only once, in April 1895 during her first inspection of the new building, did Eddy spend one night in a folding bed in her room (her attendants had to sleep on the pews). She visited the building only two more times—Sunday morning sermons in May 1895 and February 1896. Because of the satirical ridicule by Mark Twain (he was both fascinated and repelled by Eddy), in 1908 the church, at Eddy's suggestion, closed the Mother's Room. Also, she used a bylaw to change her title from "Mother" to "Leader" as a way of countering criticism that she claimed divine status. Unfortunately the revered new sanctuary soon proved much too small for the Boston congregation, leading to a new building fund and a much larger "annex" in 1906, with a seating capacity of 5,000. This addition, with its large dome, is what most people now consider the mother church, not the original building that is in its shadow.

Because of the rapid increase in the number of members and in material prosperity, Mary Baker Eddy was able to spend the last years of her life in near-seclusion. She was one of the best-known women in America. She relished the fame, the sense of power and influence, and the wealth. She remained at Pleasant View in Concord and in effect ran her church from her study. Church officials consulted her on every important issue, yet spared her administrative details. In some ways her last years must have been lonely. Her adopted son, Foster-Eddy, eventually proved a disappointment. She had to dismiss him in 1896 as head of publications (a lucrative job) because of poor record keeping and managerial incompetence and even a hint of indiscretions with a woman. He no longer held any office of significance or lived in her household. Her staff largely consisted of loyal disciples, who accepted her demands that they serve her for three years. Calvin Frye managed all her properties, which were extensive. Her publications ensured a rising flood of royalties as the church expanded. She was a millionaire by 1907 and worth over $2 million at her death.

For Christian Scientists, most of whom joined the church after her retirement to Concord, Eddy was a near-god. She almost never appeared in pubic, except for a 1:00 P.M. daily drive around the streets of Concord, which was as regular and soon almost as famous as Immanuel Kant's strolls through the streets of Konigsberg. In November 1898, to the surprise of everyone, Eddy announced a new and final class for selected students, a type of advanced or normal class. Sixty-one awed students attended free for two sessions and gained fame within the movement for this unrepeated privilege. Since she chose not to come to her church, its members tried to come to her. She sent communications to each annual meeting, and a hushed audience listened to her precious words. In 1895 she invited the attendees of the annual communion service at the mother church (she later abolished this special communion) to Pleasant View, and 180 took the train and visited in her home, in a rare reception. When she repeated the invitation in 1897, 2,500 came, some walking a mile from the train station. With no invitation in 1898, a large group came to Concord anyway to stand outside the home and along the streets to catch a glimpse of Eddy on her afternoon ride. This became an annual ritual. She was in Boston for the annual meeting in 1899, and with the completion of a new Christian Science meetinghouse in Concord, she invited the annual communicants to visit it in 1904. Very old and visibly ill, she could only greet them from her carriage. At that point she wrote a bylaw prohibiting attendance on her drives or the haunting of her house by members. Few regular members ever saw her after 1904.

Her last two years in Concord were doubly sad. She finally began action against Augusta Stetson in New York City, who had planned a sanctuary larger than the one in Boston. Once again one unrefutable charge pressed by the board of directors was mental malpractice. Eddy thus finally eliminated her strongest rival. Even more agonizing was a new misunderstanding with her son, George Glover. She allowed him a brief visit at Pleasant View in 1907, along with his daughter. He picked a bad time. She was weak, almost incoherent, and paranoid, with wild stories about her enemies. George apparently believed that she was incompetent and under the control of Frye and the directors. Thus, after seeking legal counsel, he and other more distant relatives, joined later by her adopted son, Foster-Eddy, brought suit to declare her incompetent and to separate her from the management of her property and the influence of her de facto guardians. This suit elicited enormous publicity and led to a visit to Pleasant View by opposing lawyers and court officials. In a last almost superhuman personal effort, she carefully prepared for the visit and seemed weak but completely competent. The lawyer for the petitioners withdrew the appeal. During the litigation Eddy placed all her property in the hands of loyal trustees and in a will left almost all her wealth to the church (George received a generous monetary gift, but no other assets).

In a move in part precipitated by these problems, and by the paranoid suspicions that had driven her to flight on earlier occasions, Eddy decided to return to Boston. In complete secrecy, in 1907 her staff purchased for her a large twenty-five-room mansion on twelve acres in a Boston suburb (for $100,000), completely refurbished it, and in January 1908 hired a special train to transport her from Concord to Boston. At this Chestnut Hill mansion she spent the last three years of her life, still in complete seclusion and very frail. On her ever-less-frequent afternoon drives, she was able to see the new annex but never entered it. She died in December 1910 at age eighty-nine. Her church did not make much ado about her death, which in her theological system was not real or even very important. The church continued to list her as pastor emeritus, and rarely has the influence of anyone deceased remained as strong in any religion. She remained the source not only of all its distinctive doctrines and of its special scripture, but, through the *Manual*, of its discipline.

The language of the *Manual* created dilemmas for the directors of the church at Eddy's death. Her consent or her veto was necessary for almost every action of the directors and all other boards or committees. She may have lived on in spirit, but legally it seemed impossible to transact business. The board of directors chose to continue as before but to act in place of Eddy wherever the *Manual* required her input. In subsequent years the directors faced challenges but squelched all of them in what often seemed arbitrary action and without any rights of due process or appeal from accused members.

In the aftermath of Eddy's death the directors faced a major challenge to their exclusive authority from the trustees of the publication society, who had their deed and authority directly from Eddy. When the directors tried to control policy and remove trustees, the trustees fought back, leading to litigation that stretched from 1918 through 1921. Charles Evans Hughes represented the trustees, and early findings were in their favor. This meant that the board of directors could not fire trustees or make policy for the publication society, leaving two centers of power in the church. During the time when the directors seemed likely to lose, the membership split, but with a majority favoring the directors, apparently because they believed this had been Eddy's intent. In reaction they dropped subscriptions to church publications and almost sabotaged the work of the publication society. Eventually the Supreme Judicial Court of Massachusetts found for the directors. Despite the language of the two trusteeships, it found that it had been Eddy's intent that the directors have ultimate control. Even though the original deeds required the consent of the First Members (later called Executive Members until abolished by a bylaw in 1908) for the directors to fire trustees, the court felt that a religious organization was free to change its governance and that since 1908 the board of directors had the full power of dismissal. This decision ended any chance of a counterbalancing power in the church, saved the publications under a reorganized publication society, and finally certified the sole authority of the directors, who collectively are more powerful than the pope in Roman Catholicism.

The church continued to grow through World War II. Its maximum worldwide membership may have approached 500,000 by the 1950s (the last reported membership in 1936 was 268,915). Since then, all the evidence points to a rapid decline, although the authorities in Boston do the best they can to conceal the evidence. The total number of branch churches today (around 2,700) is only slightly larger than in World War II (around 2,300). Observers in Boston believe the active membership is no more than half what it was in 1950, with some estimates as low as 100,000. Impressions of branch churches suggest an ever-greater preponderance of women, particularly older women. The sharpest decrease has been in practitioners, which peaked at over 10,000 but by 1995 had decreased to less than 3,000.

Financial woes and new controversies have embarrassed the board of directors. The church overextended itself in publications and broadcasting and by the early 1990s had drastically to retrench. It had to close a new television ministry and its television station in Boston. It also had to suspend some publications. At present it retains its worldwide Monitor radio, but many fear that it may have to close its most prestigious organ, the unprofitable *Christian Science Monitor*. Such financial problems and allegations of mismanagement have led to an unusual number of member criticisms and challenges, with damaging publicity in Boston newspapers. At present it is difficult to sustain any optimism about the church in the future. Much of its appeal seems dated. Its highly centralized polity, which may have helped it early in the century, is now an embarrassment to many members.

Perhaps above all, its approach to healing seems dated, not because of any decrease of interest in nonscientific forms of healing, but because of the straitjacket of Eddy's metaphysics and her rigid rules for practitioners.

One final, recent controversy highlights an underground problem that has haunted Christian Science from the beginning. This involves the highly publicized, much criticized decision of the directors in 1991 to permit the publication of the Knapp manuscript. Bliss Knapp, the son of Ira O. Knapp, one of Eddy's most loyal disciples and a longtime director, was very active in the church (president and first reader in the Boston church) and a practitioner. He had vivid memories of Eddy, who had adored him when he was a child. Before his death he completed a book titled *The Destiny of the Mother Church*. Because of its controversial content, the directors rejected its publication in 1948. But according to a will by Knapp's widow and sister-in-law, the church was to receive almost $100 million if it published the manuscript by 1993. It did so but then refused to promote the book, even at times making it unavailable. The anger among members forced resignations and left a suggestion of hypocrisy or of a sellout by a board beleaguered by financial woes. What was most objectionable in the book, beyond Knapp's slavish adoration of Eddy, was his bold claim, tied to prophetic passages in Daniel and Revelation, that Eddy was the second Christ and that her ministry fulfilled the promise of a second coming. Such claims were not new, had remained the belief of a minority within the church, and had some support from the writings of Mary Baker Eddy (she identified herself with the woman clothed with the sun in Revelation 12:1). Thus the issue of her identity and role is a good place to end a discussion of Christian Science.

If Knapp's beliefs were to become normative in the church (they will not), then Christian Science would represent the third intramillennial church in America. The disciples of Emmanuel Swedenborg interpreted his new revelations about the spiritual nature of the promised kingdom as opening the millennial age and thus launched the Church of the New Jerusalem (a tiny, fractured sect in America today). Ann Lee, the founder of the Shakers, left no literary remains, but after her death her disciples, early in the nineteenth century, came to believe that she was the returning Christ, this time appropriately in feminine form, and that her communal and celibate church was a millennial church. At times in her writings Eddy came close to such a claim. Clearly she believed her writing, or at least *Science and Health*, was inspired by God and that the recovery of Christian healing represented a promised new age for the church. On a few occasions, by word or in one case by a drawing in a book for children, she at least insinuated her equality with Jesus, but when challenged on this issue she always retreated to a much less lofty claim. She then emphasized that her "Science," not herself, was divine, and when her students came per-ilously close to making her a deity, she always, sooner or later, rebuked them, in part in reaction to the outrage or ridicule of outside critics, most of all Mark Twain. Only by some quotations taken out of context could Knapp use her to sustain his claim of her divine status and role.

In any case, the directors of the church have consistently rejected the full deification of their leader. Neither have they been receptive to the type of apocalyptic proof offered by Knapp. Christian Scientists, much as Mor-mons, have tried to emphasize areas of commonality with mainstream Protestantism, and thus from a public relations standpoint Knapp's book was dangerous. In no literal sense did Eddy believe in a millennium, but she did look forward to the complete spiritualization of humankind, which made meaningless any literal concept of a thousand-year reign by Jesus. Thus the majority view among Christian Scientists is that she was indeed a special prophet, with a liberating and inspired message, not a god. In fact, gods have no place in Christian Science. Even Jesus was not a god, but to an extent as yet unattained by any other human, including Eddy, he did reflect the divinity (the Christhood) that makes up the true but as yet un-realized reality of any human. Everyone is divine in essence and potentially divine in realization. Eddy offered this liberating message to humans. Thus her role in Christian Science was different only in scale, not in kind, from that of Ann Lee for Shakers and Ellen G. White for Seventh-day Adven-tists. These three make up the great trinity of female prophets in American Christianity.

NEW THOUGHT AND UNITY

At least until 1895 the number of Christian Scientists did not begin to rival all the other people attracted to a vague New Thought movement. Many of these also used the label "Christian Science" for their beliefs, particularly those who practiced some form of healing. As a whole, the quite varied spokespersons for New Thought were better educated, more accom-plished, and much more logical than Mary Baker Glover Eddy. But most did not aspire to church building, did not license practitioners, and were so broadly eclectic in religion as to move beyond the boundaries of Christian-ity. Thus they built cults that never grew into sects. Some did leave endur-ing organizations. An International New Thought Alliance still exists, with offices in Arizona, a periodical, and around 200 affiliated societies, some of which still use the label "church." Two other avowedly religious forms of New Thought have at least a tenuous present existence: Divine Science, with headquarters in Denver, and the Church of Religious Science in Los Angeles. These and even smaller New Thought or New Age societies pose no challenge to Christian Science. This is not true of Unity.

Unity was the creation of Charles and Myrtle Fillmore. Charles, a distant relative of President Millard Fillmore, was born in Minnesota in 1854. Injured as a child and sickly for years, his career had some uncanny resemblances to that of Mary Baker Eddy. Largely self-educated, he sought various employments in the West and in Colorado met his future wife, Mary Caroline "Myrtle" Page, nine years his elder and much better educated. They married in 1881 and settled in Kansas City in 1884. By then both were periodically ill, with Myrtle soon seemingly doomed with tuberculosis. In 1886 she sought help from a local healer, a disciple of the type of Christian Science taught by Emma Curtis Hopkins, an apostate student of Mary Baker Eddy. Myrtle was soon well. She converted her husband to this type of New Thought healing, and in 1890 in Chicago both took Hopkins's course on healing. Hopkins became their mentor and frequently visited them in Kansas City on lecture tours to that city.

Even before the trip to Chicago, Charles had left his real estate business and began a small New Thought periodical, then called *Modern Thought*. In 1891, under the influence of Hopkins, he renamed it *Christian Science Thought* but had to give up that title because of protests by Mary Baker Eddy. This periodical eventually became *Unity*. Even by 1890 Charles and Myrtle had begun healing on their own and began meeting with a small band of disciples at 9:00 in the evening, for silent prayer or communion. Soon a growing number of attendees began to report healing, and the testimonies that ensued resembled those in Christian Science.

The first years for the Fillmores as healers and ministers were very difficult, with bankruptcy always looming, but love offerings, soon expertly solicited, kept the small movement afloat. In 1891 Charles broke into one of the silent meditations with a single word, "unity." He immediately saw its potential and made it the key term in his developing movement. He renamed his magazine *Unity* (it remains the flagship periodical of the Unity School). Gradually more and more people in Kansas City attended the evening meditations, and a handful of disciples began assisting in a growing publishing effort. For a time Charles and Myrtle were much esteemed in the larger New Thought movement. Both attended the New Thought gathering at the World Parliament of Religions in Chicago in 1893. Here they were especially influenced by Hindu thought. Only in 1906 did Charles announce that he would no longer be a part of the New Thought movement, choosing instead to develop Unity as an independent religion.

In 1903 the Fillmores renamed their developing ministry the Unity School of Practical Christianity and in 1914 incorporated the Unity School of Christianity, the legal vehicle of the continuing movement. In Kansas City they developed a training school, a very successful correspondence course, a publishing house, and a large Unity temple or church. In the summer in Colorado they offered courses for students (the Summer School of Metaphysics), who in turn went into healing for themselves. Such disciples used the name "counselor," not "practitioner." Many of them, in turn, offered local instruction, thus imitating the early Christian Science movement, but with most of the new Unity circles in the West. At the core of the movement in Kansas City was an evolving product of the earliest evening sessions, or what the Fillmore's called Silent Unity. As early as 1891 Charles had invited special prayer requests for their evening meditations, and soon some of these came to him by letter. Gradually the requests required assistants and longer periods of prayer. Today this means over 750,000 telephone calls, and over 2 million letters each year. A large staff of over a hundred, working in shifts, keeps the prayers going twenty-four hours a day. The prayers promise help for people who have problems, including everything from illness to business reverses. This prayer outreach was (and is) open to anyone and largely involved people in various Christian denominations, most unaware of the beliefs of Fillmore. Knowledge of Unity came from word of mouth, from its numerous publications, or, later, from radio and television broadcasts.

The beliefs of the Fillmores were eclectic. They proclaimed the unity of humans with a rather vague or spiritual god; the unity of all religions (close to Bahai); the unity of soul, spirit, and body; and the unity of all people of the world in truth and love. They denied that they had formed a new sect or denomination and welcomed people to their meditation and prayer meetings from all denominations and all religions. They had no creed or confession. Their emphasis on God as mind or spirit resembled the teachings of Mary Baker Eddy. They also emphasized healing and eschewed conventional medicine, were technically unitarian and universalist in their beliefs, gave leadership roles as often to women as to men, eliminated all material sacraments in worship, and used the same synonyms for God as did Mary Baker Eddy. But they distinguished themselves in several ways: they less fully denied the reality of matter and evil, organized no church, and wrote no scripture comparable to *Science and Health*, although in 1909 Charles published his own guide to healing, simply named *Christian Healing*. As Eddy, Fillmore emphasized his faith in the healing Christ but made clear that this Christ principle encompassed other major religious prophets, such as Krishna in Hinduism. Fillmore drew on an array of non-Christian religious literature, incorporated some mystical or occult elements, and believed in reincarnation. He was also a vegetarian, although this has never been an obligatory practice among Unity Christians. In fact, Fillmore, although honored and still the source of many Unity beliefs and practices, never assumed the semidivine role of Eddy and did not leave such a centrally controlled church. Unity members vary widely in beliefs.

In 1920 Fillmore purchased a thirty-eight-acre farm southeast of Kansas City, near Lees Summit (now a Kansas City suburb). He first constructed family dwellings on these acres and then by 1929 had completed a dam, a water tower with enclosed offices, and a partially completed building for Silent Unity. But the depression and then war prevented completion of a planned Unity village, with the site used mostly as a retreat center. It was only after the war, and Charles's death in 1944 (at almost ninety-four), that his sons, who continued to head a family dynasty, completed the present village and moved to it all the Kansas City operations—training school, publication and broadcast facilities, extension division, and Silent Unity. By the 1930s Unity resembled a religious denomination, with extension units or centers in most major cities, particularly in the western United States. Trained workers or ministers began meeting in annual conferences, and Unity ordained many full-time workers. In part to protect the original purpose of the Unity School of Christianity and its nondenominational appeal, the ordained clergy first created a legally separate entity, the Unity Ministers Association, and later turned this into the Association of Unity Churches. Although legally not a division of Unity School of Christianity, these churches nonetheless use its literature, celebrate its history, still teach the philosophy of Fillmore, and recruit their ministers from its training school.

Most Americans do not confront Unity in organized churches but in its literature. They do not think of it as a denomination but as a source of meditative and devotional guides. Its daily devotional magazine, the *Daily Word*, begun in 1924, remains one of the most popular in the United States (250,000 annual subscriptions), in part because of its noncreedal, positive, therapeutic emphasis. In 1893 Myrtle Fillmore began *Wee Wisdom*, a periodical for children that also gained a large circulation, but Unity recently had to suspend this magazine to the regret of millions of adults who had enjoyed it as children. Charles Fillmore early appreciated the potential for radio, for a time owned a Kansas City station, and began a continuing mission on both radio and television. Such publications and broadcasts created clients for Silent Unity. Today, unlike at the beginning, Unity charges for its periodicals and seemingly collects abundant love offerings for its prayers.

Visitors also tour the beautiful Unity Village, on 1,400 acres, and leave their contributions.

Approximately 400 Unity churches seem to be thriving. Unity makes up one of the hundreds of small religious sects that have sprouted and grown in America, but its future seems brighter than most. In another generation it may well rank as a major new American religion, and by then its members may outnumber those in Christian Science. Its congregations exemplify a religion nominally Christian but so open ended as to appeal to non-Christians. Except for an opening affirmation (a brief statement) and silent or guided meditation, its worship services follow the simple, free worship of nineteenth-century Protestantism. But its appeal is therapeutic, not doctrinal; it promotes self-help, self-realization, and personal success. Its congregations are warm, loving, all embracing, but light on theology and without any creed or doctrine. Much more than Christian Science congregations, they have been involved in social outreach and offer a wide range of courses and support groups not permissible under the tight discipline of Christian Science. Its churches are many things to many people and are never exclusive or judgmental. Each congregation is, in a sense, a large support group, and thus Unity appeals to individuals or families with problems, or to lonely people seeking a warm and supportive community. Healing, although an important motif, is not nearly as central as in Christian Science, and most Unity members choose to use conventional medicine along with meditation and prayer. It seems that there is a very large market for religion as therapy, and Unity fills a unique niche in contemporary America. One example does not a rule make, but it may be significant that my own city has a weak Christian Science congregation but a booming Unity church, with a new sanctuary and an overflowing parking lot on Sunday morning.

READING GUIDE

Anyone interested in Christian Science faces both opportunities and frustrations. One can find plenty of literature at the nearest Christian Science Reading Room. It is hard to avoid *Science and Health*, so avidly does the church advertise its scripture. But much more than with Adventists or even Mormons, an air of apology, a certain defensiveness, marks all the official literature on Christian Science. Most of the archives of the church are closed to all but clearly sympathetic outside historians. One result of this is a literature sharply divided, in content and tone, between that approved by the church and the often shrill criticism of those who write from the outside. One consequence of this is that, to an extent not paralleled in other equally large American denominations, Christian Science suffers from the lack of even one rigorous scholarly history.

Another problem is the close identification of Eddy and her church. This identification was intentional on her part. Thus almost all the scholarship on Christian Science, even within its membership, has focused on Eddy. So does the forgoing chapter. What is not well known is the church outside Boston and the experience of members in local branches. The historiography on Christian Science still circles around the controversial Eddy and on almost all issues remains inconclusive or sharply divided.

Perhaps the most famous early accounts of Christian Science were among the most devastating. In 1899 Mark Twain published his cruel attack on Eddy, *Christian Science* (New York: Harper and Brothers), and kept reissuing new editions, with updates. A series of attacks on her had preceded his book, but no one with his literary reputation had waded into the fight. In 1907–8 *McClure's Magazine* carried a series of muckraking articles, *The Life of Mary Baker G. Eddy and the History of Christian Science*, published in book form by Doubleday in 1909. The acknowledged author was Georgine Milmine. But in a persuasive new edition of this older book (Lincoln: University of Nebraska Press, 1993), David Stouck argues that Willa Cather, then an editor at *McClure's*, completely rewrote the raw manuscript and thus was most responsible for the final form of the series. This means that two of America's ablest writers devoted time and artistry to shaping the public image of Mary Baker Eddy. It was not a flattering image, but at least Milmine did a lot of work, particularly on the childhood of the still-living Eddy. Even Christian Science biographers have had to acknowledge the value of her work. Of more modern critical views of Christian Science, the most penetrating but no less devastating is Charles S. Braden's *Christian Science Today: Power, Policy, Practice* (Dallas: SMU Press, 1958). This book, now dated, is unique in focusing most of its criticism not on Eddy but on her creation, the board of directors that, at her death, assumed her dictatorial power.

Given the almost always highly critical or even satirical treatment of Eddy by outsiders, it is no wonder that Christian Scientists rushed to her defense. They, in a sense, created a woman almost unrecognizable by outside critics. Typical of the more adulatory books is Norman Beasley's *The Cross and the Crown* (New York: Duell, Sloan, Pearce, 1952). The definitive biography, loving but open to scholarly nuances, is a trilogy by Robert Peel, *Mary Baker Eddy: The Years of Discovery* (New York: Holt, Rinehart, and Winston, 1966); *The Years of Authority* (1977); and *The Years of Trial* (1971). All the known events are here, but Peel, on interpretive issues, gives at least a strained benefit of doubt to Eddy. But for one who wants to know her life well, this is the best source.

A more theological and interpretive study is Stephen Gottschalk's *The Emergence of Christian Science in American Religious Life* (Berkeley: University of California Press, 1978). The most recent biography, by a non–Christian Scientist, Robert D. Thomas, *"With Bleeding Footsteps": Mary Baker Eddy's Path to Religious Leadership* (New York: Knopf, 1994), is in many respects more of an apology than the work of Peel. Thomas is very sympathetic to Eddy and uses psychological insights to explain her career and influence. He did have complete access to church archives. Another, more quixotic recent book, by Martin Gardner, *The Healing Revelations of Mary Baker Eddy: The Rise and Fall of Christian Science* (Buffalo: Prometheus Books, 1993), documents Eddy's plagiarism, interprets the rage of Mark Twain, and looks carefully at some New Thought successors. Gardner spends little time tracing the decline of Christian Science but does survey the Knapp affair. Stuart E. Knee, in *Christian Science in the Age of Mary Baker Eddy* (Westport, Conn.: Greenwood Press, 1994), offers a detached but very episodic treatment of Eddy, with much attention to the critique of other Christians.

The Unity movement has not yet become the subject of critical scholarship. Hugh D'Andrade, in *Charles Fillmore: Herald of the New Age* (New York: Harper and Row, 1974), celebrates the intellectual guru of Unity. In a very superficial and glowing book, *The Unity Way of Life* (Englewood Cliffs, N.J.: Prentice Hall, 1962), Marcus Bach offers a firsthand account of life at Unity Village. Most books on either the New Thought movement or on contemporary New Age religion offer a brief introduction to Unity.

6

ECSTATIC **CHRISTIANITY**

The

Holiness

and

Pentecostal

Movements

In the last twenty years the fastest-growing component of American Christianity has been the Pentecostal denominations. About half of these had their roots in earlier holiness denominations or independent holiness congregations, and these in turn developed out of Methodism. Both the holiness parent and the Pentecostal offspring reflect very innovative and influential American religious movements. Today no one can list all the Pentecostal denominations. They number close to 200, with over 125 largely black Pentecostal sects, some with only one or two congregations. But even those denominations that report their membership to the National Council of Churches (approximately thirty, and including all the largest) have a reported membership of approximately 10 million. Denominations that are holiness but not Pentecostal account for another 1.5 million. These membership claims may be too large or may include inactive or casual members. But they do not include over a hundred small denominations and an incalculable number of independent holiness and Pentecostal congregations. Finally, the doctrine of holiness, at least in some of its meanings, has gained support among many evangelical denominations that have never used the holiness name, while numerous mainline Protestants and Roman Catholics have affirmed the charismatic gifts that distinguish Pentecostals.

Holiness and Pentecostal Christians have identifying markers. In this sense they are easy to locate. Yet behind the distinctive doctrines or practices there remains great diversity, particularly among Pentecostals. The holiness denominations all stress modern versions of John Wesley's doctrine of Christian perfection (or complete holiness or sanctification). All Pentecostals believe in the baptism of the Holy Spirit and in the spiritual gifts that follow such a baptism, with speaking in tongues as the testimony to this special baptism. If such Pentecostals also accept the holiness doctrine, then they see the baptism of the Spirit as a special experience that follows both regeneration and sanctification.

THE HOLINESS MOVEMENT

John Wesley first preached a distinctive new doctrine about holiness, and it was early Methodists in America who first made it a vital part of their religious life. Beginning with the first Methodist societies in the decade before the American Revolution, lay preachers stressed the doctrine and carefully recorded the people in congregations who gained the second step, who claimed full sanctification. In the Methodist Episcopal Church, founded in 1784, the dominating early bishop, Francis Asbury, required all his circuit preachers to render full reports on the number of conversions and sanctifications that occurred each year in their congregations, thereby giving almost equal emphasis to both steps. The discipline of the Methodist Episcopal Church required aspiring ministers not only to affirm the doctrine of holiness but to seek it for themselves, requirements that remained in effect throughout the nineteenth century. In this sense the first holiness denomination in America was the Methodist Episcopal Church. But this is not to argue that Wesley's doctrine of holiness was perfectly clear or that all Methodists had the same understanding of it.

Wesley believed that Christians could, through time and constant moral effort and with the help of the Spirit, move from regeneration, and thus the secure promise of salvation for those who remained faithful, to complete holiness or sanctification, to the perfection realized by all Christians at the moment of death or at the resurrection. In his early Methodist movement, Wesley preached a rather generalized theory of perfection, one not tied to any second, conversion-like, or instantaneous experience. After about 1760, when highly experiential attainments of holiness became widespread in his societies, Wesley recognized the possibility of such a second step, but he never clearly confessed the attainment of such holiness himself. Although Wesley wrote more about perfection than about any of his other doctrines and came to see it as the most distinctive emphasis within Methodism, his exact position remained elusive, even to his closest friends. He seemed rather frequently to shift his emphasis or slightly to change his conception of holiness.

By holiness Wesley meant not an absence of human weakness or ignorance, not even the absence of temptation, but a perfect and complete or even childlike love of God and thus the ability to resist all temptation and avoid sin, in the sense of willful misdeeds. He at times defined Methodist holiness not as an escape from human ignorance or weakness but as a state in which one would not voluntarily transgress any known law of God. The attainment of such holiness need not be uncertain or problematic but could be marked by an intense sense of joy and liberation, by an experience comparable in its emotional intensity to an earlier conversion.

Because Wesley wrote so much about holiness, and over such a long period of time, he left plenty of room for later disagreements. In his early ministry it is clear that he conceived of holiness or perfection as a compelling goal for his converts, something to strive for even if one had to await death to attain it fully. Thus holiness, as a goal and a promise, informed and motivated the devotional life of Methodists. This was consistent with his freewill outlook in all areas involving salvation. Calvinists, whom he repudiated, saw saving grace as a gift, not a choice, and thus emphasized the doctrine of perseverance (once saved, an individual could not lapse from grace, and thus one's salvation was secure). Calvinists indeed tried to grow in the faith, to approach sanctification, with scriptural study, prayer, and the sacraments all God-given aids in that growth toward sainthood; but only God could grant such perfection, and he did so only after death. Wesley, in his approach to Christian living, was closer to Roman Catholicism and placed much more emphasis on what Christians could achieve through the aid of the Spirit. His voluntarism was so complete that he could not limit what a Christian might attain in this life. If one could "attain" (note the language) perfection at the end of life, why could not at least a few very devout Christians attain it before death? In this continuum of effort, perfection seemed only reasonable.

Wesley never made attained sanctification a criteria of salvation. He never suggested that all Christians should expect such a level of love and devotion, only that all should seek it and move toward it. It is not clear what percentage of early Methodists claimed to have attained holiness, and the importance of the doctrine, the expectations that accompanied it, and the types of experience that came to characterize the second step seem to have been influenced both by the understanding of ministers and by the experiential patterns in congregations. Some ministers preached a hotter religion and stressed sanctification; others remained closer to the early Wesley, with sanctification a normative standard but one rarely achieved by individuals. This might mean that only a few, often elderly and sainted Methodists, could attain it before death. This position was closer to that of Calvinists, who made sanctification an impossible but still important goal for Christians.

Wesley certainly stressed the role of the Spirit in sanctification, but he did not refer to this second step as baptism by the Spirit, and he did not link the attainment of holiness with the experience of the apostles at the day of Pentecost. It seemed that Wesley, like his Calvinist colleagues, believed that all converts received this promised gift of the Spirit. It helped them grow toward holiness. It was in nineteenth-century America that holiness advocates began to tie sanctification to the Pentecost experience, or to equate it with the baptism of the Spirit (or in a few cases to a baptism by fire).

No American Methodists in the early nineteenth century repudiated Wesley's doctrine of perfection. It was a defining doctrine of the church. Yet Methodists soon differed in the stress they placed on the doctrine and the extent to which they made the attainment a climactic experience, comparable to conversion. It seemed, at least to an emerging holiness faction within the church, that too many ministers and congregations neglected the holiness doctrine and that this accompanied less moral rigor and a degree of worldly accommodation. In 1843 a small group (twenty-two) of New York Methodist ministers, upset at the failure of the larger denomination to take a strong stand against slavery, separated into a new denomination rather than obey their bishop's order to mute their abolitionist or free soil witness. This small Wesleyan Methodist Church (today the Wesleyan Church) is now recognized as the first holiness denomination in America, although in 1843 it did not, by any express doctrine, distinguish itself from its parent church, which was, in theory and discipline, also a holiness denomination. The small Wesleyan denomination simply continued the older tradition, while the parent church gradually moved away from it (today only a minority holiness faction remains in the United Methodist Church). The founders of the new Wesleyan church were not only for free soil but desired a more republican polity (they had no bishops and admitted lay delegates to conferences) and stressed a much more rigorous and antiworldly morality. This led them to stress Wesleyan holiness.

A second splinter from Methodism, coming just before the Civil War, led to another denomination that is now part of the holiness movement. This was the Free Methodist Church, which split from the then-northern Methodist church because of a stronger commitment to abolition, opposition to the rented pews recently permitted (not recommended) by the General Conference, and a desire to have a more republican form of church government. As the Wesleyan Methodists, they also rejected membership in the Masonic order and placed great emphasis on holiness. It is worth noting that these small holiness splinters were in the North, were greatly concerned about the evils of slavery, and combined an intensely evangelical witness with compelling goals for the larger society.

The main path toward an organized holiness movement after the Civil War came not from these small splinter movements but from within the much larger Methodist Episcopal Church (the largest Protestant body in America). In early stages of self-consciousness the holiness movement largely attracted reasonably affluent northern, urban Methodists, with women in key leadership roles. But in time, as holiness groups developed parachurch institutions of their own (an echo of early Methodism within the Anglican Church), the holiness doctrine had its greatest appeal in the Midwest, West, and upper South, among small farmers and mill workers. As an upper-class phenomenon, the early holiness prayer groups resembled charismatic circles within mainline churches today.

By 1830, at least according to Methodist bishops with strong holiness leanings, the Wesleyan doctrine of a second step was rapidly losing its centrality in Methodism. A majority of Methodists neither attained sanctification nor had much concern for it. It is impossible to measure the alleged decline, but such a perception began to increase the self-consciousness and the sense of alienation of Methodists who still made this a critical and defining doctrine. At least the issue was very alive by 1835.

An emphasis on holiness soon spread beyond Methodism. Not only did perfectionist doctrines inform John H. Noyes's infamous commune at Oneida, New York, but in 1836, as a new professor at Oberlin, the great revivalist Charles Finney had an intense experience of holiness and within four years published a book in support of the doctrine of complete sanctification. As with Wesley, with whom he professed only partial agreement, Finney's beliefs and those of colleagues at Oberlin marked the beginning of a broader holiness emphasis among American evangelicals. Perhaps because of his Calvinist background, Finney emphasized the empowering role of the Holy Spirit and taught at Oberlin a type of holiness that led to a full consecration of one's life to service. This tied his perfectionism to more traditional Calvinist ideas of a vocation, and particularly to the claim of a special calling that often marked the original commitment of young men to the ministry. In a sense Finney generalized this special calling, with all its emotional undertones, and asked all Christians to move forward to such a level of devotion. Consistent with his step-by-step approach to conversion in his earlier revivals, he now held out the prospect that Christians could and should move on to perfection, and he offered guidelines for that journey. In the wake of Finney, various subtly different conceptions of holiness circulated widely among revivalists, from both an Arminian and a Calvinist heritage.

Even as Finney converted to perfectionism, two sisters in New York City launched an enduring and distinctive holiness movement within Methodism. One sister, Sarah Worrall Lankford, a member of a Methodist congregation, gained the experience of holiness in 1835. In the aftermath of this transforming experience, she began to convene special prayer meetings in her home, or what became the famous and ritualized "Tuesday Meetings for the Promotion of Holiness." In the context of these first meetings Lankford's sister, Phoebe Worrall Palmer, also achieved the second step. She and her physician husband, Walter Palmer, soon transferred many of the Tuesday meetings to their home, where they further developed an American institution of vast influence. In 1839 Phoebe Palmer began admitting men to what had begun as a women's movement. She became the key spokesperson for what she believed to be the Wesleyan doctrine of holiness, but a position much influenced by Finney and by the practical, methodical steps that he made normative for bringing people to conversion. Palmer made holiness into a special commitment or sacrifice, a consecration freely chosen by individuals. Drawing on Methodist atonement doctrines, she talked about the sacrifice of self upon the altar, or a full and complete surrender to the atoning Christ. In a crucial step beyond Wesley, she made this commitment normative for all Christians, since perfection and the special work of the Spirit were available to any who would offer themselves fully to God. Thus, in subtle ways, she transformed the older Methodist doctrine into an expected attainment for all devout Christians, into a step that originated in choice and commitment, and into an achievement that gave new purpose and power to individuals, enabling them to live on a higher plane, or what some would soon refer to as the "higher life" doctrine.

Palmer never intended her Tuesday meetings to lead to any separation from Methodism, although a few bishops early feared this as a consequence. Her hope was that the holiness doctrine would become, once again, completely normative in the Methodist Church. But despite her demurrals, her Tuesday meetings soon grew into something unique. They attracted non–Methodists and even foreign visitors. Palmer wrote a book and edited a popular periodical to promote holiness. Her meetings overflowed, as affluent and even famous people joined in the testimonies to the work of the Spirit in their own lives. Such personal testimonies dominated the content of the periodicals. In effect, the Palmer meetings, and soon dozens of similar prayer circles, replaced the older Methodist classes, which were less and less prominent in Methodist congregations. The first impact of her promotion was a reconsideration of holiness within Methodism and an increasing array of church leaders who applauded Palmer's work. Non-Methodists soon seemed as persuaded as Methodists. Ministers from all the denominations attended, gained the desired holiness, and promoted the doctrine in an informal way within their own churches. Palmer was not dogmatic and not given to narrow doctrinal controversies and thus rejoiced in the spread of holiness among all evangelicals. She saw in holiness the glue that might enable all evangelical denominations to merge into one larger church.

In 1858 William E. Bordman, a Presbyterian minister who capitulated to the holiness doctrine, published a very influential book, *The Higher Christian Life*. In it he celebrated a general doctrine of holiness, gained in part from the Tuesday meetings. In England it helped spark a holiness movement that often used the term "higher life" and that later gained a label from annual meetings at Keswick. After the Civil War Bordman traveled to England and, with two powerful holiness revivalists from America, Robert Pearsall Smith and Hannah Whitall Smith, helped convene the first major British holiness conference at Brighton in 1874 and again at Oxford in 1875, the institutional beginnings of a holiness movement in Britain.

Walter and Phoebe Palmer traveled widely, to camp meetings, conferences, or citywide revivals. They were much involved in nationwide revivals in 1857–58. During the Civil War they toured England and Scotland. They ministered to separating Methodist congregations that made holiness a key doctrine and became close friends of William and Catherine Booth, founders of the Salvation Army in Britain (after 1880 it sent units to the United States). Phoebe Palmer helped persuade Catherine Booth to become a minister, and the Palmers helped solidify the holiness emphasis within the army. Today the Salvation Army may well be the best known of all the holiness (but not Pentecostal) denominations.

A disciple of the aging Palmers, John H. Inskip, helped lead in the next institutional development of holiness. A Methodist minister, Inskip rallied other ministers of similar commitment in New York City in 1867 to plan a national camp meeting to promote holiness. This first distinctively holiness camp took place at Vineland, New Jersey, in July 1867. Earlier, holiness Methodists had often convened separate holiness prayer circles at regular Methodist camp meetings but often felt marginalized at the increasingly fashionable eastern camps. The Vineland meeting was unprecedented in size, lasted for ten days, and gained the support and participation of some Methodist bishops. Many of the sponsors met at its end to form an enduring organization, which became the central organization of most holiness advocates in America, the National Camp Meeting Association for the Promotion of Holiness (NCMAPH). Inskip became its president. The next camp meeting, in 1868, at Manheim, Pennsylvania, attracted large numbers of non-Methodists among a crowd estimated at 25,000 and first won over some evangelically inclined Mennonites to the holiness cause. Subsequently the association held at least one, and soon multiple, camps each year. By 1870 these were the most dynamic camp meetings in America, and as the century waned it was the holiness groups, Methodist and non-Methodist, who did the most to keep alive the enthusiastic camp meetings that had typified early nineteenth-century Methodism. To this day, camp meetings remain institutionally strongest in holiness and Pentecostal denominations.

The national camp meetings spawned numerous local imitations. Locally, holiness advocates formed camp meeting associations, or holiness bands, thus linking people of like mind. Even by the mid-1870s one could detect a growing rift in the holiness movement. Phoebe Palmer, who died in 1884, and Inskip had tried to keep the movement within Methodism or in other mainstream evangelical denominations. They wanted holiness revivals to be within churches and wanted order and decorum. They also represented comfortable, middle-class, largely urban constituencies. But gradually this mainstream holiness advocacy lost ground in a growing movement that such leaders could not begin to control. Outside the Northeast the holiness movement had greatest appeal among small farmers or new rural migrants to cities. Dozens of itinerant evangelists spread the holiness gospel, soon creating a network of associations. At first most still functioned loosely within denominational congregations, most of which were Methodists, but with a scattering of Baptists and Presbyterians. The holiness factions cut across denominational lines, and for a time the distinctively holiness meetings did not compete with Sunday morning worship services. Holiness people gathered in revival meetings or met on Sunday afternoon. But as some denominational ministers correctly predicted, these holiness meetings soon became more important to participants than regular church services, reminiscent of early Methodism in Britain. Many converts in holiness revivals had no church affiliation, and thus the informal and often wild and undisciplined holiness meetings became their only church. By 1880 many holiness bands were, in effect, substitute churches, and many local holiness congregations had begun to organize as independent congregations. Out of such independence came the later holiness and subsequently many Pentecostal denominations. Even to this day, the centers of the most independent holiness bands—the Kansas-Missouri-Oklahoma area, Illinois and Indiana, and southern California—are the heartland of Pentecostalism.

In the 1880s three enduring holiness denominations came out of older confessions. The first and today the largest of these is the Church of God (Anderson, Indiana). Its founder, Daniel S. Warner, first began preaching in a Methodist congregation but soon affiliated with a small, formerly German sect, the (Winebrennian) Church of God (today the Churches of God, General Conference). This was an intensely revivalistic splinter from the German Reformed Church, one which had rejected all denominational organization. It had moved close to earlier Anabaptists, for it baptized only adult converts by immersion, and like the Church of the Brethren it adapted the ordinance of feet washing. To this mix Warner tried to add the holiness doctrine but was unable to persuade the leaders of this small denomination. At first they disciplined him and then in 1878 withdrew his license to preach. In 1881 he and his disciples met in Indiana to form a new church, one that still repudiated denominationalism (congregational ordination of ministers, no formal membership). It has survived as a unique part of the larger restoration movement. Warner not only embraced the second step or holiness but also drew some of his key doctrines from Mennonites and Adventists. Doctrinally the church was the holiness version of a very tiny Christadelphian movement—congregational, evangelical, adventist, and separatist.

The second separating sect had its origins largely in the often wild holiness bands in the Missouri-Kansas area. The leader in this come-out movement was John P. Brooks, who began his holiness evangelism in Illinois. In the Southwest Holiness Association independent congregations formed as early as 1882. It was Brooks, through his doctrinal writing, who helped persuade such congregations to accept the same congregationalism espoused by Warner and even to assume the name Church of God (Holiness). But these loosely related congregations never expanded into a national church, and most would be absorbed later into other holiness and Pentecostal sects. What made this small and ephemeral Church of God so important was the extent to which its congregations were a seedbed of later Pentecostalism.

The third independence movement was, in a sense, an offspring of midwestern holiness bands. From Illinois and other states holiness people moved to southern California after the Civil War. In 1880 these migrants formed the California and Arizona Holiness Association. One of the association's leading evangelists, James F. Washburn, moved from his home in Azusa Valley to the Los Angeles area and helped form a small circle of holiness congregations, in Azusa, Pomona, San Bernardino, Santa Barbara, and, largest of all, the Downey congregation in Los Angeles. As early as 1884 these congregations became independent and in the religiously eclectic California setting drew members not only from Methodism but other evangelical denominations. The style was primitive (plain chapels, no organs, and no formal ordination of both male and female evangelists) and emotional, with Spirit or fire baptism. The membership was biracial and mostly poor. Unlike in Methodism, membership depended on a confession of sanctification, meaning that one had to experience the second step before admission to communion. These congregations often used the label "Pentecostal" and saw the baptism of fire as a repetition of what occurred on the day of Pentecost. Despite the fervor of their meetings, they apparently did not yet speak in tongues. In time these congregations formed the Holiness Church of California, which in 1946 merged with the Pilgrim Holiness Church.

The rise of independent holiness congregations and denominations horrified the older holiness leaders in the tradition of Palmer and Inskip and those who still controlled NCMAPH. As they expected, such separatism, plus the undisciplined preaching and exercises, confirmed the view of many in the Methodist Episcopal Church that the holiness movement was schismatic and dangerous. As early as 1894 a bishop in the Methodist Episcopal Church, South, openly denounced the holiness doctrines that lay behind the separatism, and from then on a growing majority in both of the main Methodist denominations condemned not the doctrine of sanctification but the interpretations of it by holiness factions, and above all the nonofficial agencies and methods they used to promote the doctrine. By 1890 the most vital holiness revivals involved largely working people, many with no past church affiliation and with a taste for a very hot form of religion.

The largest holiness denominations slowly coalesced out of a confusing array of local missions and independent congregations. But versions of the holiness doctrine gained much wider currency in America. Of greatest significance, Dwight L. Moody accepted one version of holiness and made it part of his evangelism and of his Moody Bible Institute. Adoniram J. Gordon, founder of the influential Gordon Bible Institute, affirmed holiness, as did Albert B. Simpson, one of the founders of the Christian and Missionary Alliance. Such advocates of holiness came out of a broader, evangelical, and often Calvinist background and, in the tradition of Finney, saw holiness as empowerment for service, not as the all-important second step of Wesley. They also repudiated the wild emotionalism that marked most local holiness revivals.

By the turn of the century at least a dozen small, local holiness missions or loosely grouped congregations existed in the United State. In fact, one formed almost every year—in Chicago, Michigan, Kansas, Nashville, and several in California. Strange doctrines marked some of these, such as the Fire Baptized Holiness Association in Kansas. Most permitted or encouraged such freeform and exuberant revivals that they gained a reputation later compressed into the unfair label "Holy Rollers." One feature identified about half the emergent sects: missions to the slums of inner cities, which often closely resembled the early work of the Salvation Army in America. Such missions combined a hot form of religion with rescue work and orphanages and often gained most converts from the most lowly members of society. Some also began mission work, sending evangelists not only all over America but to foreign counties. The outcome was not clear at the time, but two of these early urban ministries led to two of the largest holiness denominations in twentieth-century America.

First was the ministry of Phineas F. Bresee in Los Angeles. Bresee was a successful Methodist minister, for a time pastor of the First Methodist Church in Los Angeles. But after becoming a convert to the holiness movement, he led such fervent revivals and directed his ministry at such low orders in society as to lose the support of his bishop. Two undesirable assignments and refusal of permission to enter mission work led Bresee to resign from the Methodist ministry. He at first joined forces with the largest of the independent holiness urban ministries, the Peniel Mission in Los Angeles, but soon rankled its leaders because of his reform proposals. Thus in 1895 he began his own small congregation, at first renting meeting places (his grown and affluent children assured him a livelihood). He quickly had enough disciples to form a church, which he called the Church of the Nazarene. He built a plain tabernacle in 1896 and a large brick building in 1903. In 1898 he began a periodical, *The Nazarene.* By 1906 this founding church had formed mission congregations in several areas of the West and even in the Midwest, sent its first foreign missionary to India, and started a training college in Los Angeles. As a result of several mergers with regional holiness sects, this original Nazarene congregation became the forerunner of what is today the largest holiness denomination, the Church of the Nazarene. The key mergers in 1907 and 1908 created the Pentecostal Church of the Nazarene (the denomination dropped the word "Pentecostal" in 1919 to distinguish itself from tongue speakers, who by then had fully usurped the name).

In Cincinnati, Martin Wells Knapp unintentionally founded a second major holiness denomination. Knapp was also a Methodist minister who converted to the holiness doctrine. At first he carried on his evangelical career in Albion, Michigan, as an effective revivalist and author of numerous holiness books and tracts. In 1891 he moved to Cincinnati, still a Methodist but soon most involved in union holiness associations. By 1895 he had decided to minister to the folk of the Appalachian mountains and established both a mission in the Kentucky mountains and a rescue mission in downtown Cincinnati. In 1897 he and his disciples formed what he wanted to be an interdenominational organization, the International Holiness Union and Prayer League. This was not, at first, a church or sect but a very ecumenical alliance of holiness people who wanted to promote urban rescue missions and foreign evangelism. Yet the league soon ordained ministers, established camps, sponsored revivals, and founded urban missions. Except for Sunday worship, it acted like a church. Its intrusive evangelicalism led to Methodist censure and to Knapp's withdrawal from the Methodist ministry (he died in 1901, still technically a member of the Methodist Church).

By 1905 the International Holiness Union and Prayer League had clearly become a church. Its missions had become, for many, a church home, and the informal, revival-type services were their only worship. In 1905 it incorporated the word "Church" into its title and in 1913 became the International Apostolic Holiness Church. It also absorbed at least six other small holiness sects and in 1922 became the Pilgrim Holiness Church, then second in size only to the Church of the Nazarene. In 1968 it and the Wesleyan Methodist Church merged to create the present Wesleyan Church.

The holiness denominations still affirm second-step sanctification and believe themselves to be in the purest Wesleyan tradition. The Church of the Nazarene now has over one-half million American members. Today the second largest holiness denomination is the Salvation Army, the one branch of the holiness movement that still focuses on the earlier and more general mission to the urban poor. These are followed by the Church of God (Anderson, Indiana) and the Wesleyan Church. The sanctification doctrine also remains central in many smaller sects, including Free, Protestant, Congregational, and Primitive Methodists; in one small Adventist sect; and in one Anabaptist sect, the Brethren in Christ. A holiness faction within the United Methodist Church has its main institutional expression in Asbury College in Wilmore, Kentucky. Today most of the holiness denominations join in a Christian Holiness Association. Yet, in the larger perspective of American Protestantism, the holiness churches have remained small, eclipsed in numbers by Pentecostals. In fact, the separate holiness movement now seems, in terms of its historical influence, largely a way station on the path to Pentecostalism.

THE PENTECOST EXPERIENCE AND CHRISTIAN DOCTRINE

All modern Pentecostals appeal to what they view as a crucial and decisive event in the origins of Christianity. The Book of Acts begins with a record of the ascension of Jesus and continues with what happened to the twelve disciples who gathered, in an upper room in Jerusalem, on the day of Pentecost, or fifty days after Passover and the crucifixion of Jesus. They suddenly heard a noise as of a great wind, while tongues of fire appeared among them and came to rest on the head of each disciple. At this "baptism" of fire, each disciple was filled with the Holy Spirit and began to talk in tongues, as the Spirit gave them the power of utterance. A crowd of devout Jews, drawn from every nation under heaven, heard the disciples in their own language. Some believed the disciples had been drinking, but Peter assured them that this was not so at 9:00 in the morning. Instead he interpreted this as a fulfillment of the prophecy of Joel, that in the last days Jehovah would pour out his spirit on everyone, and then the sons and daughters would prophesy, and young men would see visions, and old men would dream dreams. Peter went on to preach a sermon about Jesus as the Christ and about repentance. Thousands converted and were baptized. This Pentecost experience marked the founding of the Church, with all converts then and henceforth promised the blessings of the Holy Spirit.

This is the foundational scripture for Pentecostals. It is a scripture honored by all Christians, yet without quite the same emphasis given it by Pentecostals. The date of its writing was probably around 90 C.E. The author is unknown; no name is on the ancient manuscripts. The Book of Acts is a sequel of the gospel attributed to Luke. This attribution, as deduced by early Church fathers, rests on two first-person passages in the Book of Acts. The only loyal disciple mentioned by Paul in his letters who was present on these two occasions was Luke the physician. The text of Luke-Acts suggests a Gentile author, or at least a very Hellenized Jew (the Greek is eloquent, and the historical conventions are those of Thucydides), and also a disciple of Paul (Paul is the hero of Acts, even though the author seems confused about some aspects of Paul's career). Since Acts is a secondary source, written long after the event and presumably based on oral sources, it is not as persuasive as Paul's own earlier and unchallenged epistles.

For Pentecostals the important aspects of the Acts account are the tongues of fire and the speaking in tongues. These document a second baptism, not by water but by the Spirit or by fire (interpretations vary). Those so baptized spoke in tongues immediately afterward, and thus one could judge such tongues as evidence or confirmation of such a baptism. Note that everyone in the pluralistic audience understood the speech of the disciples. The speech was clearly miraculous, for the speakers had no knowledge of the varied languages. All early American Pentecostals insisted that this was not a type of ecstatic speech, without syntax or conventional meaning, but a miraculous ability to speak other languages. It was not an example of glossolalia.

Acts contains a later account of what might have been tongue speaking. Paul, at Ephesus, preached to converts who had received only the baptism of John, not that of Jesus. Thus Paul rebaptized them into the name of Jesus and laid hands on them, and they spoke in tongues of ecstasy and prophesied. This seems to be a later example of the Pentecost experience. It seems also to contain a baptismal formula. But the reference to ecstatic speech does not mention foreign languages. This passage in Acts would later be very important to Pentecostals and also the occasion for divisions within the movement.

The third important text for Pentecostals is 1 Corinthians 12–14. This is a small sermon on the gifts of the Spirit, which Paul offered to an always divisive and contentious and at times rather wild congregation at Corinth. It is a commentary on contemporary events in Corinth, at least a generation removed from the day of Pentecost (Paul makes no reference to the Pentecost experience and may not have known the story as told later by Luke). The occasion for Paul's sermon was some undisciplined behavior in the early worship services at Corinth. Paul began by listing some gifts of the Spirit. The language does not allow a clear count, but many Pentecostals acknowledge seven or even nine such gifts. Paul mentioned preaching or speaking, faith, healing and other miracles, prophecy, divination, ecstatic speech, and the interpretation of such speech. In a climactic and famous passage, Paul emphasized that love was the greatest gift of all. It is clear that Corinthians had been much involved in ecstatic speech, at times at the expense of the other gifts. Paul did not deny such speech as a gift. He even professed to be more gifted in ecstatic speech than any of them, and it is likely that Paul used such speech to persuade Gentiles of his apostolic status. Nonetheless, he did not value such speech as highly as prophecy, simply because it was not edifying. No one present could understand the speakers. To listeners, it was gibberish. Even the speakers could not understand its meaning. Paul valued rational gifts, for they could build up the church. Ecstatic speech was a wonderful gift to one so inspired, and Paul commended it; but he wanted such speech limited to two or at most three speakers at every worship service (a rule followed today by most Pentecostals) and desired that someone be present who could interpret the speech for the edification of all. His climactic advice: do not forbid ecstatic speech, but let it be done decently and in order.

It is almost impossible to correlate these various texts. Were Paul and the author of Acts talking about the same phenomena in their references to tongues and to ecstatic speech? No one can say for sure. Maybe the oral traditions or the legends about the Pentecost experience developed after Paul wrote his letter to Corinth. One can, by a series of rather unlikely assumptions, reconcile the two accounts. It is conceivable that the disciples at Pentecost did indeed speak ecstatically and that the miracle was on the part of those who heard their own language. Thus Acts does in fact record the beginnings of glossolalia. Conversely, it is conceivable that Paul's references to glossolalia are to people who spoke a syntactical and grammatical language, even though none of the audience at Corinth could recognize it as such. Paul's concerns about its unintelligibility related only to that particular context. Thus his ecstatic speech is in fact a speaking in unknown tongues. Of course, early Pentecostals so interpreted the letter to Corinth, while most present charismatic Christians outside the Pentecostal movement, and many within it, believe the disciples enjoyed the gift of ecstatic speech, a nonsyntactical form of utterances, at Pentecost.

As far as I know, tongue speaking had no subsequent role in Christianity. This was not necessarily so for ecstatic speech, although this issue begs enormous problems of definition. No one knows what the ecstatics at Corinth sounded like. Various sounds provoked by intense feelings remained a subordinate tradition in Christianity, breaking out in periods of great enthusiasm among Roman Catholics and later among some Protestants. Boundaries are blurred because various sounds and even types of chanting or singing may accompany intense feelings. Only in specific religious communities do these take on a ritualistic form with common and shared features. In America types of unintelligible verbalization occurred in the revivals around 1740 and again in the revivals in the West in 1800–1801. We find references to moans and to holy laughter and even to barking like dogs. But these were spontaneous outbursts, and no one, as far as I can discover, linked them to the Pentecost experience or to the ecstatic speech at Corinth. Thus, none became conventional, a part of worship.

The first sect in America to make ecstatic speech normative was the Shakers. With roots in the French Prophets (a wild offspring of the French Reformed Church) and in Quakerism, the followers of Ann Lee affirmed the gifts of the spirit, indulged prophecy, and made glossolalia a part of their unconventional worship, which included special forms of dancing. Glossolalia appeared frequently among both early Adventists and Mormons. Yet while both sects long condoned such speech, neither made it a required aspect of worship. In time it all but disappeared in their congregations. Among many evangelical Christians, and particularly Methodists, either uncontrolled or conventional forms of shouting marked times of religious happiness at revivals or camp meetings. Among black evangelicals, shouting and other forms of verbal worship were so common as to be normative. These were at times clearly ecstatic utterances, but Christians who accepted such verbal expression did not connect it to either Pentecost or the glossolalia at Corinth. More critical, they did not see such ecstatic outbursts as evidence of any special baptism by the Spirit. Often the shouts of joy came at the time of conversion or in the aftermath of water baptism.

American Pentecostals honored all the gifts of the Spirit. Tongues was special only in one sense—it was the evidence of Spirit baptism. This was the one distinctive or defining belief of early Pentecostals. They, of course, based it on their reading of events on the day of Pentecost. This evidentiary understanding of tongues (or in some cases glossolalia) has given an un-Pauline flavor to Pentecostal Christianity. It is quite clear in 1 Corinthians that Paul, without rejecting ecstatic speech, certainly tried to deemphasize it, in a sense to place it at the bottom of the hierarchy of gifts, with love first and prophecy of greatest value to the Church.

Next to tongues the gift that has most distinguished Pentecostals has been healing. In fact, the origins of Pentecostalism in America are almost as closely linked to healing as to tongues. Healing, much more than tongues, is at the core of the New Testament story. Jesus healed continuously, both physically and mentally. According to Luke-Acts, the apostles frequently healed people. In various forms healing has remained a central emphasis in the Church. At the most general level, Christians everywhere, in all denominations, pray for the sick and ask God to heal them. In the Roman Catholic Church such prayers and other intercessions for the sick have remained a vital part of popular devotion, joined by more miraculous examples of healing, such as by individuals later canonized as saints or at shrines such as Lourdes. But such special or miraculous healing remained exceptional in Catholicism and lost credibility among the leading Protestant reformers, who generally repudiated saints, relics, shrines, or the miraculous interventions of Mary.

In the nineteenth century, large numbers of American Protestants tried to come to terms with a ministry of healing. The mainstream denominations remained very cautious, although even such a prominent theologian as Horace Bushnell was almost persuaded of the possibilities of faith healing. Mary Baker Eddy elevated divine healing to a central place in Christian Science. Among the various holiness groups a new emphasis on healing often joined with a sense that Christians were living in the last days and that the Christ would shortly return to earth. In the 1890s, holiness healers prepared the way for an embryonic Pentecostal movement.

Healing admits of degrees. Belief in divine healing can begin with a confidence that the Christian God does control the destiny of all humans and that he will heal those whom he wills, but usually in conjunction with natural means and even medical science. Humans have a duty to use such means and should not expect miraculous interventions when healthy habits and medical knowledge are sufficient. Other Christians took the next step. Evangelical and holiness leaders, such as A. J. Gordon and A. B. Simpson, still affirmed medical science for most people but believed sanctified Christians could receive healing directly from God. They began healing ministries, at times even anointed the sick with oil or laid on hands, but still tried to avoid sensationalism. In both Europe and America healing homes or retreats, or missions that involved faith healing, proliferated until the total numbered in the hundreds. In a sense such faith missions competed with other, non-Christian therapies or, as in the great sanatoriums of Seventh-day Adventists, with a religiously sanctioned hydrotherapy. For general ailments, for epidemic diseases, and above all for mental illness, such therapies were often as successful, or as unsuccessful, as the ministrations of licensed physicians. Most people regained their health though natural processes but possibly gained a sense of relief from either prayer, anointings, dubious medications, or special regimens. In some cases religiously based therapies protected patients from harmful folk remedies or from the well-intended but mistaken cures of physicians. Prayer was better than bleeding.

Beyond such overt healing ministries is what Americans now identify as faith healing. Perhaps a better label would be apostolic healing. In this case, ministers with special powers or special access to God perform healing in public arenas, usually with prayer and a laying on of hands. Of course, they always attribute the result to God. But in effect they are shamans or holy men, modern miracle workers. People come to them as they came to Jesus or as they travel to Lourdes, with expectations of a miracle. Such healing was especially congenial to holiness Christians, who believed that individuals could attain full sanctification or a special baptism of the Holy Spirit. Such full love and faith seemed likely to affect all aspects of one's life and particularly help individuals be rid of diseases that had been part of a non-sanctified life. This expectation could be heightened if one believed one lived in the very last days before the return of the Christ. In fact, some advocates of healing acknowledged that the apostolic faith had indeed lapsed for centuries and was being revived in these latter days (often called the latter-rain doctrine).

One fascinating precursor of Pentecostalism was John Alexander Dowie. He came to America from Australia, where he first began a healing ministry. He grabbed the headlines in 1893 when he sat up his tent across the street from "Buffalo Bill" Cody at the Chicago Columbian Exposition. Dowie denounced all medicine and invited people to come forward for healing. He referred to his labors as a way of building Zion and in 1894 established a tabernacle and divine healing home in Chicago. In the next five years he added new healing homes, published a periodical, and gathered disciples. He called his movement the Christian Catholic Church (it survives as a tiny denomination distinguished among Pentecostals by triune immersion) and in 1900 began building his Zion City forty miles north of Chicago on the shores of Lake Michigan. He soon claimed 25,000 members for his church, and eventually about 6,000 moved into Zion. He was an Adventist in the sense that he expected the early return of the Christ and believed the more miraculous gifts of the spirit were a latter-day blessing. Prophetic and denunciatory, he had enormous influence within the holiness movement, for hundreds of ministers came to visit Zion. Typical of early Pentecostals, Dowie enlisted women and blacks for his special ministry or for missionary work.

Less ambitious in goals but more prophetic of contemporary Pentecostal healers was Maria Woodworth-Etter, one of the most successful revivalists at the turn of the century. She found a friendly religious home only among holiness Quakers, who welcomed a female witness. As she began her ministry, she affiliated with the Church of God (Winebrenner) but was mostly on her own as a traveling evangelist who soon made healing central (the Church of God later dismissed her). She attracted large audiences, reported thousands of conversions, and because she was a woman attracted much publicity and criticism. Only belatedly did she accept tongues, but in her last years she preached as a Pentecostal.

CHARLES F. PARHAM AND THE BEGINNINGS OF PENTECOSTALISM

The origins of Pentecostalism have taken on a legendary quality. The stories of Topeka and Azusa Street function as founding myths for modern Pentecostals. The problem is that these legends contain as much fiction as fact, and such is the nature of the sources that no one will ever be able to separate the two. What is incontrovertible is that what happened at Topeka in 1900–1901 had a direct relationship to events on Azusa Street in 1906, and that the key individual in these beginnings was Charles F. Parham.

Parham was a gifted, sensitive, often sickly, mentally beset young preacher born in rural Iowa in 1873. In 1878 the parents of Charles moved south to the then-booming wheat lands of south-central Kansas, close to Wichita. He later remembered a typical conversion, an early commitment to the ministry and to missionary work in Africa, and a serious role as a teenage teacher in a nearby Methodist Sunday school. He spent three years at a struggling Southwest College and briefly shifted his career plans to medicine. But ill health beset him and persuaded him to shift back to the ministry. As a college student he preached and held evangelistic services. He early had an intense and affecting speaking style and could attract large audiences. After quitting college (the reasons are not clear), he gained a license as a Methodist minister in 1893 and acquired his first church in Eudora, Kansas, at age twenty. It is clear that his bishop considered him a promising minister, unusually well educated among rural Methodists at that time.

Given his seriousness, it is not surprising that Parham identified with the holiness faction in Methodism. His problem in the denomination was his restlessness and what soon matured into unorthodox doctrines. Parham was not content to work in a parish but soon traveled widely to conduct revivals and organize new congregations. He was little concerned whether they became Methodist. More damaging, he began to articulate non-Wesleyan doctrines. He minimized (and in one period rejected) water baptism and emphasized Spirit baptism (a good holiness emphasis). Through conversations with a Quaker, he absorbed two doctrines largely restricted to Adventists: conditional immortality (no soul survives the body at death) and a final death as the punishment for sin (no hell or eternal torment). These joined with a near-certainty that humans lived in the last days and that the advent was near. He never repudiated these doctrines, and the churches that later derived from his form of Pentecostalism were, technically, Adventist churches. In 1895, before his ordination, Parham withdrew from his Methodist conference and soon felt liberated at the prospect of a career as an independent evangelist.

In 1896 he married the daughter of his Quaker friend. The first of a series of babies followed nine months later. Parham preached where he could and in 1897 suffered a periodic bout of illness (apparently a weak heart tied to an earlier siege of rheumatic fever). At this time he converted to faith healing, with the standard claim that his prayer and faith had led to his own miraculous cure. In 1898 he moved to Ottawa, Kansas, and began a new ministry tied to healing. This proved a winning strategy, as hundreds of people soon flocked to his revivals, many seeking restored health. He soon had plenty of personal testimonies to his success, and these he always advertised. Late in 1898 he opened Beth-el in Topeka. This was a combination church, hospital, and hotel, for he charged people who came for the healing or for rest. Soon he advertised classes, making it a Bible school. He preached to interdenominational audiences on Sunday. He created a temporary orphanage. Thus he formed what was a rather typical holiness urban mission, except he was not affiliated with any holiness band or denomination.

His early success in Topeka seemed self-limiting. He barely earned a living for a growing family. A periodical succumbed for lack of subscribers. Once again, as throughout his life, he suffered both a physical and a mental breakdown. This led him into a deeper investigation of various holiness and healing ministries and to some journeys critical to his "discovery" of Pentecostalism. At his own back door he came into contact with the Kansas Fire-Baptized Holiness Church, a movement founded by Benjamin Irwin in Iowa a few years earlier. Parham never accepted Irwin's distinctive doctrines, but he confronted, for the first time, what might be called a three-step system. The Irwinites believed not only in conversion and then sanctification but, beyond that, a special fire baptism. At this low time in his career Parham needed a new step and new inspiration. He publicized the doctrine of fire baptism in his periodical but never professed this baptism for himself.

In June 1900 Parham left Topeka to learn more about other holiness and healing ministries. He traveled east, first visiting Downie's Zion missions in Chicago, then stopping at Simpson's Christian and Missionary Alliance school in Nyack, New York. But his destination was Maine, where he wanted to visit Frank W. Sandford in Durham. Sandford might be considered the grandfather of Pentecostalism. Two of Sandford's disciples had already visited Parham in Topeka. Sandford had his own idiosyncratic doctrines. He was a healer and a millennialist. He accepted a zany racial theory that Anglo-Saxons were descendants of the lost tribes of Israel and thus that they would be part of the restoration that preceded the Christ's return. A faithful group of these Anglo-Saxons would be the "Bride of Christ," a chosen minority who had a special role in bringing the gospel to the whole world. This elite (echoes of Jehovah's Witnesses) would experience an early rapture and join Jesus in ruling and judging during the millennium. Sandford established his own Christian utopia—Shiloh—in 1895 and there trained evangelists and missionaries. Shiloh reportedly had 600 residents by the time Parham visited, although Sandford had gained almost too much notoriety by purportedly raising a young woman from the dead.

What was most important to Parham in Sandford's ministry was a novel aspect of his missionary school. According to the story told by Sandford and even publicized in the holiness press and featured in an article by Parham, in 1895 one of his missionary trainees, already committed to work in Africa, had an ecstatic experience and began speaking in African dialects. Even when the trancelike experience was over, she reputedly continued to speak these languages fluently and was thus miraculously prepared for her mission assignment. She thus duplicated the experience of the apostles on the day of Pentecost. Here at Sandford's Shiloh lurked all the important contributions Parham would make to early Pentecostalism: a third-step baptism of the Spirit, speaking in foreign tongues as evidence of this baptism, and the use of such tongues for mission work in the last days before the advent.

Parham returned to Topeka healed and inspired. Other holiness preachers now controlled his healing house, and Parham did not try to regain control. Instead he was determined to found a missionary school like Shiloh. In October 1900 he established Bethel Bible College and rented a fifteen-room, three-story, turreted mansion at the edge of the city as its campus. Over thirty students moved in, for a mixture of lectures by Parham, evangelical services, and an intense devotional life. The students were former associates in his healing house or holiness workers from the surrounding area, all under the almost hypnotic sway of Parham. It was in this hothouse atmosphere that the first Pentecostal movement, and eventually the first denomination, had its origins.

The legendary story of origins came from the later writings of Parham. According to him the community at Bethel had met and discussed one dominating issue: what evidence confirmed the Pentecostal experience recorded in Acts? He left his students in late December, inviting them to search for answers to this question while he was away. He returned the morning before the Watch Night service (an old Methodist institution) on New Year's Eve. He then asked his students what they had concluded, and lo and behold all were in agreement—the proof of the Pentecostal blessing was speaking in tongues. Then, as other holiness people joined them for the Watch Night service, a spiritual power filled the room in the old mansion (many locals had long believed it haunted), and tongues of fire were visible. At this point a student, Agnes N. Ozman, asked that Parham lay on hands, for she wanted to receive the Holy Spirit and go to foreign mission fields. He laid his hands on her, prayed, and very shortly she began speaking in the Chinese language and did not speak English again until three days later. Two days later, in a new century, several of the students spoke in tongues, and the first Pentecostal revival was under way.

This was a disingenuous report. At least since his visit to Shiloh, Parham had believed such utilitarian tongue speaking was the evidence of spiritual baptism. He had even written about it in his periodical. In fact, anyone who knew the scriptural account of Pentecost already knew that the experience was marked by tongue speaking. That he left his students to find something as obvious as this is unbelievable. As for Ozman, her later accounts include references to one earlier experience of ecstatic speech and do not confirm the exact chronology offered by Parham. No one ever explained how the students or Parham knew that she spoke in Chinese. Later some of the students also did spirit writing, purportedly with Chinese characters, but one photograph of such writing makes clear that it was only random marks. Parham made frequent claims that immigrant neighbors heard students speak in their native language, with perfect syntax and accents (it is probable that some of the student did blend foreign words, which they had heard in their youth, into their ecstatic speech). He also made frequent but undocumented references to scholars and government translators, who also purportedly testified to the authenticity of the languages spoken. About all that is certain, for this is backed by local newspaper reports, is that by early January of the new century Parham's students were caught up in a near-ecstatic frenzy, with many of them uttering sounds that seemed sheer nonsense to other nonecstatic students and to newspaper reporters.

Tongue speaking brought notoriety to Parham and his students. It did not bring him early success as a minister. Some disillusioned students soon left Bethel, and Parham and his most faithful set out on a mission tour to persuade holiness people everywhere that they had found the biblical evidence of spiritual baptism. In cities such as Kansas City, the student tongue speaking did attract reporters, but mostly for ridicule. It did not draw sustained crowds or lead to expected gifts of money. Parham suffered the death of a son and soon retreated back to Bethel. By the fall of 1901 Parham and his remnant of loyal disciples had to vacate their castle (the owner sold it), and soon afterward it burned. Parham gave up his "college" and moved his family to Kansas City, where a second Bible school failed in four months. In early 1903, after two years of frustration, he moved his family to Nevada, Missouri, or just across the border from southeastern Kansas. Here he had some enduring success.

From the first episode of speaking in tongues, Parham had referred to his little band by the title "Apostolic Faith." So far, he had been unable to form any lasting congregations and in fact after 1902 had reverted back to healing as the only successful means of rallying crowds for evangelistic services. Now, in this four-state area (Missouri, Kansas, Arkansas, and Oklahoma), among immigrant lead, zinc, and coal miners and small farmers, Parham was able to form viable congregations and to create the first Pentecostal denomination. He had his first great revival in Galena, Kansas, just west of Joplin, Missouri. He held others at nearby Baxter Springs, in the farthest southeast corner of Kansas; in Joplin; and in Eldorado Springs, Arkansas. From these beginnings developed a scattering of Apostolic Faith congregations in the four-state area. But as so often for Parham, success led to overwork, a minor scandal involving a girl who died after he discouraged her recourse to medical care, and another physical and mental breakdown.

Parham decided to go south, to near Houston, Texas, both in response to interested holiness Christians there and in hopes of regaining his health. In the small town of Orchard his host, a former convert from Galena, helped rally fellow holiness converts to what quickly became a great and wild revival, with both healing and tongues at its center. His health miraculously improved, Parham next launched his crusade in Houston. Here his group (about fifteen strong) staged well-publicized revivals, using Palestinian robes to attract attention. As it had earlier back in Topeka, the small band created a viable urban mission. Soon his group had organized several small congregations around Houston, even as Parham returned to his four-state congregations for very successful revivals in the summer of 1905.

Parham's Houston crusade proved critical for the history of Pentecostalism. Although unwilling to perceive or treat blacks as equals, Parham admitted a few black holiness workers to his "school" in Houston. Among these students were William Joseph Seymour and Lucy Farrow, Seymour's female minister in a local holiness church. Seymour was not a preacher but had filled in for Farrow and, in the loose holiness context, had become a lay preacher. Notably, his five weeks of "courses" with Parham did not lead to the expected baptism of the Spirit and tongue speaking. He left Houston in February 1906 when a former Parham convert invited him to Los Angeles to help in a small holiness mission. Parham helped pay his way. Unsuspected by either Parham or Seymour, the work in Los Angeles would quickly expand into a great Pentecostal revival that very quickly eclipsed the founding efforts of Parham.

In a sense, the subsequent career of Parham was anticlimactic. He continued to move back and forth from Kansas to Houston and at first underestimated the scope and the nature of the revival in Los Angeles. By the time he finally arrived to help Seymour, the dynamics of events there had long since passed him by, and he was both jealous of that revival and resentful of departures from what he considered correct Pentecostal doctrines and practices. He was rebuffed in Los Angeles in the fall of 1906, tried for a time without success to take over Zion City in Illinois, and then in 1907 faced arrest because of widely publicized charges of sodomy. Whether the charges were justified or were falsely made by enemies remains unproven. The criminal charges were dismissed, but Parham never regained his reputation among even his own congregations in Texas. He retreated back to Baxter Springs, and in his old environment he retained the support of several congregations. He published his own periodical, went on frequent evangelistic crusades, continued a ministry of healing, and until his death in 1929 held fast to the idea that he and his converts spoke in real foreign languages. His small Apostolic Faith denomination later split, and both wings now number less than 100 congregations.

AZUSA STREET

William Seymour came to Los Angeles to assist in a small holiness mission. Fresh from his courses with Parham and full of the beliefs of the Apostolic Faith movement, he tried to convert his holiness hosts to the new doctrines and to evidentiary tongues as a mark of Spirit baptism, although he had not yet gained this experience. The holiness leaders of the mission were horrified at his teachings and dismissed him. Seymour, on his own in a strange city, sought sympathetic friends and preached from two homes. In early April 1906 he first gained the gift of tongues. He attracted a following, but the wild services dismayed neighbors. Thus Seymour sought and soon found a sanctuary—a deserted, rundown, two-story former Methodist mission on Azusa Street. Here he could hold services without restrictions. And what services! On 18 April the *Los Angles Times*, alerted to wild meetings and ecstatic speech, carried a sensational and mocking article about the new Azusa Street revival, and within two months the almost continuous revival was famous among holiness people throughout America. Thus Azusa became the shrine of American or even international Pentecostalism.

In a sense the revival on Azusa Street was well reported. Hundreds, then thousands of people came to the meetings, which scarcely had a beginning or even a daily ending. Seymour was soon joined by other preachers, most of whom were white. Time and place favored the revival. A day after the *Times* article, San Francisco was devastated with a great earthquake, lending a peculiar apocalyptic quality to the latter-rain doctrines preached at the mission. Los Angeles was full of insecure working-class families, many just arrived from the Midwest and trying desperately to cope with the problems of a city. They were ripe for new religious innovations. Many were so near the bottom of the economic ladder or so open to religious enthusiasm that normal symbols of status meant little. Thus, for one of the few times in American history, blacks and whites, men and women, joined in complete equality in exhilarating and exhausting religious services. Song, group prayers, shouts of joy, and multiple tongue speaking mingled, with people coming and going at will. Seymour tried to remain loyal to the doctrines of Parham, but it was soon evident to many observers that the ecstatic speech could not reflect any human language. Also, Seymour either had not understood or had rejected the Adventist doctrines of Parham (soul sleep and annihilationism). In any case, doctrines were not important in this revival. Presumably, people of quite diverse beliefs or those with no previous religious convictions joined in the absorbing exercises, with over 13,000 people reported to have experienced tongues in the first year.

The movement spread rapidly in the Los Angeles basin and then across the country. One effect of the baptism of the Spirit, and the ecstasy, was a strong mission urge. Some parents left children behind to testify, as groups of early converts fanned out over the city and the nation. Other mission congregations formed in Los Angeles, some with competing doctrines. Factions rose and fell. One trend, after the first few heady months, was for whites to move to their own congregations, leaving blacks in others. News from Azusa excited holiness Christians throughout America. The publicity made it imperative that ministers or representatives of congregations come to observe, to seek spiritual baptism, and then to carry the news back home. The effect in the next few years was a deep and lasting split among holiness sects, with some rejecting the wild exercises and the tongues of Azusa, but others sooner or later capitulating. The largest body to resist was the Pentecostal Church of the Nazarene, which had to drop the label "Pentecostal" from its name because the word soon identified only those who affirmed tongue speaking as evidence of spiritual baptism. Almost all present Pentecostal denominations have a tie to Azusa Street and by way of it to the early innovations of Parham.

For the first year Seymour and his associates kept the name "Apostolic Faith." After October 1907 this did not mean a continued association with Parham and his churches in Kansas and Missouri. When Parham finally arrived in Los Angeles in September, he was appalled at the racial mixing, at the disordered and wild nature of the exercises, and at the gibberish exhibited in tongue speaking. He tried to control the revival and was quickly rebuffed by the local leaders. Seymour also proved unstable and, as a result of some egoistic decisions at Azusa, lost control of the movement in the West, except for his small mission. Yet small and independent Apostolic Faith denominations, all of which repudiated Parham's leadership, coalesced in the Northwest, in California, and in Texas and Arkansas. From these small, emergent sects came many future leaders in other Pentecostal denominations, particularly the Assemblies of God.

A CONFUSION OF TONGUES—MODERN
PENTECOSTAL DENOMINATIONS

The largest Pentecostal denomination today is the one most often ignored by historians. The Church of God in Christ had a direct tie to Azusa. Two black holiness ministers, Charles Price Jones and Charles H. Mason, had organized a small denomination, the Church of God in Christ, in Mississippi in 1895. They soon moved their headquarters to Memphis. Mason was half-persuaded of the new Spirit baptism by a white missionary from Azusa who visited Memphis. He then joined two ministerial colleagues for a visit to Azusa and quickly converted to Seymour's doctrines. He returned to Memphis to try to move his denomination to Pentecostalism but only partly succeeded. Jones was already open to tongues but would never accept their necessity for Spirit baptism, and thus split the tiny denomination. Mason's faction, which retained the same denominational name, was vitally important in the first decade of an emergent Pentecostal movement. Because Mason's holiness denomination descended directly from Methodism, he kept an episcopal government (with overseers or bishops) and gained a state charter, which enabled his churches to license ministers. At the time, such credentialed ministers alone gained free rail passes. Since none of the early Pentecostal movements had a corporate charter or could legally license or ordain ministers, many white as well as black Pentecostal evangelists came to Memphis to gain a license and thus free railroad passes, which were a great help in their continuous missionary journeys.

Mason remained the presiding bishop of the Church of God in Christ until his death in 1961. Despite his efforts, he was not able to hold on to most of the white ministers, and thus today this huge denomination (an estimated 5 million or more members) is an almost all-black church, one that has enjoyed very rapid growth since 1960, making it by far the largest of many black Pentecostal denominations. Since it grew out of Methodism and the holiness movement, it is the largest Pentecostal denomination that still honors the three-step doctrine—regeneration, sanctification, and then baptism in the Spirit as evidenced by speaking in tongues.

The Pentecostal movement proved very appealing among black and white tenants or textile workers in parts of the South. There the early movement seduced a majority of former holiness Christians. Whites, in only slightly less ratios than blacks, converted. At about the same time as Mason, a North Carolina white holiness leader, Gaston B. Cashwell, visited Azusa. At first dismayed by the mixing of blacks and whites, he soon converted and received his spiritual baptism when Seymour laid on hands. Back home he preached the new message to both whites and blacks and soon was able to form small congregations all over the South. In Nashville he converted two ministers in a large holiness mission but ultimately failed to win the mission, which became a part of the Church of the Nazarene. Cashwell formed loose associations, out of which developed at least three small Pentecostal denominations. One such association, centered in North Carolina, had begun as a holiness denomination in 1898, the Pentecostal

Holiness Church. Cashwell converted most of its congregations to tongues after 1906, and in 1911 it merged with the Fire Baptized Holiness sect. A subsequent merger with another small southern sect created the present Pentecostal Holiness denomination, the second largest white three-step Pentecostal body. The Pentecostal Holiness denomination has remained heavily southern; became well known after World War II for its healing evangelists, such as Oral Roberts; and was later embarrassed by the indiscretions of popular television evangelists such as Jimmy Swaggart.

In 1908 Cashwell visited and preached in Cleveland, Tennessee, at the home church of a dynamic, at times authoritarian holiness minister, Ambrose J. Tomlinson. Tomlinson had in 1903 become a minister in a small denomination—the Holiness Church—which had begun in the mountains of Tennessee and North Carolina in 1886 under the name Christian Union. As early as 1896 some members of this very emotional denomination spoke in tongues, but as yet no one interpreted this as evidence of spiritual baptism (such priority in tongue speaking allows this denomination to claim to be the first Pentecostal church in America). Cashwell converted Tomlinson to Spirit baptism and evidential tongues, and in turn Tomlinson was able to win most of the small but growing denomination to a three-step form of Pentecostalism. Although largely white, this denomination, which took the new name Church of God, with doctrines close to those of Mason's Church of God in Christ and with a similar episcopal organization (overseers), accepted black members and, at least for a time, had integrated congregations.

The charismatic but authoritarian style of Tomlinson plus some financial indiscretions led to later schisms. In 1923 a majority of Church of God congregations overthrew the leadership of Tomlinson and has usually listed itself as the Church of God (Cleveland, Tennessee). Today it is the largest predominantly white three-step Pentecostal denomination, with a membership of over 700,000 in the United States, and even more abroad. The minority (the Tomlinson Church of God) in this split remained loyal to Tomlinson until his death in 1943, when two of Tomlinson's sons assumed the leadership of two surviving Churches of God, with one still headquartered in Cleveland, Tennessee. This has meant much confusion. In 1952 the Cleveland denomination, which is almost equally black and white and has a large number of female ministers, took the name Church of God of Prophecy, while the other wing is still known simply as Church of God, with headquarters in Huntsville, Alabama. To add to the confusion, a very small sect with its roots in the Christian Union before Tomlinson joined is now called the Church of God, Inc. (Original).

George W. Hensley, a former Baptist, was converted to Pentecostalism in 1908 during a revival conducted by Tomlinson's young son. In the next

few years (dates and details are contested) he began handling snakes in services and soon also drank poison, while others submitted parts of their
bodies to fire. In a long ministry, Hensley, an erratic, wandering man who
deserted his first two wives and married four times, helped spread these
dangerous practices throughout the Appalachians and, often through the
migration of members, south to Florida and north to Indiana, Ohio, and
Michigan (most congregations today are in twelve states stretching from
Florida to Michigan, with the highest concentration in the southern Appalachians). At least a dozen very tiny denominations, with locally varied
doctrines, have continued these practices despite state prohibitions, with
snake handling the most visible and the most controversial rite.

Tomlinson at first cautiously approved such miraculous signs, and snake
handling spread to many early Church of God congregations. For about a
decade, before he backslid and temporarily resumed earlier moonshining,
Hensley was a licensed Church of God minister. In time Tomlinson became more cautious about the fanaticism connected with snake handling,
and after about 1930 the now-divided Churches of God all repudiated it.
Today most Pentecostals are embarrassed by the continued publicity about
snake handling. They note, correctly, than no more than 5,000 people are
members of snake-handling congregations, and the number actually involved with snakes was never more than a few hundred. These congregations worship in small, plain meetinghouses, both in remote rural areas
(typical place names are Grasshopper Valley, Owl Holler, Indian Creek,
Carson Springs, Dolly Pond, Harmon's Lick, Sam's Fork, and Greasy
Creek) and in working-class neighborhoods in cities.

The justification of these practices is biblical, but with some unusual
qualifications. To the gifts of the Spirit, which are normative among all
Pentecostals, these most ecstatic Christians add another and in part overlapping test—the five signs of the Spirit as enumerated in Mark 16:15–18.
This ending of the Book of Mark contains the great commission—to pro-
claim good news to all creation—with a promise of salvation to those who
believe and receive baptism. Mark then notes that such redemptive faith
will bring with it five miracles: believers will cast out devils, speak in
strange tongues, come to no harm if they handle snakes, be able to drink
any deadly poison, and cure the sick by laying on of hands. Snakes and
poison are unique to this passage and thus provide the justification of what,
almost alone, distinguishes such Christians from other Pentecostals. The
widespread taking up of fire (usually provided by blow torches) draws support from other biblical passages. Those who subject themselves to snake-
bites or poison believe that such practices are a necessary part of Christian
witness. Thus such death-defying feats are an integral part of highly emotional worship or revivals, with people under the anointment of the Spirit

taking up snakes or drinking poison in protected areas in the front of small churches. By all reports, even by the most skeptical outsiders, many do in fact survive without apparent harm, while the awe and danger heighten to a near frenzy the religious experience of believers.

Space does not allow an extended description of these small sects. In the last few years, sympathetic outside observers have tried to do justice to their beliefs and to the honest people who find meaning in such modern-day miracles. Those who follow this ending of Mark also frequently exorcise devils, heal all manner of illnesses and in a few cases have reported the resurrection of the dead, and of course speak in tongues. The critical last verses of the Book of Mark, as contained without qualification in the Authorized or King James translation of the New Testament, have the same binding authority over these people as any part of the Bible. This is the only Bible they know and use. But of all extended parts of the New Testament, this most likely involves an adulteration of early Greek texts. Of the five or six earliest codices of Mark, only one contains this ending. Some end with verse eight, and others include shorter endings that do not include the five signs of faith. Modern translations at least identify these textual problems, and some snake-handling preachers have become aware of these scholarly issues. But none are willing to concede any authority to modern biblical scholars in a cultural context in which the King James Bible has canonical status.

The distance between snake handlers and other Pentecostals is one of degree, not of kind. All are open to modern miracles, such as healing. Apart from the translation problem, snake-handling Christians can accuse other Christians of ignoring a part of the New Testament. Other Pentecostals, who accept the validity of this scripture, take exception on only one issue. The conditional wording of the references to snakes and poisons ("if" they handle snakes or drink poisons) means, to them, that faith is a protection but that Christians have no obligation to test God, deliberately to invite harm when not accidentally exposed to it. Yet from the standpoint of snake handlers, its seems odd to distinguish these two signs from exorcism or healing or to suggest that no act of will is involved in handling snakes. Thus, to them, this is a Christian obligation.

The outsider has another question. How do such Christians either escape bites from pit vipers or seemingly suffer no harm when bitten? Or how can they drink strychnine water without dying? No fully satisfying answer is possible. In many cases the snakes do not bite (no one has removed their poison sacs), and pit vipers do not always inject venom when they strike. Even when they do, the amount of venom can vary immensely and is less if they strike repeatedly. Some people are more sensitive to the venom, and this sensitivity can vary through time. In adults an average bite from a pit viper, even when not treated, is rarely fatal and, except for those with extreme sensitivity, need never be fatal with early medical intervention. Routinely, religious snake handlers refuse all medical attention, but because of intense pain some have conceded on this issue. With strychnine the usually unknown factor is the amount of dilution in the drink. But the important qualification is that in all cases some of the most faithful advocates of these practices, including about half of the most active preachers (around seventy-five), have died, and even more have suffered lifelong injuries. Maybe faith wavered at the critical moment. Even the originator, Hensley, died of a snakebite at age seventy-five. This is not to pronounce judgment on whether some handlers miraculously survive bites or not, but to add a somber reminder that the dangers are real, and few escape them if they indulge such practices over a long period of time.

In the North and West the history of Pentecostalism varied from that in the South or in the Appalachians. Here Pentecostal missionaries invaded holiness congregations with some local or partial success, but they never captured any holiness denomination. They did create conflict and divisions. As a result of this failure to win over denominations, the Pentecostal movement remained somewhat anarchic, with most activity in small, independent congregations that at times formed loose local associations. Major centers included Chicago and parts of the Southwest where Parham first preached the new gospel. Out of several such local clusters of Pentecostals came the largest white Pentecostal denomination—the Assemblies of God. One nucleus was the Texas and Arkansas congregations originally organized by Parham. After his "disgrace" in 1907, the Texas congregations repudiated his leadership. A loosely organized and growing number of congregations in Texas and Arkansas kept the name "Apostolic Faith" but apparently forgot, or dropped, some of Parham's more distinctive Adventist doctrines.

Notably, Walter Durham, the most prominent Pentecostal leader in Chicago and pastor of a large congregation, rejected the three-step or holiness form of Pentecostalism. He denied not the goal of Christian holiness but sanctification as a crisislike experience. The only baptism of the Spirit came at the time of tongue speaking, and this experience was open to all converted Christians, not to a sanctified elite. One of Durham's converts, Eudorus N. Bell, a former Baptist, moved from Chicago to join the Texas Pentecostals and at least introduced a doctrinal variation into the Apostolic Faith. But at this time the varied Pentecostal congregations had nothing resembling a creed or confession, and most hoped that the intense experience of Spirit baptism would foster a unity across doctrinal boundaries.

Since the Apostolic Faith congregations were not legally a denomination, white ministers in the Southwest often accepted a license from Mason in Memphis, and by 1910 some began to use the label "Church of God in Christ." By 1913, 361 white ministers made up what amounted to an affiliated but quite distinct fellowship in the Church of God in Christ. They did not closely associate with Mason and black congregations and began considering some new form of association. Bell took the lead in convening a special convention in Hot Springs, Arkansas, in 1914, a meeting that took place in an auditorium above a saloon, just after a rousing revival by Woodworth-Etter. Bell was distinguished among fellow ministers by extensive college work. He helped form a general council of the Assemblies of God, which was to be governed in intervals between councils by an executive presbytery. This movement to formal denominational organization provided a focus for several regional Pentecostal groups, who moved into a very eclectic denomination that was quickly racked by doctrinal controversy. Today it claims over 2 million members.

The Assemblies of God began with no creed or confession. Clearly, it gathered people of varied doctrinal traditions. The Apostolic Faith members from the Southwest, or those ministers who had affiliated with the Church of God in Christ, had Methodist and holiness roots and had generally expected sanctification to precede spiritual baptism and tongue speaking. This meant three critical stages in the life of a Christian, although in their congregations everyone was expected to move as soon as possible to spiritual baptism. Others in the church, such as Bell, came out of a Baptist tradition and, although in favor of holiness, had never accommodated a crisislike sanctification experience. This was also true of a faction within the Christian and Missionary Alliance. Several converted to spiritual baptism in the wake of Azusa and for a while made a bid to win this small, evangelical sect over to Pentecostalism. They lost this fight, for Simpson and other leaders were never persuaded that tongues was the necessary evidence of spiritual baptism, although they allowed members to speak in tongues. Gradually the leadership in the Assemblies of God shifted from the dominant southerners present at its founding to more northern, and often better-educated, ministers. The council of the Assemblies of God never ruled decisively on this doctrinal issue, but notably it never required sanctification as a precondition for spiritual baptism. In time this meant that the church moved very clearly to a two-step position and is so identified today. In comparison with mainstream Christianity, the Assemblies of God Church, with its doctrine of evidentiary tongues, with its formalized use of tongue speaking in worship, and with its great summer campgrounds and revivals, is prototypically Pentecostal. But within American Pentecostalism this largely white, increasingly middle-class denomination has moved closest to the mainstream. It has a better-trained ministry, more colleges, and a better-established denominational headquarters (at Springfield, Missouri), and it probably accepts more accommodations with the customs of the outside world than most other Pentecostal denominations.

The second largest two-step Pentecostal denomination—the International Church of the Foursquare Gospel—was, in a sense, an offspring of the Assemblies of God. Its founder, Aimee Semple McPherson, was for a time the best-known Pentecostal evangelist in America. Born in Ontario, Canada, her mother an officer in the Salvation Army, Aimee Kennedy married a Pentecostal missionary, Robert J. Semple. He was a convert and disciple of William Durham's two-step doctrines and took his young wife with him on a mission trip to China in 1910, where he soon died. Aimee returned home with a new daughter and in 1912 married Harold McPherson, from whom she was later separated and eventually divorced.

In 1915 Aimee Semple McPherson began her career as an evangelist, often accompanied by her mother (only briefly by a long-suffering husband). She preached to huge audiences in a tent and became both famous and notorious. She was a born showperson and used her beauty, her speaking talents, her white robes, and eventually numerous theatrical props and her unrivaled record as a healer to promote her campaigns. By 1919, now separated from her husband, she settled in Los Angles and because of doctrinal affinities joined the Assemblies of God. On New Year's Day 1923 she dedicated her 5,300-seat Angelus Temple in Los Angles and preached weekly to standing-room-only audiences. By then she was too powerful and too independent to suffer the restrictions of any denomination. She founded her own separate denomination in 1927. The "foursquare" in the title, a word much used in holiness and Pentecostal circles, stood for the fourfold ministry of Jesus as savior, healer, baptizer, and coming king, or in McPherson's doctrinal statements, for salvation, divine healing, baptism in the Holy Spirit (with tongues), and the early second coming of the Christ. Scandals, one involving a nationally publicized but probably faked kidnapping in 1926, followed by a sensational trial, and a third, irrational marriage in 1932 to a womanizing husband, followed by a subsequent divorce, dimmed her luster within the larger Pentecostal movement but did not alienate her most loyal followers.

By the 1930s McPherson was comparable in many ways to Hollywood stars and just as beautiful and famous. She turned her Sunday service into a performance, helped sustain a large and vital ministry to the poor of Los Angeles, but suffered increasingly from both fame and loneliness. Her health was fragile; she endured several nervous breakdowns. Financial problems joined with interminable lawsuits and family quarrels, finally leading to the alienation of both her mother and her daughter. Such problems and a complete lack of executive ability finally cost her direct control over her temple and a growing number of Foursquare congregations. In the last seven years of her life she functioned as a minister under close control of what amounted to a guardian she had hired to run the financial affairs of her church. In this he succeeded. McPherson died in 1944 from an overdose of powerful sleeping pills. Most newspapers described this as a suicide, but the preponderance of evidence supports the legal finding: accidental death. By then her son, Rolf, had already assumed leadership in the denomination; he had the business skills and the personal maturity so lacking in his mother. What he lacked was her charisma, her almost hypnotic ability to sway audiences. At her death her church numbered less than 500 congregations. Under Rolf's leadership it expanded to over 2.5 million reported members worldwide, with over 200,000 in the United States.

The most important doctrinal split within American Pentecostalism involved baptismal formulas and, closely related to that, the Trinity doctrine. Once again the New Testament was the occasion for the controversies. At the two critical events for Pentecostals—the day of Pentecost and, later, when Paul baptized at Ephesus—baptisms seemed to be in the name of Jesus only. In Acts 2:38, a key scripture for Pentecostals as well as for Alexander Campbell and the Restoration movement, Peter, just after the coming of the Holy Spirit, commanded the multitudes to repent and be baptized in the name of Jesus the Christ for the forgiveness of sins and in order to receive the Holy Spirit. According to Acts, Paul at Ephesus also baptized converts in the name of the Lord Jesus. Thus the author of Luke-Acts, a devout disciple of Paul, seemed to certify the correct baptismal formula, one used by Paul. At least Paul's epistles do not challenge, although they do not overtly endorse, this formula. But the gospel attributed to Matthew contains at its end a very different formula, one that became orthodox in almost all Christian traditions. In a final commission the risen Jesus commanded the disciples to go forth and baptize people everywhere in the name of the Father and Son and Holy Spirit. Once again, there is no easy way to correlate these two quite different formulas. Maybe by the time of Paul's mission journeys Christian congregations baptized in the name of Jesus rather than that of John the Baptist, but in the ceremony they may have already used the three-name formula. No one can know for sure. It is possible—some scholars believe probable—that the ending of Matthew was an interpolation, added perhaps in the second century as an emerging baptismal formula became established in the dominant congregations.

The early Pentecostal movement took its departure from the Book of Acts, as did other restorationist movements. Thus Parham, at the very beginning, agonized over the correct baptismal formula, even as at times he wanted to dispense with water baptism. His final solution was a compromise. He immersed candidates "in the name of Jesus, into the name of the Father, Son, and Holy Ghost." Thus he merged Acts and Matthew, and presumably so did many of his early Apostolic Faith congregations. The issue seemed to die out until a great 1913 Apostolic Faith camp meeting near Pasadena, California, which featured the preaching of Woodworth-Etter. As in most such meetings, Woodworth-Etter and dozens of other ministers emphasized the work they did in the name of Jesus. Expressions like "Jesus only" were a part of popular devotion. One attendee at this revival not only marveled at the healing and other miracles performed in the name of Jesus, but in an inspired dream realized the great power that rested in the name of Jesus and by this emphasis began a fascinating doctrinal tradition, or what many now call the Jesus-only doctrine. Literally, it led to a unitarian branch of Pentecostalism, but because of the associations already attached to the word "unitarian," its Pentecostal advocates have not favored the label.

The person who did most to develop the Jesus-only movement was a former Australian Baptist, Frank Ewart. Notably, he was in the two-step tradition, and so would be almost all unitarian Pentecostals. In a sermon at the camp meeting a colleague of Ewart preached in favor of a Jesus-only baptismal formula, to the horror of many in the audience. It was Ewart who concluded that the titles "Father," "Son," and "Holy Ghost" were counterparts of the titles "Lord," "Jesus," and "Christ." The correct proper name for a god that functioned as father, son, and spirit was simply Jesus. The Jehovah of the Old Testament was simply the Jesus of the New. Ewart used this "new" understanding to launch a tent revival and had spectacular success. The converts—those that seem always receptive to a new revelation—provided Ewart all the proof he needed that he was correct and that most of Christendom was involved in an unintended trinitarian heresy. Soon Ewart and his disciples began rebaptizing converts to this new doctrine, this time correctly in the name of Jesus only.

This "new" doctrine had some of the same impact as the revival of tongues did at Azusa. It led to a new, even if somewhat ephemeral, revival among lagging Pentecostals and attracted converts from among all the existing Pentecostal denominations. Within two years it sharply divided the new Assembles of God, in part because its prime leader, E. B. Bell, temporarily capitulated to the new doctrine and accepted rebaptism. In 1916 this two-year-old denomination adopted a doctrinal statement that precluded many of the doctrines that accompanied the Jesus-only movement (it recommended the Matthew formula but did not forbid baptism in Jesus' name). Up to one-fourth of its membership left to join one of several emerging Jesus-only denominations. Today four or five denominations reflect the Jesus-only doctrines, but by far the largest and most influential is the United Pentecostal Church, International, a product of a 1945 merger of two smaller sects. This very strict, antiworldly denomination now claims over 500,000 members in the United States. It is the fourth largest Pentecostal denomination in America (behind only the Church of God in Christ, Assemblies of God, and the Church of God [Cleveland, Tennessee]).

This brief survey of the varieties of Pentecostalism does not do justice to the complexities of the subject. Neither does it tell much about the nature and appeal of Pentecostalism. Despite doctrinal controversies and schisms, the central appeal of Pentecostalism has never been an issue of belief but a special quality of experience. Outsiders know Pentecostals for their emotionalism, for the seeming chaos of their worship services, for tent revivals and old-fashioned camp meetings, for an emphasis on faith healing, and above all for what outsiders perceive as the gibberish that constitutes tongue speaking. They may also note the relative lack of social involvement on the part of Pentecostals, even the lack of a leadership role on conservative social issues that they support. All such observations involve at least half-truths.

Pentecostal denominations, by all polling data, draw from the lowest income groups of any major segment of American Christianity. Approximately half of all Pentecostals are black, and in the last two decades a surprising number of converts have been Hispanics. Characteristically, Pentecostal denominations often claim more foreign than United States members, which is only to testify to their continued commitment to missions. They have been particularly successful in Latin America among largely unchurched and nominal Roman Catholics, particularly those at the bottom of the social and economic hierarchy. In this sense Pentecostalism is a Christianity for the underclasses of the world. Its members do not remain at the very bottom. If devout Pentecostals, they are abstentious and hard working. In the United States the second generation has almost always moved up into the lower middle classes. But in a meritocratic society, even second- and third-generation families have rarely moved into higher income brackets or achieved prominence or power. Such a move requires the quality of higher education not yet supported by Pentecostals and which would undoubtedly subvert their beliefs and values should they gain such colleges and universities. By choice most Pentecostals, with the possible exception of the Assemblies of God, maintain such a degree of separation from and repudiate so many beliefs and values that are part of the general culture that they remain, in many senses, marginal. Thus, theirs is a religion of people dispossessed and alienated. It is all the more important to them for that reason and brings, in the quality of religious experience and in the supportive nature of their church communities, many compensatory and deserved rewards.

Other observers have noted, often with approval, the openness of Pentecostals to interracial worship and to ministerial roles for women. Once again, appearances can deceive. It is true that American Pentecostals, well before any other Christians, accepted a degree of interracial cooperation that went well beyond tokenism. They took seriously the idea that all people are spiritually equal and that all can gain the baptism of the Spirit. Also, as at Azusa, they were at first so close to the bottom of the social hierarchy, so lowly or alienated, that most social distinctions seemed unimportant, particularly during the heady days of their great revival. But white Pentecostals reflected the same prejudices as other Americans. These, plus a considerable cultural divide between blacks and whites, proved decisive. With some exceptions, among the smaller and more radically separatist sects, black and white Pentecostals swirled out of revival beginnings into their own segregated congregations, even when they remained within integrated denominations (as in the smaller branches of Tomlinson's Churches of God). Today, all the largest Pentecostal denominations are predominantly white or black, with only limited minorities still bridging the color and cultural barriers, led by the Church of God of Prophecy.

The role of women is a complex, at times paradoxical issue for Pentecostals and for Holiness sects. As in most Christian denominations, women have been disproportionately attracted to Pentecostalism. They had early vital leadership roles, as the above record demonstrates. Yet Pentecostals were and are as biblical as possible. One must not read into the record of Pentecostal women evangelists any beliefs at all related to feminism or even to any social equality for women. On these issues Pentecostals are likely to be completely resistant to change. What Pentecostals did believe in was a prophetic role for women and their right to participate in all the gifts of Spirit. Since speaking in tongues is a vital part of Pentecostal worship, women had to be included in the audible and visible aspects of a very spontaneous type of worship, and they always have been in all Pentecostal denominations. They speak in tongues and they interpret such speech, even as they prophesy and heal. Well before denominations formed or church governments made decisions or ordination became an issue, women converted, received spiritual baptism, and moved out to carry the word as evangelists or foreign missionaries. In fact, they usually outnumbered men. Thus, as Pentecostals began to form denominations, they were confronted with all those women, in roles that often seemed inconsistent with New Testament teaching. What were they to do?

They equivocated. Generally, as in the Assemblies of God, the Pentecostal denominations continued to license women for missionary or evangelical roles. Such women were vital to their survival and growth. But at first the Assembly council did not license or ordain women as pastors or permit them to administer the sacraments. It, in a sense, grandfathered in some existing pastors, made exceptions when male candidates were unavailable, and eventually relaxed the rule enough to allow the full ordination of women. But neither in the Assemblies nor in other Pentecostal denominations did women assume administrative positions (they were not over men). As time passed, the great women evangelists, such as Woodworth-Eddy and McPherson, gave way almost completely to men. Generally, Pentecostals follow scriptural advice about the role of women: women are subject to husbands in the home and to male leadership in the churches. Even Aimee Semple McPherson passed on the powerful presidency of the Foursquare Gospel to her son, not her alienated daughter. As far as records indicate, most women ministers, unlike McPherson, were modest in their claims and in a sense endorsed the political dominance of males. But even yet, women's roles tend to be greater in the smaller, more radical sects, black and white, and more restrictive in the better-established and larger Pentecostal denominations. Growth and maturity has meant churches much more conventional in gender roles and very resistant to contemporary changes in the status of women. In this, Pentecostals join evangelicals and fundamentalists.

After World War II, baptism in the Spirit as evidenced by tongues became widespread in the older, mainline denominations, Protestant and Roman Catholic. Beginning in 1959 in two Episcopal congregations in California, such charismatic experience and small fellowships or prayer groups that grew up around it expanded rapidly. As a well-publicized phenomenon, charismatic prayer groups probably peaked by the mid-1970s, although the number of individuals influenced by the phenomenon may have remained stable. With two or three marginal and ephemeral exceptions, this form of charismatic Christianity has not led to separate denominations. Rather, those involved in such experiences tried to bring spiritual renewal to existing churches, or what amounted to a contemporary form of pietism. In many respects the phenomenon resembled the early holiness movement in pre–Civil War America.

Charismatics in respectable mainstream Protestant denominations and in Roman Catholicism (the largest group of all) do not constitute new religions in America. This is as yet a story of the mainstream churches and of a degree of inclusiveness that permitted them to accept and retain such charismatics. Notably, the movement began in the Episcopal Church and soon flowered in Roman Catholicism. It attracted attention and led to prayer circles in all the more liberal or latitudinarian denominations, including even a very small group within the UUA. In time such charismatics may form new denominational splinters as they move from para-church institutions and national alliances to independence. If so, this would be an old story repeating itself. In a sense the charismatic style of piety has been very ecumenical, relating people across wide gaps of doctrine and polity. Resistance to it has been strongest among evangelical, fundamentalist, or doctrinally very conservative denominations. The large Southern Baptist Convention has consistently denounced as unbiblical the modern forms of charisma. Such a conservative fellowship as the Churches of Christ has strenuously resisted the movement, and the majority of its churches have denied fellowship to congregations that flirted with charisma. The same opposition has marked the smaller, confessional Lutheran churches and, of course, the traditional holiness denominations.

The ties between mainline charismatics and the major Pentecostal denominations have been quite limited. The cultural gap is immense, as are the class differences. But the boundaries have always overlapped. The major organizational bridge has been the Full Gospel Business Men's Fellowship International. Founded in Los Angeles in 1951 by a wealthy dairyman and Oral Roberts, this organization helped publicize the upward mobility and the business and professional success of members of largely white Pentecostal denominations, with most originally from the Assemblies of God or the Pentecostal Holiness denominations. Roberts was anxious to build bridges between the Pentecostal denominations and the charismatic fellowships developing in mainline denominations. Subsequently he left his own Pentecostal Holiness denomination and joined the United Methodist Church. Soon the Full Gospel organization circulated its publications among the mainline churches and recruited members from such churches.

In the 1950s David du Plessis, from South Africa, moved to the United States and gained ministerial status in the Assemblies of God. He had begun his ministry in South Africa in an Apostolic Faith mission and in 1947 attended the first Pentecostal World Conference, serving as secretary for subsequent conferences. In this capacity he attended and witnessed to Pentecostalism at the World Council of Churches in 1951. He was warmly received and in the next decade became an unofficial representative of

Pentecostalism in several ecumenical settings. Most officials in the mainline churches wanted to learn more about Pentecostalism and to maintain a dialogue with its leaders. As a result of his ecumenism, du Plessis suffered a period of suspension from his Assemblies of God ministry and hostility from the major Pentecostal denominations. As one would expect, mainline charismatics welcomed his bridge building. As some of the older, white Pentecostal denominations, particularly the Assemblies of God, move closer to the Protestant center (more decorous services, more affluent members, accredited colleges and universities), such contacts are bound to increase, and the boundaries between denominational Pentecostals and mainstream charismatics will further blur.

Despite the mainstream flowering of the Pentecostal gifts and the size and rapid growth of the five or six largest Pentecostal denominations, Pentecostals are still relatively unknown in the larger society. Their social status, or their race, has helped keep them invisible. Few white, mainstream church members have even heard of the Church of God in Christ and are astounded to learn that it has more members than the Episcopal Church; American Baptists; the Presbyterian Church (USA); the United Church of Christ; and possibly the Evangelical Lutheran Church. Despite numbers, Pentecostals remain at the margins of American Protestantism. But from an international perspective they are among the most potent purveyors of a certain type of American culture and have had enormous impact in Latin America.

READING GUIDE

Slowly, ecstatic Christianity is gaining its deserved scholarly attention. Until after World War II, except on sensational figures such as Aimee Semple McPherson, Holiness and Pentecostal scholarship was limited to the work of poorly trained historians within the various sects.

In 1962 a major historian of American religion, Timothy L. Smith, published a history of the formation of his own church, *Called unto Holiness, the Story of the Nazarenes: The Formative Years* (Kansas City: Nazarene Publishing House). Within a decade Charles Edwin Jones was at work on a dissertation, which led in 1974 to an even more inclusive book, *Perfectionist Persuasion: The Holiness Movement and American Methodism, 1876–1936* (Metuchen, N.J.: Scarecrow Press).

After early scholarship on small sects in the South, both white and black, David E. Harrell published a popular survey in 1975, *All Things Are Possible: The Healing and Charismatic Revivals in Modern America* (Bloomington: Indiana University Press). This opened up aspects of American religion largely unknown by those outside a Pentecostal culture. Harrell subsequently wrote the sympathetic biographies *Oral Roberts: An American Life* (Bloomington: Indiana University Press, 1985) and *Pat Robertson: A Personal, Religious, and Political Portrait* (San Francisco: Harper and Row, 1987). In 1986 Wayne E. Warner published another revealing biography, *The Woman Evangelist: The Life and Times of Charismatic Evangelist Maria B. Woodworth-Etter* (Metuchen, N.J.: Scarecrow Press).

The literature on Pentecostalism is growing but much is of poor quality. I find weak Vinson Synan's *The Holiness-Pentecostal Movement in the United States* (Grand Rapids: Eerdmans, 1971). The most influential but often contested story is Robert Mapes Anderson's *Vision of the Disinherited* (New York: Oxford University Press, 1979). By far the most nuanced and subtle study is by Donald W. Dayton, *Theological Roots of Pentecostalism* (Metuchen, N.J.: Scarecrow Press, 1987), but it is an interpretive study, not a survey. Edith L. Blumhofer fits the story of the Assemblies of God into the larger story of Pentecostalism in *The Assemblies of God: A Chapter in the Story of American Pentecostalism*, vol. I (Springfield, Mo.: Gospel Publishing House, 1989) and in 1993 published the most religiously informed biography of McPherson, *Aimee Semple McPherson: Everybody's Sister* (Grand Rapids: Eerdmans).

James R. Goff Jr. has finally written a very informed biography of the founder of American Pentecostalism, *Fields White unto Harvest: Charles F. Parham and the Missionary Origins of Pentecostalism* (Fayetteville: University of Arkansas Press, 1988). No comparable biography exists for William Seymour, although all the histories of Pentecostalism emphasize his role. A recent book by Mickey Crews, *The Church of God: A Social History* (Knoxville: University of Tennessee Press, 1990), offers some insight into the Church of God (Cleveland, Tennessee), but without much attention to doctrinal issues. The small snake-handling sects in the Appalachians have already invited significant scholarship, with the best account of origins in Thomas Burton, *Serpent-Handling Believers* (Knoxville: University of Tennessee Press, 1993), while the 5-million-member Church of God in Christ has, as of yet, no scholarly history.

Richard Quebedeaux has become the historian of mainstream charismatic movements: *The New Charismatics, II: How A Christian Renewal Movement Became Part of the American Religious Mainstream* (San Francisco: Harper and Row, 1983). Harvey Cox, the distinguished theologian, has written a challenging interpretation of all forms of Pentecostalism in *Fire from Heaven: The Rise of Pentecostal Spirituality and the Reshaping of Religion in the Twenty-First Century* (Reading, Mass.: Addison-Hensley, 1995).

AFTERWORD

One conclusion is clear after spending years with these six varieties of Christianity. Their creators were all very innovative and thus very threatening to orthodox denominations. Each repudiated crucial doctrines that remained normative in Roman Catholic, Lutheran, Anglican, and Reformed traditions. Although quite divergent in doctrines and practices, the founders of all six originals shared some common enemies. One of these was what they all called Calvinism. Scholastic Calvinism, as codified at Dort and Westminster, was the most convenient point of reference for the reformers or prophets who created these six new religious traditions in America. What they did not always realize is that in rejecting Calvinist doctrines such as limited atonement, divine election to salvation, human depravity, irresistible grace, or the perseverance of the saints, they also essayed critical changes in the two most central doctrines of Christianity: belief in a personal, creative, and providential god, and that such a divine person became incarnate in Jesus of Nazareth.

It took over four centuries for the Church of the Roman Empire to find formulas to express maturing beliefs about the nature and status of the Christ. These became the basis of the central creeds of Western Christianity. The decisions at Nicaea and Constantinople led to the orthodox Trinity formula. Only at Chalcedon in 451 did the Church settle divisions over the human and divine traits of Jesus. Neither of these settlements were fully consensual. The winning factions excommunicated dissident Arian and Nestorian Christians. Zwingli, Luther, and Calvin, who revolted against the Church of Rome and helped found new state churches, reaffirmed the core doctrines from these earlier councils. Not so some Anabaptist sects. Not so most American reformers in the nineteenth century.

All the leaders in the six traditions surveyed in this book affirmed a freewill or voluntaristic position. They rejected all versions of predestination, all conceptions of perseverance, and by implication all the strongest versions of divine omnipotence. One can speculate about the reasons for this. But whatever the necessary conditions that were in the background, each new version of Christianity provided room for individual choice and made salvation at least in part something chosen even if not deserved. Such a voluntaristic stance united groups that seemed otherwise almost opposites—rationalistic Unitarians and affectionate Pentecostals, spiritualistic Christian Scientists and corporealist Mormons.

Another, to me unexpected, finding was how poorly the orthodox Trinity formula fared among new American religions. An orthodox understanding of the Trinity was not crucial to any of the new denominations, and some within four of the six traditions completely rejected it. Unitarians, Universalists, early Adventists, Jehovah's Witnesses, and Christian Scientists all affirmed unitarian or Arian positions. Most early restorationists and one wing of the Pentecostal movement concurred. Today most within the restoration tradition and Seventh-day Adventists affirm something close to the traditional formula, but notably in each case they have not stressed it and have been unwilling to spend much time in clarifying or defending it. This leads to the surprising conclusion that, in America, those who tried to reform the Church, to go back to a truer form of Christianity, either largely ignored or openly repudiated the most central achievement of the great councils. What was so conspicuously absent in the founders of all these new religions was any concern about, or commitment to, the great creeds of Western Christianity (Nicene, Apostles', or Athanasian).

Both the radicalism and the diversity of American reformers were most apparent in their views about gods. At this most cosmic level, almost all dissented from the dominant concepts or images of divinity present in Roman Catholic, Lutheran, and Reformed versions of orthodoxy. To use the jargon of philosophers, they tangled in fascinating ways with cosmological and ontological issues. One way to identify their heterodoxy is to argue that American religious prophets created, or identified, new gods. The plural fits, since I find almost nothing in common between the fully corporeal gods of Mormonism and the ultimate divine Spirit of Christian Science. From the orthodox perspective, both these conceptions of ultimate reality were blasphemous. Neither view was close to the god affirmed by Thomas Aquinas or John Calvin.

The deeply rooted preference for monotheism in all the Semitic religions impedes clarity in any discussion about a god or gods. For example, it seems to me a given, in the pluralistic diversity of American Christianity, that avowedly monotheistic Christians have, in fact, affirmed or created many different gods. Yet most, excluding Mormons, believe that only one God is real or exists. Therefore, they note the different images but describe these as varied and more or less adequate characterizations of the one and only true god. From their perspective the characterizations all refer to one subject. Even the use of the generic term, "god," as something close to a proper name, "God," illustrates the underlying, rarely challenged assumption. Jehovah's Witnesses, almost alone, condemned such a misuse of the generic term and insisted on a proper name for their god. But their Jehovah, as they describe him (note the masculine pronoun), is not at all the same god affirmed by most other Christians. In some cases he has almost no shared characteristics (again think of Mary Baker Eddy). Here the gods are not even cousins. If, despite the differences, one still insists that both Jehovah's Witnesses and Christian Scientists are referring to the same god, but that one or both have mistakenly described him or her or it, then one simply is confessing one's own monotheistic or unitary belief about ultimate reality. Such a claim can be very confusing, for it often illegitimately suggests commonalities where none exist.

I have illustrated a plurality of gods by noting polar conceptions. It is easy to grasp the gulf between the material, personlike, limited, and monarchical god of Apocalyptic Christians and the fully spiritual, mindlike god of Transcendentalists and Christian Scientists. One could argue that the traditional orthodox theism of the Western Church has always involved a tension-producing blending of these two extremes. The great councils worked to merge competing conceptions, and the subsequent history of orthodox theology has involved the effort to maintain and update the compromises affirmed by the great councils. The orthodox, in defense of their creeds, have always appealed to canonized scriptures. But so do Adventists and Christian Scientists. The Christian Bible, composed before the full assimilation of pagan philosophies and practices by the early Church, surely provides as much or more support for a finite, monarchical god as for any divine mind or spirit.

American prophets and reformers had to deal, often in original ways, with the tensions within traditional Christian theism. The background, for most, was the dominant Reformed denominations, whose theologians affirmed what might be called the heart doctrine of Christian orthodoxy: the God of Christianity is alone real, the ground of all being, with no beginning and no ending. All finite being and all events depend on his will and purpose (that God is properly addressed as "he" is a revealed truth, not an essential or analytical truth). He is in full control. Yet such a lofty being has revealed some aspects of his nature and, particularly, his will for humans. The ultimate nature of such a god is beyond full human understanding, and thus any full description is impossible. But such a god has revealed enough about his will and purpose that humans are able to understand what is required for their salvation. In his revelations and in his direct interventions into human history this god has shown himself to be humanlike, or at least kinglike, and functions in universal history as an actor, not just a ground or source. In this respect the Christian god is closely related to early Jewish images of Yahweh, including their earliest concept of a finite, tribal deity, the master of his plantations in Eden and more powerful than the gods of the Canaanites. Yet it is not clear that one can reconcile a god as ultimate being with a governmental deity who exercises control over events on earth.

American reformers, except Mary Baker Eddy, were much more attracted to a governmental deity than to some ultimate, incomprehensible being. They were closer to Moses than to Plotinus. And even their governmental gods never seemed quite so absolute, so sovereign, as did the god of John Calvin. An Arminian position is very difficult to reconcile with omnipotence. Functionally, if not in theory, the departure point for new American prophets was the specter of a Calvinist god (too arbitrary or too cruel), and in reaction to such a god they affirmed the existence of a deity who, by nature, either was finite and thus limited in power or so opened up the course of human history as to allow a degree of self-direction by humans. In a sense, this meant a humanized god, save for Mary Baker Eddy, who deified humans. Either way, humans have some control over their own fate, not in the sense of choices that affirm their developed identity (Calvinism), but even in the choice of that identity. This position may not be logically coherent and may not make full sense, but it expressed a longing for a world in which gods, however powerful, and humans, however weak, can negotiate about or mutually control events.

Humanized gods have great appeal. By the same token, so do multiple gods. The major, historical religions, save for a mature Judaism, have always been much more polytheistic than their affirmed beliefs would seem to allow. The infinite One of Plotinus and the Brahma of early Indic religions have intellectual appeal (unity, consistency, and exemption from the contingencies of time and space). But as demonstrated in the history of Hinduism, and to a lesser extent in Christianity, such a lofty, metaphysical principle has rarely offered solace and comfort to humans. They need limited, finite, sexed, passionate, approachable, even imperfect gods, and they have created such gods to meet the need. For early Christians, Jesus was such a limited deity, literally the son of Jehovah. So was the Spirit that worked in the heart of Christians. And soon, at least for some Christians, other limited deities served some of the same roles: Mary, the mother of God; great martyrs whose spirits lived on; saints whose divine merit could help gain forgiveness for humans; or guardian angels who could protect against harm. Such are the religious needs of most humans that they cannot be satisfied with a solitary and perfect and thus necessarily aloof god or even with a single, all-powerful sovereign. One of the most appealing aspects of Mormonism is a frank acceptance of finite, limited, but multiple gods.

In the early history of what became largely a Gentile church in a Hellenistic intellectual environment, it was necessary to develop doctrines that did justice to the craving for unity as well as those that satisfied the human need for approachable, helpful deities. It was also necessary to find a synthesis of the corporeal, practical, moralistic god of the Jews and the immaterial, redemptive gods of pagan mystery religions. The synthesis of such opposites turned out to be one of the great intellectual creations of human history: the basic theology of the Church. But by the nineteenth century in America, this great intellectual achievement seemed, to many, abstract and unscriptural. In a sense, all the major American reformers except Eddy moved back toward the early Jewish church and away from the Greek or pagan theological imports that had become dominant by the fourth century, and which had considerable impact on many New Testament authors. Even those American prophets, such as Ellen G. White, who eventually affirmed the full deity of the Christ never really accepted the Nicene formula. Alexander Campbell would not even use the nonscriptural term "Trinity." In the context of corporealist beliefs, Seventh-day Adventist doctrines about the three persons of the Trinity took on a meaning very different from that found in the context of a belief in separable spirits and the possibility of a spirit's incarnation in a body. Pentecostals, more than representatives of other forms of Christianity, gave emphasis to the work of the Spirit, even as the Jesus-only Pentecostals conflated Spirit, Father, and Son into one Jesus.

The originality of American prophets and reformers lurked most clearly in the richness and variety of their attempts to come to terms with the problem of gods. An outsider has to acknowledge their ingenuity in creating new gods, some well fitted to the American context. With their creations, American religion became much more varied, and the gods competing for acceptance much more diverse, than ever before. The reasonable, logical god of the Restoration sects clarified, in the pages of the New Testament, his clear but demanding plan for human salvation. The unitary god of Unitarians and Universalists, ever more ethereal in the hands of Transcendentalists, tended to vaporize through time, leaving no god at all. The physical, tangible god of Adventists and Jehovah's Witnesses lived in a real heavenly kingdom and would soon send Jesus to earth to perfect a related kingdom for all his faithful saints. The finite, world-specific gods of the Mormons provided a difficult but achievable pathway to divinity for all humans. The Divine Spirit of Christian Science was, in essence, continuous with our own truest reality; humans thus participated in divinity. The god of Pentecostals was above all a god of miracles, and he empowered humans, as he did the apostles of old, to receive, experience, and use all the wonderful gifts of the Spirit. Which of these gods most appealed to Americans depended on the needs and aspirations of people, and perhaps also on their taste in gods. If American religious experience demonstrates anything at all, it is that this taste varied immensely from person to person, even in the already culturally constrained context of Western Christianity.

What about the future? Will there be other American originals and other new gods? Undoubtedly, although I cannot even suggest what the new beliefs or new gods will be like. But who in 1800 could have predicted the doctrines of Joseph Smith? Every time I observe some obscure new sect, I find on close investigation that it fits within one of the European-derived categories—Catholic, Lutheran, eastern Orthodox, Reformed, Anabaptist, or inspirationist like the Quakers—or fits one of my six originals. African Americans have joined each of these groups and have added nuances of belief and practice to each one, but I cannot conceive of a comparable category of Christianity tied to ethnicity or race. Some New Age prophets at least borrow some Christian beliefs, but they do not claim to be Christian. When they do, as in the Unity churches, they fit one of my categories. It is conceivable that, in the future, most creativity on the part of American religious prophets will eventuate in non-Christian religions. If so, this will demonstrate the degree to which Christian, or even more broadly, Semitic assumptions have lost their hegemony in the West.

I close with some indication of the size and strength of these six American originals. In very approximate terms, their members number about 21 million in the United States, with Pentecostals making up almost half of that total. They constitute about 15 percent of all Christians, active and inactive, and 25 percent of all Protestants. These American originals exceed the combined membership of all the following mainstream Protestant confessions: United Methodist, Presbyterian Church (USA), Evangelical Lutheran Churches, American Baptists, and the United Church of Christ. Admittedly, a few Restoration Christians are now in the United Church of Christ, meaning a small overlap. These American originals considerably exceed in total the membership of the Southern Baptist Convention, the largest Protestant body in America. The only grouping of Protestants that is larger would be a somewhat incoherent pooling of all non-Pentecostal American evangelicals and fundamentalists. Finally, these originals have been the most successful in exporting American Christianity. Today over half of all Christians in the world who owe their conversion either directly or indirectly to American mission efforts are Mormons, Adventists, Jehovah's Witnesses, or Pentecostals.

INDEX